West Bengal TET

Paper 2 : Science & Mathematics

Latest Edition
Practice Kit

10 Tests

10 Practice Test

Based On Real Exam Pattern

✓ Thoroughly Revised and Updated

✓ Detailed Analysis of all MCQs

<table>
<tr><td>Title</td><td>: West Bengal TET Paper 2 : Science & Mathematics</td></tr>
<tr><td>Author Name</td><td>: Mr. Rohit Manglik</td></tr>
<tr><td>Published By</td><td>: EduGorilla Community Pvt. Ltd.</td></tr>
<tr><td>Publishers Address</td><td>: 12/651, First Floor Opp. Arvindo Park, Near Jama Masjid,
Indira Nagar, Lucknow, Uttar Pradesh-226016, India</td></tr>
</table>

TABLE OF CONTENTS

Practice Test 01

1. By motor development we mean the development of in the use of arms and legs' by:
(a) Mind and Spirit
(b) Learning and Education
(c) Training and Learning
(d) Strength and speed

2. Which of the principles of development is defined by the below given example?
Sufi has appropriate weight and height for her age. She also has a self-esteem.
(a) Development involves change.
(b) Development follows a fixed pattern/sequence.
(c) Development proceeds from general to specific.
(d) Development is correlated.

3. Which of the following is not true regarding heredity and environment?
(a) Influence personality
(b) Influence physical and intellectual development
(c) Influence health
(d) Influence the economy

4. Schools teach new behaviours and rules to children and expect them to act accordingly. The school is acting as an agency of _____ socialisation.
(a) primary   (b) constructive
(c) secondary   (d) analytic

5. "At a particular stage children begin to use primitive reasoning and want to know the answer to all sorts of questions." Piaget called this "intuitive". As per Piaget, which of the following stage, he means?
(a) Concrete operation
(b) Pre-operation
(c) Formal operation
(d) None of these

6. Lawrence Kohlberg's theory of moral reasoning has been criticized on several counts. Which of the following statements is correct in the context of this criticism?
(a) Kohlberg has based his study primarily on a male sample.
(b) Kohlberg has not given typical responses to each stage of moral reasoning.
(c) Kohlberg has duplicated Piaget's methods of arriving at his theoretical framework.
(d) Kohlberg's theory does not focus on children's responses.

7. Curricular goals in progressive education emphasize:
(a) Rote-memorisation
(b) Conformity to authority
(c) Critical thinking
(d) Recall and drill

based upon its reflection of which current classroom strategy?
(a) Differentiated instruction
(b) Inclusive Education
(c) Socialization
(d) Discovery Learning

9. A child has ability to understand and effectively interact with others. He is showing which type of intelligence?
(a) Verbal
(b) Mathematical
(c) Interpersonal
(d) Intrapersonal

10. In _____ thinking, a child do simplification/ generalization on the one hand and truth and accuracy on the other.
(a) Reflective   (b) Critical
(c) Aesthetic   (d) Creative

11. Children acquire gender roles through all of the following, except:
(a) Media   (b) Socialization
(c) Culture   (d) Tutoring

12. A teacher should _______ if learners display individual differences.
(a) Enforce strict discipline in the class
(b) Increase the number of tests / examinations
(c) Provide a variety of learning experience
(d) Provide a variety of learning materials

13. Which one of the following would be the most effective way of conducting an assessment?
(a) Assessment is an inbuilt process in teaching-learning
(b) Assessment should be done twice in an academic session at the beginning and at the end
(c) Assessment should be done by an external agency and not by the teacher
(d) Assessment should be at the end of the session

14. A teacher asks his/her students to draw a concept map to reflect their comprehension of a topic. He/She is:
(a) Jogging the memory of the to summarise the main points
(d) Trying to develop rubrics to evaluate the achievement of the students

15. In progressive-education children are seen as:
(a) Passive imitators
(b) Active explorers
(c) Blank slates
(d) Miniature adults

16. What instructional adaptations should a teacher make while working with students that are 'Visually Challenged'?
(a) Use a variety of visual presentations.
(b) Orient herself so that the students can watch her closely.
(c) Focus on a variety of written tasks especially worksheets.
(d) Speak clearly and use a lot of touches and feel materials.

17. Which of the following enrichment programmes is suitable for gifted children in the school?
(a) Mathematics or Science Olympiad
(b) Challenging home assignments
(c) Map work during studies
(d) All of the above

18. Which of the following is the best example of creativity?
(a) Writing a script for role play in class
(b) Preparing an origami structure
(c) Making a Rangoli
(d) Making a painting

19. Which of the following is a method to teach Autistic children?

(a) PECS

(b) Braille

(c) Taylor Frame

(d) None of these

20. In order to address learners from diverse backgrounds, a teacher should:

(a) Draw examples from diverse settings.

(b) Use standardized assessment for all

(c) Use statements that strengthen negative stereotypes

(d) Avoid talking about aspects related to diversity.

(b) Ponder over the present attitude of students in a calm manner.

(c) Think about using some interesting techniques for teaching.

(d) Try to understand the reasons and try to eliminate them.

22. Alternate conceptions and misconceptions hold by children represent:

(a) Inability to learn

(b) Intuitive ideas about particular concept

(c) Baseless assertions

(d) Permanent conceptional stagnation

23. Which of the following statements about students' errors is correct?

(a) Errors help the teachers in labelling students as 'weak' or 'bright'.

(b) On the basis of their errors, the teacher can fail students and save her time.

(c) Errors offer an opportunity for the teachers to understand students' thinking.

(d) Errors should be immediately rectified by asking the students to repeatedly rewrite the 'correct answers'.

24. Which of the following is correct regarding emotion ?

(a) Emotion is subjective in nature

(b) Emotion is both subjective and objective

(c) Physiological changes in emotions may not be noticed

(d) Emotions are basically an affective process that is simple in nature

25. Which of the following example shows that intrinsic motivation is better than extrinsic motivation for learning?

(a) A student want to participate in a sport because it's fun and she enjoys it.

(b) A student did homework because he did not want to get scolded by teacher.

(c) A teacher in a private school is taking more responsibility at work in order to receive a raise or promotion.

(d) A child is speaking wrong

.... learning.

(i) emotional
(ii) cultural content
(iii) maturation
(iv) interest

(a) (iii), (iv)

(b) (ii), (iii), (iv)

(c) (i), (ii), (iii), (iv)

(d) (ii), (iv)

27. Which one of these factors plays a very important role in learning?

(a) Genetic make-up alone

(b) Physical infrastructure

(c) Social context and emotions

(d) Maturation and physical appearance

28. Which of the following is not correct regarding teaching-learning process?

(a) Processes of learning move from the simple to the complex

(b) Readiness and motivation to learn are the important to designing instructional activities

(c) Skills of problem solving are integral parts of the internal conditions of learning

(d) None of these

29. Which of the following is a property of "Deductive method"?

(a) In this method, there is no opportunity to develop powers like logic, thinking and investigation.

(b) In this method, children work mechanically because they do not know why they are doing such a thing.

(c) By this method all the children

of the class can be taught at the same time.

(d) All of the above

30. Characteristics of thinking are:

(a) It depends on both - perception and memory

(b) Thinking is a mental process that starts with a problem and concludes with its solution

(c) It is a symbolic behavior

(d) All of the above

Language - I: English

Ques (31-39): Direction : Read the given passage and answer the questions that follow.

Th......... ....

.. ..

to tackle the menace of black money, corruption, terror funding, and fake currency. From a market perspective, we think that this is a very welcome move by the government and which has taken the black money hoarders by surprise. The total value of old Rs.500 and Rs.1000 notes in circulation is to the tune of Rs.14.2 trillion, which is about 85% of the total value of the currency in circulation. This means that the total cash has to now pass through the formal banking channels to get legitimacy. The World Bank in July 2010 estimated the size of the shadow economy for India at 20.7% of the Gross Domestic Product (GDP) in 1999 and rose to 23.2% in 2007. Assuming that this figure has not risen since then (quite unlikely though) and that the cash component of the shadow economy is also proportional (it could be higher), the estimated unaccounted value of the currency could be to the tune of Rs.3.3 trillion. Now, post the announcement of demonetization by the government this money would have to either account for by paying the relevant tax and penalties or would get extinguished. There are higher chances of a larger proportion of this unaccounted currency getting extinguished as the tax rate and subsequent legal issues could be prohibitively high for such money.

This move by the government is likely to have long-term benefits for the economy. The extinguishing of the major proportion of unaccounted currency would reduce the liabilities of the government and would add to its finances. This move is likely to lead to better tax compliance, raise the Tax to GDP ratio and improved tax collection. The move is also likely to have a habit-changing impact on the Indian populous and there could be an increased belief in keeping cash in the banks rather than stashed at home and using formal banking channels for their spending needs. It will improve the medium to long-term Current Account and Savings Account (CASA) ratio of the banks. Another element of the demonetization would be a reduction in cash transactions in real estate which has been acting like a cash cow for the corrupt. This is likely to reduce real estate prices and make it affordable to some extent. This may be visible more in the rural belt, where many non-farming entities purchase fertile farmland, not for farming but for money parking purposes. The demonetization and consequent reduction in the shadow economy would bring the demand for such farmlands down.

31. How will the demand for fertile farmlands be brought down by

(b) Higher investments in real estate

(c) Cash hoarding

(d) Low agricultural output

32. What percentage of the total value of currency in circulation is made up by the old Rs.500 and Rs.1000 notes?

(a) 80%   (b) 85%

(c) 75%   (d) 60%

33. What does cash cow mean?

(a) Cash that buys cows

(b) People with low income from land

(c) Approximate estimate of cost of land

(d) A product or service that is a regular source of income for someone

34. Why will the demonetization move have a habit-changing impact on the Indian population?

(a) Indians will stop using black money for their daily needs and rely more on white money for day to day transactions.

(b) The Indian population generally uses mostly UPI for transactions and is not in the habit of saving. Demonetisation will make them wary of the future and grow their expanding habits altering their lifestyles.

(c) Demonetisation will affect the spending habits of the foreigners.

(d) The demonetization has affected all Indians and in the future, the scheme would make them wary

and help to create an atmosphere where banks and other legalized avenues will make their savings secure and easily accessible.

35. What is the main idea discussed in the passage?

(a) How black money is hid in the economy.

(b) The effects of demonetization on the Indian economy.

(c) Demonetization and its effect on the next elections.

(d) Demonetization and common man's woe.

36. Choose the correct synonym of the word 'formal'.

(a) Official   (b) Ceremonial

Action

(b) Current Affirmation and Savings Affirmation

(c) Current Account and Savings Account

(d) Current Act and Savings Account

38. According to World Bank estimates what percentage of the GDP did the shadow economy have in 2007?

(a) 20.7%   (b) 21.4%

(c) 22.6%   (d) 23.2%

39. Choose the correct antonym of the word 'compliance'.

(a) Agreement   (b) Assent

(c) Defiance   (d) Consensus

Ques (40-45): Direction : Read the poem given below and answer the questions that follow.

I was angry with my friend;
I told my wrath, my wrath did end.
I was angry with my foe:
I told it not, my wrath did grow.
And I waterd it in fears,
Night & morning with my tears:
And I sunned it with smiles,
And with soft deceitful wiles.
And it grew both day and night.
Till it bore an apple bright.
And my foe beheld it shine,
And he knew that it was mine.
And into my garden stole,
When the night had veild the pole;
In the morning glad I see;
My foe outstretched beneath the tree.

40. What did the poet water with his fears?

(a) Tree   (b) Plant

(c) Poison   (d) Anger

41. Which device is used in the

following lines?
And I sunned it with smiles,
And with soft deceitful wiles.
And it grew both day and night.

(a) Consonance

(b) Anaphora

(c) Satire

(d) Personification

42. What does the poet mean when he says 'My foe outstretched beneath the tree.'?

(a) Poet's enemy was using the tree

(b) Poet's enemy was trying to steal the fruits from the tree

(c) The enemy was relaxing under poet's tree

(d) The enemy was lying dead under the tree

(b) The dark night covered the pole

(c) Night had covered the pole

(d) The dark night was all around the tree

44. Which literary device is used throughout the poem?

(a) Personification

(b) Simile

(c) Extended Metaphor

(d) Assonance

45. What does the garden refer to in the poem?

(a) Anger   (b) Kindness

(c) Forgiveness   (d) Apology

46. Consider the correct statements regarding language learning.

I. Input-rich communicational environments are a prerequisite for language learning.

II. It helps in bridging the gap between the burden of incomprehension and language learning.

(a) Only I

(b) Only II

(c) Both I & II

(d) None of these

47. The 'acquired system' or 'acquisition' of a language is the:

(a) Formal skills development

(b) Subconscious process of learning

(c) Input output process

(d) Self monitoring of learning

48. One of the principles of materials preparation for language learning is that:

(a) Complex materials should be chosen for each age group

(b) Materials need to be graded appropriately.

(c) Any kind of materials can be selected.

(d) Materials should be short and limited.

49. Principles of sequencing in teaching a foreign language, does not include:

(a) Grammatical sequence

(b) Lexical sequence

(c) Semantic sequence

(d) Phonetic sequence

50. Grammatical rules are________ for learning a language.

(d) mandatory

51. Given below are two statements, one leveled as Assertion (A) and the other leveled as Reason (R).
Assertion (A): Grammar is the backbone of any language, it is the womb that gives birth to sentences.
Reasoning (R): Grammar rules are made easier if the teacher teaches grammar using a standard textbook.

(a) Both (A) and (R) are correct and (R) is the correct explanation of (A).

(b) Both (A) and (R) are correct, but (R) is not the correct explanation of (A).

(c) (A) is correct, but (R) is not correct.

(d) (A) is not correct, but (R) is correct.

52. When child has difficulties in understanding or expressing language that is called:

(a) Grammatical language problem

(b) Delayed Language

(c) Language Disability

(d) All of the Above

53. The order advocated for learning the language skills is:

(a) writing, reading, speaking, listening

(b) reading, writing, listening, speaking

(c) listening, speaking, reading, writing

(d) speaking, listening, reading, writing

54. Through which of the following

language skills should be taught?

(a) Through imitation

(b) In isolation

(c) Through detailed explanation

(d) In an integrated manner

55. Rohit, a English teacher, is planning to evaluate the speaking skills of his students. What should be the main focus for evaluating speaking skill?

(a) Accuracy of pronounciation

(b) Adequacy of fluency

(c) Communicative competence

(d) Accuracy of pronounciation and adequacy of fluency

56. Decoding in evaluating language proficiency refers to:

build and write words.

(c) The ability to read individual words and to sound out unfamiliar words accurately.

(d) The ability to provide remedial classes.

57. ________ is of great utility in teaching English pronunciation, accent and intonation.

(a) Epidiascope (b) Films

(c) Linguaphone (d) Radio

58. The objective of remedial teaching in English language is/are:

(a) Provides learning activities and practical experiences to pupils according to their abilities and requirements.

(b) Designs individualized teaching with intensive remedial support

(c) Help the pupils to get rid of their common or specific weaknesses.

(d) All of the above

59. The main purpose of using oral drill is:

(a) To assess the comprehension skills of learners

(b) To improve pronunciation and accuracy

(c) To enhance the speaking skills of learners

(d) To improve retention capacity of learners

60. A smartboard is a:

(a) A visual aid

(b) An audio aid

(c) An audio-visual aid

(d) None of these

61. Direction : What will come in place of question mark '?' in the following question?
$$\sqrt{324} + 9^2 - 7^2 = 2 \times (?)^2$$

(a) 25 (b) 5

(c) 10 (d) 125

62. Two pots contain equal quantity of mixture of Alcohol and water. The ratio of alcohol and water in these pots is $2:3$ and $4:1$, respectively. Radha mixed content of the two pots together. Find the ratio of Alcohol and water in new mixture.

(a) $4:3$ (b) $2:3$

(c) $3:2$ (d) $3:4$

11 years. Find the present age of B.

(a) 33 years (b) 32 years

(c) 28 years (d) 35 years

64. Raj sells a cricket bat of marked price Rs. 500 at a discount of 10% and gives a ball costing Rs. 10 free with each bat. Still, he makes a profit of 25%, the cost price of the bat is:

(a) Rs. 410 (b) Rs. 458

(c) Rs. 352 (d) Rs. 450

65. The sum of the radius and height of a cylinder is $19m$. The total surface area of the cylinder is $1672m^2$. What is the volume of the cylinder?

(a) $3080m^3$ (b) $2940m^3$

(c) $3420m^3$ (d) $2860m^3$

66. A number is as much greater than 36 as is less than 86. Find the number.

(a) 61 (b) 71

(c) 81 (d) 51

67. A rectangular field of length $242m$ has an area of $4840m^2$. What will be the cost of fencing if the cost of fencing is 50 paise/meter?

(a) Rs 262 (b) Rs 270

(c) Rs 320 (d) Rs 258

68. The area of four walls of a room is $660m^2$ and length is twice the width, height being $11m$. Find the area of ceiling of the room?

(a) 200 (b) 190

(c) 210 (d) 220

69. If a man travels with a speed of $\frac{2}{5}$ times of his original speed and he reached his office 15 minutes late to

the fixed time, then the time taken with his original speed will be:

(a) 10 min (b) 15 min
(c) 20 min (d) 25 min

70. If the mode of the following data is 7 , then the value of k in the data set $3, 8, 6, 7, 1, 6, 10, 6, 7, 2k+5, 9, 7$, and 13 is:

(a) 3 (b) 7
(c) 4 (d) 1

71. The mean of 20 observations is 15 , On checking it was found that two observations were wrongly copied as 3 and 6 . If wrong observations are replaced by correct values 8 and 4 , then the correct mean is:

(a) 15 (b) 15.15

is 28 cm.

(a) 11 (b) 22
(c) 33 (d) 44

73. If $\sqrt{y} = \sqrt{4} - \sqrt{6}$ then find the value of $\left(y^2 - 20y + 12\right)$?

(a) 4 (b) 8
(c) 10 (d) 12

74. Two chords, AB and CD of a circle meet at a point O , outside the circle. It is given that $AB = 7\,cm, CD = 4\,cm, OB = 5\,cm$. What is length of OD ?

(a) 5 cm (b) 6 cm
(c) 7.5 cm (d) 10 cm

75. If $x\left(3 - \frac{2}{x}\right) = \frac{3}{x}$ then the value of $x^2 + \frac{1}{x^2}$ is:

(a) $2\frac{1}{9}$ (b) $2\frac{4}{9}$
(c) $3\frac{1}{9}$ (d) $3\frac{4}{9}$

76. If $(a + b) = -1$, and $a^2 + b^2 = 25$, then find the value of $(a - b)^2$.

(a) 16 (b) 64
(c) 36 (d) 49

77. What is the sum of digits of the least number which when divided by 21, 28, 30 and 35 leaves the same remainder 10 in each case but is divisible by 17?

(a) 11 (b) 13
(c) 14 (d) 10

78. What is the least perfect square that is a multiple of 7, 11 and 12?

(a) 45000 (b) 853776
(c) 213444 (d) 8100

79. The HCF and LCM of two numbers are 24 and 168 and the numbers are in the ratio 1 : 7. Find the greater of the two numbers.

(a) 168 (b) 144
(c) 108 (d) 72

80. Sum of the measure of the interior angles of a polygon is 1620°. Find the number of sides of the polygon.

(a) 14 (b) 13
(c) 12 (d) 11

81. Which of the following statements is incorrect about nature of mathematics?

(a) Mathematics has its own language.

(b) Mathematics is an exact science.

(c) Mathematics is changeable in the

82. Which of the following options are correct in the context of nature of Mathematics?

(a) Mathematics' is a broad term that encompasses many branches and components.

(b) Mathematics is a way of thinking and it is related to our life on daily basis.

(c) Mathematics should be visualised as the vehicle to train a child to think, reason, analyse, and articulate logically.

(d) All of the above

83. Which among the following statement is true regarding mathematics?

(a) Boys easily learn mathematics in comparison to girls.

(b) Mathematics is very hard to understand at the primary stage.

(c) Everyone can learn and succeed in mathematics.

(d) Mathematics takes a lot of time to be understood in comparison to other subjects.

84. The important role of Mathematics in the syllabus is:

(a) Intellectual value
(b) Moral development
(c) Cultural development
(d) All of the above

85. The subject Mathematics is important in curriculum because it:

(a) Helps in the study of science subjects

(b) Improves logical thinking

(c) Is useful in daily life

(d) All of the above

86. Which of the following is/are characteristics of language of mathematics?

(a) Simplicity
(b) Accuracy
(c) Precision
(d) All of the above

87. Which of the following is not one of the merits of mathematical language?

(a) It is well defined

(b) It is clear

(c) It is highly compact and focussed

(d) It does not require other ordinary languages for its use

error will be:

(a) Lack of practice of these types of questions in the class.

(b) Lack of concrete experience of representation of decimal number on the number line.

(c) Careless attempt by the students.

(d) Misconception regarding the significance of zero in ordering decimal.

89. A learner has not understood certain concepts in a maths subject, to help him/her understand these concepts, the teacher will conduct:

(a) Diagnostic Assessment
(b) Formative Assessment
(c) Placement Assessment
(d) Summative Assessment

90. We may say that _______ implies a detailed study of learning difficulties to locate and identify the areas of learning difficulties.

(a) Drill work
(b) Remedial testing
(c) Diagnostic testing
(d) Evaluation and assessment

91. Identify the correct statement about the nature of science.

(a) The methodology of science and its demarcation from other fields continue to be a matter of philosophical debate.

(b) Even the most established and universal laws of science are always regarded as provisional, subject to modification in the light of new observations, experiments and analyses.

(c) Speculation and conjecture also have a place in science, but ultimately a scientific theory, to be acceptable, must be verified by relevant observations and/or experiments.

(d) Science is considered as value-natural and objective, and the laws of science are viewed as fixed.

92. Which approach adopted by a Science teacher reflects scientific temper on their part?

(a) Maintaining perfect discipline in the class

(b) Covering the prescribed syllabus as quickly as possible

(c) Encouraging students to ask

science in daily experience

(b) Understanding the principle of science through familiar experience and with the help of activities and experiments

(c) Developing questioning and enquiring skills

(d) Nurturing curiosity in children about the world around.

98. At secondary level, teaching science is a____.

(a) composite discipline

(b) segregated discipline

(c) discovery discipline

(d) None of these

99. Which of the following type of investigation is used by a teacher

105. Which of the following is the main thinking part of the human brain?

(a) Hind-brain

(b) Cerebrum

(c) Mid-brain

(d) None of the above

106. Which of the following contains Citric acid?

(a) Tomato   (b) Orange

(c) Tamarind   (d) Sour milk

107. If soft iron is used as a core in a solenoid, then it is called:

(a) electromagnet

(b) bar magnet

(c) ferromagnet

(d) iron magnet

93. Which one is an aural aid?

(a) Picture   (b) Slide

(c) Radio   (d) Greenboard

94. The evaluation that is concerned with the performance of the individual in terms of what he can do or the behavior he can demonstrate is termed as:

(a) Formative evaluation

(b) Norm-referenced evaluation

(c) Summative evaluation

(d) Criterion-referenced evaluation

95. Remedial teaching cannot be done for ____ students.

(a) dyslexic

(b) gifted

(c) showing lower than average performance

(d) showing above average performance

96. Which of the following tasks illustrates 'Science as inquiry'?
A. Identify a mammal from a picture of 4 animals.
B. Find out if ice cubes melt at the same rate in hot and cold water.
C. Enlist various units to measure temperature.
D. Explore factors which determine the floating or sinking of objects in liquids.

(a) C and D   (b) A and D

(c) Only D   (d) B and D

97. Which of the following is not an objective of science at upper primary level?

(a) Exploring various elements of science and start making sense of

III. Investigating Models

(a) II and III   (b) I, II and III

(c) I and II   (d) I and III

100. Which one of the following is not true about the nature of science?

(a) Science is always tentative.

(b) Science promotes scepticism.

(c) Science is a process of constructing knowledge.

(d) Science is static in nature.

101. An electrical device is used to separate irons from a heap of garbage. That device uses __________.

(a) electrical effect of current

(b) heating effect of current

(c) magnetic effect of current

(d) None

102. Which is the most electropositive stable element in the periodic table?

(a) Helium   (b) Sodium

(c) Francium   (d) Cesium

103. In medium, the nature of sound waves is:

(a) only transverse

(b) both longitudinal and transverse

(c) neither longitudinal nor transverse

(d) only longitudinal

104. Deficiency of vitamin ______ lowers the rate of calcium absorption from the food.

(a) Vitamin D   (b) Vitamin C

(c) Vitamin B   (d) Vitamin K

(c) Force   (d) Friction

109. Choose the correct group of conventional sources of energy from the following.

(a) Hydro power, geothermal energy, tidal energy

(b) Nuclear energy, solar energy, hydel power

(c) Oil, natural gas, firewood

(d) Coal, firewood, biogas

110. The shaking and trembling of earth is called:

(a) tsunami

(b) volcano

(c) earthquake

(d) none of these

111. Which of the following is a thermosetting plastic?

(a) Polythene   (b) Bakelite

(c) PVC   (d) Polyester

112. Which of the following gas is used in arc-welding?

(a) Helium   (b) Neon

(c) Oxygen   (d) Radon

113. Ruhi is from Kashmir, she likes to eat fish. Once she had gone to Goa and ate fish there but it tasted very different. Why do you think it tasted different?

(a) it was made in mustard oil

(b) it was made in coconut oil

(c) it was made in coconut curry

(d) None of the above

114. An ammeter is used to:

(a) measure the electric potential

(b) measure the electric current

flow
(c) measure the electric field value
(d) measure velocity of a body

115. The instrument used for detecting the small flow of electric current through a circuit is:
(a) Ammeter
(b) Voltmeter
(c) Galvanometer
(d) Rheostat

116. When two prism, one up and one down in contact receive white light. What is the colour of light that will emerge out?
(a) White colour (b) Red colour
(c) Blue colour (d) Green colour

			Bhature
(B)	Kashmir	II	Cooked snakes
(C)	Kerala	III	Boiled tapioca with any curry
(D)	Hong Kong	IV	Sea fish cooked in coconut oil
		V	Fish cooked in mustard oil

The correct match of the items of column I and II is-
(a) A - IV, B - III, C - V, D - II
(b) A - IV, B - I, C - III, D - II
(c) A - IV, B - V, C - III, D - II
(d) A - IV, B - III, C - II, D -V

118. Which of the following is true for light as it travels from air into water?
(a) Its velocity increases.
(b) Its frequency decreases
(c) Both its wavelength and frequency increases.
(d) Both its wavelength and velocity decrease.

119. A living organism is unexceptionally differentiated from a non-living structure on the basis of__________.
(a) reproduction
(b) growth and movement
(c) interaction with environment
(d) responsiveness

120. Which of the following changes when a body performs uniform circular motion?
(a) Speed
(b) Mass
(c) Direction
(d) Kinetic energy

// Hints and Solutions //

1(D). Motor development refers to the development of motor skills that makes children able to explore and manipulate their immediate environment.
Motor development is divided into two groups:
• Gross motor development: Development of gross motor skills is concerned with strength and speed as it refers to the development of larger muscles like arms and legs for bigger movements such as walking, jumping, etc.

wrists and fingers fir smaller movements such as writing, grasping small objects, etc.
So, it becomes clear that by motor development we mean the development of in the use of arms and legs strength and speed.

2(D). Development is correlated: All types of developments, i.e. physical, mental, social, and emotional, are related to each other e.g. a physically healthy child is likely to have superior sociability and emotional stability. The child develops as a unified whole. Each area of development is dependent on the other and thus influences the other developments. Sufi has appropriate weight and height for her age. She also has a well-developed language ability that enables her to communicate with everyone. She is loved by all and has positive self-esteem.
So, we can conclude that Development is correlated is the correct answer.

3(D). The growth and development of the child influenced by heredity and environment. Heredity is discussed as an internal factor and environment as an external factor.
Heredity:
• Heredity is the sum total of the traits potentially present in the fertilized ovum. All the qualities that a child has inherited from the parents are called heredity.
• Heredity consists of all the structures, physical characteristics, functions or capacities derived from parents and other ancestors
Environment:
• Environment means the totality of the stimuli that impinge on the organism from without whatever found around the individual may be called by the term

environment.
• The environment consists of various types of forces like physical, social, moral, economic, political cultural and emotional forces.
Thus from the above-mentioned points, it is clear that influence the economy is not true regarding heredity and environment.

4(C). Secondary Socialization:
• It occurs once the infant passes into the childhood phase and continues into maturity. It refers to the process that begins in the later years through agencies such as schools and peer groups.
• During this phase more than the family, some other agents of socialization like the school and peers' group begin to play a role in socializing the child.
interaction. Schools teach new behaviors and rules to children and expect them to act accordingly.
So, it could be concluded that the school acts as an agency of secondary socialization.

5(B). Piaget's Pre-operational stage is from 2 - 7 years. In this stage, the child faces problems with the concept of conservation and struggles with the idea of centration and irreversibility.
Preoperational stage (2-7 yrs): It is categorized into two parts:
• Pre-conceptual stage (2-4 yrs): In this, they began to pretend play; egocentrism and animism are controlled.
• Intuitive (4-7 yrs): In this, the child begins to be curious, wants to use primitive reasoning to know the things work.
So, we conclude that by the intuitive stage, Piaget refers to the pre-operational stage.

6(A). Criticisms of Kohlberg's Theory of Moral Development:
• Carol Gilligan has suggested that Kohlberg's theory was gender-biased since all of the subjects in his sample were male.
• Kohlberg has based his study primarily on a male sample.
• Critics have pointed out that Kohlberg's theory of moral development overemphasizes the concept of justice when making moral choices.
So, the statement 'Kohlberg has based his study primarily on a male sample', is correct in the context of this criticism.

7(C). Curricular goals in progressive education emphasize critical thinking as progressive education focused on developing critical thinking and problem-solving skills among the learners by enabling them to think or analyze the concepts beyond traditional ways.

Critical thinking is a skill that focuses on the analysis, evaluation and synthesizing of various available facts through experience, reflection, reasoning, communication, and arguments that allow us to make the best decision that could be possible.

So, it is clear that curricular goals in progressive education emphasize critical thinking.

8(A). Howard Gardner's multiple intelligences theory:
- The theory of multiple intelligences offers support for instructional approaches that incorporate a variety of connections for teaching and learning that validate the unique experiences, interests, and cultures of all students.
- Given that individuals gravitate to the support and enhance a differentiated classroom.
- This theory of multiple intelligence given by Gardner is useful in giving differentiated instruction to the students as they all are different in their capabilities so they are required to be instructed differently.
- Gardner initially formulated a list of seven types of intelligence and visual-Spatial Intelligence is one of them. Later, two more types of intelligence are added by Gardner.

So, it is concluded that Howard Gardner's multiple intelligences theory impacts classrooms today in schools in terms of differentiated instruction.

9(C). Interpersonal skills: The ability to understand and effectively interact with others. It is an ability to notice and make distinctions among the moods, temperaments, motivations, and intentions of other people and potential to act on this knowledge (teachers, mental health professionals, parents, religious and political leaders)

So, we can conclude that a child has the ability to understand and effectively interact with others. The child is showing interpersonal intelligence.

10(B). Critical thinking aims at simplification/ generalization on the one hand and truth and accuracy on the other. It adheres to establish canons of logic. Logic is the science of thinking. It offers general rules for thinking.

Critical thinking is described in psychology as convergent thinking because anyone and everyone who wants to arrive at truth must conform to the canons of logic.

11(D). Children acquire gender roles through media, socialization, culture and not by tutoring.

Acquiring Gender Roles:
- Socialization: Through socialization, the child learns that men are supposed to go and work, while women are supposed to take care of household work and other responsibilities regarding home.
- Media: It highly influences gender role because when a girl or a boy admires someone as their role model, they try to adapt their style which they observe in the movie, advertisement and news and they mould up their lifestyle by following them.
- Culture: It influences gender in several ways such as one's education, skill, thinking, language, emotions and behaviour.

12(C). Individual difference refers to the difference which distinguishes an mental, etc.

A teacher should provide a variety of learning experience if learners display individual differences as it will help in:
- selecting relevant prompts to be suitable for their ability level.
- combining different types of prompts to make them inculcate skills.
- catering to the range of learning needs and requirements of diverse learners.
- making learning effective for students who learn differently either visually, auditory, etc.

So, it could be concluded that a teacher should provide a variety of learning experience if learners display individual differences.

13(A). In order to know what children understand and are able to know, assessment is done. It is a systematic process of using data to measure skills and knowledge. By assessment, a teacher documents the improvements by a student and his endeavors towards learning.

With assessments as an inbuilt process in teaching-learning, teachers can understand the needs of the learners better and accordingly change or adjust the quality of their instruction during the process of teaching the unit itself.

14(B). From the above-mentioned situation, it could be interpreted that the teacher is assessing the students by conducting the formative assessment as it refers to monitor the child's progress throughout the teaching-learning process. In this case, it will help the teacher to know the children's learning needs regarding that topic and then meet the needs by remedial teaching.

Assessment for Learning (Formative Assessment):
- It is also referred to as internal evaluation.
- In this form of assessment, a teacher embeds various forms of assessment all through the teaching and learning process. Therefore, it is an ongoing assessment that allows teachers to monitor students on a day-to-day basis and modify their teaching based on what the students need to be successful.

So, we can conclude that a teacher asks his/her students to draw a concept map to reflect their comprehension of a topic. He/She is conducting the formative assessment.

15(B). In progressive-education children are seen as active explorers as progressive education:
- emphasizes to enhance skills and understanding of the learners by use their knowledge and talents effectively.
- ensures the active participation of students by working in a group and applying practical knowledge to complete an activity.

So, it could be concluded that in progressive-education children are seen as active explorers.

16(D). A visually challenged child is the one who has a problem seeing with the naked eyes or is not able to see completely. Instruction adaptations that a teacher can follow while working with students who are 'visually challenged' are:
- Should speak clearly and audibly to help them learn through listening or auditory learning
- Use a lot of touches and feel materials.
- Make use of material adaptations according to the individual needs, the actual degree of functional vision, presence of any other disabilities
- Using a variety of tactile materials like rough or smooth, cold or hot, wet or dry, vibrate or stationary helps the students to touch, feel, and understand the differences between the materials

So, we can conclude that a teacher should speak clearly and use a lot of touches and feel materials while working with students who are 'Visually Challenged'.

17(D). A gifted child is the one who displays consistently remarkable performance in various physical or cognitive aspects and exhibits superiority in general intelligence levels.

Map work during studies, Challenging home assignments, and Mathematics or Science Olympiad are the enrichment programs that are suitable for gifted children in the school as these programs:
- can satisfy and utilize their intelligence.

- can give enriched learning experiences to them.
- Can develop the ability to visualize the spatial relationship.
- Can allow students to express their interests in the subject.
- Can give students the opportunity to try new things and explore.

So, it could be concluded that all of these are true in the context of the question.

18(A). Creativity is a mental and social process involving the generation of new ideas or concepts , or new associations of the creative mind between existing ideas or concepts. An alternative conception of creativeness is that it is simply the act of making something new.

- From a scientific point of view, the products of creative thought (sometimes generate or recognize ideas, alternatives, or possibilities that may be useful in solving problems, communicating with others, and entertaining ourselves and others. Ability to generate, create, or discover new ideas, solutions, and possibilities. divergent thinking: the opposite of convergent thinking, the capacity for exploring multiple potential answers or solutions to a given question or problem (e.g., coming up with many different uses for a common object)

So, it is concluded that writing a script for role play in class is the best example of creativity.

19(A). PECS is a method to teach Autistic children.

- It is a type of augmentative and alternative communication technique where individuals with little or no verbal ability learn to communicate using picture cards.
- Children use the pictures to "vocalize" a desire, observation, or feeling.
- Many children with autism learn visually, and therefore, this type of communication technique has been shown to be effective in improving independent communication skills.

Thus from above-mentioned points, it is clear that PECS is a method to teach Autistic children.

20(A). Effective strategies to address learners from disadvantaged and deprived backgrounds:

- Inclusive education is a movement to empower the vulnerable and marginalized groups to overcome the disadvantages of unequalized socialization and give them examples from diverse settings.
- The curriculum should to be specific and related to the needs and real-life experiences. Emphasis should be on learning manual skills, life skills and technical efficiency.
- Sometime the teacher should talk to the learners to understand their needs and challenges faced by them.
- Interest in learning has to be, created by the teacher, effort should be towards developing self-confidence, self-respect and a sense of cultural identity.
- Form collaborative groups to work on activities and encourage students to support each other.
- Motivate the students to set moderately challenging goals and provide appropriate instructional support.

Thus from above-mentioned points, it is clear that in order to address learners from diverse backgrounds, a teacher should students actively involved in learning. A few of the effective teaching practices include:

- Delivering lessons in an interesting manner by connecting the content being taught with real-life situations
- Using appropriate teaching techniques such as brainstorming, group learning, activity method, role plays, etc. that allows students to actively participate in the learning process
- Making use of audio/visual aids to cater to all the different senses
- Motivating students to learn more effectively through inquiry, experimentation, questioning, application, and reflection, leading to the creation of ideas.
- Providing opportunities to question, enquire, debate, reflect, and arrive at concepts or create new ideas.
- Employing flexibility and creativity while imparting knowledge rather than being rigid.

So, students can be encouraged to attend regular classes if teachers ensure to make use of interesting techniques.

22(B). Alternative conceptions are generated as a concept is understood from different aspects, while the misconception is a thought process that goes in the wrong direction due to a lack of complete information or just ignorance.

- Alternative conceptions and misconceptions are not always baseless rather they represent children's intuitive ideas about particular concepts and the world around them as it shows their thinking and they can think and put forward their views.
- The formation of alternative conceptions and misconceptions is very natural among children as well as adults because it is a natural thought process and no two minds can think alike exactly.

- A teacher should definitely attend to these alternative conceptions and misconceptions as they are significant in process of teaching-learning because they are very helpful; in developing critical thinking. Without this, a child would not be able to put forward one's own views and would end up mugging things.

Thus, it is concluded that alternate conceptions and misconceptions hold by children represent intuitive ideas about particular concepts.

23(C). All learners make mistakes. As someone has said: "You can't learn without goofing". Whether you are learning how to ride a bicycle, how to fly a kite or learn a language, everyone does make mistakes.

- An error is an incorrect form and a sure teachers to understand students thinking or thought processes since they are a window to children's thinking.
- Errors are necessary for the learning process to give insight into children's thinking. It helps the teacher to be aware of learners' learning styles and to cater to them according to their needs.
- Making an error cannot be just due to negligence and carelessness. It may be so that students are thinking about it in a different manner other than what is the right process.
- To understand this, a teacher should analyze what mistake the students are doing, how the mistake is generated, and where exactly they tend to make mistakes.

So, it is clear that errors offer an opportunity for the teachers to understand students' thinking.

24(B). Characteristics of emotions

- Emotions are comparatively more complex in nature.
- Any emotional experience is preceded and accompanied by feelings. For example, the feeling of pleasure will lead or will be accompanied by the emotion of happiness/ joy.
- Emotion is an effective process that is much more active.
- Emotion is both subjective and objective.
- Emotions are of different types, for example, anger, joy, jealousy, and so forth.
- Physiological changes are experienced.

So, we can conclude that emotion is both subjective and objective statement is correct regarding emotion.

25(A). Learning is most effective when there is intrinsic motivation - a desire to learn from within, which finds satisfaction in the achievement itself and does not bother about other factors.

- Intrinsic Motivation refers to motivation that is driven by an interest or enjoyment in the task itself, and exists within the individual rather than relying on any external pressure. Intrinsic Motivation is based on taking pleasure in an activity rather working towards an external reward. Intrinsic motivation results in high-quality learning and creativity For example; preparing any project in science/ mathematics, participating in a sport may give pleasure to the pupil as a result of which he/she is motivated to undertake similar activities on his/her own.

Thus, it is concluded that student wants to participate in a sport because it's fun and she enjoys it is an example that shows

society. learning such qualities as sharing, cooperation, waiting for one's turn, respecting other people and things, and so on, forms a part of learning through social context.

- Emotions are the feelings or affect of an individual towards a person, object, or situation, which may generate physiological arousal, conscious experience, and/or behavioral expressions.
- Learning involves the acquisition of new knowledge, skills, values, and dispositions and as it takes shape in the young child's life it is more than intellectual in nature. It is a process located in and influenced by the social and emotional experiences and characteristics of the environment.
- The nature and quality of emotional

Features of the Deductive method are:
- General to particular or abstract to concrete.
- Facts are given to the child and the principle of growth is not considered.
- The formula is decided and children are made to memorize it without applying logic to it.
- Children are made to learn and a lot of emphasis is given to the rote learning process.
- It starts with a rule and the application part is more in it, does not appreciate or follow the principle of learning by doing.
- It requires individual learning and in this process, the child is inactive and is a one-way process.
- Less interaction between teacher and student, the student only listens but does not know why we are doing this or

includes:
- Cultural content: Cultural content and its value are significant influencers in the process of learning. A child who is aware of his culture and is motivated to preserve the cultural integrity of the society develops an interest in learning more about the society and thinks about the ways towards the betterment of the society.
- Maturation: Maturation is the process by which we change, grow, and develop throughout life. The maturation of the learner affects learning because maturation is related to the structure and potential capacity.
- Interest: Interest refers to a feeling that keeps learners involved and attentive while learning or doing a specific task. Subjects in which a learner is interested reflect his motivation, attraction, and attentiveness in favor of that subject. If a learner is disinterested in learning a particular subject it shows that he/she has a feeling of demotivation against that subject.
- Emotional factor/Emotions: Emotion impacts our levels of motivation. Positive emotions can help a student engage with learning longer because they stay motivated. Emotions during learning also impact our feelings toward education. If we have positive experiences, we are more likely to enjoy our schooling and develop a love for learning.

So, it is clear that all (i), (ii), (iii) and (iv) factors influence learning.

27(C). Characteristics of Social-emotional Development
- The social context involves the interpersonal relationships of an individual, her acquired social skills, values, and how an individual adjusts to

are crucial for the learning to take place. Thus from the above-mentioned points, it is clear that social context and emotions play a very important role in learning.

28(D). The teaching-learning process is the heart of extension education, and the fulfillment of the aims and objectives of development depends on it.
- Prerequisite behavior: Gagne advocated that processes of learning move from the simple to the complex. The learner has to develop, prerequisite capabilities before s/he acquires new terminal behavior. Thus the use of a hierarchy of learning and task analysis are integral parts of instructional transactions.
- Learners' characteristics: Learners' individual differences, readiness, and motivation to learn are the important issues to be considered before designing instructional activities.
- Cognitive process and instruction: The transfer of learning, the self-management skills of the learner, and teaching learners the skills of problem-solving are integral parts of the internal conditions of learning, applicable to instruction. The skill of learning 'how to learn' should be developed in the learner and the emphasis should be on the learner's individuality.

So, we can conclude that none of the above is incorrect regarding teaching-learning process.

29(D). Deductive learning is a more teacher-centered approach to education. Introduction of Generalizations and concepts is firstly given to learners, and to support the learning examples and activities are suggested. Minimum interaction is there between teacher and student, and the teaching method which is generally used is the lecture method.

30(D). Thinking is a pattern of behaviour in which we make use of internal representations (symbols, signs, etc.) of things and events for the solution of some specific, purposeful problem.
Characteristics of thinking are:
- It is one of the most important aspects of one's cognitive behaviour.
- It depends on both – perception and memory.
- It involves trial and error; analysis and synthesis; foresight and hindsight.
- It is a symbolic behaviour.
- It is always directed to achieve some purpose.
- Thinking is a symbolic activity. (e.g.: engineers use mental symbols to design the plan for buildings).
- Thinking is a mental process that starts with a problem and concludes with its solution.
- There is mental exploration instead of motor exploration.

So, we can conclude that all of the above is true.

31(A). According to the passage, "This may be visible more in the rural belt, where many non-farming entities purchase fertile farmland, not for farming but for money parking purposes. The demonetization and consequent reduction in the shadow economy would bring the demand for such farmlands down."
The paragraph clearly states that most black money hoarders utilize their hoarded cash to buy fertile agricultural land as means of turning the black to white, which is a part of the shadow economy.

32(B). According to passage, "The total value of old Rs.500 and Rs.1000 notes in the circulation is to the tune of Rs.14.2 trillion, which is about 85% of the total value of the

currency in circulation."
So, it is concluded that 85% of the total value of currency in circulation is made up by the old Rs.500 and Rs.1000 notes.

33(D). The idiom 'cash cow' refers to any products or services that yield a profit or income on a regular basis.

34(D). According to the passage, "The move is also likely to have a habit-changing impact on the Indian populous and there could be an increased belief in keeping cash in the banks rather than stashed at home and using formal banking channels for their spending needs."
As per the paragraph, Indians are well-known for not availing of proper banking services and since people have been mightily inconvenienced because of this

government and its effect on the economy.

36(A). The meaning of the given words:
• Formal: Officially sanctioned or recognized
• Official: relating to an authority or public body and its activities and responsibilities
• Ceremonial: relating to or used for formal religious or public events
• Informal: 'unorthodox' or 'unofficial'
• Traditional: existing in or as part of a tradition; long-established
So, from the meaning of the given word we can say that official is the correct synonym of the word 'formal'.

37(C). According to passage, "It will improve the medium to long-term "Current Account and Savings Account (CASA)" ratio of the banks."
The full form of CASA is Current Account and Savings Account.

38(D). According to passage, "The World Bank in July 2010 estimated the size of the shadow economy for India at 20.7% of the Gross Domestic Product (GDP) in 1999 and rising to 23.2% in 2007."

39(C). The meaning of the given words:
• Compliance: the state or fact of according with or meeting rules or standards
• Defiance: open resistance; bold disobedience
• Agreement: harmony or accordance in opinion or feeling
• Assent: the expression of approval or agreement
• Consensus: a general agreement
So, from the meaning of the given word we can say that defiance is the correct antonym of the word 'compliance'.

40(D). According to the given lines,

"And I waterd it in fears"
Here the 'it' refers to wrath which means anger. The poet is comparing suppressed anger to a tree that kept growing over years into a garden.
Therefore, the poet watered 'anger' with his fears.
Hence, the correct option is (D)

41(B). The poet is representing two scenarios in his poem.
• First, when he confessed his anger to his friend and it subsides.
• Second, when he suppressed his anger and how it kept growing over years and became poisonous.
• If we read both the lines carefully, we will easily notice the repetition of (And I).
• Such repetition of the same phrase at the

• Foe: Enemy
• Outstretched: It means that something is stretched to its capacity.
When a person is outstretched it means they are lying on the floor.
But in the last stanza of the poem, the poet is narrating how his enemy sneaked into his garden.
Since the tree and its fruit were poisonous, the enemy died and that's why he was outstretched under the tree.
Therefore, from all the points given above, we can infer that the last line of the poem means 'The enemy was lying dead under the tree.'

43(D). The line given in the question is from the last stanza of the poem.
• Velid is an archaic use of the word veiled which means to cover.
• The word pole refers to the tree of wrath that the poet has cultivated.
• So, through this line, the poet is describing the nighttime.
Therefore, the expression When the night had veild the pole means 'The dark night was all around the tree.'

44(C). The poem uses simple language to present its readers with a powerful message.
• The poet believes that anger that stays with an individual for a long time is dangerous.
• A metaphor is when two things are compared directly.
• An extended metaphor is simply a metaphor that extends over lines, paragraphs or stanzas.
• In this poem, the extended metaphor is a tree and it is used for anger.
Therefore, from all the points given above, we can infer that the literary device used throughout the poem is 'Extended Metaphor'.

45(A). In the whole poem, the poet is actively cultivating his anger with fears, tears and smiles:
• And I waterd it in fears,
• Night & morning with my tears:
• And I sunned it with smiles
Eventually, his tree turned into a garden as he expressed in the last stanza "And into my garden stole"
Therefore, from all the points given above, we can infer that the garden in the poem refers to anger.

46(C). Language teaching is the process in which a child gains communicative comprehension or fluency over a language. It involves practice by learners where facilitation is provided by a teacher.
Language learning:
• It is a result of deliberate and conscious communication.
• Input-rich communicational environments are a prerequisite for language learning. It arouses the interest and curiosity of learners to learn a specific language.
• Inputs include textbooks, learner-chosen texts, and class libraries allowing for a variety of genres. For example, Big Books for young learners, parallel books and materials in more than one language, radio/audio cassettes, and "authentic" materials.
• Also, these inputs and the environment that is enriched with these types of resources can help to minimize the gap between incomprehension and language learning i.e., the disability to interpret and comprehend a language and the ability to comprehend and use a language practically.
So, both statements regarding language learning are true.

47(B). Language is a symbolic, rule-governed system, shared by a group of people to express their thoughts and feelings. In a child, language development takes place through language acquisition and language learning.
Language acquisition:
• It refers to the subconscious process of learning a native or second language because of the innate capacity of the human brain.
• It is a natural process whereby children acquire language by observing and repeating what they hear in their native environment.
• Language acquisition does not require any formal instruction, children acquire the language without being taught.
• Language acquisition is a natural process so, one does not forget one's native language.

Language learning:
- It refers to the result of deliberate and conscious effort for a better understanding of foundational skills of language learning.
- It refers to have a basic knowledge of grammatical rules and their use in communication.

So, it could be concluded that the 'acquired system' or 'acquisition' of a language is the subconscious process of learning.

48(B). Language teaching is less about the school and more about the process of learning English. The modern approach to all language learning and teaching is the scientific one and is based on sound linguistic principles.
- Principle of Graded Patterns is one of the principles of materials preparation for

do not include phonetic sequence.

50(C). Grammar is defined as a theory of language. We consider language as rule-governed behavior, relating to sounds, word formation, and structure. Here grammar constitutes a subset of rules relating to morphology and syntax.
- It takes time to learn a language, even if it is by acquisition. It requires context to learn a language, for example, children speak the language when they have previous knowledge or experience.
- Grammatical Rules instruct a language user that how language should be used correctly and clearly. But it is widely known that effective language learning takes place from practicing it in real context rather than following the accurate rule.

- The disorders that come under language disorders/disabilities include Stuttering, Specific Language Impairment, Developmental Phonological Disorders, Aphasia, Dyspraxia, etc.

Thus, it is concluded that when a child has difficulties in understanding or expressing language that is called language disability.

53(C). Language skills are necessary for effective communication in any environment and to interact with others. It allows an individual to comprehend and produce language for proper and effective interpersonal communication.

The four basic language skills and their natural order are listening-speaking-reading-writing. These foundational skills of language are divided into two categories

system of complex habits, and habits are acquired slowly." So, language patterns should be taught gradually, in cumulative graded steps.
- This means the teacher should go on adding each new element or pattern to previous ones. New patterns of language should be introduced and practiced with vocabulary that students already know.

So, we can conclude that one of the principles of materials preparation for language learning is that materials need to be graded appropriately.

49(D). Language teaching is the process whereby a child gains communicative comprehension or fluency over a language. It involves practice by learners where facilitation is provided by a teacher. Some of the Principles of Language Teaching are the Principle of Graded Patterns, the Principle of Selection and graduation, etc.

Principle of Selection and Gradation:

Selection of the language material is considered as the first requisite of good teaching. It should be done in respect of grammatical items and vocabulary and structures.

Gradation of the language material means placing the language items in order. It involves grouping and sequence.
- Grouping the system of language means what sounds, words, phrases, and meanings are to be taught. Thus we have Phonetic grouping, Lexical grouping, Grammatical grouping, Semantic grouping, and Structure grouping.
- Sequence means what comes after what. In teaching a foreign language, the sequence should be there in the arrangement of phrases (grammatical sequence) words (lexical sequence), and meaning (semantic sequence).

So, we can conclude that the principles of sequencing in teaching a foreign language,

language. It is the womb that gives birth to sentences. These sentences are fertilized using grammar to form correct and appropriate speech.
- Grammar is defined as a theory of language. We consider language as rule-governed behavior, relating to sounds, word formation, and structure. Here grammar constitutes a subset of rules relating to morphology and syntax.
- Grammar rules are made easier if they are given in a context using examples and teaching grammar in context provides accuracy in the target language.
- Learning grammar in context using examples will allow learners to see how rules can be used in sentences.
- Providing the chance to practice grammar in context will allow learners to understand how language works and this will improve their communication skills.

Thus, it is concluded that (A) is correct, but (R) is not correct.

52(C). Language is the rule-based use of speech sounds to communicate. Language disorders or language disabilities involve the processing of linguistic information.
- Problems that may be experienced can involve grammar (syntax and/or morphology), semantics (meaning), understanding or expressing language, or other aspects of language.
- Disordered language may be due to a receptive problem, that is, a difficulty in understanding speech sounds (involving impaired language comprehension).
- It can also be due to an expressive problem, i.e., a difficulty in producing the speech sounds (involving language production), that follow the arbitrary rules of a specific language.

skills can measure learner's ability to produce language.
- Both skills are concerned with language product or output through speech or written tests.

Receptive skills:
- The receptive skills of language are listening and reading because these skills don't require the production of language.
- These skills focus on an individual's ability of understanding and comprehending language.

So, from the above-mentioned points, it becomes clear that the order advocated for learning the language skills is listening, speaking, reading, writing.

54(D). Language is a purely human and non-instinctive method of communicating ideas, emotions, and desires by means of voluntarily produced symbols.
- Language skills should be taught in an integrated manner. In order to provide more focused and significant learning situations, teachers must integrate the four language skills while teaching and practicing the language.
- When we speak, we also listen simultaneously. When we write we are also reading. This engagement with language enables us to internalize the underlying grammaticality of the language.

Thus, it is concluded that language skills should be taught in an integrated manner.

55(C). Communicative competence refers to a learner's ability to use language to communicate successfully. This competence can be oral, written, or even nonverbal.
- It is an inclusive term that refers to possessing the knowledge of the language as well as the skill to use the

language in real-life situations for fulfilling communicative needs.

- It includes the ability to use grammatical structures in different situations to convey and interpret messages and to negotiate meanings.
- Teachers can use information gap and role-play activities to evaluate learners' competence for speaking. It includes accuracy, fluency, complexity, appropriateness, and capacity.

Thus, it is concluded that communicative competence should be the main focus for the evaluation of speaking skills.

56(C). Decoding: This refers to the ability to read individual words and to sound out unfamiliar words accurately and automatically. Most reading problems are related to difficulty with decoding.

- Reading of nonsense words to eliminate memorization of words,
- Reading in context.

So, we can conclude that decoding in evaluating language proficiency refers to the ability to read individual words and to sound out unfamiliar words accurately.

57(C). Linguaphone: Speaking a language is an active skill, something you learn by doing, not just studying. This is the practical approach taken by Linguaphone to language learning. Linguaphone enables understanding of the language and is able to converse with and understand real people speaking the language. It helps in teaching pronunciation, accent and intonation.

So, it becomes clear that Linguaphone is a utility in teaching English pronunciation, accent and intonation.

58(D). Remedial Teaching is an integral part of the teaching-learning program, also known as compensatory or corrective teaching.

Objectives of Remedial Teaching in the English language:

- To eliminate ineffective habits
- To make learners learn better by giving additional help
- To provide learning activities and practical experiences to pupils according to their abilities and requirements.
- To teach again the language items not properly learned
- To arise learners' interest in learning with stimulating approaches
- Help the pupils to get rid of their common or specific weaknesses.
- To transmit practical experiences to learners according to their diverse needs
- To provide individualized teaching with

intensive remedial support.

So, we can conclude that all of the above are the objectives of remedial teaching in the English language.

59(B). The main purpose of using oral drill is that they help students gain confidence, and they help the teacher draw learners' attention to phonological features (i.e., accuracy and pronunciation) of the target language.

60(C). A smartboard is an audio-visual aid that maximizes learning with the help of the auditory and visual systems.

- Smartboards in classrooms allow teachers and students to access a wide range of educational resources that are available online, from videos to texts to animations and apps.
- Audio-visual aids activate the sense of independence.
- Being an audio-visual learning aid video is used to present the lesson effectively involving both sound and pictures for heightening learner's intellectual abilities to make learning meaningful.

So, from the above-mentioned points, it becomes clear that smartboard is an audio-visual aid.

61(B). Given,
$$\sqrt{324} + 9^2 - 7^2 = 2 \times (?)^2$$
$$\Rightarrow 18 + 81 - 49 = 2 \times (?)^2$$
$$\Rightarrow 50 = 2 \times (?)^2$$
$$\Rightarrow \frac{50}{2} = (?)^2$$
$$\Rightarrow 25 = (?)^2$$
$$\Rightarrow ? = \sqrt{25}$$
$$\Rightarrow ? = 5$$
$\therefore$ The value of (?) is 5.

62(C). Given,
The Ratio of Alcohol and water in two pots respectively $= 2 : 3$ and $4 : 1$
Let the quantity of mixture in each pot $= x$ liters
Then the quantity of alcohol in each pot respectively $= \left(\frac{2}{5}\right)x$, and $\left(\frac{4}{5}\right)x$
And the quantity of water in each pot respectively $= \left(\frac{3}{5}\right)x$, and $\left(\frac{1}{5}\right)x$
Required ratio
$$= \left[\left(\frac{2}{5}\right)x + \left(\frac{4}{5}\right)x\right] : \left[\left(\frac{3}{5}\right)x + \left(\frac{1}{5}\right)x\right]$$
$$\Rightarrow \left(\frac{6x}{5}\right) : \left(\frac{4x}{5}\right) = 3 : 2$$
$\therefore$ The ratio of Alcohol and water in new mixture is $3 : 2$.

63(D). Given,
Ratio of ages of A and B after 5 years $= 5 : 8$
Sum of their ages after 8 years $= 71$ years
Let the ages of A and B after 5 years be $5x$ and $8x$ respectively.
Age of A after 8 years $= 5x + 3$
Age of B after 8 years $= 8x + 3$

According to the question,
$$5x + 3 + 8x + 3 = 71$$
$$\Rightarrow 13x + 6 = 71$$
$$\Rightarrow 13x = 65$$
$$\Rightarrow x = 5$$
Age of B after 5 years $= (8 \times 5) = 40$ years
present age of B $= (40 - 5) = 35$ years
$\therefore$ Present age of B is 35 years.

64(C). Given,
Marked price of a bat $=$ Rs. 500
Discount percentage $= 10\%$
Selling price $= 500 - 500 \times \frac{10}{100} = 450$
Total selling price $= 450 - 10 = 440$
Profit percentage $= 25\%$
125% of cost price $= 440$
Cost price $= 440 \times \frac{100}{125} = 352$
$\therefore$ His cost price of the bat is Rs. 352.

According to the question,
$$\Rightarrow 2\pi r(r + h) = 1672m^2$$
$$\Rightarrow 2 \times \frac{22}{7} \times r \times 19 = 1672m^2$$
$$\Rightarrow r = \frac{(1672 \times 7)}{(2 \times 22 \times 19)}$$
$$\Rightarrow r = 14$$
$$\therefore h = 19 - 14$$
$$= 5m$$
Volume of the cylinder $= \pi r^2 h$
$$= \frac{22}{7} \times 14 \times 14 \times 5$$
$$= 3080m^3$$

66(A). Given,
A number is as much greater than 36 as it is less than 86.
Let x be the number.
According to the question,
$$\Rightarrow x - 36 = 86 - x$$
$$\Rightarrow 2x = 122$$
$$\therefore x = 61$$

67(A). Given,
Length of the rectangular field $= 242m$
Area of the rectangular field $= 4840m^2$
Cost of fencing $= 0.50$ Rs. per meter
Area of the rectangular field $= ($ length $\times$ breadth $)$
$$\Rightarrow 4840 = (242 \times \text{breadth})$$
$$\Rightarrow \text{breadth} = 20m$$
Perimeter of the rectangular field $= 2 \times$ (length $+$ breadth)
$$= 2 \times (242 + 20)$$
$$= 524m$$
Total cost of fencing of the rectangular field $= ($ Perimeter $\times$ cost of fencing per meter $)$
$$= (524 \times 0.50)$$
$$= 262$$
$\therefore$ The total cost of fencing of the rectangular field is Rs. 262.

68(A). Given,
Area of four walls of a room $= 660m^2$
Height of the room$(h) = 11m$
Length $=$ twice the width

As we know,
Area of four walls of a room $= 2(l + b) \times h$
 where 'l' is length of the room and 'b' is breadth of the room and h is the height of the room.
Area of ceiling of a room $= (l \times b)$
Let the length and breadth of the room be $2x$ and x respectively.
Area of four walls of a room $= 2(l + b) \times h$
$\Rightarrow 2 \times (2x + x) \times 11 = 660$
$\Rightarrow 2 \times (3x) \times 11 = 660$
$\Rightarrow x = 10$
Area of ceiling of a room $= (l \times b)$
$= (2x \times x)$
$= 200$
$\therefore$ The area of ceiling of the room is $200 m^2$.

69(A). Given,
Speed of man $= \frac{2}{5}$ of his original speed

time taken by him be t minutes.
Distance $=$ Speed $\times$ Time
Distance $= 5x \times t = 5xt$ ...(1)
Reduced speed $= \frac{2}{5}$ of $5x$
Reduced speed $= 2x$
New time taken $(t') = t + 15$
Distance $=$ Reduced speed $\times t'$
$\Rightarrow$ Distance $= 2x \times (t + 15)$
$\Rightarrow$ Distance $= 2xt + 30x$ ...(2)
By equating (1) and (2) we'll get
$5xt = 2xt + 30x$
$\Rightarrow 3xt = 30x$
$\Rightarrow t = \frac{30x}{3x}$
$\Rightarrow t = 10$
$\therefore$ Time taken with original speed is 10 minutes.

70(D). Given data values are $3, 8, 6, 7, 1, 6, 10, 6, 7, 2k + 5, 9, 7$, and 13.
In the above data set, values 6, and 7 have occurred more times i.e., 3 times But given that mode is 7.
So, 7 should occur more times than 6.
So, the variable $2k + 5$ must be 7.
$\Rightarrow 2k + 5 = 7$
$\Rightarrow 2k = 2$
$\therefore k = 1$

71(B). Given,
The mean of 20 observations $= 15$ and two observations was wrongly copied as 3 and 6 instead of 8 and 4.
As we know,
New mean $=$ Old mean $+$
$\frac{(\text{Sum of right observation - the sum of wrong observation})}{\text{Number of observation}}$
$= 15 + \frac{[(8+4)-(6+3)]}{20}$
$= 15 + \frac{(12-9)}{20}$
$= 15 + \frac{3}{20}$
$= 15 + 0.15$
$= 15.15$

So, the correct mean is 15.15.

72(B). Given,
$r = 28$ cm
As we know,
Circumference $= 2\pi r$ (for a central angle of $360°$)
For a central angle of $45°$, length of arc
$= 2\pi r \times \frac{45}{360} = \frac{\pi r}{4}$
$= \frac{22}{7} \times \frac{28}{4}$
$= 22$ cm

73(B). Given,
$\sqrt{y} = \sqrt{4} - \sqrt{6}$
Square the equation, we get
$\Rightarrow (\sqrt{y})^2 = (\sqrt{4} - \sqrt{6})^2$
$\Rightarrow y = (\sqrt{4})^2 + (\sqrt{6})^2 - 2 \times \sqrt{4} \times \sqrt{6}$
$= 4 + 6 - 4\sqrt{6}$
$\Rightarrow y = 10 - 4\sqrt{6}$
$= 100 + 96 - 80\sqrt{6}$
$\Rightarrow y^2 = 196 - 80\sqrt{6}$
By putting the value of y and y^2 in equation, we get
$= 196 - 80\sqrt{6} - 20(10 - 4\sqrt{6}) + 12$
$= 196 - 80\sqrt{6} - 200 + 80\sqrt{6} + 12$
$= 208 - 200$
$= 8$

74(B). $OA \times OB = OD \times OC$
Let the length of OD be x.
$\Rightarrow 12 \times 5 = x \times (4 + x)$
$\Rightarrow x^2 + 4x - 60 = 0$
$\Rightarrow (x + 10)(x - 6) = 0$
$\Rightarrow x = -10$ or $x = 6$
We take the value of $x = 6cm$ ($\because$ Length is always positive)

75(B). Given,
$x\left(3 - \frac{2}{x}\right) = \frac{3}{x}$
$\Rightarrow 3x - 2 = \frac{3}{x}$
$\Rightarrow 3x - \frac{3}{x} = 2$
$\Rightarrow 3\left(x - \frac{1}{x}\right) = 2$
$\Rightarrow x - \frac{1}{x} = \frac{2}{3}$
$\Rightarrow \left(x - \frac{1}{x}\right)^2 = \left(\frac{2}{3}\right)^2$
$\Rightarrow \left(x - \frac{1}{x}\right)^2 = \frac{4}{9}$
$\Rightarrow x^2 + \frac{1}{x^2} - 2 = \frac{4}{9}$
$\Rightarrow x^2 + \frac{1}{x^2} = \frac{4}{9} + 2$
$\Rightarrow x^2 + \frac{1}{x^2} = \frac{4+18}{9}$
$\Rightarrow x^2 + \frac{1}{x^2} = \frac{22}{9}$
$= 2\frac{4}{9}$

76(D). Given,
$(a + b) = -1$
$a^2 + b^2 = 25$
As we know,
Now,
$(a + b)^2 = a^2 + 2ab + b^2$
$(a - b)^2 = a^2 - 2ab + b^2$

Now,
$(a + b) = -1$
Squaring both the sides, we get
$(a + b)^2 = (-1)^2$
$\Rightarrow a^2 + 2ab + b^2 = 1$
$\Rightarrow 2ab + 25 = 1$
$\Rightarrow 2ab = 1 - 25$
$\Rightarrow 2ab = -24$
$\Rightarrow ab = \frac{-24}{2}$
$\Rightarrow ab = -12$
$(a - b)^2 = a^2 - 2ab + b^2$
$= 25 - 2 \times (-12)$
$= 25 + 2 \times 12$
$= 25 + 24$
$= 49$

77(B). Given,
Least number when divided by 21, 28, 30, and 35 leaves 10 as a remainder in each then their LCM also divisibly by that number
On Taking L.C.M of 21, 28, 30, and 35 = 420
Least number 420k + 10 is divisible by 17 = $420 \times 2 + 10 = 850$
Least number which when divided by 21, 28, 30, and 35 leaves 10 as a remainder in each case but divisible by 17 = 850
$\therefore$ Sum of digits of this least number $= 8 + 5 + 0 = 13$

78(C). Given,
The numbers = 7, 11, 12
As we know,
LCM = The LCM of the numbers is the smallest number that is the multiple of every one of the numbers
Let the least perfect square be X.
$\Rightarrow 7 = 7 \times 1$
$\Rightarrow 11 = 11 \times 1$
$\Rightarrow 12 = 2 \ 2 \times 3$
$\Rightarrow$ The LCM of (7, 11, 12) $= 2^2 \times 3 \times 11 \times 7$
The least perfect square $= 2^2 \times 3^2 \times 11^2 \times 7^2 = 213444$
$\therefore$ The required result will be 213444.

79(A). Given:
HCF = 24
LCM = 168
Ratio of numbers = 1 : 7
As we know,
Product of numbers = LCM $\times$ HCF
Let numbers be x and 7x.
x $\times$ 7x = 24 $\times$ 168
$\Rightarrow$ x^2 = 24 $\times$ 24
$\Rightarrow$ x = 24
$\therefore$ Larger number = 7x = 24 $\times$ 7 = 168

80(D). Given,
Sum of the measure of the interior angles of a polygon is 1620°.
Sum of interior angles of a polygon = (n – 2) $\times$ 180°
Where n is the number of sides.
Applying the formula, we get

$1620° = (n - 2) × 180°$

$\Rightarrow (n - 2) = \dfrac{1620°}{180°}$

$\Rightarrow (n - 2) = 9$

$\Rightarrow n = 11$

Number of sides = 11

81(C). The nature of Mathematics is enlisted in the following points:
- Mathematics is based on understanding.
- Mathematics has its own language.
- Mathematics puts great emphasis on the child's own methods of calculating and solving problems and rejects the previous practice of heavy emphasis on standard written algorithms.
- Mathematics is a science of discovery and logical reasoning.
- Mathematics is regarded as a powerful tool for interpreting the world and

- Mathematics with reason is rooted in action – learning through doing.
- Mathematics with reason puts less emphasis on representing numbers on paper as 'sums' and more emphasis on developing mental images in the child.

Thus, it is concluded that Mathematics is changeable in the universe is incorrect about nature of mathematics.

82(D). The nature of mathematics highly influences the nature of the teaching-learning process in mathematics.

Nature of mathematics:
- Mathematics should be visualised as the vehicle to train a child to think, reason, analyse, and articulate logically. Apart from being a specific subject, it should be treated as a concomitant to any subject involving analysis and meaning.
- 'Mathematics' is a broad term that encompasses many branches and components. It is a science that involves dealing with numbers, measurement of shapes and structures, organisation and interpretation of data and establishing relationship among variables, etc.
- Mathematics is a way of thinking and it is related to our life on daily basis. Mathematics, as an expression of the human mind, reflects the active will, the contemplative reason, and the desire for aesthetic perfection.
- Mathematics is the "queen of all sciences" and its presence is there in all the subjects. Mathematics acts as the basis and structure of other subjects. Its basic elements are logic and intuition, analysis and construction, generality and individuality".

So, it is concluded that all of the above are correct in the context of nature of Mathematics.

83(C). Mathematics is the study of

numbers, shape, quantity, and patterns. Mathematics is the 'queen of all sciences' and its presence is there in all the subjects. It acts as the basis and structure of other subjects.
- Mathematics is an important subject and is not hard in comparison to other subjects.
- It is just a myth that boys easily grasp problems in mathematics while girls take more time.
- It is the same for all and everyone can learn and succeed in mathematics by practicing.
- It is also a myth that mathematics takes a lot of time to be understood in comparison to other subjects.

So, from the above-mentioned points, it becomes clear that everyone can learn and succeed in mathematics.

potential to range across all the three values, but due to inappropriate teaching-learning process, its potential is not being utilized to its optimum level.
- Mathematics provides an effective way of building mental discipline and encourages logical reasoning and mental rigour and moral development.
- In addition, mathematical knowledge plays a crucial role in understanding the contents of other school subjects such as science, social studies, Cultural Studies.
- Mathematics has always been praised for its usefulness and significance in life. It plays a key role in deciding how individuals deal with various problems of life.
- According to National Curriculum Framework-2005, the main goal of Mathematics education in school is the mathematisation of the child's thought process.
- Mathematics relies on logic, reasoning, problem-solving, creativity and mathematical way of thinking. These skills can be useful in many other subjects.

So, we conclude that the important role of Mathematics in the syllabus is all the above points.

85(D). Mathematics is the study of numbers, shape, quantity and patterns. It relies on logical thinking and connects learning with children's day to day life.

The subject Mathematics is important in the curriculum since it:
- Improves logical thinking.
- Helps in the study of science subjects.
- Connects learning with children's day to day life.
- Develops skills such as speed, accuracy, estimation.
- Improves reasoning power, analytical and, critical thinking.

- Enhances scientific attitude like estimating, finding and verifying results.

So, we conclude that the subject Mathematics is important in the curriculum for the above-mentioned reason.

86(D). The main characteristics of mathematical language are
- the simplicity of the concepts so that the learner can easily understand them.
- accuracy is also needed in mathematics so that students can learn to commit fewer mistakes and be accurate in doing calculations.
- through precision, students learn exactly how to use formulas and under what situations these formulas are correct.

On the other hand, ordinary language can be ambiguous, vague, and emotive.

the language that used to express mathematical thoughts, expressions, and ideas.
- Language of mathematics makes learners able to reason logically, assimilate mathematical terms, and recognize and employ patterns of mathematical thought.
- Mathematical language should be well defined, clear, and should be highly compact and focussed.

Language of Mathematics Includes:
- Sign, symbol, graphs
- Formulae, syntax
- Number variable
- Greek alphabet
- Letter convention

So, we can conclude that it does not require other ordinary languages for its use is not one of the merits of mathematical language.

88(D). The most probable reason for writing 0.50 is larger than 0.5 is a misconception regarding the significance of zero in ordering decimal.
- They would not have a clear concept about dealing with zero right to the decimal.
- The only time you would want to keep zeros is when dealing with money. Monetary amounts require two place values after the decimal to indicate cents to the Hundredth place.
- Writing .5 cents is not appropriate; it should be Rs0.50.
- The concrete experience of representation of decimal numbers on a number line is required for abstract problems.
- Such misconceptions can be cleared by several examples.

So, we can conclude that students often make a mistake in comparing decimal numbers. For example, 0.50 is larger than

0.5. The most probable reason for this error is a misconception regarding the significance of zero in ordering decimal.

89(A).
Diagnostic Assessment: It is the assessment that is conducted along with formative assessment during the instructional process.
- It is carried out based on the data obtained from the formative assessment. Diagnostic assessment is specially conducted for investigating and removing the learning permanent difficulties of learners.
- For example, if it is found that a learner has not understood certain concepts in a particular subject, then to help him/her understand these concepts, diagnostic assessment is conducted and

difficulties.
So, we can conclude that a learner has not understood certain concepts in a maths subject, to help him/her understand these concepts, the teacher will conduct diagnostic assessment.

90(C). Diagnostic teaching: It is a process of informal teaching and using different methodologies for enough practice until they get mastery over the topic.
- After diagnosing the learning gaps or errors of children, the teacher teaches those concepts or topics again by using different techniques or methods.
- In this type of test, no scores are made for a right answer, only wrong answers are taken into view in the sequence of contents.
- The main purpose of diagnostic teaching is to identify the areas of learning difficulties of children which helps to find out the weakness or deficiency of a child in learning.
- A diagnostic test helps us to identify the trouble spots and discovered those areas of students' weakness that are unresolved by formative test.
- It works as an effective tool in planning remedial teaching as during remedial teaching, teacher provides learners with necessary help and guidance to overcome the problems which are determined during diagnostic teaching.
So, it can be concluded that We may say that Diagnostic testing implies a detailed study of learning difficulties to locate and identify the areas of learning difficulties.

91(B). Nature of science:
- Science is a particular way of looking at nature.
- Science is a rapidly expanding body of knowledge: One of the most important characteristics of science is that even the

most established theories can be modified, or even abandoned if new experimental results do not fit into the existing theories.
- Science is an interdisciplinary area of learning: The methodology of science and its demarcation from other fields continue to be a matter of philosophical debate.
- Science is always tentative.
- Even the most established and universal laws of science are always regarded as provisional, subject to modification in the light of new observations, experiments, and analyses.
- Science is a truly international enterprise.
Thus from the above-mentioned points, it is clear that the statement 'Even the most established and universal laws of science

92(C). The question-answer method helps in attaining inquiry-based understanding and may involve deconstruction of pre-existing ideas. As, science is a subject of inquiry, so the teacher has to encourage students to ask questions in the classroom.
The teacher has to create and sustain an intellectually stimulating classroom environment and encourage students to participate actively. S/he has to:
- Choose a topic suitable for being taught by this method
- Plan significant questions that direct the teaching-learning process and challenge students
- Ask probing questions to stimulate critical and deep thinking
- Ensure that the questions are specific and challenging
- Ensure that the discussion is focused
- Ask students to elaborate if answers are not clear
- Ensure that all students participate
Thus from the above-mentioned points, it is clear that encouraging students to ask questions in the classroom is correct in the context of the question.

93(C). Aural aids: Aural aids are known as audio aids.
Aural TLMs: These TLMs primarily stimulate the hearing sense of the learner. It includes – the human voice, telephonic conversation, audio discs/tapes, gramophone records, Radio broadcast.
So, it can be concluded that the Radio is an aural aid.

94(D). Criterion-referenced evaluation is related to the performance of the students in a well-defined learning task.
- In contrast to a norm-referenced evaluation, we can refer an individual

performance to a pre-determined criterion which is well defined.
- In criterion-referenced evaluation, a criteria is fixed i.e. a fixed standard in a learning task, say 50% or 60%.
- In it, the individual's status is ascertained with respect to some performance standard. The standard is the measure representing the criterion, the criterion itself being a specified performance.
- In criterion-referenced evaluation, there is no question of comparing one student with the other in it.
So, It is clear that t he evaluation that is concerned with the performance of the individual in terms of what he can do or the behavior he can demonstrate is termed as Criterion-referenced evaluation.

average performance:
- The students who are performing above average are usually understood the concepts in depth.
- Therefore, the mistakes done can be due to their carelessness or negligence. So, it is believed that they will auto-correct their mistakes by learning and practicing more by themselves.
So, it can be concluded that remedial teaching cannot be done for the students who are showing above-average performance.

96(D). Scientific inquiry is a holistic process. All processes in science are done with a specific purpose, evidence is collected with reliable and valid methods, and they are examined critically by controlling different variables.
Some of the processes involved in science as inquiry:
- Observing (patterns), wondering about objects, events, phenomena, experiencing & sensing discrepancies & dissonance, becoming curious & uncomfortable.
- Reflecting on various decisions & processes, aiming for better & contextually appropriate solutions, doing thought experiments, and assessing personal development.
- Deciding purpose, asking answerable questions, refining questions, hypothesizing, predicting.
- Planning, visualizing & designing collecting evidence testing evidence, considering variables, defining ideas, and measuring.
Since many processes listed above like doing experiments, testing evidence, and drawing conclusions are done in B & D.

97(D). Main objectives of science at upper primary level:

- Developing questioning and enquiry skills & relating classroom learning to life outside the classroom.
- Learners have the opportunity to explore various elements of science and start making sense of science in daily life experiences i.e. science education transits from environmental studies from science and technology.
- Learners understand the principle of science through familiar experiences and working with hands to design modules, scientific concepts are to arrive from experiments and activities.

Thus from the above-mentioned points, it is clear that to nurture curiosity in children about the world around them is not an objective of science at the upper primary level.

---

discipline, in working with hands and tools to design more advanced technological modules than at the upper primary stage, and in activities and analysis on issues surrounding environment and health.

99(B). Investigate has the broad meaning "to enquire into; to study carefully", in current science education literature the word investigation has become more focused.

Types of investigations:

- Fair testing: These investigations are concerned with observing and exploring relations between variables. Systematic changes in the independent variable are compared with changes in the outcome, or dependent, variable.
- Exploring: Pupils either make careful observations of objects or events or make a series of observations of a natural phenomenon occurring over time.
- Investigating Models: These investigations are usually technological in nature, where pupils design an artifact or system to meet a human need.

So, we can conclude that all the above points are types of investigation is used by a teacher while teaching science in the classroom.

100(D). Science refers to the study of structure and behaviour of the physical and natural things through observation and experimentation.

Nature of science:

- Science is always tentative.
- Science promotes scepticism.
- Science as an approach to investigation.
- Science is an interdisciplinary area of learning.
- Science is a particular way of looking at nature.
- Science is a process of constructing

knowledge.

- Science demands perseverance from its practitioners

So, it could be concluded that the statement 'science is static in nature' is not true in the context of te question.

101(C). An electrical device is used to separate irons from a heap of garbage. That device uses magnetic effect of current.

- The flow of current in a circular coil generates a magnetic field around it. It is known as an electromagnet.
- The magnetic field attracts the magnetic material.
- The electromagnet is a temporary magnet. Shown in the figure given below.
- Until the current flow in the coil, it will produce the magnetic field.
- Then this device is moved closer to a heap of garbage.
- An electrical device behaving as an electromagnet will attract the iron from the garbage heap.

102(D). The most electropositive stable element in the periodic table Cesium. Electropositivity can be defined as the tendency of an atom to donate electrons and form positively charged cations." Electropositivity is primarily exhibited by metallic elements, especially the alkali metals and the alkaline earth metals.

103(D). In medium, the nature of sound waves is only longitudinal.

- Sound wave: The longitudinal wave in an elastic medium that produces an audible sensation is called a sound wave.
- As sound waves are longitudinal waves, the air particles vibrate to and fro in the direction of propagation of sound.
- It is a wave of compression and rarefaction.
- Compressions and rarefactions are part of a sound wave.
- Compression: A region in a longitudinal wave where the particles are closest together is called compression. Compression has high density and high pressure.
- Rarefaction: A region in a longitudinal wave where the particles are furthest apart is called rarefaction. The rarefaction has a low density and low pressure.

104(A). Vitamins help in protecting our bodies against diseases. Vitamins also help in keeping our eyes, bones, teeth, and gums healthy.

- Our body needs all types of vitamins in small quantities.
- Vitamins help in protecting our bodies against diseases.

- Long-term deficiency of one or more nutrients in our diet may result in certain diseases or disorders.
- Vitamin D helps our body to use calcium for bones and teeth.
- Vitamin D is required for calcium absorption. Sunlight is the best source of vitamin D.
- When you don't get enough vitamin D, your body's calcium absorption lowers. This usually occurs if you are malnourished or do not get enough sun exposure.
- Our body also prepares Vitamin D in the presence of sunlight. Nowadays, insufficient exposure to sunlight is causing Vitamin D deficiency in many people.

105(B). The main thinking part of the speech, emotions, and planned muscle movements like walking.

- The cerebrum (a major part of the forebrain) is the main thinking part of the brain. It has sensory, motor, and association areas.

106(B). The fruits containing citric acid are termed as citrus fruits. eg: lemon, orange, grapefruit, etc.

- These are sour in taste and are a good source of Vitamin C, thus help in preventing the disease caused by the deficiency of Vitamin C, i.e., Scurvy.
- Grapes contain a lesser amount of citric acid than lime.
- Banana is a rich source of fiber, potassium, and Vitamin B6.
- Mango is a food source of fiber and Vitamin A and C.

107(A). It is a long straight coil of wire that can be used to generate a nearly uniform magnetic field similar to that of a bar magnet.

- When the electric current passes through the coil, it creates a relatively uniform magnetic field inside the coil.
- The soft iron inside the coil makes the magnetic field stronger because it becomes a magnet itself when the current is flowing. It is then called an electromagnet.
- Soft iron is used because it loses its magnetism as soon as the current stops flowing.
- Hence, soft iron is said to form a temporary magnet.
- The solenoid can be used as an electromagnet, as an inductor, or as a miniature wireless receiving antenna in a circuit.
- At the centre of a long solenoid, B (magnetic field strength) μnI, where μ is permeability, n is the number of turns,

and I is the current flowing through it.

108(C). In science, a push or a pull on an object is called force.
- Force: The interaction which after applying on a body changes or try to change the state of rest or state of motion of the body is called force.
- In science, a push or pull is on an object is called force.
- Actions like picking, hitting, kicking, opening, shutting, lifting, pushing, and pulling are used to describe certain tasks.
- These actions result in some or the other kind of change in the motion of an object.
- The motion which is imparted to objects is due to the action of a force.

109(C). Oil, natural gas, firewood are

- It is available in limited quantity apart from hydro-electric power.

Non-Conventional Sources:
- It is also known as renewable sources of energy
- It uses again and again without depletion.
- Examples include solar energy, bio-energy, tidal energy, and wind energy.

110(C). The shaking and trembling of earth is called earthquake.
An earthquake (also known as a quake, tremor or temblor) is the shaking of the surface of the Earth resulting from a sudden release of energy in the Earth 's lithosphere that creates seismic waves.

111(B). Bakelite is a thermosetting plastic.
Thermosetting plastics:
- These are the polymers which when condensed have a permanent change on heating.
- On heating they undergo extensive cross-linking in molds and become hard and infusible; therefore, they cannot be reused.
- Its examples are Bakelite, glyptal.

112(A). The arc welding uses electricity to create an arc which creates a very high temperature.
- This high temperature melts the metal which is to be welded.
- The melted metals when cool result in a binding of the metals.
- It is a type of welding that uses a welding power supply to create an electric arc between a metal stick ("electrode") and the base material to melt the metals at the point of contact.

113(B). Ruhi ate the fish in Goa but it tasted very different because it was cooked in coconut oil.
- Different regions have different food.
- Depending on what grows easily at which place, different things are eaten at places.
- Goa is situated on the west coast of India.
- Goa has a high yield of coconut oil and sea fish.
- Sea fish cooked in coconut oil is popular in Goa.

114(B). Ammeter: An ammeter is an instrument that is used to measure the current flowing through the circuit.
- It has low resistance, ideally zero.
- The connecting ammeter in series allows all of the circuit current to pass through it and so measure it.

potential difference between two points in an electric circuit.
- The rheostat is a device that helps in varying the current by varying the resistance in the circuit.
- The ammeter is used to measure the magnitude of current through a circuit.
- A galvanometer can detect the presence of current. The deflection on the galvanometer indicates the direction of the current in that circuit.
- Thus, the instrument that can detect the direction of flow of current is a galvanometer.

116(A). The passage through a triangular glass prism, the white light is separated into its component colors - red, orange, yellow, green, blue, indigo and violet. The separation of visible light into its different colors is known as dispersion. The light that will emerge out of the combination of the two prisms, will be white in colour.

117(C).

I (Place)		II (Most liked food)	
(A)	Goa	I V	Sea fish cooked in coco nut oil
(B)	Kashmi r	V	Fish cooked in mustard oil
(C)	Kerala	I I I	Boiled tapioca with an y curry
(D)	Hongko ng	I I	cooked Snakes
		I	Chholay Bhature

- Goa is situated on the west coast of India. Due to the high yield of coconut oil and fish, fish cooked in coconut oil is popular in Goa.
- Jammu and Kashmir is a state located in North India. Jammu and Kashmir's climate is cold. Mustard oil has healing properties, Fish cooked in mustard oil is popular in Jammu and Kashmir.
- Hong Kong cuisine is inspired primarily by Cantonese cuisine. Most of the dishes in Cantonese cuisine is based on Snake. Cooked snake and snake soup are popular in Hong Kong.
- Boiled tapioca with any curry is very popular in Kerala.

118(D). Refraction of Light:
- When a ray of light propagating in a medium enters the other medium, it deviates from its path.
- This phenomenon of change in the direction of propagation of light at the boundary, when it passes from one medium to another medium, is called drawn on the boundary of two media at the incident point.
- The entity that doesn't change is the frequency.
- The entity that changes are wavelength and velocity.
- Refractive index is also equal to the velocity of light c of a given wavelength in empty space divided by its velocity v in a substance,

119(D). All organisms, from primitive prokaryotes to most advanced and complex eukaryotes, are able to sense and respond to environmental factors. The stimuli are perceived by sense organs in higher animals through sensory receptors e.g., eyes, ears, nose. Plants do not possess such sense organs. However, they do respond to external factors such as light, water, temperature, pollutants, other organisms, etc. Human beings have an additional facility of self-consciousness (awareness of self). Consciousness and response to stimuli are said to be the defining properties of living organisms.

120(C). The direction of centripetal acceleration changes each and every moment. So the acceleration will also change.
- Similarly, the velocity keeps on changing because the direction of velocity is changing.
- In a uniform circular motion, the magnitude of the velocity is always the same and, the direction always changes. So option 3 is correct.
- Since the magnitude of velocity is same so kinetic energy and speed will remain the same always in a uniform circular motion.

Child Development and Pedagogy

1. "A child may utter a sound which is common for every object and person s/he sees in the environment, like 'inna', but later on s/he starts pronouncing words denoting objects or persons, like maa, pa, and so on." This is the principle of
   (a) Continuity
   (b) Generalization to Specialization
   (c) Differentiation
   (d) Integration

socialization?
   (a) Secondary Agent
   (b) Primary Agent
   (c) Anticipatory Agent
   (d) Both Primary and Secondary Agent

3. Nupur is studying in class V. She can classify types of triangles in different categories but has difficulty in understanding the abstract proof for the exterior angle is equal to sum of opposite interior angles.
   According to Piaget, Nupur lies in
   (a) Sensory Motor Stage
   (b) Pre-operational Stage
   (c) Concrete-operational Stage
   (d) Formal-Operational Stage

4. In a classroom, students are experiencing and interacting with the curriculum, and all students are availing the opportunity to take part in their own learning. They are relating the information to prior experiences, thus deepening the connection with new knowledge. The above-mentioned phenomenon could be attributed to which kind of education?
   (a) Special education
   (b) Progressive Education
   (c) Inclusive Education
   (d) Integrated Education

5. Which of the following is not an effective practice adopted by a teacher in the classroom to address gender stereotypes?
   (a) Counter gender bias.
   (b) Separate seating arrangement

for boys and girls in the class.
   (c) Discussions on gender discrimination.
   (d) Use of examples which show boys and girls in non-conformist roles.

6. Kritika is ready to solve the problem given by the teacher, most of the time she also finds a solution to the problem. Kritika belongs to a poor background. Despite that, which of the following motivation is strong in him?
   (a) Approval motivator
   (b) Power motivator
   (c) Achievement motivator

rivers, planets. She tries to think how these things are looking, what does Shivani do-
   (a) Concept Mapping
   (b) Imagination
   (c) Investigation
   (d) Reflection

8. Which of the following is NOT a characteristic of a teacher-centered approach?
   A. The students are writing down the dictation given by the teacher.
   B. The students are developing different models using clay and paper in groups.
   (a) only A
   (b) only B
   (c) neither A nor B
   (d) A and B both

9. Authoritative teaching strategies are associated with what students identify as "good teachers." Identify which one of the following educators is demonstrating authoritative techniques in the classroom.
   (a) When Rashmi failed to take her seat upon entering the room, her teacher reminded her of the class rules and consequences.
   (b) Pooja, a shy new student to the class, was forced by the teacher on her first day in her new school to give a speech about her past experiences in school
   (c) Disha was allowed by her teacher to skip recess and play inside by herself because she did not have any friends.
   (d) Mr. Tapesh allowed the students

to have two free days at the beginning of the year in which to become acquainted with their peers in the classroom.

10. When a child with a disability first comes to school the teacher should?
    (a) Refer the child to a special school according to the disability
    (b) Seclude him from other students
    (c) Discuss with the child's parents to evolve collaborative plans
    (d) Conduct an admission test

11. Learners who are very sensitive to sounds and have difficulty in

    (c) Autism
    (d) None of these

12. Many schools are working to become "child-friendly", why the concept of being child-friendly is such important?
    (a) To improve every child's participation and learning in school
    (b) To make children skilled
    (c) To motivate children on multiple aspects
    (d) To create a friendly situation in school

13. 'Dysgraphia' means
    (a) difficulty in reading
    (b) difficulty in writing
    (c) difficulty in grasping spoken language
    (d) None of the above

14. The term 'inclusive-education' refers to:
    (a) Education of Children belong to Scheduled Caste and Schedules Tribes
    (b) Education of children with disabilities along with normal ones
    (c) Education in multigrade setting
    (d) Education of children from minority groups

15. In an inclusive classroom with diverse learners, cooperative learning and peer-tutoring
    (a) should not be practised and students should be segregated based on their abilities
    (b) should be used only sometimes

since it promotes comparison with classmates

(c) should be actively discouraged and competition should be promoted

(d) should be actively promoted to facilitate peer-acceptance

16. Which of the following statement is incorrect about the principles of child development?

(a) Development follows a definite and predictable pattern.

(b) All individuals are similar in their development.

(c) Development is a product of hereditary and the environment.

(d) Development works on the principle of integration.

(c) Cognitive   (d) Sensory

18. The most useful term for describing the linguistic input to the language learning child is ____.

(a) motherese

(b) infant-directed speech

(c) child-directed speech

(d) caregiver speech

19. Assertion (A): A child's development progress can be accurately measured by comparing her rate of development with the other children of some age.

Reason (R): Pattern and the rate of development of children is uniform and remains some for all children across cultures.

Choose the correct option.

(a) Both (A) and (R) are true and (R) is the correct explanation of (A).

(b) Both (A) and (R) are true but (R) is not the correct explanation of (A).

(c) (A) is true but (R) is false

(d) Both (A) and (R) are false

20. A child learns to hop and jump before learning to play football. Which principal of development does this illustrate?

(a) Cephalocaudal

(b) Pronimodistal

(c) Reversibility

(d) Equilibration

21. Which of the following statements about development is NOT correct?

(a) Development is a product of heredity and environment.

(b) Development is somewhat

predictable.

(c) Rate of development is uniform and universal.

(d) Development proceeds from general to specific.

22. Assertion (A): Children pick up ways of behaving appropriately as per their culture from their friends media and various other source.

Reason (R): Socialization is a complex process that takes place through various formal and informal means.

Choose the correct option.

(a) Both (A) and (R) are true and (R) is the correct explanation of (A).

(b) Both (A) and (R) are true but (R) is not the correct explanation of

23. For children who are in concrete operational stage teachers should-

(a) Gave a lot of practice to deal with abstract concepts

(b) Provide opportunities to classify objects and ideas on increasingly complex levels

(c) Present problems that require higher order abstract thinking

(d) Give problems that require logical and scientific thinking

24. According to Jean Piaget , at which stage of cognitive development does the child understand that symbols can be used to represent objects - 'bicycle' will generate an image even when absent?

(a) Pre-conventional stage

(b) Pre-operational Stage

(c) Concrete operational Stage

(d) Formal operational Stage

25. Aanav struggles with addition of three-digit numbers on his own but is able to do so with support from the teacher. In Lev Vygotsky's theory, this highlights-

(a) Zone of proximal development

(b) Reinforcement

(c) Maturation

(d) Symbolism

26. According to Lev Vygotsky learning is-

(a) An active process of constructing knowledge

(b) A passive process of reception of knowledge

(c) A function of drill and practice

(d) A function of stimulus-response

associations

27. Which of the following tools should a teacher use to assess children's learning?
(i) Classroom interaction
(ii) Projects
(iii) Portfolios
(iv) self-assessment

(a) (ii) and (iii)

(b) (ii), (iii) and (iv)

(c) (i), (ii), (iii) and (iv)

(d) (i), (ii) and (iii)

28. By encouraging students to reflect on their cognitive abilities to reach a specified goal, a teacher is facilitating the development of:

(a) Declarative knowledge

29. To scaffold students in solving a problem, a teacher should-

(a) confuse students by highlighting extraneous information.

(b) directly tell the answer to students and ask them to copy it.

(c) give cues that activities the relevant schemas.

(d) split the information in disconnected chunks.

30. Assertion (A): During teaching-learning process, a teacher should give opportunities to students for sharing their misconceptions and alternative conceptions.

Reason (R): Misconceptions and alternative conceptions are always baseless and are insignificant in process of learning.

Choose the correct option.

(a) Both (A) and (R) are true and (R) is the correct explanation of (A).

(b) Both (A) and (R) are true but (R) is not the correct explanation of (A).

(c) (A) is true but (R) is false.

(d) Both (A) and (R) are false.

Language - I: English

Ques (31-39): Direction : Read the passage given below and answer the questions/complete the statements that follow by choosing the best options from the given ones.

(1) The Public distribution system, which provides food at low prices, is a subject of vital concern. There is a growing realization that though India has enough food to feed its masses two square meals a day, the monster of starvation and food insecurity continues to haunt the poor in

our country.

(2) Increasing the purchasing power of the poor through providing productive employment leads to rise in income, and thus good standard of living is the ultimate objective of public policy. However, till then, there is a need to provide assured supply of food through a restructured, more efficient and decentralized Public Distribution System (PDS)

(3) Although the PDS is extensive- it is one of the largest systems in the world-it has yet to reach the rural poor and the far-off places. It remains an urban phenomenon, with the majority of the rural poor still out of its reach due to lack of economic and physical access. The poorest in the cities and the migrants are left out, for they generally do not possess ration cards. The allocation of PDS supplies in big cities is

stock of food grains combined with food subsidy on one hand and the continuing slow starvation and dismal poverty of the rural population on the other, there is a strong case for making PDS target-group oriented.

31. Read the following statements:
(a) India is a poor country and lacks resources to feed every citizen
(b) Food insecurity is one of the main concerns for the poor in the country
(a) (a) is true and (b) is false.
(b) (a) is false and (b) is true.
(c) Both (a) and (b) are true.
(d) Both (a) and (b) are false.

32. What should now be the objective of public policy on PDS?
(a) to improve the food production.
(b) to provide better fertilisers to the poor.
(c) to reduce administrative cost.
(d) to let the rural poor enjoy the food subsidy.

33. Read the following statements.
(a) The public distribution system is a system which is very popular in India only.
(b) It enables the government to provide food to the people in remote areas of the country successfully.
(c) People have to procure ration card to avail of this facility.
(a) (a) is true and (b) and (c) are false.
(b) (a) and (b) are true (c) is false.
(c) (a) and (b) are false and (c) is true.

(d) (a) and (c) are true and (b) is false.

34. What would be the purpose of making PDS target-group oriented?
(a) To remove the inequality between the rich and poor.
(b) To provide food to poor rural population.
(c) To improve the purchasing power of the people.
(d) To improve the standard of living of the people.

35. Study the following statements:
(a) There is less production of food grains in India.
(b) The poor do not have enough purchasing power.

(b) (b) is right but (a) and (c) are wrong.
(c) (c) is right but (a) and (b) are wrong
(d) (a) is wrong but (b) and (c) are right.

36. 'In growing realization' in para 1, growing is used as a/an
(a) Verb　　(b) Adverb
(c) Adjective　　(d) Noun

37. In 'purchasing power' (para-2), the underlined word means the same as
(a) authority　　(b) capacity
(c) energy　　(d) will power

38. The word 'system' in 'public distribution system' stands for
(a) procedure
(b) outlook
(c) thought process
(d) routine

39. 'Streamlined' in para 4 is used as a/an
(a) noun　　(b) verb
(c) adverb　　(d) adjective

40. Which of the following is defined as regional dialect?
(a) Speech characteristics of a language in a region.
(b) Language of a state or country.
(c) Language with a script of a region.
(d) The written language and literature of a region.

41. Which of the following is true of Sign Language?

(a) Sign Language does not have a grammar.
(b) Sign Language has a grammar.
(c) Sign Language is set of gestures.
(d) Only one Sign language used across the world.

42. Language learning is
(a) natural and subconscious
(b) deliberate and conscious
(c) both natural and deliberate
(d) innate and involuntary

43. What does it mean to use 'multilingualism as a strategy' in the classroom?
(a) Using the common language of learners for translating the content in an English medium

(c) Not letting the learners to use their languages except the medium of instruction in the classroom.
(d) Learning of many languages in school to become multilingual speaker.

44. Which of the following you would not accept as authentic materials?
(a) A cartoon from a magazine.
(b) An advertisement in a newspaper.
(c) An essay on the COVID 19 written by textbook writer.
(d) A short story by the well-known writer Premchand.

45. A teacher asks her learners of class VIII as a follow up task of the reading lesson to list the events and ideas of the story in a sequence. What does she do?
(a) Asking her students to create a sub-text.
(b) Asking her students to read the story again.
(c) Reinforcing their writing skills.
(d) Promoting their skill to recall.

46. Which of the following statement is NOT true teaching of literary texts in language classroom?
(a) Literary texts should be used to teach grammar.
(b) Literary texts are for appreciation, pleasure and enjoyment.
(c) Literary texts are inputs for language learning.
(d) Literary texts develop critical

thinking.

47. Ravi reads an article from a newspaper so as to present the overall idea of the text to his group the next day. What is his reading known as?

(a) Reading between the lines.

(b) Reading beyond the lines.

(c) Scanning

(d) Skimming

48. Words one recognizes while reading but is not able to use on her own. What is this vocabulary known as?

(a) Active vocabulary

(b) Passive vocabulary

(c) Listening vocabulary

(a) using language for here-and-now and on familiar topics

(b) using language for higher order thinking

(c) using language to convey abstract ideas and concepts

(d) using language for reporting scientific research on a topic

50. Which approach to writing gives scope for learners to undergo different stage of writing in order to learn to write?

(a) Product Approach

(b) Process Approach

(c) Communicative Approach

(d) Lexical Approach

51. Arul Rahul, a teacher in his grammar class introduces rules of the grammar item, voice and tenses first and makes them understand how the form behaves and how to use it contexts. He then gives lots of tasks for learners to practice the language item. What is this process of teaching-learning grammar known as?

(a) Content knowledge

(b) Procedural knowledge

(c) Process knowledge

(d) Declarative knowledge

52. Which of the following is an input based task for language learning?

(a) Learner read a story in groups of five.

(b) Learners write a dialogue for skit to be enacted in an event.

(c) Learners enact a role play on the issue of climate change.

(d) Learners asks questions to understand the ideas of the talk they listened to.

53. Which of the following is NOT a concept from language education?

(a) grammar translation method

(b) wavelength of sound

(c) first language interference

(d) error correction

Ques (54-59): Direction: Read the following stanzas and answer the questions/complete the statements by choosing the best options from those given below

In friction land there is a family
With some confusions as you will see.
There is Raghu aged fifteen and others all

home?'
Crazy! What adventures! Bah teenagers!
Papa saw the threat
They think they can manage everything on their own - 8
'Look at your clothes, looks like you haven't bathed in years,
Cut your hair, you look like a scream!'
Raghu was in tears.
'Why can't I live like I wanna be?
I won't change! My friends love it and the girls-look at me.' - 12
Days passed by, things looked better, sometimes worse.
'Papa, there is a band, that wants me to sing a verse.'
"Join a band! yelled flabbergasted papa
'you've surely gone mad'.
Think of a career, for things gonna be sad. - 16

54. 'friction land' here stands for

(a) a mysterious island

(b) a confused family

(c) a desert

(d) wonderland

55. saw red' in line 5 means

(a) was angry

(b) was in danger

(c) was excited

(d) was nervous

56. Which of the following is not a point of clash between Raghu and his father?

(a) different lifestyle

(b) different interests

(c) different food habits

(d) age difference

57. Which line shows the dilemma faced by Raghu?

(a) Line 2   (b) Line 4

(c) Line 6   (d) Line 6

58. What is the rhyme in 1st stanza?

(a) abab   (b) abcd

(c) acbd   (d) abcc

59. In 'flabbergasted papa' flabbergasted is used as a/an

(a) verb   (b) adverb

(c) adjective   (d) noun

60. Which one of the following would you adopt in your language classroom to enhance critical thinking among the learners?

(a) Read aloud the textbook in the classroom.

(b) Write the answers to the

(d) Organising a handwriting competition.

61. The highest four-digit number which is divisible by each of the numbers 16, 36, 45, 48 is:

(a) 9180   (b) 9360

(c) 9630   (d) 9840

62. What will be the LCM of 48 and 65?

(a) 48   (b) 1

(c) 3120   (d) 65

63. What is the remainder when the sum $1^5 + 2^5 + 3^5 + 4^5 + 5^5$ is divided by 4 ?

(a) 0   (b) 1

(c) 2   (d) 3

64. Two positive numbers differ by 1280 . When the greater number is divided by the smaller number, the quotient is 7 and the remainder is 50 . The greater number is:

(a) 1585   (b) 1458

(c) 1558   (d) 1485

65. If $3^{x+3} + 7 = 250$, then x is equal to:

(a) 5   (b) 3

(c) 2   (d) 1

66. If $\frac{2a+b}{a+4b} = 3$, then find the value of $\frac{a+b}{a+2b} = ?$

(a) $\frac{5}{9}$ (b) $\frac{2}{7}$

(c) $\frac{10}{9}$ (d) $\frac{10}{7}$

67. It is necessary for our body but it does not provide a nutrient ____.

(a) minerals   (b) water
(c) fats   (d) Fibre

68. The process of nitrogen fixation by bacteria does not take place in the presence of:
(a) Molecular form of hydrogen
(b) Elemental form of oxygen
(c) Water
(d) Elemental form of nitrogen

69. Two lines AB and CD cut each other at O. If $\angle AOC = 50°$, then $\angle BOC$ is equal to:

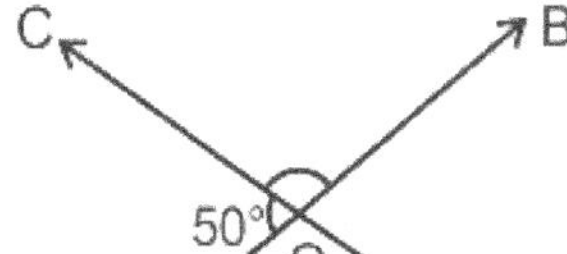

(a) $40°$ (b) $50°$
(c) $140°$ (d) $130°$

70. Two straight lines intersect at a point. If the sum of the measures of any three angles of the four angles produced is $290°$, then the measures of the four angles are:
(a) $120°, 60°, 120°, 60°$
(b) $110°, 70°, 110°, 70°$
(c) $110°, 70°, 110°, 70°$
(d) None of these

71. The measure of an angle for which the measure of the supplement is four times the measure of the complement is:
(a) $20°$ (b) $30°$
(c) $45°$ (d) $60°$

72. An amount of sum is to be divided between A, B and C in the ratio of $3 : 7 : 12$. If the difference between the shares of A and B is Rs. 3000, Find the total amount of sum?
(a) 16500   (b) 17000
(c) 17500   (d) 15500

73. A circular grass lawn of 35 metres in radius has a path 7 metres wide running around it on the outside. Find the cost of gravelling the path if the cost of gravelling is Rs. 75 per m^2.
(a) Rs.135200   (b) Rs. 120570
(c) Rs. 135450   (d) Rs. 127050

74. A solid sphere of radius 3 cm is melted to form a right circular cone such that the height of the cone is half the radius of the cone. Find the radius of the cone.

(a) 3 cm   (b) 4 cm
(c) 5 cm   (d) 6 cm

75. $(\sqrt{72} - \sqrt{18}) \div \sqrt{12}$ is equal to:
(a) $\dfrac{\sqrt{3}}{2}$ (b) $\dfrac{\sqrt{2}}{3}$
(c) $\sqrt{6}$ (d) $\dfrac{\sqrt{6}}{2}$

76. 80% of $CP = 60\%$ of SP. Find the profit or loss $\%$
(a) 33.33% profit
(b) 25% loss
(c) 30% profit
(d) 10% loss

77. Shaurya said to his brother, "I was as old as you are at present at the time of your birth. "If the Shaurya

78. If $\sqrt{a} - \sqrt{b} = 2$ and $\sqrt{a} + \sqrt{b} = 4$, find the value of $a^2 b$.
(a) 45   (b) 76
(c) 38   (d) 81

79. A sample of soil is mixed with water and allowed to settle. The clear supernatant solution turns the pH paper yellowish-orange. Which of the following would change the colour of this pH paper to greenish-blue?
(a) Lemon juice   (b) Vinegar
(c) Common salt   (d) Antacid

80. In science, a push or a pull on an object is called as ______.
(a) Pressure   (b) Gravitation
(c) Force   (d) Friction

81. 1 hertz is equal to :
(a) 1 vibration per minute
(b) 10 vibrations per minute
(c) 60 vibrations per minute
(d) 600 vibrations per minute

82. Which of the following has the largest brain in proportion to its body size?
(a) Ant
(b) Elephant
(c) Dolphin
(d) Human Being

83. The largest sense organ of our body is:
(a) Eyes   (b) Skin
(c) Ears   (d) Lungs

84. Select the material in which non-polar compounds will be soluble.

(a) Ethanol   (b) Water
(c) Butanol   (d) Benzene

85. A true species consists of a population which is__________.
(a) sharing the same niche
(b) interbreeding
(c) feeding over the same food
(d) geographically isolated

86. Consider the following terms:
A. Lightning
B. Landslide
C. Thundering
D. Tsunami
E. Floods
Earthquakes can cause:
(a) B, D and E   (b) A, B and C
(c) B only   (d) B and E

grade III learners?
(a) What is the place value of 4 in 543?
(b) Identify the next shape in a given pattern of shapes.
(c) Solve $\dfrac{1}{3} + \dfrac{1}{4}$
(d) Show that 2×5 is the same as 5×2.

88. Mr. Govind wants to build 'pattern recognition' skill in his Grade 3 students. Which of the following activities can BEST help?
(a) Asking students to make their family tree and compare it to that of their friend's family tree.
(b) Asking students to observe the night sky and describe what they saw, in class the next day.
(c) Asking students to find the national emblem of India in all their textbooks.
(d) Giving building blocks and asking students to arrange them in stacks of increasing height.

89. Ms. Priya taught the concept of division. Which of the following is the best example of an 'authentic task' to assess students on this?
(a) What will you get when you divide 65 by 13?
(b) What does division of one number by another mean? Explain using examples.
(c) Distribute 100 available drawing sheets among 25 students of your class equally.
(d) Make a flag for your class where one-third of the flag is blue

90. 'Identify the correct sequence of

geometrical thinking levels as per Van Hieles' 'theory of geometrical development'

(a) Visualisation--Analysis--Deduction--Relationships

(b) Relationships--Deduction-Analysis-Visualisation

(c) Visualisation--Analysis--Relationships-Deduction

(d) Analysis--Relationships--Deduction--Visualisation

91. Majority of students in a class says,

270 + 34 is equal to
$$\begin{array}{r} 270 \\ +34 \\ \hline 2104 \\ \hline \end{array}$$

Revisiting which of the following concepts will best remediate the

(d) Place value of three digit numbers

92. What is the mean of first 99 natural numbers?

(a) 100   (b) 50.5

(c) 50   (d) 99

93. The mean of 50 items was 24. Later on, it was discovered that two items were misread as 83 and 17 instead of 38 and 77. The correct mean is:

(a) 24.3   (b) 23.4

(c) 24   (d) 22.5

94. Mode of the data 7.5, 7.3, 7.2, 7.2, 7.4, 7.7, 7.7, 7.5, 7.3, 7.2, 7.6, 7.2 is

(a) 7.3   (b) 7.5

(c) 7.2   (d) 7.6

95. The nature of mathematics is:

(a) Ornamental

(b) Logical

(c) Difficult

(d) Not for common

96. Which is not true in the context of the mathematics classroom?

(a) Emphasis should be laid on mathematical reasoning

(b) Teaching mathematics requires thinking about concepts

(c) It should be child-centred

(d) It should be teacher-centred

97. Why we need mathematics in society?

(a) For transaction

(b) For business

(c) For calculation

(d) All of the above

98. Which of the following is NOT an appropriate reason for fear of mathematics?

(a) Cumulative nature of mathematics.

(b) Symbolic language of mathematics.

(c) Methods of assessment and language used in textbook.

(d) Mathematical Inabilities of learners.

99. Which of the following statements is NOT appropriate with regard to the nature of mathematics?

(a) It is hierarchical in nature.

(b) Mathematical concepts are abstract in nature.

(c) It is like science which is based

joins your class, which predominantly has local students. You want to use this as an opportunity to teach students about adaptation.

Which of these activities is BEST suited for the purpose?

(a) Have the local students share with the new student the rules in their school.

(b) Have a discussion in the class about different changes in the new student's life and how he handled them.

(c) Tell the class about how difficult it is for the new student to adjust and how they all should help him.

(d) Have the new student tell the class about rules in his old school and how they are different from the new school rules.

101. Which of the following is the BEST example of students engaging in active learning?

(a) Students in pairs discuss the impact of decline of traditional crafts on the livelihoods of the craftsmen.

(b) Students draw the structure of a honeycomb from the textbook, after the teacher introduces the topic.

(c) In pairs, students list down the different colours of leaves that were mentioned in the EVS textbook.

(d) After completion of a lesson, students write the definitions of certain terminologies.

102. Deficiency of which vitamin lowers the rate of calcium absorption from the food?

(a) Vitamin D   (b) Vitamin C

(c) Vitamin B   (d) Vitamin K

103. Heating effect produced by current is due to the ______.

(a) Collision of electrons

(b) Movement of electrons

(c) Resistance in electrons

(d) Lose of energy

104. The direction of electric current is always opposite to

(a) direction of conventional current in metallic conductors

(b) one ohm

(c) the electric work done

(a) Less than one

(b) More than one

(c) More than 10

(d) More than 100 or 1000

106. What happens when light travels from air to glass?

(a) It bends towards the normal line

(b) It bends away from the normal line

(c) There is no change

(d) It becomes parallel to the normal line

107. A car travels some distance at a speed of 8 km/hr and returns at a speed of 12 km/hr. If the total time taken by the car is 15 hours, then what is the distance (in km)?

(a) 48   (b) 60

(c) 56   (d) 72

108. Which of the following is/are the 'push factor' affecting migration?
(A) Better opportunities for work
(B) Better health facilitie
(C) Poorer health facilities
(D) Absence of good educational institution
Choose the correct option.

(a) Only (A) and (B)

(b) Only (C) and (D)

(c) Only (A), (B) and (C)

(d) Only (A), (B) and (D)

109. Bleaching powder contains

(a) nitrogen   (b) iodine

(c) chlorine   (d) bromine

110. The hardest substance available on earth is-

(a) Platinum   (b) Coal
(c) Diamond   (d) Gold

111. Which one of the following is not true of the nature of science?
A. Science is always tentative.
B. Science promotes scepticism.
C. Science is a process of constructing knowledge.
D. Science is static in nature.
(a) D   (b) B
(c) C   (d) A

112. Which of the following is a NOT true w.r.t. the nature of Science?
(a) Science is an interdisciplinary area of learning
(b) Science is always tentative
(c) Science promotes scepticism

diseases
(c) A debate on environmental issues
(d) Project work on nature of sound

117. Which amongst the following is incorrect about science?
(a) Science is a particular way of looking at nature
(b) Science is a rapidly expanding body of knowledge
(c) Science is an interdisciplinary area of learning
(d) Science is always an independent enterprise

118. While teaching the topic 'Electricity' in class VIII, the

statements is true about nature of science?
(a) Scientific knowledge has a tentative character.
(b) Scientific knowledge can be proved through experimentation.
(c) Science is value-neutral
(d) Scientific knowledge is an objective.

114. Choose the correct statement:
(a) Science is a blend of logic and imagination
(b) Science is a process and not a product.
(c) Science is all about the experimentation.
(d) Only science can inculcate values among students.

115. Which of the following statements is/are regarding divergent question in science.
A) They promote critical thinking in learners.
B) They help in identifying individual differences in students.
C) They are very objective in nature.
(a) A, B   (b) A, C
(c) B, C   (d) A, B, C

116. Science is considered to be questioning, exploring, doing and investigating. Which of the following activities, carried out by Dipika in the teaching of Science, is best suited to satisfy these criteria?
(a) Unit test on microorganisms
(b) A group discussion on common

used as a filament of a light bulb. Which of the following aspects is the teacher highlighting above?
(a) Subjectivity in Science
(b) Tentativeness of Science
(c) Empirical nature of Science
(d) Cultural embeddedness of Science

119. A teacher can inculcate the essence of the scientific enterprise among students by all of the following practices,
(a) Students should be made conversant with multiple methods of science.
(b) Nature of science to be made an integral part of teaching-learning.
(c) Students must be required to memorize facts and reproduce when needed.
(d) Historical aspects of the development of scientific concepts should be emphasized.

120. The chemical name of vitamin B12:
(a) Folic acid
(b) Thiamine
(c) Cyanocobalamine
(d) Acetic acid

// Hints and Solutions //

1(B). Principle of Continuity: Development follows the principle of continuity which starts with conception and ends with death. It is a never-ending process in life.
Principle of Generality to Specificity: The development process starts with general responses shown by the child as s/he passes through the later stages s/ he starts exhibiting specific behaviours. For example, a child may utter a sound which is common for every object and person s/he sees in the environment, like 'inna', but later on s/he starts pronouncing specific words denoting specific objects or persons, like maa, pa, and so on.
Principle of Interaction: The principle of interaction suggests that an individual is the product of heredity and environment. In other words, the interaction takes place within and outside forces of the child.
Principle of Differentiation in Rate: Differentiation in rate indicates that individuals differ in the rate of development. There is a difference in the rate of development in girls and boys like various aspects of development like physical, mental, emotional, social and moral.

2(B). Primary socialization was implicitly understood as taking place in the family and during the first part of childhood. In this perspective, the socializing agents in the primary process are the parents, especially the mother.
Parents along with the family are the most important agents of socialization. Within the family, it is the mother who first begins to socialize the child. Socialization in basic values such as love and affection, manners, and etiquette are first taught in the family.
The situation within the family whether affectionate or disturbed will affect the growth of a child accordingly.
For example:- A child is crying on seeing his mother who is busy in working on the laptop. A child wants love and affection from his mother.
Thus, it is concluded that The socialization of child is affected by primary agent of socialization.

3(C). He made a systematic study of cognitive development in his theory.
He believed that children are the little scientist and they actively and gradually construct their understanding of the world through Cognitive transformation.
In this stage, Children gain the abilities of conservation of number, area, volume, and orientation.
Children can conserve numbers (age 6), mass (age 7), and weight (age 9). Conservation is the understanding that something stays the same in quantity even when its appearance changes.
Children enjoy the company of friends in this stage so, this stage is also referred to as gang age, where the feeling of class inclusion dominates in a child.

Unable to understand abstract thinking. Reversibility, seriation, transitivity also developed in this stage

The ability to conserve is one of the major accomplishments of the concrete operational stage.

4(B). Dewey has proposed the concept of 'Progressive Education' which emphasizes that learning takes place through 'hands-on' approach so the students must interact with their environment to adapt and learn.

Dewey had a specific idea regarding how education should take place within the classroom. He criticized the undue importance given to the curriculum, which leads to the inactivity of the student in the entire process of learning.

Progressive Education:

In Progressive Education, students thrive in learning.

Content is presented in a way that allows the student to relate the information to prior experiences, thus deepening the connection with this new knowledge.

Dewey advocated for an
the educational structure that strikes a balance between delivering knowledge while also taking into account the interests and experiences of the student.

Progressive Education is a continuous process of adjustment, having as its aim at every stage an added capacity of growth.' He advocated the importance of education not only as a place to gain content knowledge, but also as a place to learn how to live.

The experience of the child occupies the central place in this method of learning; 'all learning must come as a by-product of actions' child learns through participation in various activities.

Hence, it could be concluded that the above-mentioned phenomenon could be attributed to progressive education.

5(B). Effective practices that should be adopted by a teacher in the classroom to address gender stereotypes

Setting tasks which have to be done together by both girls and boys.

Use of examples that show boys and girls in non-conformist roles.

Providing equal opportunities in the classroom related to asking questions, responding in the class.

Developing the habit of respecting each other's gender in students and assigning equal opportunities to every student in the class.

Involving students in discussing gender issues and countering gender bias by engaging them in solving gender-related issues in society.

Hence, it could be concluded that separate seating arrangements for boys and girls in the class is not an effective practice adopted by a teacher in the classroom to address gender stereotypes.

6(C). Mastery of needs: An individual prefers jobs that are challenging, intellectually demanding, and thought-oriented. He or she enjoys playing a leadership role in groups and is able to complete tasks already started.

Work orientation: An individual takes a proactive attitude toward work and loves what he or she does. He or she obtains a sense of satisfaction from work and pursues self-realization and growth.

Competition: An individual hopes for victory and has the desire to win over others.

Personal unconcern: An individual does not conclude that the motivation present is the Achievement Motivator.

7(B). Imagination develops the thought process of the students, their thoughts became divergent.

It improves the cognition of the student by using their knowledge, and analogies, in different conditions.

Children become fully active during imagination, it covers all the possible aspects of the problem for image formation. So we can say that when the teacher explains about rivers, mountains, etc. Shivani tries to form an image in her mind, this is an example of imagination.

8(B). It focuses on the discipline of students.

The emphasis is given to the right answer by students.

The teacher gives instructions while students only listen to teacher not give any responses.

Courses prescribed for a class can be completed in a time because all activities are controlled by the teacher.

Power is primarily with teachers and the teacher is the only person who will give instructions and students will follow the instructions.

Acquisition of knowledge is focused.

So, in a teacher-centered approach, the student will not develop the ability to develop the ability to create different models using clay and paper in the group. because the teacher-centered approach focuses on imparting the knowledge and students passively grasp the knowledge.

9(C). Good teachers have positive interpersonal relationships.

They care about their students.

They keep the classroom organized and maintain authority without being rigid or "mean."

They are good motivators, they can make learning fun by being creative and innovative so students learn something.

Thus, it is concluded that Disha was allowed by her teacher to skip recess and play inside by herself because she did not have any friends-educator is demonstrating authoritative techniques in the classroom.

10(C). Disabled Child: A child with a disability is unable to perform certain functions properly than other children. The disability may be physical, it may involve senses like hearing or seeing, it may involve mental health.

To deal with the disabled child in teaching, the teacher should discuss with the child's parents to evolve collaborative plans, to know exactly about the problem and the possible ways to teach the child with other Hence, it becomes clear that when a child with a disability first comes to school the teacher should discuss with the child's parents to evolve collaborative plans.

11(B). It is also known as Central Auditory Processing Disorder, which affects how sound travels unimpeded through the ear is processed and interpreted by children's brain. Children with this disorder cannot recognize subtle differences between sounds in words, even when the sounds are loud and clear enough to be heard. Children suffering from this disorder are unable to block out background noise or to tell where the sound is coming from.

- A student with APD may also have Language Processing Disorder (LPD), which is a specific type of APD in which students find it difficult to attach meaning to sound groups that form words, sentences and stories. These disorders can, in turn, affect expressive (what someone says) and receptive (understanding what was said) language as well.

Disability	Key Points
APD (Auditory Processing Disorder)	<ul><li>very sensitive to sounds and have difficulty in filtering out background noises.</li><li>hearing disorder</li><li>easily distracted</li></ul>
ADHD (Attention Deficit Hyperactivity Disorder)	<ul><li>difficulty staying focused and paying attention.</li><li>the tendency to get distracted easily, difficulty controlling behaviour and hyperactivity.</li></ul>
Autism	<ul><li>challenges with social skills, repetitive behaviours, speech and nonverbal communication.</li></ul>

12(A). Many schools are working to become child-friendly, where children have the right to learn to their fullest potential within a safe and welcoming environment. The aim is to improve every child's participation and learning in school, rather than concentrating on the subject matter and examinations. Being "child-friendly" is very important, but it is not complete.

13(B). Dysgraphia refers to a learning disability which:

affects learners' ability to write coherently.

hinders in organizing letters, numbers, or words on papers.

leads to problems with poor spelling, impaired handwriting, etc.

Remedies useful for treating students with Dysgraphia:

giving extra time for writing assessment, the learners to assimilate the idea easily and will help them in putting their thoughts on paper.

providing low-stress opportunities will allow the learners to learn and write at their own pace and to foster their own strategy of learning and writing.

Hence, it could be concluded that 'Dysgraphia' means difficulty in writing.

14(B). Inclusive-education values the diversity, each child brings to the classroom and facilitates all with equal opportunities to learn and grow.

Inclusive education improves the quality and makes provisions of education for all. It welcomes and celebrates diversity.

It provides a provision to include disabled children along with normal children in a regular classroom environment.

It refers to an education system that accommodates all children regardless of their physical, intellectual, social, emotional, linguistic, or other conditions.

15(D). It refers to an education system that accommodates all children regardless of their physical, intellectual, social, emotional, linguistic, or other conditions.

It provides a provision to include disabled children along with normal children in a regular classroom environment.

Inclusive classroom refers to an education system that includes children regardless of physical, intellectual, social, linguistic, or other differently-abled conditions.

In an inclusive classroom with diverse learners, cooperative learning and peer-tutoring should be actively promoted to facilitate peer-acceptance.

Cooperative learning: It refers to a heterogeneous group where students work collaboratively to achieve learning outcomes. It develops critical thinking, brainstorming, communication, and life long learning skills.

Peer tutoring: It refers to the learning process where fellow students teach each other. In this strategy, a higher-performing student is paired with a lower performing student to teach specific skills.

An inclusive classroom is not limited to children with a disability but also gifted children, economically disadvantaged children, children from remote populations, children belonging to ethnic, linguistic, or cultural minorities or children from other marginalized groups.

Therefore, in an inclusive classroom with diverse learners, cooperative learning, and peer-tutoring should be actively promoted to facilitate peer-acceptance.

16(B). Development refers to an increase in structure for better and enhanced

- Principle of integration: By proceeding from general responses to specific responses again, these specific responses are integrated from the whole it means there is a movement from whole to parts and again from parts to whole.
- Principle of individual difference: With respect to development, the rate and quality of development in various dimensions differ from person to person. There is a difference in the growth rate between boys and girls. Girls mature earlier in comparison to boys.
- Development follows a pattern: Prenatal (before birth) and postnatal (after birth) development of human beings follow a pattern or a predictable sequence. Physical development, motor or language development and intellectual development take place in definite sequences.
- Product of hereditary and environment: Hereditary and environment play a vital role in determining the development of an individual.

So, it could be concluded that the statement 'All individuals are similar in their development' is incorrect about the principles of child development.

17(D). Emotion is a mental state associated with fear, anger, love, etc. The emotional states of an individual are the combination of cognitive experience, physiological change, and behavioral changes. Together, these are known as the elements of emotion.

Three elements of emotion are as follows:

- Cognitive experience: Emotions also involve cognitive processes such as memorials, perceptions, expectations, and interpretations. Our appraisal of an event plays an especially significant role in the meaning it has for us. Thinking of life events can produce emotions.
- Physical changes: Emotions involve the brain, nervous system, and hormones so that when you're emotionally aroused the hormone secretion is more to give us instant energy. Each emotion has a specific characteristic of physiological aspects. Fear may cause blood pressure to rise, pupils to dilate, etc.
- Behavioral changes: Emotions also involve behavioral reactions, both expressive and instrumental. Facial expressions such as smiles and frowns, as well as gestures and Lories of voice, all serve to communicate our feelings that may enhance our chances for survival. Overt expressions such as smiles, or frowns to reveal emotions.

So, we can conclude that Sensory is not an

18(C). The most useful term for describing the linguistic input to the language learning child is child-directed speech.

19(D). Development involves the processes that are genetically programmed as well as those that are influenced by the environment.

- Development takes place in all aspects such as physical, cognitive, language, social, emotional, and others.
- Let us understand the assertion and reason statement:- Differences in the rate of development can be seen in many areas-the acquisitions of teeth, the age at which the child sits stands walks, becomes pubescent, etc.
- Development occurs at different rates for different parts of the body neither the growth of different parts of the body nor the mental growth takes place at the same rate. The different aspects of physical or mental growth take place at different rates and reach maturity at different times. In some areas, the body growth may be rapid, while in others relatively slow.
- A child's development progress can not be accurately measured by comparing her rate of development with the other children of some age a s patterns and rate of development are not the same or uniform for everyone.

Hence, it can be concluded that Both (A) and (R) are false .

20(A). Development is a process that creates growth, progress, positive change, or the addition of physical, economic, environmental, and social. and demographic components.

- Human development refers to the physical, cognitive, and psychosocial development of humans

- Principle of Sequential development- The principle of sequential states that every individual although exhibiting the difference in the change follows the same sequence of change. Cephalocaudal and Proximodistal tendencies are found to be followed in maintaining sequence and direction of development.
- The cephalocaudal tendency exhibits that the development proceeds in the longitudinal direction that is from head to foot. That is the reason why the child first gains control over head before he/she starts walking.
- Infancy develops control of the head and face movements in the first two months. In the next few months, they are able to lift themselves up by using their arms and then gain control over the toe and he

Thus, it is concluded that when a child learns to hop and jump before learning to play football, this illustrates the Cephalocaudal principle of development.

21(C). Development involves the processes that are genetically programmed as well as those that are influenced by the environment.
- Development takes place in all aspects such as physical, cognitive, language, social, emotional, and others.
- Although all individuals grow and develop in their own unique way and in their own contexts, there are some basic principles which underlie the process of development and can be observed in all human beings. These are called the principles of development .
   - Development is a product of heredity and environment:- Heredity and the environment plays an important role in the development of the individual. From the earliest moments of life, the interaction of heredity and the environment works to shape who children are and who they will become.
   - Development proceeds from general to specific : In all the phases of pre-natal (before birth) development and post-natal (after birth) life, the child's responses are from general to specific. General activity proceeds to a specific activity. For example, when Sufi was less than 3 months of age and was shown a rattle, she would get excited and move her arms and kick her legs. This is a general response. At 5 months of age, she would reach out to hold it in her hand. This is a specific response.
   - Development is predictable - The rate of development is fairly constant for

each child. This shows that it is possible to predict the future level of development of the child and to what degree he will exhibit particularly so for height, weight, cognitive ability, etc.
- Principle of differentiation of rate - Differences in the rate of development can be seen in many areas-the acquisition of teeth, the age at which the child sits, stands, walks, becomes pubescent, etc.
   - Development occurs at different rates for different parts of the body, neither the growth of different parts of the body, nor the mental growth takes place at the same rate. The different aspects of physical or mental growth take place at different rates and reach

Therefore, it can be concluded that Rate of development is uniform and universal is not correct statements about development.

22(A). Socialization is also considered as the passing of culture from one generation to the next.
- During the process of socialization, children learn about their family traditions from their elders and preserve them and pass them on to the next generation as they grow older.
- Socialization helps children to learn and perform the different roles and responsibilities which they have learnt from their elders.
- Children pick up ways of behaving appropriately as per their culture from their friends, media, and various other sources:- It is secondary socialization. **Secondary socialization is a type of socialization that refers to the growing child who learns a very important lesson in social conduct from his peers. Friends, media, and peer groups are the agents of secondary socialization which take place throughout one's life.**
- It helps children to learn appropriate social attitudes such as how to like and enjoy social life and group activities.
- Socialization is a process that continues throughout life from birth till adulthood. However, there are different phases in which the process takes place. These phases are usually spread across different age groups and have been categorized as the different types of socialization.
- It includes formal and informal means. Socialization is done by parents, teachers, peers, neighbors, and educational and religious institutions.

Thus, it is concluded that Both (A) and

(R) are true and (R) is the correct explanation of (A).

23(B). Jean Piaget's stage theory describes the cognitive development in children.
- Cognitive development involves changes in cognitive processes and abilities. In Piaget's view, early cognitive development involves processes based upon actions and later progresses into changes in mental operations
- Concrete Operational Stage:
   - 'Concrete Operational Stage' lasts around 7 to 11 years of age which refers to the late childhood stage of child development.
   - In this stage, children can classify objects into groups and subgroups and gain the abilities of conservation
   - Children can conserve numbers (age 6), mass (age 7), and weight (age 9). Conservation is the understanding that something stays the same in quantity even when its appearance changes.

Thus, it infers that according to Jean Piaget, for children who are in the concrete operational stage teachers should provide opportunities to classify objects and ideas on increasingly complex levels

24(B). Piaget's stage theory describes the cognitive development in children.
- Cognitive development involves changes in cognitive processes and abilities. In Piaget's view, early cognitive development involves processes based upon actions and later progresses into changes in mental operations
- 'Preoperational period' lasts around 2 to 6 or 7 years of age .
- In this stage, the child assumes that other people feel, see, and hear exactly the same as the child does.
- It refers to the child's inability to infer the perspective of other people or to see a situation from other's points of view.
- The child has mental representations and are also able to understand things symbolically (playing house, having a tea party).
- The child during this stage engages in what is called a symbolic play that is, the wooden box is considered as a car, a rounding, the steering wheel and the stick, a gun. That is during play an object takes the place of or represents something else in the child's mind.
- Piaget noted that children are unable to take the point of view of other people, which he termed egocentrism. Egocentrism is when children experience difficulty in experiencing

another person's perspectives.

Thus, it infers that according to Jean Piaget, at the Pre-operational Stage of cognitive development the child understand that symbols can be used to represent objects - 'bicycle' will generate an image even when absent.

25(A). Lev Vygotsky, a Russian psychologist, proposed a theory of cognitive development known as 'Socio-Cultural Theory'. He believed that children gain knowledge through social and cultural experiences.

- When the child is having interactions with peers and adults, they learn the values, beliefs, customs, and language of their culture. As per his socio-cultural theory, development takes place due to the intermingling of culture, social

- the gap between what the child can do independently and with assistance.
- difference between what a learner can do on his/her own and what he/she can do with someone's help.
- range of tasks too difficult for the child to do alone, but possible with the help of adults and more skilled peer.
- distance between learners' actual development level and his/her level of development under someone's guidance.

Therefore, it is concluded that Aanav struggles with addition of three digit numbers on his own but is able to do so with support with teacher, In Lev Vygotsky's theory, this highlights Zone of proximal development.

26(A). Lev Vygotsky was a Russian psychologist who believed that social interactions play a key role in development.

- According to him, learning occurs when children interact with people and the environment.
- Lev Vygotsky, a Russian psychologist, proposed a theory of cognitive development known as 'Socio-Cultural Theory'. He believed that children gain knowledge through social and cultural experiences.
  - When the child is having interactions with peers and adults, they learn the values, beliefs, customs, and language of their culture. As per his socio-cultural theory, development takes place due to the intermingling of culture, social interaction, and language.

Therefore, It infers that according to Lev Vygotsky learning is an active process of constructing knowledge.

27(C). Assessment is a process of collecting, receiving, and using data for the purpose of improvement in the learning process.

- Assessment is a systematic way of collecting information to make a judgment about student learning.
- It is integral to the teaching-learning process which helps in facilitating student learning and improving instruction.
- The assessment provides feedback on the performance of the student specifying his/her strengths and areas for improvement which provides insights for taking appropriate steps for improving the learning.
- Following are the tools a teacher uses to assess children's learning:-
  - Classroom interaction:- The students

more objective when the assessment is based on a shared set of assessment schedules. This assessment can further develop cooperative learning and team skills. The learners can overcome their difficulties easily and do better in their studies.

- Projects:- It is a method that emphasizes the active participation of students by working in a group to complete a specific project. It encourages students to think creatively and assesses their intelligence and their representation.
- Portfolio assessment Portfolio is a collection of students' work representing a selection of performance. It often documents a student's best work. It may also include information such as drafts of his/her work, his/herself assessment of work, and parents' assessment.
- Self-assessment:- It is the ability of a person to accurately evaluate or assess his/her performance, and his/her strengths and weaknesses.

Thus, it is concluded that all the given options are the tools should a teacher use to assess children's learning.

- Following are the tools a teacher uses to assess children's learning:-
  - Classroom interaction:- The students, in a group, share their experiences and learn better from each other. The students sharing each other's experiences and assessments can be more objective when the assessment is based on a shared set of assessment schedules. This assessment can further develop cooperative learning and team skills. The learners can overcome their difficulties easily and do better in

their studies.

- Projects:- It is a method that emphasizes the active participation of students by working in a group to complete a specific project. It encourages students to think creatively and assesses their intelligence and their representation.
- Portfolio assessment Portfolio is a collection of students' work representing a selection of performance. It often documents a student's best work. It may also include information such as drafts of his/her work, his/herself assessment of work, and parents' assessment.
- Self-assessment:- It is the ability of a person to accurately evaluate or assess his/her performance, and his/her strengths and weaknesses

28(C). Knowledge: Knowledge is a complex one because the range of what constitutes knowing or knowledge is very wide.

- Knowledge can be used to mean a variety of things, such as familiarity with people, places, persons, skills, and competencies of performing various tasks, beliefs, faiths, and everyday experiences.
- Meta-cognition: A learner needs to be aware of the processes he/she is engaged in during the course of learning. This helps him/her to learn the new learning task effectively. This awareness of one's processes of learning a new learning task is understood as metacognition.

Thus, by encouraging students to reflect on their cognitive abilities to reach a specified goal, a teacher is facilitating the development of metacognition.

29(C). Vygotsky is known as the proposer of social constructivism . Social Constructivism approach talks of the importance of social interaction and context in learning.

- He believes that learning is social in nature. Through interactions, children shared their views and make their own meaning. It does not focus much on individual learning rather it emphasized social context; knowledge is mutually built and constructed.
- Scaffolding: A technique to provide the right kind of support in the right amount at right time to increase a child's competence.
  - Scaffolding can be defined in simpler terms as "a technique to provide the right kind of support in the right amount at right time to increase child's competence."
  - scaffolding is not only a technique to

support learners to achieve their goals but it also helps in filling the 'learning gaps' i.e. what a learner has learned and what was expected to learn.

○ It helps a learner to move from a Zone of Actual Development to a Zone of Proximal Development and finally reach to Zone of Desired Development, with the help of a more experienced person like peers, elders in the family, or teachers.

○ When a teacher starts supporting the learner initially for learning, and gradually reduces the support till the learner reaches a situation, where s/he can develop his/ her own meaning and understanding independently. The teacher is scaffolding the learner. Thus, to scaffold students in solving a

acquiring and integrating knowledge. Learners develop an in-depth understanding through the process of extending and refining their knowledge (e.g. by making new distinctions, clearing up misconceptions, and reaching conclusions).

- In knowledge creation, one cannot be free from one's own context. The social, cultural, and historical contexts are important for individuals because such contexts give the basis to individuals to give meaning to them.
- That is why limited interaction with the environment and externalization of personal knowledge can lead to misconceptions.
- The teacher needs to explain the difficulties and resolve the misconceptions among learners. After many such settings, learners may be assigned some challenging problems also to find out the solution.
- Inquire into the learner's understanding of concepts, exploring misconceptions and untrue ideas'
- Misconceptions are not always baseless and are insignificant in process of learning. It plays a significant role in the teaching-learning process.
- For example , there is often a belief that seasons change based on the earth's proximity to the sun. In reality, seasons change as the earth tilts toward or away from the sun at different times of the year.
- To counter this misconception, a teacher can implement a Think-Pair-Share activity. Where, first, she asks learners what causes the seasons, in order to assess their prior knowledge and potential misconceptions. Learners then pair with a partner to discuss answers and share as a class. The teacher then presents a well-organized lesson on this

topic directly addressing the misconception. Learners again pair and explain the seasons. Learners harboring the misconception may experience cognitive dissonance during the activity as they learn. Further activities continue to restructure and confirm their knowledge.

Thus, (A) is true but (R) is false.

31(B). Refer to the following lines from the passage:

1. "There is a growing realization that though India has enough food to feed its masses two square meals a day, the monster of starvation and food insecurity continues to haunt the poor in our country"

2. "The Public distribution system, which provides food at low prices, is a subject of vital concern. There is a growing realization

From the above sentences, it is clear that statement (A) is false as there is no mention in the passage whether India is a poor country or not and it also doesn't lack resources to feed every citizen.

Statement (B) is true as inspite of having enough food to feed our citizens, our country doesn't have a streamlined PDS due to which the poor is not getting required amount of food timely.

32(D). Refer to the following line from the passage:

1. "Also considering the large stock of food grains combined with food subsidy on one hand and the continuing slow starvation and dismal poverty of the rural population on the other, there is a strong case for making PDS target-group oriented".

From the above sentence, it is clear that the objective of public policy on PDS should now be to let the rural poor enjoy the food subsidy.

33(C). Refer to the following lines from the passage:

1. " The Public distribution system, which provides food at low prices, is a subject of vital concern".

2. "Although the PDS is extensive- it is one of the largest systems in the world-it has yet to reach the rural poor and the far-off places. It remains an urban phenomenon, with the majority of the rural poor still out of its reach due to lack of economic and physical access".

3."The poorest in the cities and the migrants are left out, for they generally do not possess ration cards".

From the above sentences, it is clear that statement (A) is false as there is no mention in the passage whether the public distribution system is very popular in India only or not.

Statement (B) is also false as it is mentioned

in the passage that PDS is an urban phenomenon, it has yet to reach the rural poor and the far-off places.

Statement (C) is true as it is mentioned in the passage that those people who have ration cards can only avail of the PDS facility.

34(B). Refer to the following line from the passage:

1. "In view of such deficiencies in the system, the PDS urgently needs to be streamlined. Also considering the large stock of food grains combined with food subsidy on one hand and the continuing slow starvation and dismal poverty of the rural population on the other, there is a strong case for making PDS target-group oriented".

From the above sentence, it is clear that the

the passage:

1. "There is a growing realization that though India has enough food to feed its masses two square meals a day, the monster of starvation and food insecurity continues to haunt the poor in our country".

2. "Increasing the purchasing power of the poor through providing productive employment leads to rise in income, and thus good standard of living is the ultimate objective of public policy".

3." The allocation of PDS supplies in big cities is larger than in rural areas".

From the first line mentioned above, it is clear that statement (A) is false as it is mentioned in the passage that India has enough food to feed its citizens two square meals a day.

From the second line mentioned above, it is clear that statement (B) is true as it is mentioned in the passage that if we increase the purchasing power of the poor people by providing productive employment to them, then the ultimate objective of PDS will be obtained.

From the third line mentioned above, it is clear that statement (C) is true as it is mentioned in the passage that allocation of PDS supplies is more in big cities than in rural areas or remote areas.

36(C). Here the underlined word 'growing' is an adjective i.e a word naming an attribute of a noun, such as sweet, red, or technical.

Growing means becoming greater over a period of time; increasing.

For example:- She added yet another item to the growing queue.

Realization is a noun and growing is modifying the same.

Thus, the part of speech is adjective here.

37(B). Power means the ability or capacity to do something or act in a particular way.

For example:-Alex was doing everything in his power to provide her with all the experiences of a natural mother.

Capacity means the ability or power to do or understand something.

For example:- He attended in his official capacity as mayor.

Hence, capacity is similar in meaning to the word power.

38(A). System means a set of principles or procedures according to which something is done; an organized scheme or method.

For example:-This system imposes additional financial burdens on many people.

Procedure means an established or official way of doing something.

For example:- New employees are taught

alphabet), movements, facial expressions, and body language to convey meaning.

- Every sign language has a comprehensive vocabulary and its own grammatical rules. These grammatical rules are different from that of spoken languages. Sign language is used by people with different degrees of hearing loss. Some people learn it as young children, while others choose to learn it later in life.
- Main features of sign language include:
  - A sign language has its own grammar , just as Hindi has its own grammar which is quite different from the grammar of Bengali or English.
  - So when a young child is being taught Hindi, he will learn the vocabulary and grammar of Hindi; and when he is taught sign language he will learn

content subjects. It ensures the inclusion of all students irrespective of their linguistic background.

- In an environment of multilingualism, students get the opportunity to not only master their primary language but also get the opportunity to efficiently learn multiple languages at the same time.
- The multilingual students make rules across languages in a stimulating environment which helps them to sharpen their skills like observing, deducting, and reasoning thus leading to greater linguistic and cognitive flexibility.

Thus, it is concluded that 'Multilingualism as a strategy' in the classroom means making use of the languages of learners to teach-learn languages and content subjects.

'streamlined' is an adjective i.e a word naming an attribute of a noun, such as sweet, red, or technical.

Streamlined means having been made simpler and more efficient or effective.

For example:- The manufacturer has streamlined the car's design.

40(A). Language is not static but is subject to variation, this variation could be due to social factors such as geographical location, socioeconomic status, caste, ethnic group, and so on. This variation in language is termed as Dialect .

Regional dialect:

- When we travel from one place to another in a particular direction, we will notice linguistic differences, from one village to another. When the areas are close to each other, the differences will be relatively small.
- However, the further we get from our starting point, the larger the differences will become from that point. These differences are known as regional dialects.
- In other words, a regional dialect is the speech characteristics of a language in a region. More particularly, we can say that dialect is regional and it comes from a region.
- Linguistically, it refers to far greater differences than mere pronunciation which pertains to accents. For instance , take the case of Hindi spoken in different parts of India. We can find differences at the level of sounds, as well as vocabulary and grammar.

From the above points, we can conclude that regional dialect is the speech characteristics of a language in a region.

41(B). Sign Language is a visual language that uses hand shapes (the shape of the hand for different words or letters of the

language by listening to it from the time he is born, sign language is acquired by the young hearing impaired child, by 'seeing' it being used by people around him.

From the above points, we can conclude that ' Sign language has a grammar' is true of Sign Language.

42(B). development takes place through language acquisition and language learning .

Language learning :

- It refers to the result of deliberate and conscious effort in a formal environment, for a better understanding of foundational skills of language learning.
- In language learning, children should move from simple to complex rules to be proficient in all aspects of language skills.
- It is effectively done by providing comprehensible inputs to make the learners actively involved in real communication.
- It refers to have a basic knowledge of grammatical rules and their use in communication.

Hence, it could be concluded that Language learning is deliberate and conscious.

43(B). Multilingualism refers to speaking more than one language competently. The term multilingualism is derived from two Latin words namely "multi" which means many and "lingua" which means language.

- Multilingualism is constitutive of the identity of a child and a typical feature of the Indian linguistic landscape must be used as a tool, resource, and classroom strategy by a creative language teacher.
- Multilingualism as a strategy means using the languages of learners for teaching and learning languages and

teaching-learning process respects the diversity among students and the teacher follows different paths to achieve the goals of learning.

- Authentic materials refer to any text, audio, video, or object developed or written in natural language and contexts. These are the reading texts that were written by native speakers and published in newspapers or magazine contexts.
- '
- Authenticity means that nothing of the original text or material is changed and also its presentation and layout are retained.
- Authentic Material gives authentic and cultural information as it includes authentic resources such as newspaper advertisements , short stories of well-known writers, cartoons from magazines , hoardings, brochures, etc.
- Authentic materials are mostly drawn from periodicals that are constantly being updated. These materials relate more closely to learners' needs and provide them with a source of relevant materials for learning.

Therefore, it is concluded that " An essay on the COVID 19 written by the textbook writer " would not be accepted as authentic material.

45(A). Reading has been defined as a process whereby one looks at and understands what has been written, the reader does not necessarily need to look at everything in a given piece of writing. The reader actively works on the text and is able to arrive at understanding it without looking at every letter and word.

- The subtext is the meaning which is hidden in the text. It provides the reader with a piece of short information about the text regarding its characters and the

plot of the story.
- The subtext is any content of a creative work that is not announced explicitly by the characters or author. It is implicit or becomes something understood by the observer of the work.
- It refers to listing the events and ideas of the story in a sequence . It creates the interest of the reader as subtext provides bits and pieces of information and helps the reader to read between the lines.

From the above points, it is clear that the teacher is asking her students to create a sub-text.

46(A). Language occupies a key position in the School curriculum. The all-round development of the learner is the ultimate aim of education. Therefore, the curriculum

techniques which focuses on reading rapidly to get the overall idea or the gist of the text.
- It looks at the keywords of the text for a general overview. It ignores or skips unnecessary information to get the main idea.
- It involves one going through the text to get the central idea. All the insignificant words are avoided and the focus is on the meaning-bearing elements.
- For example, a reader reads an article from a newspaper to present the overall idea of the text to his group the next day.

Hence, it is clear that the above-mentioned type of reading is known as Skimming .
- Scanning involves quickly glancing through the text to find out a specific piece of information. It is used when looking into a dictionary, invoices,

skills are needed in social situations.
- It is a cognitively undemanding language, i.e. it is easy to understand, deals with everyday language and occurrences, and uses a simple language structure.
- It refers to using language for here-and-now and on familiar topics, for day-to-day living, including conversations with friends on day-to-day routines, and informal interactions.
- It is context embedded. Context embedded means that the conversation is often face-to-face, and offers many cues to the listener such as facial expressions, gestures, and concrete objects of reference.

Hence, it is clear that Basic Interpersonal Communication skills are using language for here-and-now and on familiar topics,

written or sometimes spoken forms.
- Literature for children is considered as an authentic source of reading as it is genuine material covering various genres. Travelogues, one-act plays, memoirs, etc. are the forms of literature.
- A literary text is one that is written for infotainment purposes, that it is for appreciation, pleasure, and enjoyment as well as it might contain some information that is useful to the learners.
- The literary text should be authorized and approved. Literary texts are of many types such as poetry, fictional & nonfictional stories, etc. "Harry Potter" is an example of a literary text.
- Literary texts are perceived as a resource and relevant input to stimulate language activities and they can be used in a language class for the teaching and learning of language functions.
- Literary texts develop critical thinking as by reading the text, the students get information about other cultural matters, and they are encouraged to read the text and form a personal opinion.
- Using literary texts in the language classroom can make the students more aware of the language they are learning, and help them in developing skills and strategies.

   Thus, it is concluded that 'Literary texts should be used to teach grammar.' is NOT true teaching of literary texts in a language classroom.

47(D). Reading sub-skill refers to the well-planned reading approach which helps the learners to comprehend and perceive the meaning of the text effectively. There are different kinds of reading sub-skill and 'Skimming' is one of them.
- Skimming is one of the reading

figures, or percentage.
- Reading between the lines refers to the phenomenon where the answers are not explicitly stated but only suggested in the text. It helps to infer literal meanings from the author's figurative language.

48(B). Vocabulary refers to the set of words an individual uses as a tool for communication. It is a collection of familiar words used or understood by an individual or group of people. There are mainly two types of vocabulary which include Active and Passive vocabulary.
- Passive vocabulary refers to the set of words that we recognize when we listen to them and read them as these words can't be recalled and used easily and frequently.
- One can recognize these words in a text or when spoken by others and can guess the meaning of these words but cannot use them confidently.
- Our active vocabulary is more limited (smaller) than our passive vocabulary. Students try their best to increase the repertoire of both active and passive vocabulary and gradually try to convert their passive into their active vocabulary.

Hence, it could be concluded that the above-mentioned types of words are known as Passive Vocabulary.

49(A). There are two major aspects of language proficiency that must be acquired by second language learners. Jim Cummins has identified these as Basic Interpersonal Communication Skills (BICS), or conversational proficiency, and Cognitive Academic Language Proficiency (CALP), or academic proficiency.

BICS:
- BICS stands for Basic Interpersonal Communication Skills. These language

different approaches to writing and the 'Process Approach' is one of them.
- Process approach to writing models the writing process rather than the written product. It involves the active participation of learners.
- It enables learners to learn how to write as it is a writing approach in which learners undergo different stages of writing fo r developing a good write-up .
- It focuses on the steps involved in creating a unique/creative piece of writing and emphasizes revising, editing, and producing a text before coming up with the final text.
- Stages involved in the process approach to writing are Brainstorming, Outlining, Drafting, Revising, Proof-reading, and Writing the final draft.

Hence, it could be concluded that the P rocess Approach to writing gives scope for learners to undergo different stages of writing in order to learn to write.

51(D). Knowledge is often considered synonymous with terms like familiarity, understanding, wisdom, education, awareness, etc. Knowledge can be expressed in the form of data, scientific formulae, product specifications, manuals, universal principles, and so forth. Knowledge may be declarative or procedural.
- Declarative knowledge comprises a number of knowledge consisting of known facts and active goals.
- Declarative encoding in learning grammar means that the information, i.e. an explicit grammar rule, is provided usually through instruction.
- The aim is for a learner to develop the language structure. It enables a student to describe a rule of grammar and apply it in structured and pattern practice drills.

- It means establishing knowledge of grammar rules or patterns in the learners' minds. In other words, here, students learn how the form behaves and how to use it in contexts.

Hence, it could be concluded that the above-mentioned process of teaching-learning of grammar is known as declarative knowledge .

52(A). Task-Based Language Learning is an approach that implies the idea that language learning takes place by using language meaningfully and contextually. It is an approach in which students use language to complete a task. There are different types of language tasks such as input-based tasks, output-based tasks, etc.

- Input-based language tasks are typically designed to engage learners in input

facilitate vocabulary acquisition receptively as well as productively. Input-based tasks have been typically operationalized as read-and-comprehend tasks and listen-and-do tasks.

- These tasks don't require the production of language. They focus on an individual's ability of understanding and comprehending language. For example, reading a story, listening to a story, etc.

From the above points, we can conclude that 'learners read a story in groups of five' is an input-based task for language learning.

53(B). Language education/teaching refers to a process whereby a child gains communicative comprehension or fluency over a language. It involves practice by learners where facilitation is provided by a teacher.

Concepts related to language education:

Grammar translation method:

- Grammar translation is a traditional method through which language is taught with a detailed study of grammar. Learners apply the rule of grammar in translating sentences from their mother tongue to the target language.
- It explains grammatical rules therefore it gives correct and accurate knowledge of English. This method tries to establish a strong link between new ideas and old ideas and focuses on reading and writing skills.

Error correction:

- Error correction refers to understanding the error patterns of children so that they can be provided with better learning experiences which will help them in developing a contextual understanding of language learning processes.
- The teacher has to identify and assess

these errors of children to identify the patterns of errors or mistakes that students make in their work so that these can be minimized or removed.

First language interference:

- The positive influence of the first language could be seen in the classroom, but sometimes, it manifests in the form of incorrect pronunciation, and the importance of pronunciation in communication can't be denied.
- It is necessary to minimize the interference/influence of the first language by using it as a support in the English classroom, and it can be done by giving inputs from the target language in a simple & graded manner and using the languages of learners.

Hence, it is clear that the wavelength of sound is NOT a concept from language

it has been used for Raghu and his father as they always have differences and their views don't match.

Friction Land means disagreement between people or groups.

55(A). **saw red:** means to be or become extremely angry.

The poem refers that Raghu took advice from his father to go mountain climbing.

When his father refused him to go there, Raghu got **saw red** at this rejection.

Means Raghu become extremely angry with his father.

56(C). Different food habits is not a point of clash between Raghu and his father.

Raghu's father used to ask him to change his lifestyle.

He wanted him to be quiet. His father wanted him to change himself.

The interests of Raghu and his father were different.

Raghu loved mountain climbing, but his father forbade him to do it.

Raghu wanted to sing poetry for the band, but even his father did not like it. He wanted him to think about his career.

It was their age difference that they could not understand each other's feelings.

Thus, we can say is that the food differences between Raghu and his father were not the subject of conflict.

57(D). Line 6 "Am I the prefect at school? or the baby at home?' shows the dilemma faced by Raghu.

He doesn't know whether he is prefect at school or at home as a kid.

Because he feels that he is liked by everyone in the school for who he is.

But at home her father wants to change him.

He want him to stay clean by wearing good clothes, washing his hair and getting his hair cut.

58(D). We look at the lines:

abcc is the rhyme in 1st stanza.

In friction land there is a family, family - a

With some confusions as you will see. see - b

There is Raghu aged fifteen and others all grown, grown - c

'Please will someone let me ever be on my own!' own - c

59(C). Here, flabbergasted is used as an adjective.

flabbergasted means overwhelm with shock, surprise, or wonder.

Flabbergasted is used for Raghu's father when Raghu asked his father to join a band to sing poetry, his father went to flabbergasted.

Adjective: a class of words that modify nouns and pronouns, primarily by

conducts such type of activity that compels the children to think, analyze, observe, experiment, etc.

Critical thinking can be developed by giving activities that involve brainstorming sessions by them, assigning a problem-solving task, and observing how they perform in it.

To enhance critical thinking among the learners the teacher should give situations and ask learners to discuss and solve them among the group.

This activity will compel the children to use their existing knowledge and previous experiences to critically think, compare and analyze the situations to solve them effectively.

Hence, it could be concluded that to enhance critical thinking among the learners the teacher should give situations and ask learners to discuss and solve them among the group.

61(B). We can write,

$\Rightarrow 16 = 2^4$

$\Rightarrow 36 = 2^2 \times 3^2$

$\Rightarrow 45 = 3^2 \times 5$

$\Rightarrow 48 = 2^4 \times 3$

LCM of the numbers = Product of highest powers of prime factors = $2^4 \times 3^2 \times 5 = 720$

Now, Highest 4-digit number = 9999

On dividing 9999 by 720, remainder = 639

∴ Required number = 9999 - 639 = 9360

62(C). Given

48 and 65

Calculation

Factors of 48 = 2 × 2 × 2 × 2 × 3

Factors of 65 = 5 × 13

L.C.M of 48 and 65 = 2 × 2 × 2 × 2 × 3 × 5 × 13

$\Rightarrow 3120$

∴ The LCM of 48 and 65 is 3120

63(B). Remainder when 1^5 divided by $4 = 1$
Remainder when 2^5 or 32 divided by $4 = 0$
Remainder when 3^5 or 243 divided by $4 = 3$
Remainder when 4^5 or 1024 divided by $4 = 0$
Remainder when 5^5 or 3125 divided by $4 = 1$.
Remainder $= 1 + 3 + 1 = 5$
Remainder when 5 divided by $4 = 1$

64(D). Given,
Two positive numbers differ by 1280.
When the greater number is divided by the smaller number, the quotient is 7 and the remainder is 50.
Dividend = Quotient × divisor + remainder
Let, the greater number be a and smaller number b.

Put the value of a from equation (2) into equation (1)
$\Rightarrow 7b + 50 - b = 1280$
$\Rightarrow 6b = 1280 - 50$
$\Rightarrow 6b = 1230$
$\Rightarrow b = \left(\frac{1230}{6}\right)$
$\Rightarrow b = 205$
Put the value of b in equation (1) we get,
$\Rightarrow a - 205 = 1280$
$\Rightarrow a = 1280 + 205$
$\Rightarrow a = 1485$
$\therefore$ Greater number is 1485.

65(C). Given,
$3^{x+3} + 7 = 250$
$\Rightarrow 3^{x+3} = 250 - 7$
$\Rightarrow 3^{x+3} = 243$
$\Rightarrow 3^{x+3} = 3^5$
$\Rightarrow x + 3 = 5$
$\Rightarrow x = 2$

66(C). $\frac{2a+b}{a+4b} = 3$ (Given)
$\Rightarrow 2a + b = 3(a + 4b)$
$\Rightarrow 2a + b = 3a + 12b$
$\Rightarrow -a = 11b$
$\Rightarrow a = -11b$
$\therefore \frac{a+b}{a+2b}$
$\Rightarrow \frac{-11b+b}{-11b+2b}$
$\Rightarrow \frac{-10b}{-9b}$
$\Rightarrow \frac{10}{9}$

67(D). Dietary fibre is found in wholegrain cereals and fruit and vegetables. Fibre is made up of the indigestible parts or compounds of plants, which pass relatively unchanged through our stomach and intestines. Fibre is mainly a carbohydrate. The main role of fibre is to keep the digestive system healthy."

68(B). Elemental oxygen is found as a gas at standard temperatures and pressures, most commonly in the O 2 form.
The process of nitrogen fixation by bacteria does not take place in the presence of the Elemental form of oxygen. Certain bacteria such as Azotobacter (occur freely in the soil) and Rhizobium (occur in root nodules of leguminous plants like pea, gram, bean, etc), convert the atmospheric nitrogen into water-soluble nitrates.
Hence, the correct option is (B)

69(D). $\angle AOC$ and $\angle BOD$ are vertically opposite angles, also $\angle AOD$ and $\angle BOC$ are vertically opposite angles.
It is given that $\angle AOC = 50°$
Thus, $\angle BOD = 50°$.
Let, $\angle AOD = \angle BOC = x°$
As we know that the sum of all angle around a particular point is $360°$.
$\angle AOC + \angle BOD + \angle AOD + \angle BOC = 360°$

$\therefore \angle AOD = \angle BOC = 130°$
Thus, it becomes clear that $\angle BOC$ is equal to $130°$.

70(B). We know that:
Vertically opposite angles are equal.
Let, two lines be AB and CD.

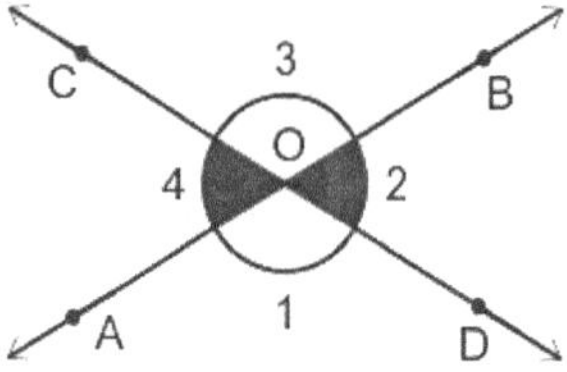

and four angles be $\angle 1, \angle 2, \angle 3$ and $\angle 4$
Sum of measures of three angles $= 290°$
Then, the fourth angle (say $\angle 1$)
$= 360° - 290° \Rightarrow \angle 1 = 70°$
$\Rightarrow \angle 3 = \angle 1 = 70°$ [Vertically opposite angles are equal]
AB is straight line,
$\therefore \angle 1 + \angle 2 = 180°$
$\Rightarrow \angle 2 = 180° - 70° = 110°$
$\Rightarrow \angle 4 = \angle 2 = 110°$ (Vertically opposite angles are equal)
So, the measure of all four angles are $110°, 70°, 110°, 70°$

71(D). We know that:
The sum of the complementary angles is $90°$.
The sum of the supplementary angle is $180°$.

Let, the angle be x.
Supplement angle $= 180° - x$
Complement angle $= 90° - x$
Given that,
The Supplement angle four times of complement angle,
$(180° - x) = 4 \times (90° - x)$
$\Rightarrow 180° - x = 360° - 4x$
$\Rightarrow 3x = 180°$
$\Rightarrow x = 60°$

72(A). Given:
The ratio of A, B and C is $3 : 7 : 12$
And the difference of the shares of B and $C = 3000$
We know that:
The total amount of the sum can be found using ratio concept.
Let, P be the amount of money share,
Then the ratios will be $3 \times P : 7 \times P : 12 \times P$
Now the sum of ratios $= 3 \times P + 7 \times P + 12 \times P = 22 \times P$
And $(7 \times P) - (3 \times P) = 3000$
$\Rightarrow 4 \times P = 3000$
$\Rightarrow P = 750$
$\therefore$ The total sum of Amount $= 22 \times P = 22 \times 750 = 16500 =$ Rs. 16500

73(D). Area of the lawn $= \pi r^2 = \frac{22}{7} \times 35 \times 35 = 3850 m^2$

$= 5544 m^2 - 3850 m^2 = 1694 m^2$
$\therefore$ Cost of gravelling $= 1694 m^2 \times$ Rs. 75 per $m^2 =$ Rs. 127050

74(D). Given:
Radius of sphere $= 3 cm$
Height of the cone = Half of the radius of the cone
Volume of Sphere $= \frac{4}{3} \times \pi R^3$
Volume of Cone $= \frac{1}{3} \times \pi r^2 h$
Now,
Applying the formula:
$\frac{4}{3} \times \pi \times 3 \times 3 \times 3 = \frac{1}{3} \times \pi \times r \times r \times h$
Put $h = \frac{r}{2}$
$\Rightarrow \frac{4}{3} \times 3 \times 3 \times 3 = \frac{1}{3} \times r \times r \times \frac{r}{2}$
$\Rightarrow r^3 = 216$
$\Rightarrow r = 6$

75(D). Given:
$(\sqrt{72} - \sqrt{18}) \div \sqrt{12}$
$= \frac{\sqrt{72} - \sqrt{18}}{\sqrt{12}}$
$= \frac{6\sqrt{2} - 3\sqrt{2}}{2\sqrt{3}}$
$= \frac{3\sqrt{2}}{2\sqrt{3}} \times \frac{\sqrt{3}}{\sqrt{3}} = \frac{\sqrt{6}}{2}$

76(A). Given:
80% of CP = 60% of SP
% Profit $= \left[\frac{(SP - CP)}{CP}\right] \times 100$
% Loss $= \left[\frac{(CP - SP)}{CP}\right] \times 100$
Let the $CP =$ Rs. x
So, we get:
$\left(\frac{80}{100}\right) \times x = \left(\frac{60}{100}\right) \times SP$
$\Rightarrow SP = \left(\frac{4}{3}\right)$
Therefore we get:
% Profit $= \left[\frac{\left(\frac{4}{3}\right)x - x}{x}\right] \times 100 = 33.33\%$
$\therefore$ There is a profit of **33.33%**

77(D). Given:
Shaurya age is 38,
Let the brother's present age be x years.
According to Question statement,
$(38 - x) = x$
$\Rightarrow 2x = 38$
$\Rightarrow x = \dfrac{38}{2}$
$\Rightarrow x = 19$
$\therefore$ Brother's age 5 years back
$= (19 - 5) = 14$ years

78(D). Given:
$\sqrt{a} - \sqrt{b} = 2$ and $\sqrt{a} + \sqrt{b} = 4$
$\sqrt{a} - \sqrt{b} = 2 \ldots (1)$
$\sqrt{a} + \sqrt{b} = 4 \cdots (2)$
Adding equations (1) and (2),
$\Rightarrow 2\sqrt{a} = 6$
$\Rightarrow \sqrt{a} = 3$
$\rightarrow a = 9$

$\Rightarrow b = 1$
$a^2 b = 81 \times 1 = 81$
$\therefore$ Value of $a^2 b$ is 81.

79(D). According to the question the solution of water and soil is acidic in nature as it is able to turn the litmus paper into yellow-orange colour. As we know lemon is a rich source of vitamin C, which is known as citric acid. Being a weak acid it will be able to turn the litmus to red. Vinegar is a combination of water and acetic acid. It acts as a mild acid and it also turns the litmus paper to red. Common salt includes the sodium and chloride ions and is not able to turn the litmus to blue as it is not a basic compound.
Antacid has its neutralizing property for acidsand it reduces the acidity with the alkaline nature of its compounds such as aluminium and sodium carbonate. So antacid would change the pH paper from yellow-orange to greenish-blue while others are acidic in nature.

80(C). In science, a push or a pull on an object is called force.

Ter m	Meaning
Pr ess ure	It is an expression of force exerted o n a surface per unit area.
Gr avi tat ion	It is a force that exists among all ma terial objects in the universe.
Fo rce	A push or a pull on an object is calle d a force.
Fri cti on	It is the force that opposes the relati ve motion between the two surfaces of objects in contact.

81(C). Hertz is the unit of frequency.
$1 Hz = 1$ vibration per $sec = 60$ vibrations per minute.

82(C). Dolphin has the largest brain in proportion to its body size.
Dolphins have the highest brain-to-body weight ratio of all cetaceans.
Bottlenose dolphins have bigger brains than humans, and they have a brain-to-body-weight ratio greater than great apes do.
Monitor lizards, tegus, and anoles, and some tortoise species have the largest among reptiles.
Among birds, the highest brain-to-body ratios are found among parrots, crows, magpies, jays, and ravens.

83(B). Skin is not just a mere outer covering but it is the largest and one of the most active sense organ of the body. It performs a plethora of functions important

Benzene is insoluble in water in normal conditions. The primary reason for the insolubility of benzene in water is that it is a nonpolar compound. This means that the intermolecular bonds between the carbon atoms of the benzene molecule are highly covalent.

85(B). As per the definition given by Ernst Mayr in : 1964
"A species is a group of actually or potentially inbreeding populations that are reproductively isolated from other such groups."

86(A). Earthquake is a sudden violent shaking of the ground, it causes great destruction over the ground surface. It is mainly due to the movement of tectonic plates of earth crust or volcanic action. Earthquakes are able to initiate landslides over mountainous regions or wet regions. If the earthquakes are under the sea bed, this sudden shake can create extreme pressure outwards and might take a shape of a Tsunami. Sometimes the earthquakes can break the dams and overflows of water can create the situation of floods.

87(D). The learner should be able to construct and use multiplication facts in daily life situations.
The learner should be able to read and write numbers up to 999 using place value and solve simple daily life problems using addition and subtraction of 3 digit numbers leader without regrouping. (What is the place value of 4 in 543?)
Analyze and applies an appropriate number operation in the situation.
Identify, make, and describe 2D shapes by several sides, corners, and diagonals and fill a given region leaving no gaps using a tile of a given shape.
Estimate and measure length and distances using standard units.

Compares the capacity of different containers in terms of non-standard units.
Comparing quantitative data like shows that 2 X 5 is the same as 5 X 2.
Identify a particular day and date on a calendar
Extends patterns in simple shapes and numbers.
Records data using tally marks.

88(D). Activities for building pattern recognition skills-
Putting the beads on a string.
Taking various shapes and sizes of building blocks and trying to maintain them in specific order to create a series. It will assist students in developing mental math skills, which will help them in many problem-solving situations.
Creating a pattern in the meals children
It's easier for kids to comprehend division if they can visualize a bunch of goods being divided evenly. for example- distributing 100 available drawing sheets among 25 students of your class equally.
Learning by doing is happening in this case.
Children will be learning division by active learning.
It will be an interesting task to engage children in the learning process.
It will help children apply their knowledge and ability to real-world situations.

90(C). Level 1: Visualization
At this initial stage, students are aware of space only as something that exists around them.
Geometric concepts are viewed as total entities rather than as having components or attributes.
Level 2: Analysis
At this level, an analysis of geometric concepts begins, through observation and experimentation, students begin to discern the characteristics of figures.
These emerging properties are then used to conceptualize classes of shapes.
Thus figures are recognized as having parts and are recognized by their parts.
Level 3: Informal Deduction.
At this level, students can establish the interrelationships of properties both within figures and among figures.
Thus they can deduce the properties of a figure and recognize classes of figures.
Level 4: Formal Deduction
At this level, the significance of deduction as a way of establishing geometric theory within an axiomatic system is understood.
A person at this level can construct, not just memorize, proofs; the possibility of developing a proof in more than one way is seen; the interaction of necessary and sufficient conditions is understood;

distinctions between a statement and its converse can be made.

Level 5: Rigor

At this stage the learner can work in a variety of axiomatic systems, that is, non-Euclidean geometries can be studied, and different systems can be compared.

Geometry is seen in the abstract.

91(A). In the above question, students will start adding the number in the one's column (0+4). By adding these numbers, the answer they get is 4.

Then, they will add the numbers in the tens column (7+3), and the answer they get is 10. However, they cannot place the 10 underneath the tens column because they can only place one digit per column.

Then, by regrouping they can change 10 into 0 tens + 1.

regrouping they will add the hundreds column(2+1), then the answer will be 304.

It means that the students are having problems with the concept of regrouping.

92(C). Concept:

Suppose there are $'n'$ observations $\{x_1, x_2, x_3, \ldots, x_n\}$

Mean

$$(\bar{x}) = \frac{(x_1 + x_2 + x_3 + \ldots + x_n)}{n} = \frac{\sum_{i=1}^{n} x_i}{n}$$

Sum of the first n natural numbers

$$= \frac{n(n+1)}{2}$$

Calculation:

To find: Mean of the first 99 natural numbers

As we know, Sum of first n natural numbers

$$= \frac{n(n+1)}{2}$$

Now, Mean $= \dfrac{\frac{99(99+1)}{2}}{99}$

$$= \frac{(99+1)}{2} = 50$$

93(A). Given

Number of items = 50

Mean = 50

Formula used

Mean = sum of observation/Number of observation

Calculation

Sum of observation = 50 × 24

$\Rightarrow 1200$

correct mean = (Sum of observation - wrong item included + right item)/Number of items

correct mean = (1200 - 83 - 17 + 38 + 77)/50

$\Rightarrow 1215/50$

$\Rightarrow 24.3$

94(C). Given:

The data = 7.5, 7.3, 7.2, 7.2, 7.4, 7.7, 7.7, 7.5, 7.3, 7.2, 7.6, 7.2

Concept:

Mean: Mean is the average or the most common value in a collection of numbers

Median: The middle value of the given numbers when arranged in an order.

Mode: The mode is the value that is repeatedly occurring in given numbers

Calculation:

When we arrange the data in a manner

$\Rightarrow$ 7.2, 7.2, 7.2, 7.2, 7.3, 7.3, 7.4, 7.5, 7.5, 7.6, 7.7, 7.7

We can see that 7.2 is frequently occurring in given data then,

The mode of the given data = 7.2

∴ The required result will be 7.2.

95(B). Mathematics is the study of numbers, shape, quantity, and patterns. Mathematics is the 'queen of all sciences' and its presence is there in all the subjects. It acts as the basis and structure of other subjects.

it visualized as the vehicle to train a child to think, reason, analyze, and articulate logically

Development of skills like speed, accuracy, estimation

Improvement of reasoning power, analytical and, critical thinking

Enhancement of scientific attitude like estimating, finding and verifying results

Remaining options are not relevant in the context as mathematics relies on logic and is suitable for every student.

So, from the above-mentioned points, it becomes clear that the nature of mathematics is logical.

96(D). Mathematics teaching often criticized for its emphasis on memorizing basic facts, rules, and formulae.

Effective mathematics takes place in an effective classroom.

So, from the above-mentioned points, it becomes clear that the mathematics classroom should not be teacher-centred.

97(D). Mathematics is the study of numbers, shape, quantity, and patterns. The nature of mathematics is logical as it relies on logic and connects learning with children's day-to-day life.

We need mathematics in society for:

Counting

Business

Calculation

Transaction

Measurement

Making budget

Financial analysis

So it could be interpreted that all the given needs are correct in the context.

98(D). Cumulative nature- Mathematics' cumulative nature is primarily responsible for anxiety and failure. All mathematical concepts are interconnected, necessitating each topic's clarity and comprehension.

Symbolic language- The prominence of symbolic language is the second major cause. When symbols are manipulated without the children's knowledge, they begin to dissociate from the subject.

The language used in textbooks- The mathematics language they acquire in the school is considerably different from their everyday speech, and it becomes a big source of alienation in and of itself.

Assessment methods- the crude methods of assessment are the barriers to effective teaching and learning mathematics.

Hence, we conclude that the mathematical inabilities of the learners are not an appropriate reason for fear of mathematics.

99(C). Mathematical concepts are abstract- mathematics uses observation, simulation, and even experimentation to never be forgotten.

The mathematical concepts are hierarchical in nature, which means that they are built on practical and conceptual knowledge from one class to the next. They are taught in a pre-determined order, such as arithmetic first, then algebra, trigonometry, and calculus.

Mathematics reveals the hidden patterns that help in our understanding of the world. Mathematics is not based on observation instead it is based on logic. It can be used to explain the things that we observe.

Hence, we conclude that the statement which is not appropriate regarding the nature of mathematics is that "it is like science which is based on observation".

100(B). he Child's adjustment to school is influenced by the classroom environment. If a student is comfortable, interested, and not afraid in the classroom, the process of adaptation is aided.

The teacher should conduct a discussion in the classroom about different changes in the new student's life and how he handled them to give children an opportunity to understand adaptation.

This activity will help children to develop friendships with their peers and feel less social tension.

This discussion will also develop self-esteem in the new child and he will not feel isolated in the classroom.

Hence, we conclude that the best activity for teaching students about adaptation is having a discussion in the class about different changes in the new student's life and how he handled them.

101(A). Active learning tasks allow children to interact with the material in a way that encourages creative thinking.

It provides students with the opportunity to have first-hand experience.

Active learning tasks encourage children to make their ideas explicit which helps teachers to assess students learning.

Students are active participants rather than passive listeners.

It encourages students to establish a connection between their existing knowledge and new concepts, allowing them to reflect on their understanding.

It places a strong emphasis on collaboration among students.

Hence, we conclude that the best example of students engaging in active learning is students discussing in pairs the impact of the decline of traditional crafts on the livelihoods of craftsmen.

102(A). Vitamins help in protecting our bodies against diseases. Vitamins also help in keeping our eyes, bones, teeth, and gums

against diseases.

Long-term deficiency of one or more nutrients in our diet may result in certain diseases or disorders.

Vitamin D helps our body to use calcium for bones and teeth.

Vitamin D is required for calcium absorption. Sunlight is the best source of vitamin D.

Our body also prepares Vitamin D in the presence of sunlight. Nowadays, insufficient exposure to sunlight is causing Vitamin D deficiency in many people.

103(A). Whenever a current is flowing in the resistance then heat is produced in it .

- The phenomenon of producing heat by the electric current is called as the heating effect of electric current .

Cause of heating effect of current:

- When a potential difference is applied across the ends of a conductor, its free electrons get accelerated in the opposite direction of the applied field.
- But the speed of the electrons does not increase beyond a constant drift speed. This is because, during the course of their motion, the electrons collide frequently with the positive metal ions.

104(A). The passage of current is due to the flow of positive charges. This is what we call the conventional flow of current, i.e. in the direction of flow of positive charges.

The direction of the conventional current corresponds to the direction of positive charge which is from higher potential(positive) to lower potential(negative).

After the discovery of electrons, it was observed that electrons are the particles that flow in a conductor.

Electrons being negatively charged flow from the negative terminal to the positive terminal of the voltage source. So, the actual

direction of the current should be from the negative to the positive terminal.

Electric current is associated with the movement of electrons which is from lower potential(negative) to higher potential(positive), therefore, the direction of electric current is opposite to that of conventional current.

Thus the direction of electric current is always opposite to the direction of conventional current in metallic conductors. So option 1 is correct.

105(D). Ferromagnetic Substances: The substances which are strongly magnetized when placed in an external magnetic field in the same direction to the applied field are called ferromagnetic substances. d lines are originated from a pole and not at the centre of the bar.

by a magnet

- It develops strong magnetization in the direction of the applied magnetic field
- By removing the magnetizing filed, it does not lose its magnetization
- When placed in a non-uniform magnetic field, it tends to move from weaker to stronger regions of the magnetic field
- When placed in a uniform magnetic field, it aligns itself parallel to the direction of the magnetic field
- Magnetic susceptibility is much greater than 1 i.e. more than 100
- Relative permeability is much greater than 1 i.e. more than 100

106(A). Refraction is the change in the direction of a wave passing from one medium to another.

A light ray refracts whenever it travels at an angle into a medium of different refractive index.

This change in speed results in a change in direction.

As an example, consider air travelling into water.

The speed of light decreases as it continues to travel at a different angle.

When light travels from air into glass, It bends towards the normal line and the light slows down and changes direction slightly.

When light travels from a less dense substance to a denser substance, the refracted light bends more towards the normal line.

If the light wave approaches the boundary in a direction that is perpendicular to it, the light ray doesn't refract in spite of the change in speed.

Laws of Refraction of Light

The incident ray refracted ray, and the normal to the interface of two media at the point of incidence all lie on the same plane.

The ratio of the sine of the angle of incidence to the sine of the angle of

refraction is constant.

This is also known as Snell's law of refraction.

107(D). Let the distance be d km.

We know that,

Distance = Speed x Time

$$\Rightarrow \frac{d}{8} + \frac{d}{12} = 15$$

$$\Rightarrow \frac{3d+2d}{24} = 15$$

$$\Rightarrow d = 72 km$$

108(D). Human migration is the movement of people from one place to another with intention of settling, permanently or temporarily, at a new location.

1. Push factors "push" people away from their homes and include things like war. Pull factors "pull" people to a new home

people to migrate, so these are the push factors of migration.

3. Better opportunities for work and better health facilities pull people and so, these are pull factors of migration.

Hence, Poor health facilities and the absence of good educational institutions are the push factors for migration.

109(C). Calcium hypochlorite is commonly known as Bleaching powder.

- Its formula is Ca(OCl) 2 .
- It is a pale yellow coloured powder with a strong smell of chlorine.

Uses of bleaching powder -

- For bleaching dirty clothes in the laundry.
- As a bleaching agent for cotton and linen in the textile industry.
- As an oxidizer in many industries.

110(C). The hardest known substance available naturally on earth is Diamond. In diamond, every layer of carbon atom is bonded with strong sigma bonds . Due to the presence of such strong covalent bonding between the carbon atoms arranged in a tetrahedral manner imparts rigidity to the substance making it the hardest known substance.

111(A). Science refers to the study of structure and behaviour of the physical and natural things through observation and experimentation. In other words, science is a classified knowledge gained from a systematic study of the behaviour of nature.

Nature of science:

- Science is always tentative.
- Science promotes scepticism.
- Science as an approach to investigation.
- Science is an interdisciplinary area of learning.
- Science is a particular way of looking at nature.
- Science is a process of constructing

knowledge.
- Science demands perseverance from its practitioners

112(D). Scientific investigations use a variety of methods.
Scientific knowledge is based on empirical evidence.
Science is tentative i.e. scientific knowledge is open to revision in light of new evidence.
Science promotes scepticism, scepticism is the act of suspending judgment (the opposite of jumping to conclusions) when evaluating an explanation or claims.
Scientific models, laws, mechanisms, and theories and explain natural phenomena.
Scientific knowledge assumes order and consistency in natural systems.
Science is a human endeavor and a way of knowing.

looking at nature- Scientist always considers eclipse a natural phenomenon, enjoys the sight and tries to understand what caused the event and investigates whether it could have any ill effects.
Science is a rapidly expanding body of knowledge- Newer disciplines are being discovered and established every day and the older ones are being enriched by researches being carried out in institutes of higher learning
Science is an interdisciplinary area of learning- It is then that knowledge was organized for convenience into disciplines like physics, chemistry, biology, geology, astronomy, etc. though no natural phenomenon falls completely under just any one of these disciplines
Science is a truly international enterprise- Science does not belong to any single country or a group of countries, and it would be morally and ethically wrong to deny the fruits of scientific development to any country in the world.
Science is always tentative- All theories, even the seemingly well-founded ones, can be revised or improved upon, or abandoned altogether whenever new evidence emerges, either as new experimental observations or as new theoretical developments
Thus from the above-mentioned points, it is clear that Scientific knowledge has a tentative character.

114(A). Science demands evidence
Science is a blend of logic and imagination
Scientific knowledge is durable
Scientific knowledge is subject to change

Scientists attempt to identify and avoid bias
Science is a complex social activity
Science is a blend of logic and imagination

115(A). It requires children to analyze, synthesize, evaluate a knowledge base and then predict different outcomes.
It encourages children to stretch their thinking beyond what they already know. They are also known as open-ended questions.
These questions encourage children to think independently and also promote critical thinking. It encourages learners to use their higher-order cognitive abilities to create new ideas or explanations by combining original and known ideas.
It helps in identifying individual differences in students as each child will come up with different answers.

116(D). Investigatory projects use the scientific method. It starts with asking questions about something learners observe. When learners frame questions about their observation, they should be encouraged to arrive at a testable and precise question or the question on which they do their project.
After researching and investigating, they frame hypotheses, i.e. the possible answers for their questions. Generally, learners use the terms like 'if'/ 'then' to convert the question into a hypothesis.
When they frame hypotheses, they started thinking of the experimentation.
While doing experimentation, learners record the observations and analyze them in order to find out the answer to their question. Sometime, the hypotheses may be right and some times it may be wrong. If the hypothesis is wrong, they again reframe a new hypothesis and test it.
Learners report their findings in clear terms in either case i.e. hypothesis is accepted or rejected.
Thus from above-mentioned points, it is clear that project work on the nature of sound is best suited to satisfy these criteria.

117(D). Science is both a body of knowledge and a process.
Science is ongoing which means Science is continually refining and expanding our horizons of knowledge of the universe.
Science is a particular way of looking at nature different from all other ways where cause and effect relationship doesn't exist.
Science is an interdisciplinary area of learning relating to more than one branch

of knowledge.
Science is a community enterprise It is a large-scale human endeavor that involves a supporting community from school children to pharmaceuticals and political parties to farmers.

118(C). Empirical nature of science- It refers to the idea that science is founded on or generated from observations of the world around us, which are then interpreted. It is based on observed and measured phenomena and knowledge is derived from actual experiences rather than theory or belief.
It emphasizes that rather than relying exclusively on prior reasoning, intuition, or revelation, all hypotheses and theories must be evaluated against observations of the natural world.

science to many elements of their lives and allows them to broaden their knowledge in a variety of subjects related to certain aspects of their environment to make the nature of science an integral part of teaching-learning.
Developing creative thinking- The teacher should encourage students to participate in tasks rather than memorizing facts.
Students should be made conversant with multiple scientific methods as they teach them how to think, study, solve issues, and make informed decisions.
Historical aspects of science should be emphasized- Studying the history of science gives you an insight into both the world's past and how we discovered everything we know about the world.

120(C). Vitamins are organic compounds required in the diet in small quantities to perform specific biological functions for the normal maintenance of optimum growth and health of an organism.
They can be classified into fat-soluble vitamins and water-soluble vitamins.
Fat-soluble vitamins – Vitamin A, D, E and K. They are stored in the liver and adipose tissues.
Water-soluble vitamins- Vitamin B and C.
Vitamin B12 is called cyanocobalamine
It is the only metal-containing vitamin.
Vitamin B12 contains cobalt metal.
It is a highly complex, essential vitamin.
It has an important role in DNA synthesis and amino acid metabolism.
Pernicious anaemia is caused by its deficiency.

Child Development and Pedagogy

1. Which of these is an external factor influencing the growth and development of a child?
(a) Physical environment
(b) Intelligence
(c) Biological factors
(d) Hereditary factors

2. Which statement about a creative child is not true?
(a) A creative child is curious
(b) A creative child is not
...

3. Which is an example of intrinsic motivation?
(a) Aspiration
(b) Praise
(c) Encouragement
(d) Prize

4. According to Kohlberg's theory of moral development, the period of pre moral state is:
(a) From birth to 5 years of age
(b) From birth to 2 years of age
(c) From the 3 years to 6 years of age
(d) From the 7 years to the early teenage

5. According to Jean Piaget, the adolescence stage of cognitive development is termed as :
(a) Pre-operational stage
(b) Concrete operational stage
(c) Formal operational stage
(d) Sensory-motor stage

6. Which among the following is correct regarding Curriculum?
i) Everything that goes on within the school, including extra-class activities, guidance, and interpersonal relationships.
ii) Everything that is planned by school personnel.
iii) A course of study
iv) A program of studies
(a) i, ii
(b) iii, iv
(c) i, ii, iv
(d) All of the above

7. Which among the following is considered as the teacher's guide for running a particular lesson?
(a) Unit plan
(b) Lesson plan
(c) Simulated plan
(d) None of the above

8. What is/are the functions of the School Management Committee as per the Right to Education Act, 2009?
i) To monitor the working of the school
ii) To monitor the utilization of grants
iii) To prepare the school development plan
(a) Only (i)

9. Which of the following statements does not represent an attribute of growth?
(a) This is a quantitative aspect.
(b) It is not measurable.
(c) It's not lifelong.
(d) It only shows physical development.

10. The sequence in which a child develops, follows two trends:
(a) Constant and correlation
(b) Learning and maturation
(c) Growth and development
(d) Cephalocaudal and proximodistal

11. In a diverse classroom, a teacher responsibility is:
(a) To teach all students together with an appropriate teaching method
(b) To provide varieties of learning experiences
(c) To make a lesson plan before starting teaching
(d) To evaluate learner's academic performance

12. Which of the following is/are the factors affecting language learning?
(a) Age (b) Motivation
(c) Aptitude (d) All of these

13. Child development emphasis on:
(a) Role of environment
(b) Role of experience
(c) Role of intelligence
(d) All of the above

14. Which of the following is not correct regarding the growth of an individual?
(a) Growth is quantitative changes in an individual
(b) Growth does not continue throughout the life
(c) Growth always brings development
(d) Changes produced by growth are subject to measure

15. On the basis of which of the following principles does the child learn the language?
(a) On the principle of multi-faceted effort
(b) On the principle of simulation
(c) On the principle of
...
are________.
(a) Genetic factors
(b) Organic and environmental factors
(c) Both (A) and (B)
(d) None of the above

17. In order to address the needs of students who are facing learning difficulties, a teacher should NOT________.
(a) Using a creative pedagogical approach
(b) Implementation of individual educational plan
(c) Practice of Rigid Structures for Teaching and Assessment
(d) Use of multiple audio-visual aids

18. A child with Learning Disability________.
(a) Needs to be put in a separate institution and not in mainstream schools
(b) Has a right to study in the regular school where there are special provisions for him
(c) Should be given vocational education, but should not be taught science and writing skill
(d) Needs to be dealt with severely and punished harshly for these mistakes

19. How would you identify a child with a learning disability?
(a) By administering intelligence tests
(b) By seeing their physical appearance
(c) By looking at their notebooks for

writing

(d) By observing how much they fight with other children

20. What is inclusive education?

(a) Increases diversity in the classroom

(b) Encourages strict admissions procedures

(c) It involves the inclusion of facts

(d) This includes teachers from marginalized groups

21. At the age of 6 - 9, children start taking interest in:

(a) Religion   (b) Human body

(c) Intimacy   (d) School

22. Who called infancy the ideal time to

23. Very young infants can either look at an object or grasp it when it comes in contract with their hands. They cannot coordinate looking and grasping at the same time. As per Piaget, the characteristics reflects the tendency of:

(a) Adaptation

(b) Assimilation

(c) Organization

(d) Accommodation

24. IQ level of extraordinary students lies between:

(a) 80-90   (b) 110-120

(c) 50-60   (d) 130-144

25. If a student frequently remains inattentive in class, he or she should be:

(a) Punished hard

(b) Expelled from school

(c) Advised to stop reading in school

(d) None of the above

26. A child falling in love with a parent of other sex is the characteristic behavior of:

(a) Anal stage

(b) Phallic stage

(c) Latency stage

(d) Genital stage

27. _____takes place when a child strikes balance between the two processes while trying to internalise the perceived object.

(a) Equilibration

(b) Adaptation

(c) Assimilation

(d) Accommodation

28. A child watches a classmate get in trouble for hitting another child. They learn from observing this interaction that they should not hit others. This is a classic example of learning by ______________.

(a) doing

(b) imitation

(c) trial and error

(d) observation

29. Baby Bhavya starts to look for her toys which was hidden by her mother. In which stage of development does Bhavya lies?

(a) Sensory-motor Stage

(b) Pre-operational Stage

develops a more profound attachment towards his mother as compared to his father. What was the term coined by Freud for this change of behaviour of child?

(a) Oedipus complex

(b) Electra complex

(c) Super ego

(d) Narcissism

Language - I: English

Ques (31-36): Direction : Read the poem given below and answer the questions that follow by selecting the correct/most appropriate options.

The cardboard shows me how it was
When the two girl cousins went paddling
Each one holding one of my mother's hands,
And she the big girl – some twelve years or so.
All three stood still to smile through their hair
At the uncle with the camera, a sweet face
My mother's that was before I was born
And the sea, which appears to have changed less
Washed their terribly transient feet.
Some twenty-thirty years later
She'd laugh at the snapshot. "See Betty
And Dolly," she'd say, "and look how they
Dressed us for the beach." The sea holiday
Was her past, mine is her laughter. Both wry
With the laboured ease of loss
Now she has been dead nearly as many years
As that girl lived. And of this circumstance
There is nothing to say at all,
Its silence silences.

31. Explain the feelings of the poet in "Both wry with the laboured ease of

loss."

(a) Sad and nostalgic

(b) Mixed sentiments

(c) Happy and nostalgic

(d) Sad and Ironic

32. The phrase "Its silence silences." means:

(a) Pain of her mother's loss

(b) Tranquility of the ocean

(c) Standing still for the picture

(d) All of the above

33. Which of the following is the synonym of the word 'transient'?

(a) Permanent   (b) Short-lived

(c) Ceaseless   (d) Dull

34. What is the figure of speech used in

(a) Repetition

(b) Alliteration

(c) Metaphor

(d) Personification

35. How old was the poet's mother when the photograph was taken?

(a) Eleven years old

(b) Twelve years old

(c) Thirteen years old

(d) Fourteen years old

36. Complete the line:

___________ later She'd laugh at the snapshot.

(a) Twenty-thirty year

(b) Twenty four year

(c) Forty- fifty year

(d) Twenty five year

37. Ravi, a English teacher, is planning remedial teaching for his student who faces problems in expressing his view while talking with someone. Remedial work for spoken English involves:

(a) Drill and studying

(b) Revision, drill, situation communicative practice and reviewing

(c) Going through situational practice

(d) Revision and practice

38. A teacher divides the class in small groups and asks them to discuss and present their views on "Save Environment".
Students are free to plan and present their choice and creativity. The teacher is facilitating them as and when required. Which approach/method is followed in

the class?

(a) Structural approach
(b) Natural approach
(c) Deductive approach
(d) Constructivist approach

39. A language teacher, while teaching grammar, writes some examples on the blackboard and with the help of students tries to point out some of the rules. She tries to stimulate the power of thinking and reasoning. Which method of teaching grammar is she adopting?

(a) Direct method
(b) Inductive method
(c) Inductive deductive method
(d) Translation method

(b) forms and structures of language
(c) communicative functions of language
(d) both structures and rules of language

41. Direction : Answer the following questions by selecting the most appropriate option.
Students of Class IV can recognize flawed usage or sentence construction when the teacher

(a) Tells them something is wrong
(b) Gives alternatives as possible corrections
(c) Lets them find the corrections
(d) Focuses on certain surface errors

42. Given below are two statements, one leveled as Assertion (A) and the other leveled as Reason (R) :
Assertion (A) - At first, the child starts listening to the sounds then observes how people speak, and then later development of reading and writing skills takes place.
Reasoning (R) - The four basic language skills and their natural order are reading-writing-listening-speaking.

(a) A is correct and R is incorrect
(b) A is incorrect and R is correct
(c) Both A and R are correct
(d) Both A and R are incorrect

43. At upper primary level, the language/languages used by children in a multilingual classroom is/are:

(a) Resource

(b) Puzzle
(c) Complex challenge
(d) Difficult problem

44. A teacher found an advertisement pamphlet for sale of biscuits. She uses it for reading and speaking activities in her class. What do you call the pamphlet?

(a) Realia
(b) An authentic text
(c) Extra materials
(d) Newspaper clipping

45. A Hindi - speaking teacher gets posted in a primary school which is situated in a remote area of Rajasthan. Since she doesn't known the local language, she faces lots of

resource while teaching

(c) Encourage the community to learn standard Hindi
(d) Try to get a positing to a Hindi speaking area.

46. Fluency in English can be developed through:

(a) Creating opportunities to use the language for communication among learners
(b) The teacher talking for most of the time
(c) The teacher being alert to spot the errors and correcting them
(d) Allowing students who are not confident to have the freedom to be quiet

47. Continuous comprehensive evaluation emphasises _______evaluation.

(a) process   (b) product
(c) term end   (d) formation

48. In which method of teaching language, the learning is based on repetition of dialogues and phrases about every day situations?

(a) Direct method
(b) Grammar-translation method
(c) Audio-Lingual Method
(d) Task based language teaching

49. Reading longer texts usually for one's 'own pleasure is known as:

(a) Skimming
(b) Scanning
(c) Extensive Reading
(d) Intensive Reading

50. Which language is a part of the

personal, social and cultural identity of a child?

(a) First language
(b) Second language
(c) School language
(d) Foreign language

51. Which one of the following is an essential characteristic of a good textbook in English?

(a) Every lesson should have a proper introduction at the beginning and a conclusion at the end.
(b) It should be based on the guiding principles of curriculum and syllabus.
(c) No difficult words should be given in the textbook at primary

Ques (52-60): Direction : Read the passage carefully and answer the questions given below.

As NASA works toward its long-term goal of establishing a human settlement on Mars, SpaceX is fleshing out its plans to help NASA make that dream a reality.

The private spaceflight company, which regularly launches cargo to the International Space Station with the Falcon 9 rocket and will soon launch astronauts up there, is currently building an interplanetary spacecraft for Mars. Known as Starship, the rocket-spacecraft combo will be able to launch 100 passengers and large amounts of cargo to and from the Red Planet.

Before Starship can launch to Mars, it will start off launching commercial satellites as early as 2021, followed by a manned flight around the moon in 2023. Although SpaceX has not given a timeline for its first missions to Mars, SpaceX founder Elon Musk has said that the first Mars base could be up and running in 2028. And while Musk shared some eye-catching artist illustrations depicting what he called "Mars Base Alpha" as an intricate network of buildings and infrastructure, SpaceX's plans for the Red Planet are not quite that extensive.

"SpaceX very much is a transportation company," Paul Wooster, the principal Mars development engineer at SpaceX, said during a speech at the Humans to Mars Summit in Washington in May. He explained that SpaceX plans to build whatever infrastructure is necessary to support the company's Starship flights to and from Mars; that could include landing pads and refueling stations for the reusable rockets.

For its very first Mars missions, SpaceX

will land at least two unmanned cargo ships on the Red Planet before sending any humans there, Wooster said. Those cargo missions would bring supplies, such as life- support systems and power generators that the first astronauts on Mars will need when they set up camp.

The first unmanned Mars missions will also be tasked with confirming the presence of natural resources that can provide fuel for future two-way missions to the Red Planet, Wooster said. SpaceX wants to use water ice from the planet's surface and carbon dioxide from the Martian atmosphere to refuel Starships on Mars, enabling the rockets to return to Earth.

After those first two cargo missions, SpaceX will launch two manned missions alongside two additional cargo-only flights

rocket's engines.

So, while SpaceX intends to set up a transportation system for humans and cargo traveling to the Red Planet, the company won't be building an entire Mars base on its own. Musk has laid out his vision to create a million-person colony on Mars, but to establish that colony SpaceX will have to work together with NASA and the agency's international partners and other commercial space companies. Several companies have already begun designing concepts for Mars habitats and have proposed orbital outposts similar to NASA's Lunar Gateway, which could serve as a waypoint for Starship and reduce the amount of fuel needed for return trips to Earth.

52. What is the name of the spacecraft that SpaceX is building that will carry passenger Falcon 9and cargo to mars?

(a) Falcon 9

(b) Starship

(c) Mars Base Alpha

(d) Lunar Gateway

53. As per the passage, what fuel will be used to power the Starship rocket while returning from Mars?

(a) Liquid hydrogen

(b) Liquid oxygen

(c) Liquid methane

(d) Both B and C

54. Which of the following statements is/are true with respect to the passage?

(a) In the first Mars mission, SpaceX will land one unmanned cargo ship on the Red Planet.

(b) A propellant production plant

will be set up on Mars in the first unmanned mission with the help of robots and A.I.

(c) SpaceX is expected to conduct a manned flight around moon in 2023.

(d) SpaceX is collaborating with Jaxa and ISRO for its Mars missions.

55. Which of the following statements is/are not true with respect to the passage?

(a) Starship is expected to start off launching commercial satellites by 2021.

(b) Only SpaceX and NASA are designing concepts for Mars habitats.

(c) In spite of primarily being a

56. As per the passage, which rocket is used by SpaceX to send cargo to the International Space Station?

I. Falcon 9

II. Falcon Heavy

III. Starship

(a) Only I   (b) Only II

(c) Only III   (d) Both I and II

57. According to Elon Musk, when could the first Mars base be operational?

(a) By 2021   (b) By 2023

(c) By 2028   (d) By 2030

58. What is the vision of Elon Musk, as mentioned in the passage?

(a) Elon Musk wants to see the human race as an interstellar species.

(b) Elon Musk wants to build a lunar base so that launch costs can be dramatically reduced.

(c) Elon Musk wants to harness the power of the sun to meet the energy needs of the human species.

(d) Elon Musk wants to build a colony of 10 lakh people on Mars.

59. What is the name of the proposed Mars base as put forward by SpaceX?

(a) Mars Base Alpha

(b) Mars Base Beta

(c) Martian Gateway

(d) Starship

60. Which of the following statements is/are correct as per the passage? I. SpaceX is currently building an

interstellar spacecraft.

II. SpaceX wants to use water ice from the Martian surface and carbon dioxide from the Martian atmosphere to power the Starship rockets.

III. NASA has a long term goal of establishing human settlement on Mars.

(a) Only I and III

(b) Only II and III

(c) Only III

(d) Only I

61. A gardener has 996 plants. He wants to plant them in the garden

(a) 38   (b) 24

(c) 28   (d) 34

62. The traffic signal lights at three different road crossings change after 48 seconds, 72 seconds, and 108 seconds, respectively. If they all change together in the 8: 20:00 hours, at what time will they again change together?

(a) 8:27:12 hours

(b) 8: 30: 00 hours

(c) 8: 54: 10 hours

(d) 8: 34: 10 hours

63. In an examination, a student scores 4 marks for every correct answer and loses 1 mark for every wrong answer. A student attempted all 200 questions and got 200 marks. How many questions did he answer correctly:

(a) 82   (b) 80

(c) 68   (d) 60

64. The ratio of two numbers is $9:11$ and their HCF is 8, then find their LCM.

(a) 792   (b) 565

(c) 765   (d) 234

65. If $(2a + 3b)(2c - 3d) = (2a - 3b)(2c + 3d)$, then:

(a) $\frac{b}{a} = \frac{c}{a}$ (b) $\frac{a}{b} = \frac{c}{d}$

(c) $\frac{a}{d} = \frac{c}{b}$ (d) $\frac{a}{b} = \frac{d}{c}$

66. If $a + b + c = 5, a^2 + b^2 + c^2 = 27, a^3 + b^3 + c^3 = 125$

, then the value of $\frac{abc}{5}$ is:

(a)　5　　　　(b)　-5

(c)　1　　　　(d)　-1

67. If $(a + c + 1) = 0$, then find the value of $(a^3 + c^3 + 1 - 3ac)$

(a)　-1　　　(b)　1

(c)　2　　　　(d)　0

68. ABCD is a trapezium in which AB is parallel to DC and ∠A = ∠B = 50°. Find ∠C and ∠D.

(a)　130°, 140°　(b)　130°, 130°

(c)　120°, 130°　(d)　100°,130°

69. If the complementary angle of x is 30° more than the 2 times of x, then find the supplementary angle of x.

75. Direction: Simplify the given equation:
$$13^2 \times \frac{210}{28} \times 44 = ? + 27^2$$

(a)　55041　　　(b)　55045

(c)　55060　　　(d)　55070

76. The ratio of income of A and B is $3 : 4$. If the ratio of expenditure of both A and B is $2 : 3$ and both of them save Rs. 200 each. What is the income of B ?

(a)　700 Rs.　　(b)　1000 Rs.

(c)　600 Rs.　　(d)　800 Rs.

Ques (77-79): Direction : Study the following bar graph and answer the following question given below.

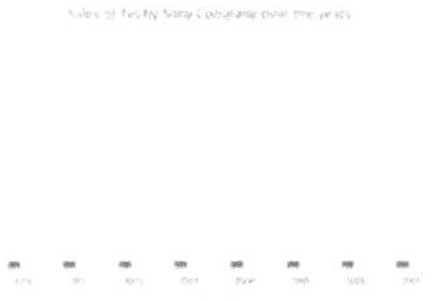

B. To introduce the new topic or lesson and new points of Mathematics.
C. To give the information regarding the historical development of Mathematics.

(a)　Project Method

(b)　Lecture Method

(c)　Problem solving method

(d)　None of the above

83. What is the role of the teacher in a mathematics teaching-learning process?

(a)　To convince students math's needs to be remembered

(b)　To convince students math's is not about rote learning

(c)　To convince them that they

∠C is equal to:

(a)　$\frac{560°}{21°}$　　(b)　$\frac{1260°}{31°}$

(c)　$\frac{560°}{31°}$　　(d)　$\frac{1260°}{21°}$

71. The water from the rain drains through the roof of length 22 m and breadth 10 m into a cylindrical vessel of diameter 4 m and height 3.5 meter. If the rain water collected from the roof fills 4/5th of the cylindrical vessel. Find how much it rained (height) in cm.

(a)　10 cm　　　(b)　16 cm

(c)　12 cm　　　(d)　15 cm

72. The curved surface area of a cylinder is 484 sq. cm. If height of the cylinder is 7 cm, then what is the volume of the cylinder (in cubic cm)? (Use π = 22/7)

(a)　2200　　　(b)　2750

(c)　2662　　　(d)　2650

73. A dealer allows his customer a discount of 35% and still gains 30%. If the cost price of an article is Rs.950, then what is its marked price (in Rs.)?

(a)　1,750　　　(b)　1,800

(c)　1,900　　　(d)　1,500

74. Present age of son and mother are in ratio 3 : 8. Four years ago ratio of daughters age to Mothers age was 1 : 9. When the son was born the ratio of age of mother and father was 5 : 6. If the present age of daughter is 8 years, find the average age of family just before the daughter is born.

(a)　28 years　　(b)　28 years

(c)　25.33 years　(d)　27.67 years

77. What is the ratio of the average sales of 2000 and 2007 to the average sales of 2003 and 2004?

(a)　$\frac{55}{52}$　　　(b)　$\frac{52}{55}$

(c)　$\frac{22}{21}$　　　(d)　$\frac{21}{22}$

78. In which year was the percentage decrease in sales maximum as compared to the previous year?

(a)　2007　　　(b)　2004

(c)　2005　　　(d)　2003

79. What is the percentage decrease in the sales of TVs over the years?

(a)　45.45%　　(b)　220%

(c)　68.75%　　(d)　145.45%

80. The aspect that are crucial in understanding the nature of mathematical ideas is:

(a)　Concrete to Abstract

(b)　Known to Unkown

(c)　General to Specific

(d)　Conceptual to General

81. Which of the following is common reasons for fear of mathematics?

(a)　Lack of encouragement from parents and/or teachers

(b)　Prior negative experiences with mathematics

(c)　Lack of positive role models

(d)　All of the above

82. Which method of teaching is suitably used to teach Mathematics for the following situations?
A. To give mathematical information.

multiplication and verification of products:

(a)　Dominoes

(b)　Cuisenaire strips

(c)　Abacus

(d)　Napier strips

85. Which of the following is a narrow aim of teaching mathematics?

(a)　To develop their scientific attitude i.e. to estimate, find and verify results.

(b)　To develop the technique of problem solving.

(c)　To develop their power of decision-making.

(d)　To develop 'useful' capabilities like numeracy related skills.

86. The subject Mathematics is important in curriculum since it:

(a)　Enhances scientific attitude like estimating, finding and verifying results.

(b)　Improves reasoning power, analytical and, critical thinking.

(c)　develops skills such as speed, accuracy, estimation and logical thinking

(d)　All of the above

87. According to NCF 2005:
"Developing children's abilities for Mathematisation is the main goal of Mathematics education.
The narrow aim of school Mathematics is to develop 'useful' capabilities. " Here mathematisation refers to develop child's abilities

(a)　To develop the child's resources to think and reason

mathematically, to pursue assumption to their logical conclusion and to handle abstraction

(b) In performing all number operations efficiently including of finding square root and cube root

(c) To formulate theorem of geometry and their proof independently

(d) To translate word problems into linear equations

88. A good teacher is one who:

(a) Gives printed notes to students.

(b) Gives students ample opportunities to learn the language of mathematics.

89. To be familiar with the laws of learning, a mathematics teacher must:

(a) Participate in professional activities

(b) Have selective academic training

(c) Understand educational psychology

(d) Possess the right attitude

90. Which one is not a source of carbohydrate?

(a) Sorghum (b) Rice

(c) Gram (d) Millets

91. Guava, Lemon, Orange and Tomato are rich in _________.

(a) vitamin A (b) vitamin B

(c) vitamin C (d) vitamin D

92. An electric cell is connected to the bulb from its one end. The other end of both bulb and cell is open. Given, the connections are correct and bulb and cell both are in working conditions, which among the following will ensure that the bulb will not glow when it is connected across both open ends?

(a) A steel spoon

(b) A key

(c) An silver wire

(d) A wooden ruler

93. Which of the following statements regarding amalgam is true?
Statement 1:It is an alloy of mercury.
Statement 2:It is an alloy of tin and lead.

(a) Only 1

(b) Only 2

(c) Both 1 & 2.

(d) Neither 1 nor 2.

94. Which of the following is an example of a green algae?

(a) Laminaria

(b) Sargassum

(c) Chlamydomonas

(d) Fucus

95. Keystone species are:

(a) important for ecosystem

(b) important for plants

(c) endangered species

(d) extinct species

96. A batsman hits a cricket ball which then rolls on a flat ground. After covering a short distance, the ball

(b) Velocity is proportional to the force exerted on the ball.

(c) There is a force on the ball opposing the motion.

(d) There is no unbalanced force on the ball, so the ball would want to come to rest.

97. Needles N1, N2 and N3 are made of a ferromagnetic, a paramagnetic and a diamagnetic substance respectively. A magnet when brought close to them will:

(a) Attract N1 strongly, but repel N2 and N3 weakly

(b) Attract N1 and N2 strongly but repel N3

(c) Attract all three of them

(d) Attract N1 strongly, N2 weakly and repel N3 weakly

98. Consider the following with regard to ultrasonic sound waves.
I. They are used to measure the depth of the sea.
II. They are used for sterilization of a liquid.
III. They are used for removal of lamp-shoot from the chimney of factories.
Which among the above is NOT an application of the ultrasonic sound wave?

(a) Only II and III

(b) Only I and II

(c) Only I and III

(d) All I, II and III are applications of ultrasonic sound waves

99. Which of the following pair of natural sources and acid is correctly matched?

(a) Tomato - Oxalic acid

(b) Orange - Acetic acid

(c) Nettle Sting - Lactic Acid

(d) Tamarind - Methanoic acid

100. When a moving bus suddenly stops, a person sitting _________.

(a) Stands up

(b) Falls forward

(c) Falls backward

(d) Is unaffected

101. Magnetism at the centre of Bar magnet is _________.

(a) Minimum (b) Zero

(c) Negative (d) Maximum

102. An optical fibre has a core material of refractive index of 1.55

(c) 3.05 (d) 0.90

103. Sulphur Dioxide when dissolved in water forms:

(a) Sulphur Trioxide

(b) Sulphurous acid

(c) Sulphuric acid

(d) Sulphur

104. In which group of the modern periodic table are halogens placed?

(a) 16th (b) 18th

(c) 1st (d) 17th

105. Which part of human respiratory system provides surface for exchange of gases?

(a) Alveoli (b) Bronchioles

(c) Bronchi (d) Trachea

106. Which vitamin-dependent clotting factors represent a homeostatic mechanism based on the hypercoagulability (thrombosis)-hypocoagulability (hemorrhagic) system?

(a) Vitamin A (b) Vitamin C

(c) Vitamin D (d) Vitamin K

107. If the frequency of a sound is below 20Hz it is known as _________ sound.

(a) Audible

(b) Infrasonic

(c) Ultrasonic

(d) None of the above

108. Which of the following is a phase of the symmetry strategy in science?

(a) Map Parallels

(b) Presentation of abstraction

(c) Interconnected concepts

(d) Experiment

109. Out of the following which innovative teaching method covers all domains of objectives of teaching?

(a) Team teaching

(b) Microteaching

(c) Brainstorming

(d) Programmed instruction

110. Advantages of integrated education includes
1) it provides an equal opportunity for education
2) children with disabilities get an

disabilities

(a) 1 and 2   (b) 1and 3

(c) 2 and 3   (d) 1, 2 and 3

111. The largest flower in the world is?

(a) Lotus   (b) Rose

(c) Rafflesia   (d) Giant flower

112. Which moves from specific to general?

(a) Deductive method

(b) Inductive method

(c) Alternative method

(d) None of these

113. The full form of 'GSM' technology used in mobile phones is:

(a) Geo Satellite for Mobile

(b) Global System for Mobility

(c) Global System for Mobile

(d) Geo Station for Mobility

114. In the process of teaching and learning a language, the textbook is:

(a) The only tool

(b) One of the tools

(c) The tool for evaluation

(d) The guidebook for teachers and policy makers

115. School based assessments ________.

(a) Encourage teaching to the test as they involve frequent testing.

(b) Focus on exam techniques rather than outcome.

(c) Offer less control to the students over what will be assessed.

(d) Improve learning by providing a constructive feedback.

116. A person having scientific attitude is:

(a) Open minded

(b) Has the spirit of curiosity

(c) Adopts a scientific method in his thinking and working

(d) All of the above

117. The first step in remedial teaching is:

(a) To give instructions

(b) To identify poor students

(c) To locate the learning difficulties

(d) To use appropriate strategy

(c) In air

(d) In vacuum

119. Om Prakash travels Bombay to Pune at a speed of 80 km/hr and returns back to Bombay by increasing his speed by 50%, then his average speed for the whole journey is ______.

(a) 96 km/hr   (b) 67 km/hr

(c) 69 km/hr   (d) 65 km/hr

120. Which of the following is not likely to cause Tsunami?

(a) A major nuclear explosion under sea

(b) Earthquake

(c) Volcanic eruption

(d) Lightning

// Hints and Solutions //

1(A). The physical environment is an external factor that affects the growth and development of a child.

The development of a child is primarily determined by two factors: heredity and environment. Heredity refers to the inborn traits and capacities. These inborn capacities are transmitted from parents to the child. The birth of a child is also considered to be a social phenomenon. The family, particularly the socialization practices and parent-child-relationship (i.e. the physical environment) has a great impact on cognitive, language, social, and personality development.

- A group of theorists, known as Behaviourists, believe that human development is controlled by these external factors and they totally ignore the significance of hereditary factors.

- Both heredity and environment interact (multiply) to influence various aspects of development.

- The effect of the two is not simple addition (heredity + environment), rather it is multiplication (heredity x environment).

- It is not easy to separate the effects of the two since dynamic interaction between them is continuous and complex.

- Therefore, we conclude that the Physical environment is an external factor influencing the growth and development of a child.

2(B). "A creative child is not an adventurer" The statement about the creative child is not correct.

Creative children express opinions and constantly ask many questions. So curiosity

3(A). Aspiration is an example of intrinsic motivation.

Intrinsic Motivation:

An intrinsically motivated activity will always be rewarded due to the direct relationship between the activity and the goal. This secures a continuous motivation to do the activity.

Intrinsic motivation is internal. It occurs when people are compelled to do something out of pleasure, importance, or aspiration.

So, it does not require an external push, unlike extrinsic motivation which requires an external motivating factor. So intrinsic motivation is more beneficial.

Extrinsic Motivation:

- When an activity is performed to accomplish the goal of an external reward, the person is said to be extrinsically motivated.

- Extrinsic motivation occurs when external factors compel the person to do something.

- This is motivation based on external rewards and has nothing to do with the activity directly. The Behaviourists' approach to motivation mainly focuses on the external rewards of reinforcement and punishment.

- Thus from the above-mentioned points, it is clear that aspiration is an example of intrinsic motivation.

4(B). According to Kohlberg's theory of moral development, the period of prior moral state is from birth to 2 years of age. At this age, children think about their needs. The relationship of moral work is socially and culturally related to what is right and what is wrong.

5(C). The adolescence stage of cognitive development is termed the formal operational stage; in this stage, an individual has the ability to think and reason from concrete visible events to an ability to think hypothetically. An individual can solve problems through abstract concepts and utilize them hypothetically.

6(D). The curriculum is that which is taught in schools, a set of subjects, Content, a program of studies, A set of mater, a sequence of courses, a set of performance objective, a course of study, everything that goes on within the school (including extra-class activities, guidance, and interpersonal relationships), everything that is planned by school personnel, a series of experiences undergone by learners in a school, it is that which an individual learner experience as a result of schooling.

7(B). A lesson plan is the teacher's guide for running a particular lesson. A lesson

learning. Details will vary depending on the preference of the teacher, the subject being covered, and the needs of the students. There may be requirements mandated by the school system regarding the plan. A lesson plan is the teacher's guide for running a particular lesson, and it includes the goal, how the goal will be reached, and a way of measuring how well the goal was reached.

8(C). According to the Right to Education Act 2009, the school management committee is prepared. This committee monitors the utilization of grants, prepares the school development plan, and monitors the working of schools. School management committees have 50% women members from the disadvantaged groups of the community.

9(B). The terms growth and development are often used interchangeably. They are conceptually different. Neither growth nor development takes place all by itself.

- Growth refers to quantitative changes in size which include physical changes in height, weight, size, internal organs, etc (which are measurable). As an individual develops, old features like baby fat, hair, teeth, etc., disappear, and new features like facial hair, etc. are acquired.
- When maturity comes, the second set of teeth, primary and secondary sex characteristics, etc., appear. Similar changes occur in all aspects of the personality. During infancy and childhood, the body steadily becomes larger, taller, and heavier. To designate this change the term growth is used.
- Growth involves changes in body proportions as well as in overall stature and weight. The term growth thus indicates an increase in bodily

dimensions. But the rate of growth differs from one part of the body to the other. Development, by contrast, refers to qualitative changes taking place simultaneously with quantitative changes of growth.

10(D). Every individual has a different rate of development. The development of all human beings follows a similar direction or sequence. Two types of sequential patterns are the cephalocaudal sequence and proximodistal sequence.

11(B). In a diverse classroom, a teacher's responsibility is to provide varieties of learning experiences. In a child-centered approach, a child learns better from experiences. So, providing varieties of learning experiences will result in active learning in which students take initiative to

etc. Learning a language is affected by all these factors, if a child is motivated and reinforced for his learning then he/she takes more interest. Proper guidance and reinforcement should be given to the learner for better learning.

13(D). Child development involves the study of the patterns of growth, change and stability that occurs from conception through adolescence and therefore its emphasis on internal and external factors for its growth. The role of environment, experience and intelligence play a major role in the development of a child.

14(C). All the options given in the question about growth are correct except option C. i.e. it is not necessary that growth always bring development for example if a child becomes fat may not bring any qualitative improvement.

15(B). The child learns language on the basis of the principle of imitation. Psychologists such as Chapini, Shirley, and Valentine have studied language learning through simulation. They had opinion that children learn by following the language of their family and peers, that is, children learn the language in the same society or family in which the language is spoken.

16(C). The causes of learning disabilities are genetic factors, biological and environmental factors. Learning disabilities can also cause problems in coordinating movements, making the child seem (and feel) awkward. Learning disabilities are disorders that affect a person's ability to understand or respond to new information, or they are disorders that affect the ability to remember information that appears to have been taken in. Learning disabilities tend to cause problems with listening skills,

language skills (including speaking, reading, or writing), and mathematical operations.

17(C). To meet the needs of students experiencing learning difficulties, a teacher should not practice rigid structures for teaching and evaluation.

- Learning difficulties can be defined as imperfect ability to listen, think, speak, read, write, spell, or do mathematical calculations.
- Learning disability is believed to be present if there is a substantial difference between expected and actual performance based on intelligence, ruling out other contributing factors such as poor learning-teaching environment, second language etc.

18(B). A child with Learning Disability is characterized by specific difficulties in learning to read (dyslexia), to write (dysgraphia), and to do grade-appropriate mathematics (dyscalculia).

19(A). Identify a child with a learning disability by conducting an IQ test.

- Learning Disability is an umbrella term that encompasses a variety of specific kinds of learning problems.
- Children with learning disabilities experience difficulty in learning and using certain skills namely reading, writing, listening reasoning, and mathematics.

20(A). A classroom/institution that welcomes diversity of categories, abilities, cultures, disabilities, etc. is an inclusive education.

The principles of inclusive education include:

- No discrimination among students
- Equal educational opportunity for all
- Adapting to the needs of students, for example, making institutions disabled-friendly
- Equal educational benefits to all students
- Individual difference is promoted among students
- The needs of the students are taken seriously.

21(D). At the age of 6-9 years, children start taking interest in school.

Developmental psychology studies the development of human emotional, intellectual, cognitive and social abilities. It studies the actions of man from infancy to old age.

The following are the stages of human development:

Infancy and Toddlerhood

- Early childhood

* Middle Childhood
* Adolescence
* Early Adulthood

22(D). Valentine called infancy the ideal time to learn.
* Human development is divided into different stages infancy, childhood (early and middle childhood), adolescence and adulthood.
* It refers to the first year or early period of a baby's development in which the baby grows rapidly after birth.
* This is a critical period of development in which the child learns to sit, crawl, stand etc.

23(C). The situation given in the above question shows the trend of the organization
~ Two Basic Inclinations and Tendencies

the arrangement, recombination and rearrangement of behavior and thought into a coherent system.
* Organization: This concept assumes that people have a tendency to organize their thinking processes into psychological structures. For example, very young children can either look at an object or hold it when their hands contract .
* Adaptation: As the term suggests this concept refers to the adjustment of man to the new environment. It can be defined as "changing one's cognitive structure or one's environment (or to some extent both) in order to better understand one's environment".

24(D). Exceptional students have an IQ level between 130-144
* Intelligence Quotient is commonly known as IQ refers to the score of a standardized test that assesses and measures human intelligence.
* The first test to measure intelligence was developed by Binet and Simon in 1905.
* Terman in 1916 revised the test and devised the concept of Intelligence Quotient.

25(D). If the teacher comes to know that a student is absent in the class, in such a case, instead of expelling/punishing/preventing him/her from attending the class, the teacher should know the reason for his/her negligence and find out the appropriate remedy.
Improving Teacher Preparation in Classroom Management
* Provide teacher candidates with instructional approaches for classroom management through coursework and guided practice with feedback, and
* Address the challenges facing teacher candidates and new teachers in creating

a positive classroom context

26(B). If a child expresses affection for a parent of the opposite sex, it will be characterized by the phalic stage.
Freud's Psychological Stages of Development: Freud proposed a five-stage model of personality development. According to him, the main aspects of a person's personality develop by the age of five and remain unchanged throughout time. Furthermore, he said that in order to move from one stage to another, a child needs to successfully resolve the conflicts of each stage.

27(A). Equilibration takes place when a child strikes balance between the two processes while trying to internalise the perceived object.
Equilibration: The process of striking a

perceived object, adaptation (a relatively stable structure) takes place.

28(D). A child sees that a classmate has gotten into trouble by hitting another child. They learn by observing this interaction that they should not kill others. This is a classic example of learning by observation.
Learning style refers to a range of principles that aim to take into account differences in individuals' learning. Many theories share the proposition that humans can be classified according to their 'style' of learning, but differ in how the proposed styles should be defined, classified and assessed. A general concept is that individuals differ in the way they learn.

29(A). In this question, Baby Bhavya starts looking for her toys that her mother had hidden because Bhavya is aware of her toys even when they are not in front of her, that is, she has developed object permanence, Hence it is in pre-operational stage or pre-operational stage.
Object permanence means that an object still exists, even if it is hidden. It requires the ability to create a mental representation of the object (i.e. a schema).

30(A). At 4 – 5 years of age, a male child develops a deeper attachment to his mother, known as the Oedipus complex, than to his father.
Psychological stages of development:
* Stage I: Oral Stage (birth to 18 months)
* Stage II: Anal Stage (18 months to three years)
* Stage III: Phallic Stage (three to five years)
* Stage IV: Latency Stage (six to twelve years)
* Stage V: Genital Stage (thirteen years to adulthood)

31(A). The line " Both wry with the

laboured ease of loss" implies that the poet and her mother both are saddened by the loss that they have experienced over time. Thus, it is clear that the feeling hidden in this line is 'Sad and nostalgic.'
Nostalgic means **feeling happy and also slightly sad when you think about things that happened in the past.**

32(A). In the above-given poem, the poet is nostalgic after seeing a photograph of her mother's childhood.
* The phrase "Its silence silences" indicates the constant pain experienced by the poet on account of her mother's loss which makes her speechless.
* The silence is prevalent in the situation and it also silences everything else at that moment.
Thus, it can be inferred that the phrase "Its

doesn't last forever.
The phrase 'terribly transient feet,' from the above-given poem, implies that human life is not eternal.
Thus, we can conclude that the correct answer is Option B.

34(B). Alliteration is a figure of speech that repeats a speech sound in a sequence of words that are close to each other. For example, "Clean your cluttered closet."
Let's look at the line:
"All three stood still to smile through their hair"
* In this line, stood, still and smile – all are beginning with the similar sound of speech -'s'.
Thus, it is clear that the figure of speech used here is 'Alliteration.'

35(B). Let's look at the line:
"And she the big girl – twelve years or so"
* It clearly indicates that the poet's mother was around twelve years old when the photograph was taken.
Thus, the most appropriate answer is 'twelve years old.'

36(A). Twenty-thirty years later She'd laugh at the snapshot.
From the given lines: "Some twenty-thirty years later,
She'd laugh at the snapshot. "See Betty"

37(B). Remedial teaching:
* During learning, a child makes mistakes. It is the job of a teacher to help students to correct those mistakes after diagnosing them.
* The method is known as remedial teaching. It helps the teacher to provide learners with the necessary help and guidance to overcome the problems.
The following are its characteristics:
* It can be used for improving language skills by revision, drill, situation

communicative practice, and reviewing.
- For example, a student is confused about the pronunciation of 'no' and 'know', he can be taught the concept of silent letters.
- It also helps teachers to know which areas are left during regular teaching. It is used by teachers to remove the weakness of the learner.
- It is carried out after the identification of problems and challenges faced by students. It is a systematic process as the teacher first diagnoses the problem of students and then applies appropriate remedial methods.

Thus, it is concluded that remedial work for spoken English involves revision, drill, situation communicative practice, and reviewing.

Thus, we can conclude that the inductive-deductive method is used to teach grammar.

40(C). Communicative competence should be the goal in language learning. This concept takes into account both the linguistic aspect of the target language and the importance of context in language acquisition.
- Communicative competence is the ability not only to apply the grammatical rules of a language in order to form grammatically correct sentences but also to know when and where to use these sentences and to whom.
- It includes the ability to use grammatical structures in different situations to convey and interpret messages and to negotiate meanings.

	Skills	Description
tive Reading		Process of looking at a series of written words/symbols and getting meaning from them.
Productive Speaking		Delivery of information through the mouth.
Productive Writing		Process of using symbols (letters of the alphabet, punctuation, and spaces) to communicate thoughts in a readable form.

principle of constructive approach refers to content-oriented language teaching and usually takes place in bilingual classes. A constructive approach to language teaching is based on the foundation that knowledge is constructed. Students are given the freedom to plan their choice and to be creative.
- Structural Approaches: Structural approach is a scientific study of the fundamental structures of the English language, their analysis and logical arrangement. Every structure expresses an important grammatical point. A sentence needs a grammatical background. The different arrangements or patterns of words are called structures.
- Natural approaches: It is the theory that is based on the notion that we learn the language in the same way as we acquire our first language. It doesn't force to utter words or phrases, much less pronounce them correctly. There are no endless drills on correct usage and no mentions of grammar rules or long lists of vocabulary to wrap the head around.
- Deductive approaches refer to developing a Hypothesis. It is testing of Existing theory.

Thus, we conclude that the above situation

39(C). Advantages of the Inductive Deductive Method
- This method is considered to be the best method for teaching grammar because it follows some sound educational principles
- Rules discovered by the pupils themselves are easily remembered. So there is no need for memorizing rules.
- It develops thinking ability among the pupils.
- It makes learning grammar interesting.
- It keeps the pupils active.

appropriateness, and capacity.
- Communicative tasks are important because they allow learners to practice the target grammar feature under 'real operating conditions.

Thus, it is concluded that Teaching grammar should focus on communicative functions of language.

41(B). For the students of class IV learning English, their learning outcomes include, reciting poems correctly, being responsive to simple announcements, they having a simple knowledge of correct punctuations in writing.
The teacher can provide possible alternative corrections for the sentence as the students can get better insight about the words, their usage and also learn about the flaws in the wrong sentence.
Thus, it is concluded that Students of Class IV can recognize flawed usage or sentence construction when the teacher gives alternatives as possible corrections.

42(A). The four basic language skills and their natural order are listening-speaking-reading-writing. These foundational skills of language are divided into two categories which are receptive and productive skills.
For example, at first, the child starts listening to the sounds of people around him and then observes how they speak and started speaking, then later development of reading and writing skills takes place.
Let's understand it briefly:

	Skills	Description
Receptive	Listening	Receiving information through the ears.

43(A). Multilingualism is the ability to use more than two languages, it refers to using the language of learners as a strategy in school.
- Multilingualism is constitutive of the identity of a child and a typical feature of the Indian linguistic landscape must be used as a resource, classroom strategy, and a goal by a creative language teacher.
- Multilingualism as a resource means using the languages of learners as a strategy in school.
- It is used as a resource to teach a new language to the child with the help of a mother tongue or other known language.

Benefits of Multilingualism (NCF - 2005):
- It emphasizes on the significance of a smooth transition between the home and school language.
- Multilingualism encourages children to believe in themselves.
- It improves cognitive flexibilities to express thought in multiple ways.

Thus, from the above points, we can conclude that at the upper primary level, the language/languages used by children in a multilingual classroom is a resource.

44(B). A teacher found an advertisement pamphlet for the sale of biscuits. She uses it for reading and speaking activities in her class.
He is using an authentic text as the advertisement pamphlet is the authentic pamphlet that a shopkeeper is using to increase his sale of biscuits.
Whereas Realia refers to the objects associated with everyday life to be used in the classroom. Using realia in the language class means bringing real objects as teaching aids.
The advertisement pamphlet is a type of realia but if we have to say it more

accurately, we will say it is an authentic text. The newspaper clipping and extra materials can be a type of realia also. But here as per the given question, the authentic text is best suited.

45(B). A teacher should overcome the language barrier to go through the process of teaching-learning.

- The basis of the communication of ideas and information to the learners is the responsibility of the teacher.
- A teacher should use the child's language as a resource and start teaching.
- As mentioned in the question above, a teacher should not apply for transfer since it shows that he wants to run away from his duty.
- Communicating in English is not the

clear that a teacher should use the child's language as a resource while teaching.

46(A). Fluency in English means that the child can use the basic skills of langauge that are listening, speaking, reading, and writing.

- One who can perform these basic skills properly and collectively with full accuracy and speed is said to be fluent in English.
- The goal of language learning is communication competence and the child who learns the basic skills of a language is able to develop real communication in a natural setting environment.
- The teacher must create opportunities to use the language for communication among learners to develop their fluency in English.
- This can be done by conducting several language-based activities such as discussions, drama, dialogues, conversations, debates, questionnaires, etc.

Thus, we can conclude that fluency in English can be developed through creating opportunities to use the language for communication among learners.

47(A). Continuous comprehensive evaluation emphasises **process** evaluation.

- Continuous Comprehensive Evaluation treats evaluation as a developmental process.
- The term 'continuous' refers to regularity in the assessment.
- The development of a child is a continuous process.
- Therefore, students' development should be assessed continuously.
- The Evaluation has to be completely integrated with the teaching and learning process.

- The term 'comprehensive' implies that evaluation of learners' performance is carried out in both scholastic and co-scholastic areas.
- CCE is comprehensive in nature as it takes care of the achievement of learners in various school subjects from science, mathematics, languages, social science, work education, and physical health activities as well as includes the assessment of co-scholastic abilities like attitude, values, life skills, interests, habits, etc.

48(C). **The Audio-Lingual Method:** This self-teaching method is also known as the Aural-Oral method. The learning is based on the repetition of dialogues and phrases about everyday situations. These phrases are imitated, repeated, and drilled to make

and speaking part of dialogues, not the written part. In this students are more focused on dialogues delivering.

- In this method, students develop correct language habits through the drilling of patterns.
- The theory behind this method is that the students can form new habits by basing them on habits of their native language.
- The Audio Lingual method is the method that focuses on the repetition of some words to memorize.
- In the execution of the learning process, the Audio Lingual method gives more practice, drill, memorize vocabularies, and the students memorize and practice some vocabulary unconsciously.

So, we can conclude that in the audio-lingual method of teaching language, the learning is based on the repetition of dialogues and phrases about everyday situations.

49(C). Reading longer texts usually for one's 'own pleasure is known as extensive Reading.

Types of reading skills:

Exte nsiv e rea ding	Extensive is a reading strategy tha t focuses on: • **Reading for pl**easure and over all understanding of the text. • Helping learners to build readi ng speed and reading fluency to understand language faster and better. • **Reading novels, discussion a bout stories, etc.**
Inte nsiv e rea ding	Intensive is a reading strategy that focuses on: • Gaining a deeper and better un derstanding of the text. • Enhancing reading comprehens ion and critical thinking skills.

	• Reading materials such as label s, reports, contracts, articles, et c.

Thus, we can conclude that reading longer texts usually for one's 'own pleasure is known as extensive reading.

50(A). The **first language** of a child is part of the personal, social and cultural identity.

- A first language (L1) is the language or are the languages a person has been exposed to from birth or within the critical period, or that a person speaks the best and so is often the basis for sociolinguistic identity.
- Language is fundamental to cultural identity.
- First Language is intrinsic to the

group identity and solidarity.

- People are also categorized by other people according to the language they speak.
- People belong to many social groups and have many social identities.
- Speaking that language/variety/jargon gives a sense of belonging to the group.

51(B). Qualities of a good textbook of English:

- Comprehensible inputs
- Age-appropriate materials
- Adequate subject matter
- Use of suitable language
- Interesting and attractive
- Use of appropriate vocabulary
- Proper introduction & Conclusion

Thus from the above-mentioned points, it is clear that **an essential characteristic of a good textbook in English is it should be based on the guiding principles of curriculum and syllabus.**

52(B). The private spaceflight company, which regularly launches cargo to the International Space Station with the Falcon 9 rocket and will soon launch astronauts up there, is currently building an interplanetary spacecraft for mars. Known as Starship, the rocket-spacecraft combo will be able to launch 100 passengers and large amounts of cargo to and from the Red Planet.

From the highlighted part, it is clear that SpaceX is building a spacecraft named 'Starship' to carry passenger and cargo to mars.

53(D). After those first two cargo missions, SpaceX will launch two manned missions alongside two additional cargo-only flights to begin setting up a propellant production plant. At that plant, water and carbon dioxide will be converted into liquid methane and liquid oxygen, which fuel the rocket's engines.

From the highlighted part, it is obvious that both liquid methane and liquid oxygen will be used to power the Starship rocket while returning from Mars. Liquid hydrogen is nowhere mentioned in the passage.

54(C). For its very first Mars missions, SpaceX will land at least two unmanned cargo ships on the Red Planet before sending any humans there, Wooster said.

The highlighted part confirms that the statement given in option A is false.

After those first two cargo missions, SpaceX will launch two manned missions alongside two additional cargo-only flights to begin setting up a propellant production plant.

Robots and A.I. were not mentioned in the passage. Besides, the highlighted part confirms that the the statement given in

make that dream a reality.

Jaxa and ISRO are nowhere mentioned in the passage, and the highlighted part confirms that SpaceX tied up with NASA.

So, the statement given in option D is clearly false.

Before Starship can launch to Mars, it will start off launching commercial satellites as early as 2021, followed by a manned flight around the moon in 2023.

Starship is being developed by SpeceX and the highlighted part confirms that the statement given in option C is true.

55(D). Before Starship can launch to Mars, it will start off launching commercial satellites as early as 2021, followed by a manned flight around the moon in 2023.

- The highlighted part confirms that the statement given in option A is correct.
- Several companies have already begun designing concepts for Mars habitats and have proposed orbital outposts similar to NASA's Lunar Gateway, which could serve as a waypoint for Starship and reduce the amount of fuel needed for return trips to Earth.
- The highlighted part confirms that the statement given in option B is not true.
- And while Musk shared some eye-catching artist illustrations depicting what he called "Mars Base Alpha" as an intricate network of buildings and infrastructure, SpaceX's plans for the Red Planet are not quite that extensive.
- The highlighted part confirms that SpaceX's plans for Mars are not quite extensive. It clearly proves that the statement given in option C is not true.
- Both the statements given in options B and C are not true.

56(A). The private spaceflight company, which regularly launches cargo to the International Space Station with the Falcon

9 rocket and will soon launch astronauts up there, is currently building an interplanetary spacecraft for Mars. Known as Starship, the rocket-spacecraft combo will be able to launch 100 passengers and large amounts of cargo to and from the Red Planet.

The second highlight part confirms that Starship is being designed to send passenger and cargo to the Mars, not the International Space Station. There is no mention of Falcon Heavy in the passage.

The first highlighted part confirms that option A is correct.

57(C). Although SpaceX has not given a timeline for its first missions to Mars, SpaceX founder Elon Musk has said that the first Mars base could be up and running in 2028.

principal Mars development engineer at SpaceX, said during a speech at the Humans to Mars Summit in Washington in May.

Nothing related to harnessing the power of the sun, creating a lunar base or 'human race as an interstellar species' is anywhere mentioned in the passage. So, option A, option B and Option C are false.

59(A). And while Musk shared some eye-catching artist illustrations depicting what he called "Mars Base Alpha" as an intricate network of buildings and infrastructure, SpaceX's plans for the Red Planet are not quite that extensive.

The highlighted part confirms that option A is correct.

60(B). The private spaceflight company, which regularly launches cargo to the International Space Station with the Falcon 9 rocket and will soon launch astronauts up there, is currently building an interplanetary spacecraft for Mars.

The highlighted part clearly shows that statement I is incorrect.

Statement II: SpaceX wants to use water ice from the Martian surface and carbon dioxide from the Martian atmosphere to power Starship rockets.

SpaceX wants to use water ice from the planet's surface and carbon dioxide from the Martian atmosphere to refuel Starships on Mars, enabling the rockets to return to Earth.

The highlighted part confirms that statement II is correct.

Statement III: NASA has a long term goal of establishing human settlement on Mars.

As NASA works toward its long-term goal of establishing a human settlement on Mars, SpaceX is fleshing out its plans to help NASA make that dream a reality.

The highlighted part clearly shows that statement III is correct.

61(C). Let a be the same number of rows and columns.

$\therefore$ Number of plants planted = Number of rows $\times$ Number of columns

$= a^2$

$\Rightarrow a^2$ must be a perfect square number that is close to 996 and greater than 996.

$\sqrt{996} = 31.56$

To make it a perfect square, $a = 32$

$\therefore$ Number of rows and columns $= 32$

Number of additional plants $= 32^2 - 996$

$= 1024 - 996 = 28$

62(A). Given,

The traffic signal lights at three different road crossings change after 48 seconds, 72 seconds, and 108 seconds respectively. They all change together at 8: 20:00.

After the L.C.M. of (48, 72, and 108) they will all change together.

Thus, they will change together after 432 seconds.

1 minute = 60 seconds

Now, 432 seconds = 7 minutes 12 seconds

They will change together at 8:27:12 hours.

63(B). Suppose he answered x question correctly.

Marks obtained by him in x questions = 4x

Wrong answer will be = 200 - x

According to the question,

4x - (200 - x) = 200

$\Rightarrow$ 4x - 200 + x = 200

$\Rightarrow$ 5x = 200 + 200 = 400

$\Rightarrow$ x = 80

Thus, he answered 80 questions correctly.

64(A). Given,

The ratio of two numbers $= 9 : 11$

Let the two numbers be $9x$ and $11x$.

$HCF = 8$

So, the numbers will be 72 and 88

As we know,

Product of two numbers $= HCF \times LCM$

$\therefore 72 \times 88 = 8 \times LCM$

$\Rightarrow \dfrac{(72 \times 88)}{8} = LCM$

$\Rightarrow 72 \times 11 = LCM$

$\therefore LCM = 792$

So, their LCM is 792.

65(B). Given,

$(2a + 3b)(2c - 3d) = (2a - 3b)(2c + 3d)$

$\Rightarrow 4ac - 6ad + 6bc - 9bd = 4ac + 6ad - 6bc - 9bd$

$\Rightarrow 12bc = 12ad$

$\Rightarrow bc = ad$

$\Rightarrow \dfrac{a}{b} = \dfrac{c}{d}$

$\therefore$ Required answer is $\dfrac{a}{b} = \dfrac{c}{d}$

66(D). Given,

$a + b + c = 5, a^2 + b^2 + c^2 = 27, a^3 + b^3 + c^3 = 125$

$a^2 + b^2 + c^2 = (a + b + c)^2 - 2(ab + bc + ca)$

$a^3 + b^3 + c^3 - 3abc = (a + b + c)$
$(a^2 + b^2 + c^2 - ab - bc - ca)$
Calculation:
$27 = 5^2 - 2(ab + bc + ca)$
$\Rightarrow ab + bc + ca = -1$
Now,,
$a^3 + b^3 + c^3 - 3abc =$
$[(a + b + c)$
$\{a^2 + b^2 + c^2 - (ab + bc + ca)\}]$
$\Rightarrow 125 - 3abc = (5)\{27 - (-1)\}$
$\Rightarrow 3abc = 125 - 140$
$\Rightarrow 3abc = -15$
$\Rightarrow abc = -5$
The value of $\frac{abc}{5}$ is -1

67(D). We know that
$a^3 + b^3 + c^3 - 3abc = (a + b + c)$
$(a^2 + b^2 + c^2 - ab - bc - ca)$
From the given data, $(a + 1 + c) = 0$

68(B). ABCD is a trapezium in which AB is parallel to DC and $\angle A = \angle B = 50°$
Concept:
Sum of adjacent angles in a trapezium is $180°$

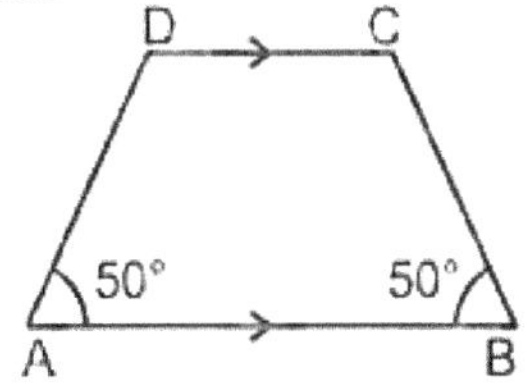

$\angle A + \angle D = 180°$
$\angle D = 130°$
Now,
$\angle B + \angle C = 180°$
$\angle C = 130°$

69(A). The complementary angle of x = 2x + 30°
If the sum of two angles is 90° then both the angles are complementary of each other.
If the sum of two angles is 180° then both the angles are supplementary of each other.
Let the original angle be x
The complementary angle of x = 90° - x
According to the question,
90° - x = 2x + 30°
$\Rightarrow 60° = 3x$
$\Rightarrow 3x = 60°$
$\Rightarrow x = 20°$
The supplementary angle x = 180° - 20°
$\Rightarrow 160°$
∴ The required value is 160°.

70(B). The Sum of all angles in a triangle is $180°$
LCM of 5,7 and 10 is 70
Dividing by 70 .
$\Rightarrow \frac{5\angle A}{70} = \frac{7\angle B}{70} = \frac{10\angle C}{70} = k$
$\angle A = 14k$
$\angle B = 10k$
$\angle C = 7k$

$\angle A + \angle B + \angle C = 180°$
$\Rightarrow 14k + 10k + 7k = 180°$
$\Rightarrow 31k = 180°$
$\Rightarrow k = 180°/31°$
$\angle C = 7k = 7 \times 180/31$
$\therefore \angle C = \frac{1260°}{31°}$

71(B). Given:
Length of roof, l = 22 m
Breadth of roof, b = 10 m
Diameter of cylindrical vessel = 4 m
Height of vessel = 3.5 m
Volume of cylinder = πr2h
Volume of cuboid = Length × Breadth × Height
Let the height be h m.
$\Rightarrow$ Volume of water from the roof = 22 × 10 × h
Now, radius of the cylindrical vessel = $\frac{4}{2}$ = 2

$\Rightarrow 22 \times 10 \times h = 45 \times \frac{22}{7} \times 2 \times 2 \times 3.5$
$\Rightarrow h = 0.16$ m = 16 cm
So, it rained up to 16 cm.

72(C). Given,
Curved surface area(CSA) of the cylinder $= 484$ cm^2
Height (h) of the cylinder $= 7$ cm
CSA of cylinder $= 2\pi rh$
Volume (V) of cylinder $= \pi r^2 h$
$r =$ radius of the base of the cylinder
$2\pi rh = 484$
$\Rightarrow 2 \times \frac{22}{7} \times r \times 7 = 484$
$\Rightarrow r = 11$
$V = \pi r^2 h$
$\Rightarrow V = \frac{22}{7} \times 11^2 \times 7$
$\Rightarrow V = 2662$
∴ Volume of the cylinder = 2662 cm^3

73(C). Given:
A dealer allows his customer a discount of 35% and still gains 30% .
Cost price of the article is Rs. 950
$CP/MP = \frac{100 - discount\,\%}{100 + profit\,\%}$
Cost price of the article is Rs. 950
CP/MP = (100− discount %)/(100+ profit %)
Rs. $950/MP = (100 - 35)/(100 + 30)$
M P= Rs. $950 \times 130 \times \left(\frac{1}{65}\right)$
M P = Rs. 1900

74(C). Given,
The present age of son and mother are in ratio 3 : 8
Four years ago the ratio of daughter's age to Mothers age was 1 : 9.
The present age of daughter = 8 years
Age of Mother and Daughter 4 years back = 36 and 4 respectively
The present age of Mother = 40 years
The present age of Son = 15 years
Age of Father and Mother when son was

born(15 years back) = 30 and 25 respectively.
Therefore, present age of father = 45 years
Age of family 8 years ago
Daughter = 0
Son = 7
Mother = 32
Father = 37
Average age $= \frac{7 + 32 + 37}{3} = 25.33$ years

75(A). Given,
$13^2 \times \frac{210}{28} \times 44 =? + 27^2$
$\Rightarrow 169 \times 7.5 \times 44 =? + 729$
$\Rightarrow 169 \times 330 =? + 729$
$\Rightarrow 55770 - 729 =?$
$\Rightarrow ? = 55041$

76(D). Given,
The ratio of income of A and $B = 3 : 4$

Income = Expenditure + Saving
Expenditure = Income − Saving
$\therefore \frac{(3x - 200)}{(4x - 200)} = \frac{2}{3}$
$\Rightarrow (3x - 200) \times 3 = 2 \times (4x - 200)$
$\Rightarrow 9x - 600 = 8x - 400$
$\Rightarrow 9x - 8x = 600 - 400$
$\Rightarrow x = 200$
∴ Income of $B = 4x = 4 \times 200 = 800$
So, the income of B is Rs. 800 .

77(D). Average sales of 2000 and $2007 = \left(\frac{80 + 25}{2}\right) = 52.5$
Average sales of 2003 and $2004 = \left(\frac{65 + 45}{2}\right) = 55$
∴ Required ratio $= \frac{52.5}{55} = \frac{21}{22}$

78(A). The percentage decrease in sales as compared to the previous year for different years are:
$2001 = \left(\frac{80 - 50}{80}\right) \times 100\% = 37.5\%$
$2003 = \left(\frac{75 - 65}{75}\right) \times 100\% = 13.33\%$
$2004 = \left(\frac{65 - 45}{65}\right) \times 100\% = 30.77\%$
$2005 = \left(\frac{45 - 40}{45}\right) \times 100\% = 11.11\%$
$2007 = \left(\frac{60 - 25}{60}\right) \times 100\% = 58.33\%$
∴ The percentage decrease in sales as compared to the previous year is maximum for the year 2007.

79(C). Sales of TV in the year 2000 = 80
Sales of TV in the year 2007 = 25
∴ Required percentage
$= \frac{(80 - 25)}{80} \times 100\% = 68.75\%$

80(A). The aspect that is important in understanding the nature of mathematical ideas is the transition from the tangible to the intangible.
Concrete to Abstract:
• The concrete experiences help students

to develop the concept of 'roundness'. As the frequency of dealing with concrete experiences increases, gradually, concepts like 'circle', 'sphere' etc. comes to their mind

Particular to General:
- Experiences with particular cases will broaden the abstractness and help individuals to arrive at a general concept.

Conceptual and Procedural Knowledge:
- When students understand a concept in a meaningful way, they are more likely to be able to correctly apply it in various situations.

81(D). The above points are true in the context of fear of mathematics.

Some very common causes of mathematics phobia are:

- Lack of encouragement from parents and/or teachers
- Lack of positive role models
- Ethnic and/or gender stereotypes
- Lack of conceptual understanding
- Pressure to score high in examinations
- Teacher's negligence towards remedial teaching
- Mathematics problems being used as punishment in school
- The pressure of taking timed tests
- The fear of looking or feeling "stupid" in front of others

82(B). Lecture Method:
- The lecture method is teacher controlled and information-centered approach in which the teacher works as a role resource in classroom instruction.
- In this method, the only teacher does the talking and the student is passively listening.
- The lecture method mainly focuses on cognitive objectives. The main emphasis of this strategy is the presentation of the content.

83(B). The role of the teacher in a mathematics teaching-learning process to convince students math's is not about rote learning.

Teachers play an interactive role in fostering the potential of young seedlings to grow and bloom. Their patience and perseverance significantly impact a child's success in the classroom. He needs to teach students:

- Every student of mathematics needs to learn the mathematics process. The best way to learn the process is to practice it.
- Mathematics is not about remembering facts and rote learning.
- Choosing a subject after 10th should be students' decision rather than someone else's.

84(D). Napier sticks are teaching material mainly used for the verification of products and multiplications.

Napier strips:
- Napier's strip is a manually-operated calculating device created by John Napier.
- Napier strips are mainly used for multiplication and verification of products.
- Napier strips can be used for multiplying a large number with a single-digit number. In this way, it reduces multiplication to a series of additions.
- This method is very similar to the Gelosia method of multiplication developed by Indian mathematicians many centuries ago.
- Each of Napier's strip is simply the multiplication table for that number.

as numerical skills is a narrow objective of teaching mathematics.

NCF-2005 is the National Curriculum Framework published in 2005, by the National Council of Education, Research, and Training (NCERT).
- It is the official document which states that the curriculum must be student-centric and beyond the textbooks.
- It also emphasized making classroom activities more flexible and related to daily life.

86(D). For all the above reasons Mathematics subject is important in the syllabus.

Mathematics has always been praised for its usefulness and importance in life. It plays an important role in deciding how individuals deal with various problems of life. It plays an important role in understanding the content of other school subjects like science, social studies, cultural studies.

Mathematics subject is important in the syllabus because it:
- Improves logical thinking.
- Science helps in the study of subjects.
- Connects learning with children's daily lives.
- Develops skills like speed, accuracy, estimation.
- Improves reasoning power, analytical and critical thinking.
- Enhances scientific approach such as estimating, finding and verifying results.
- Provides an effective way of building mental discipline and encourages logical reasoning, mental and moral development.

87(A). Mathematisation refers to the act of interpreting or expressing mathematically or the state of being considered or explained mathematically.

- In other words, mathematization is nothing but converting a given situation in a more specific way using numerals, symbols, and mathematical facts satisfying the given conditions with the help of logic. Logic is the backbone of the mathematization of any given situation.
- The teaching-learning of mathematics stresses much on developing the skill of mathematization.
- It is expected that children should expand the horizon of cognition by incorporating abilities that help them manage situations mathematically.
- Here, children should make use of the knowledge, facts, and principles of Mathematics to arrive at a judgment. This is referred to as the mathematization of the mind.

good teacher-
- He gives children ample opportunities to learn the language of mathematics.
- Teachers foster children's learning and development best by building on the existing knowledge, abilities, interests, needs, styles of learning, and strengths of the children in the class.
- giving a democratic climate so that the child gets maximum opportunities for interaction with other children in the class, with the teacher, and with a variety of teaching-learning material.
- Effective teachers emphasize healthy social and interpersonal development
- their orientation is towards discovery learning (active) rather than reception (passive) learning

89(C). Educational psychology refers to the scientific study of a learner's learning process, including learning difficulties, teaching methods, guidance, classroom environment, and learner's maturity.

Functions of Educational Psychology:
- Educational Psychology emphasizes 'Child-centred education' that gives primacy to children's experiences and needs.
- It is the application of the principles of psychology to the solution of problems encountered in the classroom.
- It is the application of principles and laws of learning to understand learners, the learning process, and the teaching methodologies that enhance learning.

90(C). Gram is not a source of carbohydrate, it is a source of protein.
- Food comprises constituents like proteins, carbohydrates, fats and supplementary substances such as minerals, vitamins and water that are vital for life.
- These constituents are known as

nutrients. For proper functioning of our body, we need to consume bodybuilding foods (e.g. milk, meat, poultry, fish, eggs, pulses, groundnuts); energy-giving foods (e.g. cereals, sugar, roots, fats and oils); and protective foods (e.g. vegetables, fruits).

91(C). Guava, Lemon, Orange and Tomato are rich in vitamin C.
Vitamin C, also known as ascorbic acid, is necessary for the growth, development and repair of all body tissues. It's involved in many body functions, including formation of collagen, absorption of iron, the proper functioning of the immune system, wound healing, and the maintenance of cartilage, bones, and teeth.

92(D). A wooden scale is a poor conductor because it is made of wood

connecting wires, switches, and electrical appliances.
- If the switch is ON, the circuit is closed and the current passes. Current will not pass through the circuit when the
- When a bulb is connected through the circuit, and it glows, that means the circuit is complete and the current is flowing.

Good and bad conductors of Electricity:
- Good Conductors are the devices that allow the electric current to pass through them easily.
- Examples are metals like copper, silver, iron, etc.
- Bad Conductors resist the flow of current across them.
- Examples of bad conductors are wood, rubber, plastic etc.

93(A). An amalgam is an alloy of mercury with another metal.
- Depending upon the proportion of mercury, it may be a liquid, a soft paste or a solid.
- Nearly all metals can form amalgams with mercury.
- The well-known exceptions are iron, platinum, tungsten, and tantalum.

94(C). **Chlamydomonas** is an example of green algae.
About Chlamydomonas-
- Class: Chlorophyceae
- Order: Chlamydomonadales
- Scientific name: Chlamydomonas
- Phylum: Chlorophyta
- Higher classification: Chlamydomonadaceae

95(A). Keystone species are plants or animals species that play a unique and crucial role in the way an ecosystem functions.
They are very important for ecosystem to

function properly.

96(C). A batsman hits a cricket ball which then rolls on a flat ground. The ball stops after traveling some distance. The ball slows to a stop because there is a force on the ball opposing the motion.
- When the ball rolls on the ground, the ground exerts a friction force on the ball in the opposite direction of its motion.
- The force of friction acts between the two surfaces by opposing the relative motion of one surface over the other.
- Due to friction, as the ball rolls, the ball loses its energy to heat and sound. As the energy is lost, the ball slows down and eventually stops. Hence statement C is correct.
- When the ball rolls on the flat surface of the ground, its motion is opposed by

97(D). Diamagnetic Substance:
- Diamagnetic substances are those which develop feeble magnetization in the opposite direction of the magnetizing field.
- Such substances are feebly repelled by magnets and tend to move from stronger to weaker parts of a magnetic field.
- Magnetic susceptibility is small and negative i.e. $-1 \leq \chi \leq 0$.
- Examples: Bismuth, copper, lead, zinc, etc.

From above it is clear that ferromagnetic substances are strongly attracted by a magnet and paramagnetic substances are feebly attracted by magnets whereas the diamagnetic substance is feebly repelled by magnets.
So, N1 attract strongly, N2 weakly and repel N3 weakly.

98(D). The various applications of ultrasonic sound waves are:
- For cleaning clothes, aeroplanes and machinery parts of clocks
- F or measurement of the depth of the sea
- In ultrasonography
- For removing lamp-shoot from the chimney of factories
- I n sterilization of any liquid
- For sending signals
- Sound waves with frequencies above 20000 Hz are known as ultrasonic sound waves.
- Human beings cannot detect these waves but certain creatures such as dog, cat, bat, and mosquito can detect these waves.

99(A). Correct Pair: **Tomato - Oxalic Acid**
- Oxalic acid is a chemical compound that occurs naturally in almost every plant to some degree, including fruit, vegetable and grain plants.
- Tomato contains more than 10 types of

acids such as citric acid, malic acid, ascorbic acid, and oxalic acid etc.
- The oxalic acid content of tomatoes is about 50 mg per 100 g serving.
- Very ripe tomatoes generally contain higher oxalate amounts than less mature fruit.

100(B). As the bus stops, the lower part of the person's body comes to rest along with the bus while the upper part of his body continues to remain in motion due to inertia and therefore the person falls forward.

101(B). Magnetism at the centre of Bar magnet is **zero** .
- Magnetism maxima and minima for a bar magnet
- Magnetism is strongest at the north poles and south poles of the magnet and
- at the poles.
- or it can be thought of as magnetic field lines are originated from a pole and not at the centre of the bar.

102(B). **Refractive index** : The ratio of the speed of light in a vacuum to speed of light in a medium is called the refractive index of that medium. It is also called an absolute refractive index.
Critical angle: When a ray of light is going from a denser medium to a rare medium then the angle of incidence at which the refraction angle is 90° is called as the critical angle.
The critical angle is given by:
$\Theta_C = \text{critical angle} = \text{Sin}^{-1}(n_2/n_1)$
Where n_2 is the refractive index of second medium in which light ray is going and n_1 is the refractive index of first medium from which light is going to second medium.
Numerical aperture (NA)
$$NA = \sqrt{n_1^2 - n_2^2}$$
Where n_2 is the refractive index of second medium in which light ray is going and n_1 is the refractive index of first medium from which light is going to second medium.
Given: Refractive index of core $n_1 = 1.55$, refractive index of cladding $n_2 = 1.50$;
Numerical aperture (NA)
$$NA = \sqrt{n_1^2 - n_2^2}$$
$$NA = \sqrt{(1.55)^2 - (1.50)^2}$$
NA = 0.39

103(B). When **sulphur dioxide is dissolved in water it forms Sulphurous acid** . The chemical formula of sulphur dioxide is SO_2.
The chemical equation is shown below.
- $SO_2 + H_2O \rightarrow H_2SO_3$
- Metallic oxides are formed when metals react with oxygen. Because they react with water to form bases, these metallic

oxides are basic in nature.

- Non-metals, on the other hand, react with oxygen to form non-metallic oxides, which differ from metallic oxides in that they are acidic. Non-metallic oxides also form acids when they react with water.
- Sulphur is a non-metallic element, and sulphur dioxide (SO_2) is acidic. As a result, it reacts with water to produce sulphurous acid (H_2SO_3)

Properties of Sulphurous acid:

- Sulphurous acid is a colourless liquid.
- Sulphurous acid is a good reducing agent.
- It is used as a mild bleaching agent for applications.
- Sulphurous acid is unstable and has never been isolated in it its pure states.

104(D). The Halogens are the elements

- It is divided into 18 groups and 7 periods running vertically and horizontally respectively.
- The periodic table accommodates a discrete combination of metal, non-metals, and metalloids.
- The elements in the periodic table are arranged horizontally in ascending order of their atomic numbers known as periods.
- Vertically the elements having identical chemical properties are clubbed together known as groups.
- The 18 groups are also known as columns and the 7 periods are also known as the rows.

105(A). The **alveoli** provide the surface for the exchange of gases.

The main function of the human respiratory system is to Inhale the air and using the Oxygen present in the air then transported to different body parts and using that oxygen food is broken down to be stored in form of energy (ATP).

- Nostril: Air is taken in via nostrils and passes through the nasal cavity.
- Trachea: It is a long tube passing through the mid-thoracic cavity.
- Bronchi: The trachea is later divided into two bronchi. The trachea and bronchi moisten the air flowing through with the help of ciliated epithelial cells and goblet cells (secretory cells)

106(D). The vitamin K dependent clotting factors represent a homeostatic mechanism at the basis of the hypercoagulability (thrombosis)-hypocoagulability (hemorrhagic) system. This vitamin is called anti-hemorrhagic factor as its deficiency produced uncontrolled hemorrhagic due to defect in blood coagulation. Vitamin K is a naphthoquinone derivative and essential for the production

of blood clotting factor. Prothrombin is a vitamin K-dependent protein directly involved with blood clotting.

107(B). If the frequency of a sound is below 20Hz it is known as Infrasonic sound. Sound waves are of three types:

- Infrasonic waves: The sound waves of frequency between 0 Hz to 20 Hz are called infrasonic waves. The sound produced by thunders, volcanoes, etc. Animals like elephants and whales can hear infrasonic sounds.
- Audible waves: The sound waves of frequency between 20 Hz to 20,000 Hz are called Audible waves. The human ear can able to listen to these frequencies
- Ultrasonic waves: The sound waves of frequency above 20,000 Hz are called Ultrasonic waves. Many animals like

- Remind students of analogy concepts they know
- Identifying relevant features of the concept
- Adding similar attributes to rules
- Indicate where the symmetry between the rules breaks down
- Draw conclusions about rules

Therefore, from the above points, it becomes clear that map parallelism is a phase of the symmetry strategy in science.

109(C). The brainstorming method covers all areas of learning objectives.

Brainstorming : It is the method that is used for creating ideas without limitations. Its name is so given since it looks for attacking problems (with ideas) just like a storm does. The following are its characteristics:

- It exploits a student's cognitive abilities to understand the problem, create an idea, evaluate if it can work, analyze so that it can be connected with the actual problem, applying it practically, remembering the same idea when it needs to be recalled.
- In this method, a group of students and teachers sit around a table and brainstorm on a problem, hence it improves social skills (one of the affective domains)
- When it comes to psychomotor domains, it should be noted that while presenting an idea, a student needs to maintain gestures and postures.

110(D). I ntegrated education:

- The concept of integrated education arises as an outcome of the National policy of education, 1986 r recommended providing equal opportunity to all not only for access but also for success. Integration signifies the process of interaction of disabled children with

normal children in the same educational setting. Integration also means 'mainstreaming' or 'Normalisation'. As disabled children are treated with normal children.

Importance of integrated education:

- It does not create a feeling of differentiation among disabled children.
- It helps to remove the inferiority complex among disabled children.
- It provides peer group help in learning from normal children.
- It provides disabled children a chance to enjoy school life with normal children and ensures social integration.
- It inculcates affection, love, and respect for disabled children among normal children.
- It ensures that learners have an understanding of and respect for the

largest bloom is the Ramesia arnoldii. This rare flower is found in the rainforests of Indonesia. It can grow to be 3 feet across and weigh up to 15 pounds! It is a parasitic plant, with no visible leaves, roots, or stem.

112(B). Inductive is used to describe reasoning that involves using specific observations, such as observed patterns, to make a general conclusion. This method is sometimes called induction.

Inductive reasoning is a method of drawing conclusions by going from the specific to the general. It's usually contrasted with deductive reasoning, where you go from general information to specific conclusions. Inductive reasoning is also called inductive logic or bottom-up reasoning.

113(C). GSM technology is used in mobile phones.

The full form of GSM is Global System for Mobile.

- ETSI (European Telecommunication Standard Institute) has developed this technology .
- The protocols for second-generation digital cellular networks are described by the GSM technology .
- In 1991 , Finland was the first country of deploying GSM .
- The global system of mobile communication became a global standard for mobile communications in 2010 .
- It achieved a market share of 90% at that time.
- A digital circuit-switched network that was optimized for full-duplex voice telephony was described by GSM global technology.
- The GSM associations own the trademark of GSM.
- It is a secured wireless system.
- A pre-shared key is used for user

authentication.
- Several cryptographic algorithms for security are used in G

114(B). Textbooks play a pivotal role in language classrooms in all types of educational institutions. Textbooks play a very crucial role in the realm of language teaching and learning and are considered the next important factor
- A textbook is **one of the tools** in the hands of the teacher, and the teacher must know how to use it, and how useful it can be for everyone.
- It is instructional material that provides facts and information.
- It is thus, a base around that a course is developed and built.

Thus, it is concluded that In the process of teaching and learning a language, **the**

Assessment (SBA) is proposed to be conducted throughout the country to assess the Learning Outcomes of all the children at the Elementary level. The purpose of the SBA is to empower the teachers to improve the learning levels of the students.

116(C). A person having scientific attitude is adopts a scientific method in his

thinking and working.

The scientific attitude is one that harnesses and directs the power of the human brain, turning it to the investigation of the observable world. Scientists learn to think in specific ways, deducing patterns and principles from observations of the way things work.

117(B). The first step in remedial teaching is to identify poor students.

Remedial education should be arranged according to a schedule and repeated as required.

Learning difficulties people face:
- Poor memorization power
- Short attention span and are easily distracted
- Low level of comprehensive control
- Motivation to learn is lacking
- Failure to understand knowledge effectively and a proclivity for mixing things up.

118(D). A free fall in true sense occurs only in a vacuum.
- A fall is considered as a free fall if only force acting on it was gravity.
- As the vacuum contains no matter, there

is no opposite force against the free fall due to gravity.
- In air and atmosphere, there is aerodynamic drag and in the sea, there is a buoyancy force of water to oppose the movement due to gravity.

119(A). Given,

Om Prakash travels Bombay to Pune at a speed (s_1) of 80 km/hr

Returns back to Bombay by increasing his speed by 50% = 50% of 80 km/hr

$= 40$ km/hr

Returing speed $(s_2) = 120$ km/hr

We know that,

If the distance is the same then,

$$\text{Average speed} = \frac{2s_1 \times s_2}{s_1 + s_2}$$

$$= \frac{2 \times 80 \times 120}{80 + 120}$$

$$\frac{19200}{}$$

120(D). Tsunami is caused due to disturbance caused deep down the sea. Lightening will not cause any disturbance for the sea whereas earthquake, A major nuclear explosion under sea and Volcanic eruption can cause disturbance in the sea.

Child Development and Pedagogy

1. Which of the following principle of development is incorrect one?
(a) There are individual differences in development.
(b) Development is the result of coincidences.
(c) It is a continuous process.
(d) It is predictable.

2. Which of the following human relationships comes under tertiary relationship?
(a) Nephew   (b) Uncle

"Where is the blue piece? No, not this one, darker one that would go here and make this shoe".
This kind of talk is referred to by Vygotsky as:
(a) Private speech
(b) Talk aloud
(c) Scaffolding
(d) Egocentric speech

4. Giving cues to children and offering support as and when needed is an example of _________.
(a) reinforcement
(b) conditioning
(c) modelling
(d) scaffolding

5. Instruction at the primary stage need to be:
(a) Teacher centered
(b) Textbook centred
(c) Student centered
(d) Teacher and Textbook centrered

6. An educational psychologist works:
(a) only within the classroom, focusing on children's behaviour.
(b) at multiple levels, with individual children, groups of children, parents and at the organizational level.
(c) exclusively with individual children with special education need.
(d) only at administration level

7. Which of the following Psychologist viewed that cognitive development of children as a socially mediated process in which children depend on assistance from adults and more expert peers?
(a) Bronfen Brenner
(b) Freud
(c) Vygotsky
(d) Jean Piaget

8. A positive or negative evaluative reaction towards a stimulus, such as a person, action, object or concept is known as:
(a) Attitude   (b) Aptitude
(c) Interest   (d) Appreciation

9. In Indian context (According to RPWD Act, 2016) a person can be considered as 'Deaf' if:
(a) He has 70 dB or more hearing
(c) He has 60 dB to 50 dB hearing loss in both ears.
(d) He has 50 dB or less hearing loss in both ears.

10. Which of the following can not be considered as a characteristic of an activity-based classroom?
(I) Children are totally involved in doing their work by collaborating with their peers.
(II) If children are asked what they are doing they could not state the objectives of that activity.
(a) Only I
(b) Only II
(c) Both I & II
(d) None of these

11. What are the critical role played by a teacher
I. Observer and diagnostician of learner
II. Provider of the environment for learning
II. Facilitator of learning
(a) Only I   (b) I and II
(c) II and III   (d) I, II, and III

12. Which of these is a planned performance of an occupational skill, scientific principle or an experiment?
(a) Jigsaw method
(b) Problem solving
(c) Synthetic method
(d) Demonstration

13. Which of the following is incorrect about Autistic Spectrum Disorder?
(a) It affects the child's ability to communicate.
(b) Frequently associated with repetitive behaviour.
(c) It appears after first 3 years of life.
(d) It affects the ability to develop inter-individual relationship.

14. The test should be reliable, valid and standardized. Here the term validity refers to:
(a) if it measures something consistently
(b) the degree to which it measures what it intends to measure
(c) comparison of a score of a person with those of others in a defined group

15. If you are unable to get a job of teacher, then you will:
(a) start giving tuition at home
(b) remain at home till you get a job
(c) take some another job
(d) continue applying for teaching

16. Which of the following is the approximate age range related to Erickson's psychological stage termed as "Initiative versus Guilt"?
(a) 3-6 years   (b) 6-11 years
(c) 1-3 years   (d) 13-18 years

17. Students should be involved in keeping their school clean to create a sense of responsibility and pride in their school environment. What can be the result of this statement.
(a) School campus will be clean and hygienic
(b) Teachers and staff have less burden to clean the school
(c) Students will keep their home clean
(d) Skills learnt in school may be carried into other environments, hopefully for many years.

18. According to Bronfenbrenner's Bio-Ecological model, 'War' can be included in which of the following system?
(a) Individual system
(b) Micro system
(c) Meso system
(d) Chrono system

**19. Which of the following things a teacher should consider while creating individual learning situation in the classroom?

I. **Communication of assignments clearly**
II. **Monitor students' work**
III. **Provide appropriate feedback**
(a) I and II   (b) I, II and III
(c) I and III   (d) II and III

20. _____ education is life oriented.
(a) Formal
(b) Non-formal
(c) Informal
(d) All of the above

21. Which of the following factor influences personality development of a child?
(a) Hereditary
(b) Physical environment
(c) Social environment

(a) Competition
(b) Praise
(c) Rewards
(d) Level of aspiration

23. In the context of education, socialization means:
(a) creating one's own social norms
(b) respecting elders in society
(c) adapting and adjusting to social environment
(d) always following social norms

24. What should a teacher do to develop spirit of labour in students?
(a) Give example of people who put in labour
(b) Teacher should indulge in labour
(c) Give detailed lectures on importance of labour
(d) Give opportunities to students to do labour often

25. Which of the following is NOT a factor that is essential for the success of work education?
(a) Positive relationship between community and school
(b) Broadmindedness
(c) Dignity of labour and pessimistic attitude
(d) Feelings of co-operation

26. As Freud observed 'Electra Complex' develops at a particular age of child. The age of developing an electra complex falls under which of the following Piagetian stage?
(a) Sensory Motor stage
(b) Pre-operational stage
(c) Concrete operational stage
(d) Formal operational stage

27. Which of the following step shall be taken to transform the assessment for school development ?
(a) The progress card of all students for school-based assessment will be completely redesigned by States/UTS.
(b) The progress card will be a holistic, 360 degree, multidimensional report that reflects in great detail the progress.
(c) Both 1 and 2
(d) Only 2

I. Graphs
II. Number and alphabet cards
III. Flash cards on different themes
(a) I and IV   (b) I and II
(c) I, II and III   (d) II and III

29. Which of the following is not the step of social learning theory of Albert Bandura?
(a) Attending to and perceiving the behaviour
(b) Remembering the behaviour
(c) Converting the memory into action
(d) Generalization of the Imitated Behaviour

30. In which principle of development, the child develops in sequence and follows two tends?
(a) Learning and Maturation
(b) Development is correlated
(c) Development is flexible
(d) Cephalo-caudal and Proximodistal

Language - I: English

Ques (31-39): Direction : Read the passage given below and answer the following questions.

Gender inequality is the main social issue in India. There is a need to accelerate women empowerment to bring men and women on par. The upliftment of women in all fields should be included in the national priority. The disparity between men and women gives rise to many problems which can pose as major obstacles in the development of the nation. It is the birthright of women that they should get equal importance to men in society. To really bring empowerment, women should be aware of their rights. Not only domestic and family responsibilities but also women should play an active and positive role in every field. They should also know the happenings around them and in the country.

Women empowerment has this power to change a lot in society and the country. She can deal with any problem in society better than men. She can understand well the loss of overpopulation for the country and the family. With good family planning, she is fully capable of managing the economic condition of the country and the family. Women are more capable of handling any effective violence than men, whether it is family or social.

Through women empowerment, it is possible that a country with female-male family can develop easily without much effort. A woman is considered very responsible for everything in the family, so she can solve all problems well. With the empowerment of women, the whole society will automatically become strong. Women empowerment is a better solution to any small or major problem related to human, economic or environmental. In the last few years, we are getting the benefit of women empowerment. Women are more conscious about their health, education, job, and responsibility towards family, country and society. She participates prominently in every field and shows her interest. Finally, after many years of struggle, they are getting their right to follow the right path.

31. What attribute of a women can bring the real empowerment?
(a) Women should know her responsibility towards family, country and society.
(b) Women should help in improvising economic condition of the country
(c) Women should be aware of their rights
(d) All of the above

32. What has the power to change a lot in society?
(a) Women health
(b) Economic condition
(c) Male influence
(d) Women empowerment

33. Choose the word which is opposite in meaning to 'influence'.
(a) Impotence   (b) Powerful
(c) Efficacy   (d) Impact

34. **Find the error.**

A women (a)/ can deal (b)/ with any problem in the society (c)/ in best way.(d)

(a) a
(b) b
(c) c
(d) d

35. **Read the following statements:**
    A. A country with female-male equality forms a strong economy.
    B. Human, economic or environmental problems can not be dealt with by Woman empowerment.
    (a) A is true
    (b) B is true
    (c) Both A and B are true
    (d) Both A and B are false

36. **Identify the part of speech of the**

    (a) Preposition   (b) Adjective
    (c) Pronoun   (d) Conjunction

37. **Which of the following is NOT true?**
    (a) The disparity between men and women gives rise to many problems
    (b) No one in the country can understand the loss of overpopulation for the country and the family
    (c) Women are active participants in every field
    (d) Women are more conscious about their health, education, job, and responsibility

38. **Identify the part of speech of the underlined word:**
    The disparity <u>between</u> men and women gives rise to many problems.
    (a) Adverb   (b) Preposition
    (c) Conjunction   (d) Verb

39. **Disparity in the line, "The disparity between men and women gives rise to many problems which can pose as major obstacles in the development of the nation." means**
    (a) Equality   (b) Similarity
    (c) Difference   (d) Unity

Ques (40-45): Directions : Read the extract given below and answer the questions that follow by selecting the most appropriate options:
I have a little shadow
that goes in and out with me.
And what can be that use of him
is more than I can see.
He is very, very like me
from the heels upto the head;

And I see him jump before me
When I jump into my bed.
The funniest thing about him
is the way he likes to grow-
Not at all like proper children,
Which is always very slow;
For he sometimes shoots up taller
like an India rubber ball,
And he sometimes gets so little that
There's none of him at all.

40. **The expression 'that goes in and out with me' refers to:**
    (a) The shadow
    (b) Child
    (c) The poet
    (d) A rubber ball

41. **Which of the following statement is not true?**

    (c) The poet finds his shadow funny.
    (d) The poet observes that his shadows goes before him.

42. **Which of the following adjectives do not apply to the shadow?**
    (a) Funny
    (b) Slow
    (c) Tall
    (d) None of these

43. **What is the meaning of the word 'coward'?**
    (a) Wimp   (b) Daredevil
    (c) Valiant   (d) Stalwart

44. **Which literary device is used in the expression 'He is very, very like me'?**
    (a) Assonance
    (b) Alliteration
    (c) Simile
    (d) Personification

45. **Name the figure of speech used in 'He stays so close beside me'.**
    (a) Metaphor
    (b) Alliteration
    (c) Simile
    (d) Personification

46. **The primary objective of teaching new words is:**
    (a) To enable the students to become better readers
    (b) To enable the students to become better writers
    (c) To enable the students to translate words into another language
    (d) To enable the students to coin new words

47. **In a constructive classroom, language learning should be based on:**
    (a) the transaction of the prescribed textbook by the teacher
    (b) learners' previous knowledge in constructing their new knowledge using authentic tasks
    (c) the assumption that the English language can only be learned if the teacher transmits it to the learners
    (d) drill and practice of grammatical items

48. **Which of the following is not the aim of language pedagogy?**

    organized and systematic way.
    (c) To enable them to use appropriate vocabulary in writing various forms of composition.
    (d) To prepare them for good handwriting

49. **Procedural knowledge helps learners _____.**
    (a) learn the knowledge about language
    (b) learn the form first and use it later.
    (c) apply the rules of grammar in communication
    (d) master the rules of grammar of a language.

50. **A language teacher is planning to teach grammar. Which one of the following might be a good strategy for teaching grammar?**
    (a) Providing the chance to practice grammar in context
    (b) Emphasizing students to note down the rules clearly
    (c) Teaching grammar using a standard book
    (d) Asking students to practice questions only to learn rules

51. **What does 'comprehensible input' means in language learning?**
    (a) Engagement with language which is comprehensible to all learners.
    (b) Engagement with written and formal language below the level current level of master of the learner.
    (c) Exposure to high level of written

and spoken language above the learner's current level of mastery.

(d) Exposure to meaningful oral and written language somewhat above the learners' current level of mastery.

52. TBLT in second language teaching is:
(a) Tool Based Language Teaching
(b) Task Book Language Teaching
(c) Task Based Language Teaching
(d) None of the above

53. A teacher "teaching again" the content that students previously failed to learn. Here, the teacher is using:

54. A teacher brings a newspaper to her class VIII students and asks them to find some advertisements. She then asks them to list out how advertisements are designed and what an advertisement contains. What is the newspaper have?
(a) For reading.
(b) An instrument of language learning.
(c) A technique of language learning.
(d) Materials for language learning.

55. Students are asked to read a short text and make points for discussion. What skills of the learners are assessed?
(a) Study skills
(b) Listening skills
(c) Speaking skills
(d) Writing skills

56. What is the status of English in India? It is:
(a) an associate official language.
(b) the official language
(c) a regional language
(d) a foreign language

57. A class VII student makes mistakes in spelling. As a teacher would you:
(a) allow the student to use a mobile dictionary?
(b) ask the student to re-pronounce the word?
(c) show him his mistakes and ask him to re-pronounce them?
(d) gnore the mistakes?

58. How can a language teacher help a

student in learning English whose exposure to the target language (English) is limited?
(a) By giving him extra remedial classes.
(b) Being extra sensitive towards his needs.
(c) By giving him supplementary reading materials.
(d) By enrolling him in language library.

59. A teacher one of his students about "what was it to study in your previous school?" This type of question is:
(a) Lower-Order Question
(b) Higher-Order Question
(c) Close Ended Question

multilingual classroom?
(a) Miscellaneous written exams
(b) More than once, linguistic assessment
(c) More than one textbook
(d) Miscellaneous text material

Mathematics and Science

61. Ensuring a good start to the students in learning mathematics, creating love, faith and interest for learning mathematics are:
(a) Broader Aims
(b) Narrower Aims
(c) Specific Aims
(d) All of the above

62. Which of the following is correct about the nature of mathematics?
(a) The results of mathematics theorems and theories are not significant and useful.
(b) Precision is the nature of mathematics that deals with accuracy and exactness.
(c) Mathematics is science of concrete objects and there is no place for logic or creativity.
(d) Mathematics deals with qualitative facts and relationships as well as problem solving.

63. Which of the following statements is NOT correct with regard to nature of mathematics?
(a) Mathematics aims at abstraction.
(b) Mathematics is illogical.

(c) Mathematics is precise.
(d) Mathematics is symbolic.

64. Which of the following is the most appropriate strategy for teaching students to solve mathematical problems?
(a) Multiple perspective approach
(b) Rigidness in problem solving
(c) Hit and trial method
(d) Memorization of formula

65. To enjoy Mathematics, a teacher must ensure that the students:
(a) Must practice their exercise
(b) Have sense of competence and fear
(c) Must do exactly as is written in their textbooks

likely to impact teaching-learning in mathematics?
(a) Providing complete solutions to students wrong answers
(b) Crude methods of assessment.
(c) Memorization and rote learning in mathematics.
(d) Providing feedback via formative assessment.

67. Mathematics can be used in-
(a) the truths that are discovered
(b) the methods used to discover truths
(c) Both A and B
(d) None of the above

68. Which among the following is true regarding Van Hiele Theory?
(a) Van Hiele Theory describes the evaluation of learner in geometry
(b) Van Hiele Theory describes how people learn geometry
(c) Van Hiele Theory describes how people learn algebra.
(d) Van Hiele Theory describes the evaluation of learner in algebra.

69. If a six digit number 738A6A is divisible by 11 and a three digit number 68X is divisible by 9, then the value of (A + X) is:
(a) 11   (b) 15
(c) 12   (d) 13

70. The number of rational numbers between 5 and 7 is:
(a) 2   (b) infinite
(c) 1   (d) 0

71. Find the greatest value of k for

which the 6 -digit number $24312k$ is divisible by 6 .

(a) 6   (b) 4
(c) 8   (d) 0

72. If $x^2 - 4x + 1 = 0$, then find the value of $(x)^6 + \dfrac{1}{(x)^6}$

(a) 2702   (b) 5774
(c) 2706   (d) 5776

73. If $(a - b) = 3$ and $ab = 70$, then find the value of $(a^3 - b^3)$.

(a) 657   (b) 783
(c) 840   (d) 580

74. If $x + \dfrac{1}{x} = 4$, then find the value of $x^4 + \dfrac{1}{x^4}$

a   triangle   and $\dfrac{\angle A}{4} + \dfrac{\angle B}{4} + \dfrac{\angle C}{5} = 41°$, then find the value of $\angle A + \angle B$

(a) 120°   (b) 100°
(c) 90°   (d) 80°

76. In the given figure, chords AB and CD are intersecting each other at point L . Find the length of AB :

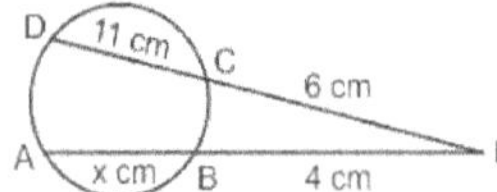

(a) 23.5 cm   (b) 21.5 cm
(c) 22.5 cm   (d) 24.5 cm

77. In the figure, ABC is a triangle. Measure of $\angle$ABD is:

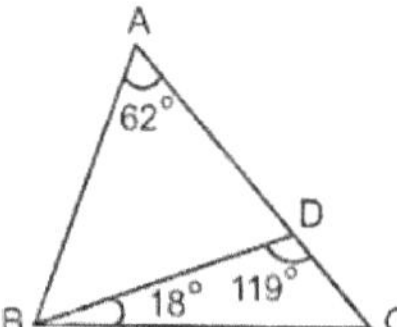

(a) 57°   (b) 61°
(c) 72°   (d) 80°

78. Find the area of the circle whose circumference is equal to the perimeter of a square of side 11 cm.

(a) 231 cm^2 (b) 140 cm^2
(c) 77 cm^2 (d) 154 cm^2

79. Height and radius of cone is 15 cm and 7 cm respectively. What is the volume of cone?

(a) 550 cm^3 (b) 660 cm^3
(c) 110 cm^3 (d) 770 cm^3

80. A man buys 10 oranges for Rs. 3 and sells 8 for Rs. 3. Calculate his gain percent.

(a) 25   (b) 20
(c) 27   (d) 30

81. The average age of A, B, C, D and E is 40 years. The average age of A and B is 35 years and the average age of C and D is 42 years. The age of E is?

(a) 46
(b) 48
(c) 32
(d) None of these

82. A helicopter covers a certain distance at a speed of 180 km/h in 6 hours. To cover the same distance in $\underline{10}$ hours, at what speed will it

83. Arun and Meena recently celebrated their golden anniversary and their daughter Seema's birthday. If the age of Seema is 18 years after her parent's marriage and her age at their golden anniversary is in the ratio 5 : 21, how many years after the marriage was Seema born?

(a) 8 years   (b) 15 years
(c) 12 years   (d) 10 years

84. The sum of two positive numbers is 240 and their HCF is 15. Find the number of pairs of numbers satisfying the given condition.

(a) 8   (b) 2
(c) 4   (d) 5

85. Simplify:
$[(7 \times 9) + (3 \times 8) + 3] \div [(9 \times 4) + (72 \div 8)]$

(a) 5   (b) 4
(c) 2   (d) 3

86. If two samples of sizes 30 and 20 have means as 55 and 60 and variances as 16 and 25 respectively, then what would be the S.D. of the combined sample of size 50?

(a) 5.00
(b) 5.06
(c) 5.23
(d) None of these

87. The mean of 13 numbers is 24. If 3 is added to each number, then what will the new mean?

(a) 24   (b) 21
(c) 27   (d) 25

88. Find the mean of the given data {a, b, a, a, b, a, b, c, a, b, a, c, a, b, a}, where a is less than b and b is less than c.

(a) $\dfrac{(3a+2b+4c)}{9}$

(b) $\dfrac{(8a+4b+2c)}{15}$

(c) $\dfrac{(8a+5b+2c)}{15}$

(d) $\dfrac{(8a+5b+c)}{15}$

89. To introduce the concept of area, a teacher can start with:

(a) Explaining of formulae for finding area of figure of different shapes.

(b) Comparing area of any figure with the help of different object like palm leaf note book etc.

(d) Calculating area of figure with the help of counting unit square.

90. Which of the following statement best describes the nature of science?

(a) scientists are totally objective in their work

(b) the scientific method is the only guide for conducting research

(c) science is a system of beliefs

(d) science is social in nature

91. The values of Science for nature is:

(a) Possibility   (b) Reality
(c) Interim   (d) Uncertainty

92. The aims of teaching science at secondary level:

(a) to know about the facts and principles of science and its applications

(b) to acquire the requisite theoretical knowledge only

(c) to criticize the issues at the interface of science, technology and society

(d) to develop the feeling of fear and prejudice.

93. Role of a teacher while using lecture cum demonstration method in science should not be:

(a) The lecture method should be planned and rehearsed well in advance.

(b) The teacher should be clear of the purpose, aims and objectives of lecture & demonstration.

(c) Teacher should conduct question answer session while or after demonstration.

(d) Teacher should handle class situation very strictly while performing the demonstration.

94. **Which of the following is not appropriate to understand science at the upper primary stage?**

(a) Observing things and recording observations

(b) Plotting graphs

(c) Hands-on experience

(d) Learn the subject through abstraction

95. **From the following, identify the statement that is not true about science:**

(a) Science is a systematic and through research.

(c) Science aims for measurable results through testing and analysis.

(d) Science is merely based upon opinion or preferences, not on facts and experiments.

96. **In order to incorporate Piaget's suggestions, a teacher must:**

(a) Initiate group discussions in the class

(b) Organize group work

(c) Schedule visits to community

(d) Give lots of manipulative to work with

97. **Which of the following is the correct sequence and steps of learning through scientific method?**

(a) creative thinking-observation-classification-evaluation

(b) observation-reflection-classification-evaluation

(c) classification-evaluation-thinking-observation

(d) evaluation-concern-observation-classification

98. **Which method is used for constructing a concept with the help of a sufficient number of concrete examples?**

(a) Analytic method

(b) Inductive method

(c) Deductive method

(d) Synthetic method

99. **Which of the following is longitudinal wave?**

(a) Sound wave   (b) Radio wave

(c) Water wave   (d) Light wave

100. **Which of the following option is correct regarding properties of a magnet?**

(a) Magnet attracts only iron, and not cobalt or nickel.

(b) A freely suspended magnet can points in any direction.

(c) Like magnetic poles attract each other and unlike magnetic poles repel each other.

(d) Magnets are used for constructing magnetic needles and mariner's compass.

101. **'Kahwa' is a special type of tea / beverage. It is popular in:**

(a) Kashmir   (b) Karnataka

(a) Rajasthan

(b) Gujarat

(c) Madhya Pradesh

(d) Chhattisgarh

103. **Which is the leading cause of blindness in children worldwide?**

(a) Glaucoma

(b) Cataracts

(c) Colour blindness

(d) Vitamin A deficiency

104. **Which of the following vitamin deficiency causes Beriberi?**

(a) Vitamin B1   (b) Vitamin B2

(c) Vitamin B6   (d) Vitamin B12

105. **Saliva helps in digestion of _____.**

(a) Starch   (b) Fiber

(c) Proteins   (d) Fats

106. **Which one of the following statements is/are correct?**
a. The number of protons in a nucleus is called its atomic number.
b. The total number of protons and neutrons constitutes its mass number.

(a) Only a

(b) Only b

(c) Both a and b

(d) Neither a nor b

107. **Some acids completely dissociated into ion. These acids are known as:**

(a) Strong acids

(b) Strong bases

(c) Conjugate acid

(d) Weak acid

108. **If a ray of light goes from a rarer medium to a denser medium, will it bend towards the normal or away from it?**

(a) Bends away from the normal

(b) Bends towards the normal

(c) Goes undeviated

(d) Is reflected back

109. **A man is stranded in the middle of a perfectly smooth island of ice, where there is no friction between the ground and his feet. Under these circumstances,**

(a) He can reach the desired corner by throwing any object in the same direction

(b) He can reach the desired corner by throwing any object in the
(c) ___________________________
by walking on the ground in that direction

110. **The most rapidly dwindling natural resource in the world is:**

(a) Water   (b) Forest

(c) Wind   (d) Sunlight

111. **Which of the following phenomenon is responsible for the twinkling of stars?**

(a) Atmosphere reflection

(b) Atmosphere refraction

(c) Reflection

(d) Total internal reflection

112. **Energy flow and energy transformation in a living system follow:**

(a) Biogenetic law

(b) Law of thermodynamics

(c) Law of limiting factor

(d) Liebig's law of minimum

113. **Which one of the following aspect is an exclusive characteristic of living things?**

(a) Perception of events happening in the environment and their memory.

(b) Increase in mass by accumulation of material both on surface as well as internally.

(c) Isolated metabolic reactions occur in vitro.

(d) Increase in mass from inside only.

114. **Aluminium foil is used in wrapping the food. Which property of aluminium is used in making its foil?**

(a) Malleability

(b) Ductility

(c) Sonorous

(d) Heat conductivity

115. A car braked suddenly near a cliff. Explain the motion of the driver.

(a) The driver remain stood up to look at how near his car was to the edge of the cliff.

(b) The driver was thrown forward when the car stopped, as he still has tendency to remain in motion.

(c) The driver tried to lean forward to balance himself.

(d) The driver was moved in the backward direction due to inertia of motion.

(d) Present examples of 2D and 3D shapes in the classroom and make a chart on it.

120. A child often recognizes multi-digit numbers, such as thirty (30) or 400 (four hundred), but he does not understand that the position of a digit determines its value. As a teacher, how will you address this?

(a) Give them lots of practice question

(b) Ask them to bring their parents in school

(c) Use manipulatives like base ten blocks

(d) Take them to field trips

'Private speech' in his Sociocultural theory, which refers to when children 'think out loud'. It illustrates that children use speech to guide their own actions.

Concept of private speech:

- Private speech refers to the speech produced aloud by young children which seems to be addressed either to the self or to others, which sometimes cannot be easily conceived by a listener.

- It has a major role in the augmentation of the self and self-consciousness.

- For example, Najma says to herself, "Where is the blue piece? No, not this one, darker one that would go here and make this shoe". This is a kind of self-talk by Najma, so it can be considered as private speech.

- This phenomenon starts in the early years of life and proceeds to the end of

(a) To generate energy

(b) In manure

(c) In boiler

(d) In the manufacture of electrical insulating materials

117. A plotting compass is placed near the south pole of a bar magnet. The pointer of plotting compass will:

(a) Point away from the south pole

(b) Point parallel to the south pole

(c) Point towards the south pole

(d) Point at right angles to the south pole

118. When a straight conductor is carrying current:

(a) There are circular magnetic field lines around it

(b) There are magnetic field lines parallel to the conductor

(c) There are no magnetic field lines

(d) None of the above

119. A teacher wants to teach about measurements like surface area and volume in 2D and 3D shapes. The best way to teach this concept is

(a) Explain all the formulas used in this concept.

(b) Ask how much paint will be required to paint their classroom if 1 litre paint is required to paint area 20 metre square.

(c) Ask the child to observe the units used in measurement of milk and vegetables.

continues gradually until reaching its maximum growth.

The rate of development is not uniform and everyone has their own particular rate of development.

It is a wide and complex process, thus there are some principles that need to be followed for a better understanding of the concept.

Principles of development include:

- Development is cumulative.
- Development is predictable.
- Development is the process of interaction.
- Development follows uniformity of pattern.
- Development is predictable and sequential.
- Development proceeds from general to specific.
- Development rate varies from person to person.

Therefore, it could be concluded that 'Development is the result of coincidences' is not a principle of development.

2(D). We conclude that friend comes under tertiary relationship.

Society is a 'web of relationship' and these relations are fundamental for understanding human behaviour and different institutions of society. Different forms of relations in family, community and society are:

Within the family, there are relations like mother, father, son, daughter, husband, wife, brother, sister which we put under primary relations

uncle, aunt, nephew, niece are called secondary relatives.

There are also tertiary relatives like friends, neighbourhood relations and many other similar relations.

3(A). Lev Vygotsky introduced the term

carry out a task, or achieve a goal through a gradual shedding of outside assistance. Scaffolding literally means the structure which is made to support the work crew while a building is constructed or repaired.

- Scaffolding is a technique that is linked to the concept of the Zone of Proximal Development (ZPD), which refers to a range of tasks that a child can achieve only with assistance from a more skilled adult or peer.

- This concept was developed by the Russian psychologist, Lev Vygotsky in his "Sociocultural Theory of Learning".

- Scaffolding refers to a technique that provides the right kind of support in the right amount at the right time to increase a child's competence.

- In other words, it is a means by which a child's 'zone width' (or potential for new learning) can be assessed, i.e. scaffolding helps with providing support to learners in their initial phase of learning, which is in the right amount and gradually decreases as the learner progresses.

- As children are given assistance or shown how to perform certain tasks, they use this information as a guide on how to perform these tasks and eventually learn to perform them independently.

- It helps a learner to move from a Zone of Actual Development to a Zone of Proximal Development and finally reach to Zone of Desired Development, with the help of a more experienced person like peers, elders in the family, or teachers.

- For example, a teacher gives a lesson on vocabulary before making the child read a difficult passage and provides necessary cues and prompts when the child faces difficulty.

5(C). At primary stage covers the children

of class I-V. At this stage, the child is very curious to learn new things. In this age group, children are not able to comprehend the learning. Therefore, at the primary stage when children have to learn basic concepts they should be taught through play and activities arid not through the 'chalk and talk' method.

Learner-Centered Instruction at the primary stage: There are demands for learner-centered methods so that learning is meaningful to learners.

- It should basically have a child-centered approach involving the interaction of children. The activities .should be interesting, relevant, based on the daily life experiences of the child.
- The age. mental level. aptitude, interest, and abilities of the child should be the main criteria for selecting the activities

initiative, courage to ask questions.

- It should encourage the child to think of solutions to problems in higher day-to-day life.
- It should develop the desired skills in children; It should help a child to develop logical thinking; It should help a child to take an active interest and participate in solving some simple problems in a limited way.

6(B). Education Psychology is a part of your course on Behavioural Sciences.

- Educational psychology by its very nature is dynamic and constantly evolving from childhood till death. Man learns by his intelligence, ability and motivation.
- It helps the teacher to foster harmonious overall development of the student.

7(C). Cognitive development is the process in which cognition (thinking) develops. It is the orderly development of mental and intellectual processes, like logical thinking, making sense of new ideas, solving problem and the like, that takes place over a period of time.

- Even the process of concept formation is a part of cognition.

Lev Vygotsky:

- The cultural theory of Vygotsky attempts to explicate this relationship between individual cognitive processes and the historical, cultural, and social settings in which it occurs.
- It sees psychological processes as culturally mediated, historically developing, and socially engendered.
- He stresses the impact of culture and language on the cognitive development. According to him, without culture, our intellectual functioning is limited to apelike, elementary mental functions. With intensive interaction with the

elements of culture and a healthy language development, we become capable of higher mental functions involved in thinking, reasoning, remembering and so on.

Therefore, Lev Vygotsky ,the famous Russian psychologist viewed that cognitive development of children as a socially mediated process in which children depend on assistance from adults and more expert peers.

8(A). Attitude: Allport (1935) defined attitude as "a mental and neural state of readiness, organised through experience, and exerting a directive or dynamic influence upon the individual's response to all objects and situations with which it is related" .

9(A). Disability: A disability is defined as

Hearing impairment :

- "deaf" means persons having 70 DB hearing loss in speech frequencies in both ears;
- "hard of hearing" means person having 60 DB to 70 DB hearing loss in speech frequencies in both ears.

10(B). Activity-based learning is a "learner-centered" approach in the teaching-learning process. In this approach, the 'learner' or 'child' is the main focus of the educational program. It emphasizes learning rather than teaching.

- During activity-based learning, the learners use their multiple senses to understand the concepts and enhance learning.

11(D). The learner is at the centre of all activities in learner-centred approach. The teacher plays the role of a facilitator of the learning process and an organizer of the learning situation to "stimulate curiosity and independent thinking, develop problem-solving skills, promote planning and execution of projects and develop self-learning involving acquisition of knowledge through observation of phenomena, creative thinking and activities." (National Curriculum for Elementary and Secondary Education-A Framework,1987). In the learner-centred approach, as a teacher, you have the following three critical roles to play:

- Observer and diagnostician of learner: You must constantly watch the behaviour and activities of learners in and out of the classroom so as to estimate and diagnose strengths, weaknesses, learning needs, and learning dispositions. This would help you in shaping and providing appropriate learning environments and learning activities for the learners.

- Provider of the environment for learning: Once you diagnose the various learning needs of the learners, it becomes your primary duty to plan a learning environment that is conducive so that each learner would find enough scope and opportunity to fulfil his/ her needs.
- Facilitator of learning: You always need to look out for occasions to help the learners while they are engaged in learning. This is more challenging than directly teaching. As we know that each learner has a distinct learning style, variations in learning dispositions, we have to provide support at the appropriate situations during their period of learning. Further, you need to encourage the learners to be engaged in learning activities whenever you find

scientific principle or experiment.

- The most effective way to teach an occupational skill is to demonstrate it. demonstrate it. one of the two most essential teaching skills is the ability to demonstrate; the other is the ability to explain. Both are vital to the success of either an operation lesson or an information lesson.
- The demonstration is defined as a method of teaching by exhibition and explanation. It implies the presence of an organized series of events or equipment to a group of students for their observation.
- It is a combination of lecture and laboratory work. The teacher makes the use of classroom and demonstration table area in the classroom to teach and demonstrate.
- Some part of the teaching is done before the demonstration, some during the demonstration, and some after demonstration to explain the purposes, articles used, underlying principles, and termination of the procedure, etc.

13(C). Autism: It is a developmental disorder that is characterised by impaired development in communication, social interaction, and behaviour.

- Autism is classified as a pervasive developmental disorder (PDD), a category of disorders that is often described interchangeably with the broad spectrum of developmental disorders affecting young children and adults called the autistic spectrum disorders (ASD).
- The behavioral symptoms of autism spectrum disorder (ASD) often appear early in development. Many children show symptoms of autism by 12 months to 18 months of age or earlier.

14(B). A psychological test is a structured technique used to generate a carefully selected sample of behavior.

15(D). If you are unable to get the job of a teacher, then you will continue applying for teaching. A person who is dedicated and passionate about teaching will continue applying for the teacher job by upgrading skills and attitude. This dedication and towards teaching will help in getting the job of the teacher. Characteristics of a Teaching Profession:
- It essentially involves an intellectual operation.
- It draws material from science.
- It transforms raw material for a practical and definite end.
- It possesses an educationally communicable technique.

- It has a high degree of autonomy.
- It is based upon a systematic body of knowledge.
- It has a common code of ethics.
- It generates in service growth.

16(A). Psychosocial development reflects an interrelationship between psychological developments, emotional needs and the way individuals interact with their environment.
Initiative vs Guilt - 3 to 6 years
- The child continues to be more accepting and take more initiative, but may become too forceful, which can lead to feelings of guilt.
- Children who are successful at this stage feel capable of leading others.
- People who fail to acquire these skills are left with a sense of guilt, self-doubt, and a lack of initiative.

17(D). Habits that are learned at a young age tend to sustain for many years. Many students learn to be obedient, sincere, and punctual. If you teach a kid, a habit of playing football, he or she may continue to pursue football, even at older ages, and may even represent the nation someday in the sport.
- Keeping the school clean also yields the same results. The habit of keeping the environment clean sustains throughout the life and tend to keep their surroundings clean whether it is a workplace or their home.

18(D). Urie Bronfenbrenner's Ecological Theory: The seminal work on ecological systems theory in 1979 asserts the role of environmental systems in human development.
- His theory described the child's ecology as comprising of levels of environmental contexts, from most proximal to the most distal systems.

- With the individual in the centre and other systems forming concentric layers, the structure is akin to the Russian nesting dolls, one level opening into another.

19(B). The aim of education is to enable every individual child to become an able learner and as such individualized learning is the ultimate goal of all teaching-learning processes used in the classroom so that each learner becomes self-reliant in acquiring learning experiences. Individualized learning, also known as self -paced learning, requires individual efforts and interest to perform a task. The teacher gives clear instruction to every learner on the carefully designed set of learning activities to be successfully completed, at his/her own pace. The following guidelines clearly, so that each student can have a full understanding of what he/she is supposed to do. If necessary, give example to illustrate your point.
- Monitor student's work: While the activity is going on, you should move around the class and provide help whenever necessary. Do not interfere else they may feel discouraged.
- Checking students' assignments: Students will work at a different speed, so the class will not finish the task at the same time. In a large class size, checking student's work is a challenging task. Sometimes, this can be accomplished by getting students' to check each other's work. This is particularly appropriate for assignment involving fixed / specific answers. But certain assignments require your careful reading.
- Provide appropriate feedback: Learning occurs when students receive feedback on the performance of their assignments. All assignments need to be corrected and feedback should be given. This should occur as soon as possible after the assignments have been handed over.

20(B). Learning is a sequence of events that we can recall for a long period, and hence, it offers experience and the behavioural changes through learning are relatively permanent.
NON-FORMAL: Non-formal Education (NFE) is any organized educational activity that takes place outside the formal educational system.
Usually, it is flexible, learner-centred, contextualized, and uses a participatory approach.
There is no specific target group for NFE; it could be kids, youth, or adults.
It is life-oriented as it is not limited to schooling.

21(D). Personality is all that a person is. It is the totality of one's behavior towards one's own self as well as others.
- Personality includes everything about the person, his/her physical, emotional, social, mental, and spiritual make-up.
- It refers to the different aspects of a person's character such as his/her interest, behavior, cognition, etc.

22(D). Motivation is usually defined as an internal state that arouses, directs, and maintains behavior.
Intrinsic motivation
- Intrinsic motivation is the natural human tendency to seek out and conquer challenges as we pursue personal interests and exercise our capabilities.
- When we are intrinsically motivated, we satisfied Spenser studies chemistry outside school simply because he loves learning about chemistry; no one makes him do it.
- Intrinsic motivation is associated with many positive outcomes in school such as academic achievement, creativity, reading comprehension and enjoyment, and using deep learning strategies.

23(C). Socialization is a process by which an individual becomes a member of a society through a mechanism of interaction. Its purpose is to prepare individuals for future roles.
- Socialization is a process of acquiring values, beliefs, and expectations.
- Socialization is a combination of personality development and cultural development.
- Socialization is a life-long process that continues throughout life from birth to adulthood.

24(D). A teacher do to develop spirit of labour in students ,Give opportunities to students to do labour often. In the present study, teachers have been asked what their goals are with regard to the development of values related to labour in their students. It shows which values related to labour teachers wish to develop in their students: which labour identity they want to construct in their students. The study focuses on the role of teachers in education: on their opinion about the pedagogical task of education.

25(C). Work education is considered purposeful and meaningful physical labor, which is organized as the inherent part of the educational process. It is deemed as the production of meaningful material and community service, in which the children share the experience of contentment and pleasure. Work education emphasizes including knowledge, understanding, practical skills in educational activities.

26(B). Electra Complex is defined as when a girl, aged between 3 -6 years, becoming subconscious sexually attached to her father but increasingly hostile toward her mother. It is first introduced by Carl Jung.

27(C). National Education Policy-

"National Education Policy is an ambitious and futuristic policy that ensures opportunities for children to hone their talents by fixing the lacunae in the education system".

- National Education Policy 10+2 system is to be replaced by a four-stage 5+3+3+4 structure.
- NEP 2020 is the third education in the history of independent India after the ~~policy of 1968 and the second policy of~~

can learn to implement the acquired knowledge and skills in their practical life.

- National Education Policy emphasis on a skill like analysis, critical thinking, and vocational subjects will diversify their learning.
- Students will be given increased flexibility and choice of subjects to study.

28(C). Aids used by the teacher to facilitate the teaching-learning process is known as teaching material/teaching-learning materials or teaching aids.

- It can be made and used by both students and teachers.
- The appropriate use of teaching material in a classroom makes the learning relatively permanent.
- It should be noted that teaching material should be used by the teachers based on the objectives of the lesson.
- The most commonly used teaching-learning materials in the classrooms are graphs, models, charts, flashcards, number cards and alphabet cards.
- Teaching materials can be classified into audio -aids, visual aids and audio-visual aids.
- Thus, we can conclude that graphs, numbers and alphabet cards and flashcards are those teaching-learning materials that are prepared by teachers and students in most schools.

29(D). Social cognitive theory is basically a social leaning theory based on the ideas that people learn by watching what others do and that human thought processes are central to understanding personality.

30(D). The term 'development' refers to qualitative changes in an individual such as a change in personality or other mental and emotional aspects. However, very often

growth and development are used interchangeably. The process of development continues even after the individual has attained physical maturity (growth). The individual is continuously changing as he/she interacts with the environment.

Development is governed by certain principles which apply to all individuals. Let us learn about these principles in this section. The various principles of development are:

The development follows a fixed pattern/sequence: Each child may have a different rate of development. However, the development of all human beings follows a similar pattern, similar sequence, or direction. Sequential pattern of development can be seen in two directions:

- Cephalo-caudal sequence: means that

could catch hold of objects, sit, crawl and later she could stand and walk.

- Proximodistal sequence: means that the development proceeds from the central part of the body towards the peripheries. In this sequence, the spinal cord of the individual develops first and then outward.

Hence, we can conclude that in the cephalo-caudal and the proximodistal principle of development, the child develops in sequence and follows two tends.

31(C). To really bring empowerment, women should be aware of their rights. Not only domestic and family responsibilities but also women should play an active and positive role in every field. They should also know the happenings around them and in the country.

32(D). Women empowerment has this power to change a lot in society and the country. She can deal with any problem in society better than men. She can understand well the loss of overpopulation for the country and the family.

33(A). Influence: The power to have an effect on people or things, or a person or thing that is able to do this

Impotence: Lack of power to change or improve a situation

34(D). "The" is missing before the superlative adjective "best" in part d of the sentence.

35(A). Through women empowerment, it is possible that a country with female-male equality of a strong economy can be replaced with a country with male influence.

36(B). The marked option is adjective which is used to qualify a noun or a pronoun.

the use of shadow.

41(B). In the above line, the poet is curious to observe how the shadow keeps changing his shape. The poet observes that sometimes, the shadow becomes taller than him like a huge rubber ball.

According to the above lines it can be deduced that the shadow becomes taller than him.

42(B). According to the above lines it can be deduced that adjective 'slow' does not apply to the shadow. It applies to the children.

43(A). 'Coward' means a person who is not brave and is too eager to avoid danger, difficulty, or pain, a person who is easily frightened.

'Wimp' means a person who is not strong, brave, or confident.

44(C). 'Simile' is a comparison between two unlike things using the words "like" or "as". It is used to compare an object or a person with something else to make the description more vivid and clear.

Similarly in the given expression ' He is very, very like me', 'Simile' is the figure of speech used as a child is comparing his shadow with himself using the word 'like'.

45(B). 'Alliteration' is the series of words which commence with the same letter. Alliteration consists of the repetition of a sound or of a letter at the beginning of two or more words.

46(A). All of the skills, such as reading, writing, speaking, and listening, are built on vocabulary. This demonstrates the importance of learning new vocabulary. Knowing a word's meaning as well as how the word blends into different contexts are referred to as vocabulary awareness. Vocabulary is learned inadvertently by

37(B). Women empowerment has this power to change a lot in society and the country. She can deal with any problem in society better than men. She can understand well the loss of overpopulation for the country and the family.

38(B). Prepositions are commonly used to show a relationship in space or time or a logical relationship between two or more people, places or things.

They are most commonly followed by a noun phrase or pronoun

39(C). Disparity means a noticeable and usually significant difference or dissimilarity; lack of similarity or equality. There is great disparity between the amount of work that I do and what I get paid for it.

indirect word experience and consciously through explicit instruction in specific topics.

47(B). Constructivism is a view of learning based on the belief that knowledge isn't a thing that can be simply given by the teacher. Constructivism is a theory based on observation and scientific study about how people learn. It says that people construct their understanding and knowledge of the world, through experiencing things and reflecting on those experiences.

Constructivist classrooms are structured in such a way that learners are immersed in experiences within which they may engage in action, imagination, invention, interaction, and personal reflection.

In language learning, constructivism is a language theory to help the students in a contribution to the education field. So, for the constructive classroom, language learning should be based on the learners' previous knowledge.

48(D). Pedagogy refers to the set of principles that influence the approaches to the teaching-learning process. It consists of a learning environment, teaching-learning arrangements, methods, general educational principles, etc.

- In Language pedagogy, a learner learns about various methods and approaches to learning language, tools, and techniques. It lets the learner know about skills required to learn a language, that is, listening, speaking, reading, and writing.

49(C). Knowledge is often considered synonymous with terms like familiarity, understanding, wisdom, education, awareness, etc. Knowledge can be expressed in the form of data, scientific formulae, product specifications, manuals, universal principles, and so forth.

50(A). Grammar is the backbone of any language. It is the womb that gives birth to sentences. These sentences are fertilized using grammar to form correct and appropriate speech.

- Grammar is defined as a theory of language. We consider language as rule-governed behavior, relating to sounds, word formation, and structure. Here grammar constitutes a subset of rules relating to morphology and syntax.

51(D). Comprehensible input' refers to using language that children are capable of understanding, and at the same time holds challenges for them. An important part of making this language comprehensible is providing it in natural, communicative situations that are meaningful to children and this will help children in meeting the challenge.

52(C). According to Willis, who supported the idea that TBLT is a learner-centred approach, "A Task can be defined as an activity where the target language is used by the learner for a communicative purpose in order to achieve an outcome".

- Task-based language teaching (TBLT), also known as task-based instruction (TBI), focuses on the use of authentic language and on asking students to do meaningful tasks using the target language.

53(B). During the teaching-learning process, you have to locate and identify the areas where the learner commits mistakes. It is the crucial stage of the teaching-learning process where you have to

54(D). Teaching Learning Material (TLM), also known as instructional aids, facilitate a teacher in achieving the learning objectives formulated by her/him before teaching-learning activities start. For example, newspaper, dictionary, sticker, etc. Accurate and realistic teaching-learning material is the one which:

- Facilitates the learning process in a meaningful and productive way.
- Makes learning more interesting and enliven by bringing the class to real-life.
- Encourages healthy classroom interaction and helps in meeting individual differences.

55(C). Speaking skills have two major components. First, there are motor perceptive skills. These are the means of perceiving, recalling, and articulating in the correct order the sounds and structure of a language. Generally, these are developed at the primary level where learners are put through the various look and say exercises, or pattern practice.

Ways of Assessing Speaking Skills: Assessing speaking skills is a complex task for a teacher. The teacher has to be more creative and vigilant in assessing speaking skills. The ways of assessing speaking skills as follows:

- Discussion: Students are asked to read a short text and make points for discussion. This would offer the students to get a deep understanding of the text which is helpful in speaking.
- The teacher can make the groups of learners and learners are asked to read the text by taking turns.
- Read aloud Task: The teacher can record the speaking of the learner and listen to a recording and evaluate the students in a series of phonological factors and fluency.
- Interactive Speaking Strategy: The Teacher can use an interactive speaking strategy, in which the student and teacher having the face to face conversation,
- Role-Play is also another way to assess the speaking skills of students while he/she producing dialogues in play.
- Story-Telling: Students are asked to tell a story of a new of something they heard or read.
- Oral Presentation: The teacher can use oral presentations for assessing the speaking skills of students.

56(A). English in India: It's Status: The English language is used in satisfying our practical need for social mobility, opportunity, power, and communication on the other hand.

57(C). If the students make mistakes in correct them while re-pronouncing the same spelling.

Ways to Overcome committing mistakes in spelling:

- The teacher should provide the etymology of each word.
- Teacher should compare the written reproduction vocabulary with the recognition vocabulary.
- Teachers should compare recognition and reproduction vocabulary to find out the common words.
- Use mnemonics to learn the spelling.
- Students should divide the words into chunks and re-pronounce it and combined it, to make a proper spell out.

58(B). India is a multi-lingual country with numerous languages and dialects. There are approximately 1652 languages and dialects that belong to the five different language families in the country. Around 40 languages are used as a medium of instruction in schools and universities and the English language is one of them.

59(B). A question is a sentence that seeks an answer for information collection, tests, and research. Right questions produce accurate responses and aids in collecting actionable quantitative and qualitative data.

Higher-Order Questions:

Higher-order questions are those that the students cannot answer just by simple recollection or by reading the information "verbatim" from the text.

Higher-order questions put advanced cognitive demand on students. For example, asking students about their previous school, its atmosphere, its strength and weaknesses etc.

They encourage students to think beyond literal questions. Higher-order questions promote critical thinking skills because these types of questions expect students to apply, analyze, synthesize, and evaluate information instead of simply recalling facts.

Lower-Order Questions:

Lower order questions are those that require "brief thought" and a basic amount of understanding of an already learned subject or area.

These kinds of questions are meant to encourage students to recall or remember basic information.

60(D). A multilingual classroom is a classroom with learners having more than one language including learners from different backgrounds.

61(C). The specific aims of mathematics education help to design suitable methods for planning effective classroom learning

achievable, etc. The following are some of the specific aims of mathematics education:
- To ensure a good start for the students in learning mathematics.
- To give clarity on the fundamental concepts and processes of the subject. To create love, faith, and interest in learning mathematics.
- To develop in them a taste and confidence in mathematics.
- To develop an appreciation for accuracy.
- To acquaint them with the relation of mathematics with their present as well as future life.
- To see aesthetics in mathematics.
- To develop in them the habits like regularity, practice, patience, self-reliance, and hard work.
- To apply mathematics in other subjects.
- To acquaint them with mathematical language and symbolism.
- To prepare them for the learning of mathematics of higher classes.
- To prepare them for mathematical exhibitions.
- Therefore, we conclude that the above points are specific aims of mathematics.

62(B). Mathematics is a study of patterns, numbers, geometrical objects, data, and information. It deals with data analysis, integration of various fields of knowledge, deductive and inductive reasoning, and generalizations.
- The teaching of mathematics should be done in the way, in which a student learns the best i.e., following the child-centered approach by engaging students actively in the learning process.
- The teacher should focus more on providing practical exercises and abstract knowledge to students to foster their individualized discovery-oriented learning.

63(B). The basic structure of mathematics includes arithmetic, algebra, geometry, and trigonometry that helps in learning the techniques to handle abstractions and structures.
- The teaching of mathematics must develop attitudes to think, reason, analyze, and articulate logically.
- The nature of mathematics highly influences the nature of the teaching-learning process in mathematics.

64(A). Mathematics is a subject matter of complex abstractions that mainly deals with patterns, shapes, sizes, figures, and data analysis. It is based on practical usability in all aspects of life.

65(A). The teaching and learning of mathematics have always been a major concern in education. The National Policy

teaching heavily depended upon rote learning which have been replaced by methods that depend upon discovery and problem-solving approaches.
- The teacher should use effective teaching methods of mathematics so that individualized discovery-oriented (or problem-solving) learning could be fostered.

66(D). Mathematics focuses on developing an understanding of numbers, shapes, and patterns by using the techniques of problem-solving and logical reasoning.
- The mathematical curriculum treats mathematics both as a tool for practical utility as well as a discipline that develops reasoning and analytical abilities.

67(C). Throughout the centuries, mathematics has been recognised as one of the central strands of human intellectual activity. From the very beginning, mathematics has been a living and growing intellectual pursuit. It has its roots in everyday activities and forms the basic structure of our highly advanced technological developments. Math's has grown largely as a result of
- social needs, as shown in everyday life, commerce, science and technology
- the intellectual need to connect together existing mathematics into a single logical framework or proof structure

Thus, the word mathematics can be used in two distinct and different senses:
- the truths that are discovered
- the methods used to discover truths

Therefore, we conclude that mathematics can be used in both distinct and different senses.

68(B). Van Hiele was famous for his

theory that describes how students learn geometry, he was born in 1909 and died November 1, 2010. It postulates five levels of geometric thinking.

69(D). Concept:

Divisibility of 11 = add digits placed on even place – add digits on odd place = 0 or 11

Divisibility of 9 = sum of all digits must be divisible by 9

Calculation:

Digits of even place = 7 + 8 + 6 = 21

Digits on odd place = 3 + A + A = 3 + 2A

Now subtract both the equations

$\Rightarrow 21 - 3 - 2A$

$\Rightarrow 18 = 2A$

$\Rightarrow A = 9$

68X is divisible by 9

6 + 8 + X

14 + X = 18

of p/q where q is not equal to zero. Any fraction with non-zero denominators is a rational number. Some of the examples of rational numbers are $\frac{1}{2}$, $\frac{1}{5}$, $\frac{3}{4}$, and so on.

The number "0" is also a rational number, as we can represent it in many forms such as $\frac{0}{1}$, etc.

You can say 5.1 is a rational number lying between 5 and 7.

More examples are $5.01, 5.001, 5.0001, 5.00001$, and so forth.

There is no quota on the number of decimal places and thus the combination of numbers in these decimal places. As long as the number starts with 5 and has a definite end when expressed in decimals, this is an example of rational numbers.

So,

The number of rational numbers between 5 and 7 is infinite

71(A). Given:

$24312k$ is divisible by 6

As we know that used:

If a number is even or a number whose last digit is an even number i.e. $2, 4, 6, 8$ including 0 ,it is always completely divisible by 2

a number is completely divisible by 3 if the sum of its digits is divisible by 3.

Now:

For divisible by 6 it must be divisible by both 2 and 3

$24312k$ must be divisible by both 2 and 3

Now, possible values of $k = 0, 2, 4, 6, 8$

$2 + 4 + 3 + 1 + 2 + 0 = 12$ divisible by 3

$2 + 4 + 3 + 1 + 2 + 2 = 14$ not divisible by 3

$2 + 4 + 3 + 1 + 2 + 4 = 16$ not divisible by 3

$2 + 4 + 3 + 1 + 2 + 6 = 18$ divisible by 3

$2 + 4 + 3 + 1 + 2 + 8 = 20$ not divisible by 3

72(A). $x^2 - 4x + 1 = 0$
Dividing the above equation by x we get,
$= x - 4 + \frac{1}{x} = 0$
$= x + \frac{1}{x} = 4 \ldots (1)$
Cubing equation,
$\left(x + \frac{1}{x}\right)^3 = (4)^3$
$\Rightarrow x^3 + \frac{1}{x^3} + 3x\frac{1}{x}\left(x + \frac{1}{x}\right) = 64$
$\Rightarrow x^3 + \frac{1}{x^3} + 3(4) = 64$
$\Rightarrow x^3 + \frac{1}{x^3} = 64 - 12$
$\Rightarrow x^3 + \frac{1}{x^3} = 52$
Now, squaring the above equation,
$\left(x^3 + \frac{1}{x^3}\right)^2 = x^6 + \frac{1}{x^6} + 2 \times x^3 \times \frac{1}{x^3}$
$\Rightarrow (52)^2 = x^6 + \frac{1}{x^6} + 2$
$\Rightarrow x^6 + \frac{1}{x^6} = 2704 - 2 = 2702$

Calculation:
$a^3 - b^3 = (a - b)^3 + 3ab(a - b)$
$\Rightarrow a^3 - b^3 = 3^3 + 3 \times 70 \times 3$
$\Rightarrow a^3 - b^3 = 27 + 630$
$\therefore a^3 - b^3 = 657$

74(A). Given:
$x + \frac{1}{x} = 4$
By squaring,
$\Rightarrow x^2 + \frac{1}{x^2} + 2 = 16$
$\Rightarrow x^2 + \frac{1}{x^2} = 14$
By squaring again,
$\Rightarrow x^4 + \frac{1}{x^4} + 2 = 196$
$\Rightarrow x^4 + \frac{1}{x^4} = 196 - 2 = 194$

75(B). Given,
$\angle A, \angle B$ and $\angle C$ are three angles of a triangle
$\frac{\angle A}{4} + \frac{\angle B}{4} + \frac{\angle C}{5} = 41°$
Formula:
Sum of all three angles of a triangle is $180°$.
$\frac{\angle A}{4} + \frac{\angle B}{4} + \frac{\angle C}{5} = 41°$
$\Rightarrow \frac{(5\angle A + 5\angle B + 4\angle C)}{20} = 41°$
$\Rightarrow \frac{(\angle A + 4/A + \angle B + 4/B + 4\angle C)}{20} = 41°$
$\Rightarrow \frac{(\angle A + \angle B + 4/A + 4/B + 4\angle C)}{20} = 41°$
$\Rightarrow \angle A + \angle B + 4(\angle A + \angle B + \angle C) = 41° \times 20$
$\Rightarrow \angle A + \angle B + 4 \times 180° = 820°$
$\Rightarrow \angle A + \angle B = 820° - 720°$
$\Rightarrow \angle A + \angle B = 100°$

76(B). Given:
$LC = 6, CD = 11, LB = 4$ and $AB = x$
Formula used:
$LC \times LD = LB \times AL$
According to the question
$LC \times LD = LB \times AL$
$6 \times (6 + 11) = 4 \times (4 + x)$
$\Rightarrow 4 + x = \frac{51}{2}$

$\Rightarrow 4 + x = 25.5$
$\Rightarrow x = AB = 21.5$

77(A). Given:
$\angle BAD = 62°$
$\angle BDC = 119°$
$\angle CBD = 18°$
Sum of all the angles made at a straight line is $180°$
Sum of all the angles of a triangle makes $180°$
Let the $\angle ABD$ be x.
Sum of angles at a straight line $= 180°$
$\Rightarrow \angle BDC + \angle BDA = 180°$
$\Rightarrow \angle BDA = 180° - 119°$
$\Rightarrow \angle BDA = 61°$
Sum of all the angles of $\triangle ABD$,
$\Rightarrow \angle BAD + \angle BDA + \angle ABD = 180°$
$\Rightarrow 62° + 61° + \angle ABD = 180°$
$\Rightarrow \angle ABD = 180° - 123°$

the square
$\Rightarrow 2\pi r = 4a$
$\Rightarrow 2\pi r = 4 \times 11$
$\Rightarrow 2 \times \frac{22}{7} \times r = 44$
$\Rightarrow r = 7$ cm
Area of the circle $= \pi r^2$
$\Rightarrow \frac{22}{7} \times 7 \times 7 = 154$ cm^2
$\therefore$ Area of circle is 154 cm^2.

79(D). Given:
Height of cone $= 15$ cm
Radius of cone $= 7$ cm
We know that:
Volume of cone $= \frac{1}{3}\pi r^2$ h
$= \frac{1}{3} \times \frac{22}{7} \times 7 \times 7 \times 15$
$= 22 \times 7 \times 5$
$= 770$ cm^3

80(A). According to the question,
Cost price of 10 oranges = Rs 3
$\Rightarrow$ Cost price of 1 orange = Rs $\frac{3}{10}$ = Rs 0.3
Selling price of 8 oranges = Rs 3
$\Rightarrow$ Selling price of 1 orange = Rs $\frac{3}{10}$ = Rs 0.375
$\Rightarrow$ Gain percent
$= \left[\frac{(\text{selling price} - cost \text{ price})}{cost \text{ price}}\right] \times 100$
$\Rightarrow$ Gain percent
$= \frac{(0.375 - 0.3)}{0.3} \times 100\% = 25\%$

81(A). Average of A, B, C, D and E is 40 years.
So, $\frac{A + B + C + D + E}{5} = 40$
$A + B + C + D + E = 200$
$A + B = 70$
$C + D = 84$
$E = 200 - 70 - 84$
$= 200 - 154$
$= 46$

82(D). Given:

The helicopter covers a certain distance at a speed of 180 km/h in 6 hours.
We know that distance covered = speed × time
The helicopter covers a certain distance at a speed of 180 km/h in 6 hours.
Total distance = 180 × 6 = 1080 km
Now, the helicopter needs to cover the same distance in $\frac{10}{3}$ hours.
Then the speed will be $= \left(1080 \div \frac{10}{3}\right)$
$\Rightarrow \left(1080 \times \frac{3}{10}\right) = 324$
$\therefore$ It has to travel at 324 km/hour speed.

83(A). Given,
The age of Seema 18 years after her parent's marriage be 5k years
Therefore,
Age of Seema at golden anniversary of her parents   (5k + 32)

$\Rightarrow 21 \times 5k = 5(5k + 32)$
$\Rightarrow 105k = 25k + 160$
$\Rightarrow 105k - 25k = 160$
$\Rightarrow 80k = 160$
$\Rightarrow k = \frac{160}{80}$
$\Rightarrow k = 2$
Now,
Age of seema = 5k
$= 5 \times 2$
$= 10$
So, Seema's age was 10, when her parents had completed 18 years of marriage.
So, Seema was born 8 years after her parent's marriage.

84(C). Given:
The sum of two number positive number is 240 and their HCF is 15.
Calculation:
Let two positive number is 15x and 15y where x and y should be coprime that means x and y should have HCH as 1.
According to the question:
The sum of the number is
$\Rightarrow 15x + 15y = 240$
$\Rightarrow x + y = 16$
Now, we have to find the number of pair in which sum of the two number is 16 but no common factor between them, such pair is
$\Rightarrow (1, 15) (3, 13) (5, 11) (7, 9)$
$\therefore$ Total possible pairs is 4.

85(C). Now:
$[(7 \times 9) + (3 \times 8) + 3] \div [(9 \times 4) + (72 \div 8)]$
$\Rightarrow [(7 \times 9) + (3 \times 8) + 3] \div [(9 \times 4) + 9]$
$\Rightarrow [(7 \times 9) + (3 \times 8) + 3] \div (36 + 9)$
$\Rightarrow [(7 \times 9) + (3 \times 8) + 3] \div 45$
$\Rightarrow [63 + (3 \times 8) + 3] \div 45$
$\Rightarrow [63 + (24 + 3)] \div 45$
$\Rightarrow (63 + 27) \div 45$
$\Rightarrow 90 \div 45$
$\Rightarrow 2$

86(D). Given:
Two samples of sizes $n_1 = 30$ and $n_2 = 20$ have means as 55 and 60 and variances as $S_1^2 = 16$ and $S_2^2 = 25$ respectively To Find:
S.D. of the combined sample of size 50

$$x = \sqrt{\frac{n_1 S_1^2 + n_2 S_2^2}{n_1 + n_2}}$$
$$= \sqrt{\frac{30 \times 16 + 20 \times 25}{30 + 20}}$$
$$= \frac{\sqrt{480 + 500}}{50}$$
$$= \sqrt{\frac{980}{50}}$$
$$= \sqrt{19.6}$$
$$= 4.43$$

87(C). Given,
Mean of 13 numbers is 24.
Now 3 added to each number

$$\text{Mean} = \frac{\text{Total of observation}}{}$$

Now 3 is added to all 13 numbers.
$\Rightarrow$ New total = 312 + 13(3)
$\Rightarrow$ New total = 312 + 39
$\Rightarrow$ New total = 351

New mean $= \frac{351}{13}$

$\Rightarrow$ New mean = 27
$\therefore$ The new mean will be 27.

88(C). Concept:
$$\text{Mean} = \frac{\text{Total sum of all values}}{\text{Number of values}}$$
Calculations:
Sum of the given data
$= a + b + a + a + b + a + b + c + a + b + a + c + a + b + a$
$\Rightarrow 8a + 5b + 2c$
Number of values $= 15$
$$\text{Mean} = \frac{(8a + 5b + 2c)}{15}$$

89(B). The area of a shape or any object is the space enclosed by it on a plane surface. For example, the area of a house will be the space occupied by it over a piece of land.
The teacher should use real-life objects to teach them the concept of "area" and "perimeter" as learning becomes more lively, purposeful, and interesting when real-life examples or objects are used in teaching.
By using real-life objects or examples, the children can become aware of the application of mathematical concepts in the real world and also they get to know the relevancy of mathematical knowledge with respect to their implications in real life.
A teacher can compare the area of any figure with the help of different objects like palm, notebook etc so that the students can understand the concept meaningfully.
Directly introducing the formulae of areas will lead the child to confusion and he will find the topic boring.
Thus, it is concluded that to introduce the concept of area, a teacher can start with comparing the area of any figure with the help of different object like palm, leaf, note book etc.

90(D). **Science** is dynamic, expanding body of knowledge covering ever-new domains of experience. It is an organized system of knowledge that is based on inquiry born out of natural curiosity, logical reasoning, and experimentation.
- It is this organized knowledge with an inquiry, logical reasoning, and experimentation as its central themes, that we call science. Science may rightly be said to be a domain of inquiry.

Nature of science:
- Science comes out from people and it can not be guaranteed if people are not biased, hence, it can not be surely said that scientists are totally objective in their work.
- Science does not rely on belief, rather it is dependent on facts.
- Science is exploited by people, hence it is social in nature.
- One of the most important characteristics of science is that even the most established theories can be modified, or even abandoned if new experimental results do not fit into the existing theories.

Thus, the statement ' science is social in nature' best describes the nature of science.

91(B). **Science** as a discipline has its unique perspective. Science is not limited to observation, experimentation, and analysis only rather it is a way of life. Science is an expanding body of knowledge through the process of inquiry.

Nature of Science:
- Science is socially and culturally embedded.
- Science is inferential, imaginative, and creative. It is subjective and theory-laden.
- Science is empirical (based on or derived from developed observation of the natural world).
- Science is not merely a collection of evidence of happenings rather it attempts to understand happening through analysis, testing, and verification.
- The value of science comes from its economical and political importance, but science seeks the truth by observing important values: a scientist must be honest, modest, always critical, rejecting any dogmatism and any fraud, but also creative, imaginative, and able to work collectively.
- The main values of science to be rigorous, rational, honest , critical , creative, can explain how science aims as far as possible at the truth (even if the scientific knowledge is always under construction) but it is impossible to say that science is the only truth in our world.

Thus, it is concluded that Reality is the value of science for nature.

92(A). NCF-2005 and Position Paper of National Focus Group on Teaching of Science (2006) have proposed 6 criteria for the validity of a science curriculum i.e. cognitive, content, process, historical, environmental, and ethical. On this basis, the following general aims of science education have been conceptualized:
Science education should enable the learner to:
- know the facts and principles of science and its applications, consistent with the stage of cognitive development,
- develop a historical and developmental perspective of science and to enable her to view science as a social enterprise,
- relate to the environment (natural environment, artifacts, and people), local as well as global, and appreciate the issues at the interface of science, technology, and society,
- acquire the requisite theoretical knowledge and practical technical skills to enter the world of work,
- nurture the natural curiosity, aesthetic sense, and creativity in science and Science Teaching-Learning technology,
- imbibe the values of honesty, integrity, cooperation, concern for life and preservation of the environment, and
- cultivate 'scientific temper'-objectivity, critical thinking, and freedom from fear and prejudice

Thus, we can conclude that the aim of teaching science at the secondary level is to know about the facts and principles of science and its applications.

93(D). The teaching method is a way to put theory into practice. The process of interpreting the world of knowledge to a pupil's mind is called the method of teaching.
- It helps a teacher to understand "what to teach", "how to teach", "how to approach it".
- It includes both strategies and techniques of teaching and involves the choice of what is to be taught.
- Science refers to the development of thinking in a specific way that involves scientific temper, scientific inquiry, and a sense of humanity.
- The main aim of teaching science is to develop the scientific attitude among learners and to foster their individual discovery.
- The conventional way of giving lectures

will not help that much but when using in combination with demonstration it brings concreteness into the classroom and also enables a child to think scientifically.

94(D). Science r efers to the study of the structure and behavior of physical and natural things through observation and experimentation. In other words, science is a classified knowledge gained from a systematic study of the behavior of nature.

- The science curriculum is organized at different levels so that it suits the cognitive levels of the learner at that stage.
- Understanding science at the upper primary stage aims at enhancing children's comprehension of scientific concepts and also acquiring basic

the experiments

- Observing things closely, recording observations
- Plotting graphs and drawing from what they observe
- Engaging learners in group discussions, hands-on activities, etc

95(D). Science refers to the study of structure and behaviour of the physical and natural things through observation and experimentation. In other words, science is a classified knowledge gained from a systematic study of the behaviour of nature.

- Science includes study of the physical and biological world around us through several approaches like observation, experimenting, inference etc. while technology involves application of that scientific knowledge for practical purposes.

Nature of science:

- Opinion or preferences, to be scientifically acknowledged, must be verified and cross checked by fact, experiment and data.
- Science aims for measurable results through testing and analysis as every conclusion in science is based upon some evidence or empirical data.
- Science is a systematic and logical approach to discover how things in the universe work as science always try to discover the scientific theory behind every physical phenomena of the universe.
- The process of science is designed to challenge ideas through research as science, with the help of laboratory research, conclusive evidence and empirical data, tries to prove or disprove a hypothesis.
- Science promotes skepticism which is a matter of questioning, seeking, inquiring the doubt. While performing any

scientific research and inquiry skepticism helps scientists to remain objective.

- Science is an interdisciplinary subject of knowledge which means different fields of study. For example, if you read a science fiction novel, you are covering two disciplines here, literature and science.

Thus, it could be concluded that the statement ' Science is merely based upon opinion or preferences, not on facts and experiments ' is not true about science.

96(D). In order to incorporate Piaget's suggestions, a teacher must give lots of manipulative to students to work with as:

- Piaget, a Swiss psychologist, emphasizes that children are curious beings and little scientists who learn through by manipulating it. It is a material that is used to provide concrete experience to learners.

97(B). The scientific method has emerged as the predominant, universally accepted approach to acquiring knowledge. As against religious faith, magic, and superstition, the scientific method is a way of arriving at an empirical, impartial, and reliable representation of the world.

Following is the correct sequence and steps of learning through the scientific method:-

- Observation and description of the phenomenon is the first step. It is necessary to first record the present data so that there is a benchmark to compare with.
- Reflection:- Formulation of a hypothesis to explain the phenomenon. In the classical scientific method of which physics is the paradigmatic example, it takes the form of a causal mechanism or mathematical relation. It is a stage where a person reflects his thought process in the form of research to analyze the observed data to think of a fruitful conclusion.
- Classification:- Using the hypothesis to predict the existence of other phenomena or the results of new observations and classifying them into categories to make subgroups of common types of studies.
- Evaluation: - Performance of experiments to test the hypothesis by several impendent researchers. If all the researchers come to the same results, then the hypothesis will become a theory or law. Experimental verification is the key to the success of the scientific method. Such type of research is the most common evaluation process of any new concept developed through the scientific method.

Therefore, it is concluded that observation-reflection-classification-evaluation is the correct sequence and steps of learning through the scientific method.

98(B). There are different kinds of teaching-learning methods in a fashion which makes learning a fruitful process . Teacher adopts any method according to the needs and interests of students.

- Teaching methods include problem-solving, lecture, inductive, deductive, analytic, synthetic, heuristic and discovery method.

Inductive Method:

The inductive approach is based on the process of induction. It is a method of constructing a formula with the help of a sufficient number of concrete examples .

Induction means to provide a universal Example: Square of an odd number is odd and the square of an even number is even.

Inductive approach proceeds from-

- Particular to general
- Known to unknown
- Simple to complex
- Example to formula

Thus, it could be concluded that the inductive method is used for constructing a concept with the help of a sufficient number of concrete examples.

99(A). CONCEPT:

- Wave: The continuous transfer of energy by vibrating the medium of propagation is called wave.
- Sound waves, light waves, waves formed due to stretched string are some examples of waves.
- Longitudinal wave: The wave in which the particles in medium vibrates to and fro motion along the line of propagation of wave is called longitudinal wave.
- Transverse wave: The wave in which the particles in medium vibrates along the perpendicular axis of propagation of wave is called transverse wave.
- Propagation of sound wave: Sound waves travels in air or any medium by vibrating the air particles along the direction of its motion.
- Sound waves creates regular compression (higher density area) and rarefaction (lower density area) along the wave of its propagation.

From the above concept, it is clear that sound is a longitudinal wave.

100(D). CONCEPT:

Magnet: An object which is capable of producing a magnetic field and attracting unlike poles and repelling like poles is called a magnet.

List of Properties of Magnet:

1. When a magnet is freely suspended, it

always points in a north-south direction.
2. Like magnetic poles (N-N and S-S) repel each other and unlike magnetic (N-S) poles attract each other.
3. A magnet attracts ferromagnetic materials like iron, cobalt, and nickel.
4. Magnetic poles always exist in pairs.
EXPLANATION:
Option (A): Magnet attracts all ferromagnetic materials like cobalt, iron, and nickel.
Option (B): A freely suspended magnet always points in a north-south direction.
Option (C): Like magnetic poles (N-N and S-S) repel each other and unlike magnetic (N-S) poles attract each other.
Option (D): Magnets are used for constructing magnetic needles and compass.

green tea (Camellia sinensis).
- It is consumed in Pakistan, Afghanistan, some Central Asian regions, and in northern India, especially in the Kashmir Valley.
- The tea is made to add a great fragrance by boiling green tea leaves.
- Saffron cultivated in Kashmir, cinnamon bark, cardamom pods, almonds and sometimes Kashmiri roses are added to it.
- Kashmiri Hindus have often referred to Mogul chai as kahwa.
- That means that this tea was introduced back then by the Mughal emperors in the valley.
- In Kashmir, the term Kahwah means "sweetened tea".
- The word also tends to be synonymous with the Turkish word for coffee (kahveh).
Thus, 'Kahwa' is popular in Kashmir.

102(B). The dish named undhiyu or upside down, in Gujrati.
The upside down here because the pot in which this food is made placed upside down.
undhiyu would be eaten with bajra rotis, freshly cooked on chulha.
The farmers of Gujrat are fond of these foods.

103(D). Vitamin A deficiency is the leading cause of blindness in children worldwide.
Deficiency of vitamin A is associated with significant morbidity and mortality from common childhood infections, and is the world's leading preventable cause of childhood blindness. Vitamin A deficiency also contributes to maternal mortality and other poor outcomes of pregnancy and lactation.

104(A). Vitamin B1 deficiency causes

Beriberi.
Beriberi is a deficiency of thiamin, more commonly known as vitamin B1. Your body needs thiamin to break down and digest the foods you eat, to keep your metabolism going, and help your muscles and nervous system do their jobs effectively. Beriberi can affect the cardiovascular system or central nervous system.

105(A). Saliva is a watery and usually somewhat frothy substance produced in the mouths of some animals, including humans.
Produced in salivary glands, saliva is 98% water, but it contains many important substances, including electrolytes, mucus, antibacterial compounds, and various enzymes.
The digestive functions of saliva include and dextrin.
Thus, digestion of food occurs within the mouth, even before the food reaches the stomach.
Saliva does not digest the proteins. fats and fibres.

106(C). Atomic number:
- The total number of protons in the nucleus of an atom gives us the atomic number of that atom. Hence, statement a is correct.
- It is represented with the letter 'Z.'
- All the atoms of a particular element have the same number of protons, and hence the same atomic number.
- Atoms of different elements have different atomic numbers.
- For example, all carbon atoms have an atomic number of 6, whereas all atoms of Oxygen have 8 protons in their nucleus.
Mass Number:
- The number of protons and neutrons combined give us the mass number of an atom. Hence, statement b is correct.
- It is represented using the letter 'A.'
- As both protons and neutrons are present in the nucleus of an atom, they are together called nucleons.
- For example, an atom of carbon has 6 protons and 6 neutrons. Thus, its mass number is 12.
- While the number of protons remains the same in all atoms of an element, the number of neutrons can vary. Thus, atoms of the same element can have different mass numbers, and these are called isotopes.
- The weight of an electron is almost negligible. Thus, the atomic mass of an atom is almost the same as its mass number.

107(A). Acids differ enormously in the

extent to which they dissociate into ions in aqueous solution. Some acids, such as hydrochloric and nitric acids, are strong electrolytes, completely dissociated into ions; these acids are known as strong acids.

108(B). Refraction is the bending of light rays after entering a medium where its speed is different. Due to refraction of light, when a ray of light passes from a rarer medium to a denser medium, bends towards the normal to the boundary between the two media. The amount of bending depends on the indices of refraction of the two media. Hence, when a ray of light from air enters a denser medium, it bends towards the normal.

109(B). Since the surface is frictionless, there would be no external force and hence no external impulse. Hence, linear velocity.

110(B). The most rapidly dwindling natural resource in the world is forest.
The most rapidly decreasing natural resource in the world is forest resource as humans are cutting the trees tremendously and causing deforestation.

111(B). The phenomenon responsible for twinkling of stars is refraction. Light from the stars has to come through a thick layer of atmosphere and also the density of atmosphere keeps on changing as gravitation increases so more dense layer of atmosphere will have greater refractive index and hence will bend light more. Since the physical condition of atmosphere is not constant and keeps on changing so the amount of star light entering our eye keeps on changing thus sometimes they appear bright while sometimes faint.

112(B). Energy flow and energy transformation in a living system follow Law of thermodynamics.
Law of themodynamics is applicable for all universe. So it will also applicable for a living system.

113(A). One of the complex characters of each living organism is the efficient manifestation of the happenings towards their surroundings or environment. Every living being is aware of their surroundings. They perceive their surroundings and store the happenings into their memory which is due to the developed nervous system.
The memory helps to make the decisions on the second occurrence of the same event.

114(A). Aluminium is metal and hence can be beaten into thin sheets.
So, aluminum foils can be made.
These foils are used in the wrapping of food and protect food from getting

contaminated.
Malleability is the property of the metal which makes it get formed as thin sheets.

115(B). CONCEPT:
- Newton's first law of motion: It is also called the law of inertia. Inertia is the ability of a body by virtue of which it opposes a change.
- According to Newton's first law of motion, an object will remain at rest or in uniform motion in a straight line unless acted upon by an external force.
- The inertia of rest: When a body is in rest, it will remain at rest until we apply an external force to move it. This property is called inertia of rest.
- The inertia of motion: When a body is in a uniform motion, it will remain in motion until we apply an external force

driver also was in motion and he is the inertia of motion.
- Due to the inertia of motion, the driver was thrown forward when the car stopped, as he still has a tendency to remain in motion.

116(B). Biogas is a mixture of inflammable gases (methane, SO_2, CO_2, etc)

produced by microbial activity that can be used as fuel.
- Cattle excreta (dung) is used as a raw material in the production of biogas.
- The biogas plant has a concrete tank (10-15 feet deep) that collects bio-wastes and dung slurry.
- An outlet distributes the produced gas to nearby homes.
- The spent slurry is removed through another outlet and used as fertiliser.
- The large-scale use of bio-waste and sewage material provides a safe and efficient method of waste disposal, as well as energy and manure.
- Biogas is used as a source of energy for cooking and lighting.

117(C). A plotting compass is placed near the south pole of a bar magnet. The pointer points in the direction of the south pole of the bar magnet. When you take the compass away from the bar magnet, it again points north.

118(A). When a straight conductor is carrying current there are circular magnetic field lines around it.
The Magnetic field lines around a straight conductor carrying current are concentric circles whose centres lie on the wire. The direction of magnetic field lines can be determined using Right-Hand Thumb Rule.

119(B). In a math class, a teacher follows a proper sequence in teaching which is usually practically followed in any classroom. This is known as classroom operations. It plays a major role in Mathematics learnings. Mathematics teachers use a variety of methods and techniques in his/her daily classroom teaching to make his/her teaching more interesting and creative. According to NCF, Mathematics should be taught in context. Hence, the best possible way to teach the concept of surface area and volume is to ask them to calculate the amount of paint required to paint their classroom.

should need to use innovative ideas to teach abstractions of mathematics.
The manipulative tools are used in the teaching of mathematics to clear the complex and abstract mathematical concepts and to arouse the interest of students while learning mathematics.

Child Development and Pedagogy

1. **Which one of the following statements best sums up the relationship between development and learning?**
   (a) Learning and development are synonymous terms.
   (b) Learning and development are inter-related in a complex manner.
   (c) Development is independent of learning.
   (d) Learning trails behind development.

   (b) Development is influenced by both heredity and environment
   (c) Development is modifiable
   (d) Development is governed and determined by culture alone

3. **For optimum development of an individual:**
   (a) Only heredity is essential
   (b) Both heredity and environment are essential
   (c) Only environment is essential
   (d) Neither heredity nor environment is essential

4. **Process of primary socialisation begins from ______.**
   (a) infancy   (b) childhood
   (c) adolescence (d) adulthood

5. **According to Piaget the child is able to apply logical thoughts to all classes of problems, this development occurs in which of the following periods?**
   (a) The sensory motor period
   (b) The pre-operational period
   (c) The formal operational period
   (d) The concrete operational period

6. **Which of the following is a sub-stage in Kohlberg's 'conventional state's of Moral Development?**
   (a) Instrumental purpose and exchange
   (b) Universal ethical principles
   (c) Morality of contract, rights and law
   (d) Social concern and conscience

7. **Child centered system of education lays major emphasis on:**

   (a) Learning without burden
   (b) Incidental learning and self expression
   (c) Activity based learning
   (d) Learning under free environment

8. **Gardner's Multiple Intelligences Theory support the idea that:**
   (a) Most students can be considered "intelligent" in some way
   (b) Intelligence changes multiple times across the life span
   (c) Creative individuals are considered to be more intelligent
   (d) Intelligence can be multiplied

   must posses with ________.
   (a) Linguisitc Intelligence
   (b) Body-kinesthetic Intelligence
   (c) Musical Intelligence
   (d) Inter-personal Intelligence

10. **The cause of downfall of a particular language is:**
    (a) Acceptance of language other than the native language
    (b) Narrow thinking
    (c) Intolerance
    (d) Both (B) and (C)

11. **Gender is a/an:**
    (a) Social Construct
    (b) Biological Determinant
    (c) Economic Concept
    (d) Psychological Entity

12. **Which of the following is NOT an effective strategy to cater to individual differences in the class?**
    (a) Reflect on one's verbal and non-verbal communication
    (b) Recognize and respect differences
    (c) Use diverse pedagogical strategies
    (d) Identify deficits in students and correct them

13. **Which one of the following is not a social-personal quality assessed under Continuous and Comprehensive Evaluation (CCE)?**
    (a) Cleanliness   (b) Painting
    (c) Co-operation (d) Discipline

14. **In absolute grading, the reference point for an assessment of students performance happens to be a:**

    (a) Pre-determined standard
    (b) Standard determined on the basis of a normal probability curve
    (c) Standard determined on the basis, of dividing the equal percentage of cases from top to bottom
    (d) Standard determined on the basis of arbitrarily chosen percentages of cases for various grading groups

15. **A teacher has to enhance the readiness level of his students. Which will be the best way to do so?**
    (a) By organizing a creational
    (c) By story telling method
    (d) By giving monitoring to one of the student of the class

16. **Hearing impaired children exhibit:**
    (a) Barriers in communication by language
    (b) Barriers in moving around
    (c) Barriers in individuals self-care skills
    (d) Barriers in tactile skills

17. **In inclusive term, exceptional children means _____.**
    (a) the children with mental disabilities
    (b) the children with low IQ
    (c) the children with maladjustment problem
    (d) the gifted, intelligent, backward, mentally retarded childrens

18. **Children with special needs should be:**
    (a) Given no education at all.
    (b) Given only vocational training.
    (c) Segregated and put in separate institutions.
    (d) Included in 'regular' set-ups with special provisions.

19. **A creative learner refers to one who is:**
    (a) Capable of scoring consistently good marks in tests
    (b) Good at lateral thinking and problem-solving
    (c) Very talented in drawing and painting
    (d) Highly intelligent

20. **The gifted children:**

(a) Are always calm and quiet

(b) Always behave extraordinarily

(c) Solve the problem quickly

(d) Perform any task quickly

21. Which one of the following is the last stage of learning?

(a) Acquisition   (b) Adaptation

(c) Fluency   (d) Maintenance

22. Rohini, a newly admitted student, is unable to adjust to the classroom, as a teacher you will:

(a) Give her small group work and supervise.

(b) Will try to find out the reason.

(c) Will leave her on time.

(d) Will call the guardians

---

process.

(b) Teaching is a tripolar process.

(c) Teaching is an effect - directed process.

(d) Teaching is a process confined only to the classrooms.

24. Children's misconceptions and errors:

(a) Are a hindrance and obstacle to the teaching-learning process.

(b) Should be ignored in the teaching-learning process.

(c) Signify that children's capabilities are far inferior to that of adults.

(d) Are a significant step in the teaching-learning process.

25. Errors made by children are indicative of:

(a) Poor intelligence

(b) Low ability

(c) Their inability to reproduce knowledge

(d) Children's thinking process which is qualitatively different from that of adults

26. What is the definition of cognition?

(a) The process of acquiring and understanding knowledge through our thoughts, experience and sense

(b) The process of biological and psychological changes

(c) Developing attitude and interest

(d) Structural and physiological changes

27. Motivation and learning are inter-related. Which among the following

---

is not true about the principle of motivation?

(a) Depends on curiosity

(b) It provides a purpose for learning

(c) Helps to get a higher position

(d) Skills and knowledge

28. Which of the following is an environmental factor which impact learning?

(a) Attitude

(b) Motivation

(c) Personality traits

(d) School

29. Learning is influenced by:
i. Psychological factors
ii. Socio-Cultural factors

(c) i, ii, iii   (d) i, ii, iii, iv

30. How should teachers promote motivation to learn among their students?

(a) Use incentives to help students learn.

(b) Give the students things to study that will be tested rather than things that won't.

(c) Give easier tests.

(d) Let the students make the test.

Language - I: English

Ques (31-39): Direction : Read the passage carefully and answer the questions that follow.

The Indus Waters Treaty is a water-distribution treaty between India and Pakistan, brokered by the World Bank, then the International Bank for Reconstruction and Development. The treaty was signed in Karachi on September 19, 1960, by Prime Minister of India Jawaharlal Nehru and President of Pakistan Ayub Khan.

According to this agreement, control over the three "eastern" rivers — the Beas, the Ravi, and the Sutlej — was given to India, while control over the three "western" rivers — the Indus, the Chenab, and the Jhelum — to Pakistan. In aftermath of the 2016 Uri attack, India reviewed the treaty and its provisions and proposed several changes. The treaty was reviewed by India to explore possible ways to use its share of water from rivers, including the Jhelum, flowing into Pakistan.

According to the IWT, India is permitted to construct water storage on western rivers -Indus, Jhelum, and Chenab -up to 3.6 million acre-feet for various purposes,

---

including domestic use.

India is currently building 3 hydro projects on the rivers that flow to Pakistan in their course. One of this projects is the 1000 MW Pakul Dul dam on Chenab. Another one includes a 120 MW on Miyar, which would be located across Miyar Nalla, a right-bank tributary of the river Chenab and a 43 MW hydro project on the Lower Kalnai Nalla; another tributary of Chenab. Pakistan objected to these projects stating that these projects are in violation of the Indus Water Treaty of 1960.

India refused to countenance any change of design of the Miyar dam in J&K, as asked by Pakistan and plans to continue utilization of its allocation under the Indus Waters Treaty.

31. Which of the following river is not included according to IWT for the

---

(c) Jhelum   (d) Chenab

32. Which of the following is not a correct pair of the eastern and western rivers according to the passage?

(a) Beas, Jhelum

(b) Ravi, Chenab

(c) Sutlej, Indus

(d) Chenab, Jhelum

33. Which of the following is refused by India as asked by Pakistan?

(a) 1000 MW Pakul Dul dam construction on Chenab.

(b) Permit to construct the water storage in eastern rivers.

(c) To allow the access to all the three eastern rivers.

(d) To countenance any change of design of the Miyar dam in J&K.

34. Choose the word which is most nearly the OPPOSITE in meaning to the word 'permit'.

(a) Allow   (b) Back

(c) Ban   (d) Authorize

35. Choose the word which is most nearly the SAME in meaning to the word 'explore'.

(a) Initiate   (b) Investigate

(c) Intimate   (d) Neglect

36. In aftermath of the 2016 Uri attack, India reviewed the treaty and its provisions and proposed several changes.
The part of speech 'aftermath' is a/ an:

(a) Adverb   (b) Adjective

(c) Noun   (d) Preposition

37. **What is the theme of the passage?**
    (a) Rivalry between India and Pakistan
    (b) River issues in both the countries
    (c) Indus Waters Treaty
    (d) Construction issues of Dam

38. **Find an error in a part of the sentence and mark the corresponding option.**
    One of this/ projects is /the 1000 MW/ Pakul Dul dam on Chenab.
    (a) One of this
    (b) projects is
    (c) the 1000 MW
    (d) Pakul Dul dam on Chenab.

39. Which of the following river is

(c) Ravi   (d) Jhelum

Ques (40-45): Direction: Read the following poem and answer the question by choosing the correct/most appropriate option.
I love to rise in a summer morn,
When the birds sing on every tree;
The distant huntsman winds his horn,
And the skylark sings with me.
O! what sweet company.
But to go to school in a summer morn,
O! it drives all joy away;
Under a cruel eye outworn,
The little ones spend the day,
In sighing and dismay.
Ah! then at times I drooping sit,
And spend many an anxious hour.
Nor in my book can I take delight,
Nor sit in learning's bower,
Worn thro' with the dreary shower.
How can the bird that is born for joy,
Sit in a cage and sing.
How can a child when fears annoy,
But droop his tender wing,
And forget his youthful spring.

40. **How does the school boy feel when he goes to school?**
    (a) Very happy   (b) Cheerful
    (c) Romantic   (d) Unhappy

41. **Whom is the school boy compared to?**
    (a) A bird
    (b) Summer
    (c) Winds
    (d) Dreary shower

42. **Which figure of speech has been used in the line?**
    sky-lark sings
    (a) Apostrophe   (b) Alliteration

(c) Assonance   (d) Simile

43. **Which figure of speech has been used in the line?**
    Under a cruel eye outworn.
    (a) Anaphora   (b) Apostrophe
    (c) Alliteration   (d) Metaphor

44. **What does the sweet company refer to in the first stanza?**
    (a) Skylark
    (b) Summer morning
    (c) Huntsman horn
    (d) Both (A) and (C)

45. **What takes away all the happiness of the child?**
    (a) Going to the school in the winter morning

46. **A child learns his/her first language in a:**
    (a) Friendly setting
    (b) Tutored setting
    (c) Formal setting
    (d) Natural setting

47. **Language learning is ____.**
    (a) Not a conscious attempt by the learner.
    (b) Conscious attempt by the learner.
    (c) An act which occurs naturally.
    (d) Conscious attempt by the teacher.

48. **Teaching a lesson, through a number of language activities connected with the topic, refers to which principle of second language teaching?**
    (a) Structural Approach
    (b) Multiple Line of Approach
    (c) Circular Approach
    (d) Bilingual approach

49. **"From small utterances, the students can easily pass on to longer sentences." Which principle of second language teaching could be associated with this statement?**
    (a) Give Priority to Sounds
    (b) Language Habit through Language Using
    (c) Present Language in Basic Sentence Patterns
    (d) Individual Differences

50. **'Decorum' in spoken language pertains to:**
    (a) Correct grammatical usage
    (b) Voice quality or loudness
    (c) Clarity and purity of style
    (d) Appropriate gestures

51. **Teaching of grammar will help the learners to:**
    (a) Differentiate the phoneme
    (b) Have a basic knowledge of phonetics
    (c) Have a good conversational skill
    (d) Know the structure of the language

52. **The principle of which of the following method is to memorize the rules of grammar?**
    (a) Structural Approach
    (b) Direct Method

53. What is the main challenge of teaching language in a diverse classroom?
    (a) Challenge of a mixed-ability group of learners.
    (b) Challenge of teaching-learning materials.
    (c) Challenges to curriculum design.
    (d) All of the above

54. **Language skills can be learnt better:**
    (a) If they are taught in an integrated manner
    (b) With the help of challenging drills
    (c) Through written tests and practices
    (d) If taught in isolation

55. **Which of the following skills comes under the productive category of language skills?**
    (a) Speaking and Listening
    (b) Listening and Reading
    (c) Reading and Writing
    (d) Writing and Speaking

56. **Evaluation of speaking consists of:**
    (a) Evaluation of pronunciation
    (b) Evaluation of intonation
    (c) Evaluation of stress
    (d) All of the above

57. **Which of the following is not a useful activity of evaluating listening skills?**
    (a) Dictations
    (b) Oral presentations
    (c) Vocabulary assessment task
    (d) Listen and Draw

58. Flannel board is useful for:
- (a) Teaching picture composition
- (b) Developing reading skill
- (c) Developing acting skill
- (d) Improving thinking skill

59. What can be used as props for dialogues to teach new lexical or structural items?
- (a) Textbook
- (b) Reference book
- (c) Realia
- (d) Dictionary

60. Remedial teaching is a:
- (a) Preparation of teaching
- (b) Systematic process
- (c) Pre-teaching program

61. The rational number lying between $\sqrt{2}$ and $\sqrt{3}$ is:
- (a) $\frac{49}{28}$
- (b) $\frac{56}{35}$
- (c) $\frac{63}{45}$
- (d) $\frac{85}{66}$

62. The numbers $x, x+2, x+4$ are all prime numbers. What is the value of x?
- (a) 3
- (b) 2
- (c) 11
- (d) 17

63. If sum of five consecutive integers is 'S', then largest of these integers in terms of S Will be:
- (a) $\frac{(S-10)}{5}$
- (b) $\frac{(S+4)}{4}$
- (c) $\frac{(S+5)}{4}$
- (d) $\frac{(S+10)}{5}$

64. If $(a-b):(a+b)=1:5$ then what is $(a^2-b^2):(a^2+b^2)$ equal to:
- (a) $6:13$
- (b) $4:13$
- (c) $5:13$
- (d) $8:13$

65. If $x+y+z=3$ and $x^2+y^2+z^2=101$, then what is the value of $\sqrt{x^3+y^3=z^3-3xyz}$?
- (a) 28
- (b) 26
- (c) 24
- (d) 21

66. If $x=\sqrt{10}+3$ then find the value of $x^3-\frac{1}{x^3}$
- (a) 334
- (b) 216
- (c) 234
- (d) 254

67. Ratio of two complementary angles is $1:5$. What is the difference between them?
- (a) $60°$
- (b) $90°$
- (c) $120°$
- (d) $160°$

68. The length of a pendulum is $60cm$. The angle through which it swings when its tip describes an arc of length $16.5cm$ will be:
- (a) $15°30'$
- (b) $15°45'$
- (c) $16°15'$
- (d) $16°45'$

69. Find the value of x in the given figure where PA is parallel to QC.

- (a) $75°$
- (b) $185°$
- (c) $285°$
- (d) $245°$

- (a) 5cm
- (b) 2.5cm
- (c) 3cm
- (d) 2.25cm

71. Circumference of the base of a $9m$ high conical tent is $44m$. Find the volume of air contained in it.
- (a) 430 m^3
- (b) 462 m^3
- (c) 472 m^3
- (d) 492 m^3

72. The average marks obtained by the students in a class are 43. If the average marks obtained by 25 boys are 40 and average marks obtained by the girl students are 48, then what is the number of girl students in the class?
- (a) 20
- (b) 25
- (c) 15
- (d) 10

73. The age of x is six times that of y. After 4 years, x is 4 times elder of y. What is the present age of y?
- (a) 4 years
- (b) 5 years
- (c) 6 years
- (d) 7 years

74. Direction : What will come in the place of the question mark '?' in the following question?
$18\frac{1}{3}+9\frac{2}{3}-10\frac{1}{3}=1\frac{2}{3}+?$
- (a) 10
- (b) 15
- (c) 18
- (d) 16

75. The LCM of two numbers is 90 times their HCF. The sum of LCM and HCF is 1456. If one of the number is 160, then what is the other number?
- (a) 120
- (b) 136
- (c) 144
- (d) 184

76. A dishonest shopkeeper used to sell onions at Rs. $30/kg$. If a customer bought $2kg$ of onions. He gave $750g$ instead of $1kg$ to a customer, find the shopkeeper's actual profit percentage.
- (a) 5%
- (b) 10%
- (c) 25%
- (d) 33.33%

77. A man is moving with a speed of $16km/h$. After every km, he takes a rest of 4 minutes. How much time will he take to cover a distance of $40km$?
- (a) $5hrs\ 8min$
- (b) $5hrs\ 6min$
- (c) $5hrs\ 10min$
- (d) $5hrs$

78. Direction : Given below is a data set of temperatures (in ºC) : -6, - 8, - 2, 3, 2, 0, 5, 4, 8
What is the range of the data?
- (a) 0 ºC
- (b) 16 ºC
- (c) 18 ºC
- (d) 10 ºC

- (a) 75
- (b) 375
- (c) 15
- (d) 70

80. In a given data, which one of the measures of central tendencies would be affected by one or two extremely large or extremely small values outside the range of the rest of the data?
- (a) Median
- (b) Mean
- (c) Mode
- (d) Frequency

81. The nature of Mathematics is:
- (a) Ornamental
- (b) Difficult
- (c) Logical
- (d) Unsystematic

82. Which one is not related to the nature of Mathematics?
- (a) Exactness
- (b) Specific sequence
- (c) Expanded expression
- (d) Pattern

83. As per NCF 2005, the goal of mathematics teaching in school curriculum is that children learn "Important Mathematics". Important Mathematics implies:
- (a) Understanding appropriate use of learnt mathematical techniques.
- (b) Verifying geometrical theorems in Maths Lab.
- (c) Knowing mathematical procedures and algorithms.
- (d) Solving mathematical games and puzzles.

84. Which one of the following does not match curricular expectations of teaching mathematics at the primary level?

(a) Analyse and infer from representation of grouped data

(b) Develop a connection between the logical functioning of daily life and that of mathematical thinking

(c) Develop language and symbolic notations with standard algorithms of performing number operations

(d) Represent part of whole as a fraction and order simple fractions

85. **Which mathematical topic that is best seen as a compact language and a means of succinct expression is introduced at the upper primary**

(d) Algebra

86. **Students often make a mistake in comparing the decimal numbers. For example, 0.50 is larger than 0.5. The most probable reason for this error is:**

(a) Lack of practice of these types of questions in the class.

(b) Lack of concrete experience of representation of decimal number on the number line.

(c) Careless attempt by the students.

(d) Misconception regarding the significance of zero in ordering decimal.

87. **Which of the following is not true about the problems in teaching and learning mathematics?**

(a) Positive attitude towards mathematics

(b) Focus on problem solving approach

(c) Cramming of all mathematical formulas

(d) Connecting real life problems to mathematics

88. **Which is the main remedial teaching strategy?**

(a) Tutorial

(b) Supervised

(c) Both (A) and (B)

(d) None of these

89. **In a class text, to the question, find out 23% of 200, two students answered in following ways:**
Student A: 23% **of** $200 = 23\%$ **of**

$(100 + 100) = 23 + 23 = (20 + 20) + (3 + 3) = 46$

Student B: 23% **of** $200 = 200 \times \dfrac{23}{100} = 2 \times 23 = 46$

(a) Since student B has used the standard algorithm, teacher gives full marks to student B and zero to student A

(b) Teacher gives full marks to both the students as they have attempted the question using their own algorithms. Both formal and informal algorithms are integral to solving problems in mathematics.

(c) Teacher gives zero marks to student A and directs him to redo the question using the algorithm taught in the Class

90. **A teacher asked the students to collect leaves and to identify symmetry patterns. This task reflects the teacher's efforts to:**

(a) Relate real life experience with mathematical concepts

(b) Introduce an intradisciplinary approach

(c) Enhance creativity amongst students

(d) Improve mathematical communication

91. **In cockroaches, air enters the body through:**

(a) Lungs   (b) Gills

(c) Spiracles   (d) Skin

92. **Read the description given below and identify the dish.**
1. It is a vegetable stew.
2. All the vegetables are put into a clay pot, along with fresh spices.
3. The pot is placed upside down.

(a) Khichdi

(b) Undhiya

(c) Thukpa

(d) Vegetable curry

93. **Mammals have _____.**

(a) glandular skin with hairs

(b) dry and non-glandular skin with feathers

(c) dry and non-glandular skin with scales

(d) dry and glandular skin with feathers

94. **The essential nutrients that the body required for normal growth and metabolism, apart from water,** protein, carbohydrate and fats, are:

(a) Minerals

(b) Vitamins

(c) Both (A) and (B)

(d) None of these

95. **The device used for producing electric current is called:**

(a) Generator

(b) Galvanometer

(c) Ammeter

(d) Motor

96. **Electric current is considered to be the flow of _______.**

(a) negative charges

(b) dielectric

(c) magnet pieces

B. Landslide
C. Thundering
D. Tsunami
E. Floods
Earthquakes can cause:

(a) B, D and E   (b) A, B and C

(c) B only   (d) B and E

98. **The major source of mineral in the soil is the :**

(a) Parent rock from which soil is formed

(b) Plants

(c) Animals

(d) Bacteria

99. **_______ are those which gets strongly magnetised when placed in an external magnetic field.**

(a) Ferromagnetic substances

(b) Diamagnetic substances

(c) Paramagnetic substances

(d) All of the above

100. **The property of light used in optical fibers is:**

(a) Dispersion

(b) Interference

(c) Total internal reflection

(d) Diffraction

101. **When acid and base is mixed together, then which of the following is formed?**

(a) Salt   (b) Base

(c) Acid   (d) Hydrogen

102. **The amplitude of a wave is a measure of its:**

(a) Height   (b) Period

(c) Length   (d) Speed

103. **In a transverse wave, the motion of the particles is ____ the wave's direction of propagation.**
    - (a) along
    - (b) perpendicular to
    - (c) opposite from
    - (d) parallel to

104. **Which vitamin Deficiency causes failure of blood clotting?**
    - (a) K
    - (b) B
    - (c) D
    - (d) A

105. **Bile Juice is formed in the:**
    - (a) Kidney
    - (b) Salivary Gland
    - (c) Liver
    - (d) Lung

106.
    - (c) Br
    - (d) I

107. **Which force makes the aircraft move in the air?**
    - (a) Lift Force
    - (b) Drag Force
    - (c) Thrust Force
    - (d) Gravity Force

108. **Which material is on the matchstick?**
    - (a) Sodium
    - (b) Manganese
    - (c) Phosphorus
    - (d) Calcium

109. **In a pressure cooker cooking is faster because the increase in vapour pressure:**
    - (a) Increases the specific heat.
    - (b) Decreases the specific heat.
    - (c) Decreases the boiling point.
    - (d) Increases the boiling point.

110. **Magnetic materials are the materials which:**
    - (a) Always get attracted towards a magnet
    - (b) Never get attracted towards a magnet
    - (c) Always move away from a magnet
    - (d) None of these

111. **Shalini has planned a field trip for Class IV students to the Science Center. Which one of the following general instructions given to the students is irrelevant for the trip?**
    - (a) Do not go anywhere without informing me
    - (b) Carry your full schoolbag for the day
    - (c) Ask question for your doubts on displays
    - (d) Take notepad and pen with you

112. **The concept of 'seed germination' can be taught best by:**
    - (a) Showing germinated seeds to the class and explaining the process of germination
    - (b) Presenting the germination stages through drawings on the board
    - (c) Asking the students to perform an activity to sow seeds, observe different stages and draw them
    - (d) Showing photographs of speed germination

113. **Ms. Priya wants to show students**
    - (a) Tapping a table and hearing the sound
    - (b) Plucking an elastic band and seeing the vibrations.
    - (c) Throwing a pebble in water and observing it
    - (d) Feeling the vibrations in your throat while speaking.

114. **Your students have just entered grade 8. If students have largely mastered the concepts taught till grade 7 as per NCERT, which of the following will they most likely NOT be able to describe?**
    - (a) Separation of fibres from cotton seeds
    - (b) Processing of synthetic fibres into different articles
    - (c) Processing of natural fibres into wool
    - (d) Process of rearing silkworms under laboratory conditions

115. **Which of the following questions is BEST suited to develop deductive reasoning in students?**
    - (a) Why does the diaphragm contract during inhalation?
    - (b) How are spiracles and tracheae comparable to nostrils?
    - (c) Plant is a living organism. Do plants respire?
    - (d) What will happen if food accidentally enters the trachea?

116. **Which of the following is the MOST appropriate instructional aid for a teacher to INTRODUCE the concept of sedimentation?**
    - (a) A filter paper
    - (b) Mixture of oil and water
    - (c) Dropping a stone in a glass of water
    - (d) A Glass of muddy water

117. **One of the students in the class said that the soil does not contain any moisture.**
    Which of the following remedial actions would be BEST suited to clarify this misconception?
    - (a) Placing a soil sample on a wooden plank.
    - (b) Comparing the weights of a soil sample before and after drying under sunlight.
    - (c) Collecting and examining a soil sample after rain.
    - (d) Mixing water and soil in a

    of chemical changes in his class. **Which one of the following is the BEST example of an 'authentic task' which he can use to assess students?**
    - (a) Asking students to burn a magnesium ribbon and observe the changes.
    - (b) Create a set up to pass gas through lime water.
    - (c) Make a protective solution that prevents rusting of iron.
    - (d) Create a cooling chamber that can maintain low temperatures for chemical changes.

119. **What type of teaching should be planned after diagnosing the learning difficulties of the students in science teaching?**
    - (a) Microteaching
    - (b) Team teaching
    - (c) Diagnostic teaching
    - (d) Remedial teaching

120. **Consider the following statements about Dyspraxia:**
    I. It is a disorder that is characterized by difficulty in muscle control, which causes problems with movement and coordination, language and speech, and can affect learning.
    II. A disorder which is usually characterized by a significant discrepancy between higher verbal skills and weaker motor, visual-spatial and social skills.
    III. A learning disability that affects a person's ability to understand numbers and learn math facts.

(a) Only I   (b) Only II
(c) Only III   (d) Only I and II

// Hints and Solutions //

1(B). Development and learning are inter-related and inter-dependent and contribute to each other.
- Development is a product of maturity and learning.
- Learning and development are inter-related in a complex manner.
- Maturity is more or less automatic, unfolding biological potential which is an irreversible sequence and entails biological changes.
- Such changes are relatively independent of environmental factors as long as environmental factors remain normal.
- Learning occurs across the entire life span, which differs from maturity.
- However, learning depends on the process of maturing i.e. individual readiness (mental and physical) for certain activities.

So, we conclude that learning and development are inter-related in a complex manner.

2(D). Principles of development include:
- Development is Life-Long/Principle of continuity: This principle defines that development is a life-long process as it does not stop at maturation and continues gradually until reaching its maximum growth.
- Development is modifiable: Development may be explained as the series of overall changes in an individual due to the emergence of modified structures and functions that are the outcome of the interactions and exchanges between the organism and its environment.
- Development follows a pattern: Prenatal (before birth) and postnatal (after birth) development of human beings follow a pattern or a predictable sequence. Physical development, motor or language development and intellectual development take place in definite sequences.
- Product of hereditary and environment: Hereditary and environment play a vital role in determining the development of an individual as all the mental and social traits depend on the environment and all the inborn traits, instincts, potentials, and I. Q. depends on heredity.

So, it could be concluded that development is governed and determined by culture alone is not a principle of development.

3(B). Heredity and environment are the elements that play a vital role in determining the personality development of an individual. How a person will develop depends on the environment but how far a person can develop depends on heredity.
- Heredity and environment play an important role in the development of the personality and other qualities in the individual.
- From the earliest moments of life, the interaction of heredity and the environment works to shape who children are and who they will become.
- While the genetic instructions a child inherits from his parents may set out a road map for development, the environment can impact how these directions are expressed, shaped or event silenced.
- In order to understand child development, it is important to look at impact on child psychology and development.
- The complex interaction of Heredity and the environment does not just occur at certain moments or at certain periods instead it is persistent and lifelong.

Thus, it can be concluded that for optimum development of an individual both heredity and environment are essential.

4(A). Primary socialization: Inculcation of norms and values within the family is called primary socialization. Here children want to know themselves and try to find their identity and learn the daily routine tasks of humans.

Characteristics of primary socialization:
- Primary socialization begins from the age of infancy.
- Self-identity formed.
- Children start to go familiar with their innate abilities and disabilities.
- Children start learning their daily needs, such as toilet training.

So, it is concluded that process of primary socialisation begins from infancy.

5(C). According to Piaget, in the 'Formal Operational Period', the child is able to apply logical thoughts to all classes of problems as in this period:
- Mental capabilities develop to the maximum level.
- Metacognition and problem-solving skills develop in children.
- Children understand world through abstract & scientific thinking.
- Children become capable of hypothetical and deductive reasoning.

So, it could be concluded that according to Piaget the child is able to apply logical thoughts to all classes of problems, this development occurs in 'Formal Operational Period'.

6(D). Stages of Moral Development: Kohlberg's theory is broken down into three primary levels. At each level of moral development, there are two stages.

Level 1. Preconventional Morality (4 to 10 years): Preconventional morality is the earliest period of moral development. At this age, children's decisions are primarily shaped by the expectations of adults and the consequences of breaking the rules. There are two stages within this level:
- Stage 1 (Obedience and Punishment): Children at this stage see "rules as fixed and absolute". Obeying the rules is important because it is a way to avoid punishment. In this children ignore the intention of others and instead focus on the fear of authority and negative consequences.
- Stage 2 (Instrumental purpose and they serve individual needs.

Level 2. Conventional Morality (10 to 13 years): The next period of moral development is marked by the acceptance of social rules regarding what is good and moral. During this time, adolescents and adults internalize the moral standards they have learned from their role models and from society.
- Stage 3 (Good-Boy Good-girl orientation): This stage of the interpersonal relationship of moral development is focused on living up to social expectations and roles. There is an emphasis on conformity, being "nice" and consideration of how choices influence relationships.
- Stage 4 (Social concern and conscience): This stage is focused on ensuring that social order is maintained. The focus is on maintaining law and order by following the rules, doing one's duty, and respecting authority.

Level 3. Postconventional Morality (13 to 16 years): At this level of moral development, people develop an understanding of abstract principles of morality. The two stages at this level are:
- Stage 5 (Social Contract and Individual Rights): At this stage, the people believe that rules of law are important for maintaining a society, but members of society should agree upon these standards.
- Stage 6 (Universal Ethical Principles): Kohlberg's final level of moral reasoning is based on universal ethical principles and abstract reasoning. At this stage, people follow these internalized principles of justice, even if they conflict with laws and rules.

So, we can conclude that social concern and conscience is a sub-stage in Kohlberg's 'conventional state's of Moral Development.

7(C). A child-centered system of education is designed to develop the individual and social qualities of a student rather than providing generalized information or training by way of the prescribed subject matter.

Characteristics of the child-centered education system:
- More focus is being placed on the holistic development of a child.
- To help the child become independent, responsible, and confident.
- Child-centered teachers engage in an 'active learning' process.
- Students actively engaged in their own learning.
- They have opportunities to investigate and discover.
- Continuous evaluation.
- Gives respect to the individuality of the

8(A). Gardner's Multiple Intelligences Theory supports the idea that", Most students can be considered Intelligent" in some way.

For example: as all individuals have some different strengths, so the Intelligence. Fish is not a good climber as that of a monkey but has strength in swimming, so we cannot expect the fish to be good climbers instead we should recognize the natural potential otherwise they may lose their essence.
- The Teachers should be aware that every class has different learners, and they learn in different ways, including their own intelligence profile.
- Should practice content using several points of entry and various strategies.
- Knowing the learners in your current teaching context, what intelligences do they have and what activities can you implement to maximize their learning potential
- Students should be encouraged to practice their strengths and opposed to practicing one universal strength.

9(B).

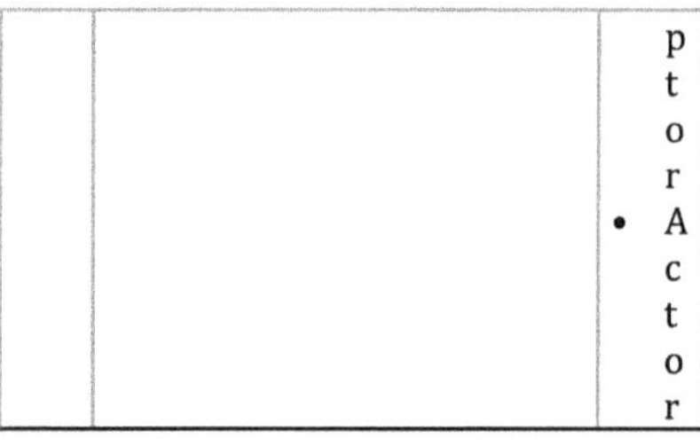

Bodily-Kinesthetic Intelligence	Persons who said to be good at body movement, performing actions, and physical control. People have excellent hand-eye coordination, Physical movement, and motor control.	• Dancer • Builder • Sculptor • Actor

So, we can conclude that Shorya is a renowned dancer. So he must possess Body-kinesthetic Intelligence.

10(D). Our attitude towards diversity in languages influences the existence of linguistic diversity or multiline quality.
- If we have a positive attitude to linguistic diversity, we help in the existence and growth of all the languages spoken in the
- For example, there are 21 sub-castes in the Naga community and about the same numbers of languages are spoken in the community. People of a particular sub-group speak to the other members of their sub-group in their mother tongue. When people of one sub-group need to talk to people of the other sub-group they use Nagameez language and when they have to speak to people outside their community (i.e. people outside Nagaland and Manipur) they use Hindi and English. This is an example of the positive attitude that Naga people have towards linguistic diversity and this is what makes them multilingual.
- On the other hand, residents of Goa keep fighting over the existence of Marathi and Konkani. Similarly, residents of Belgaon in Karnataka are arguing over the existence of Kannada and Marathi.

So, we conclude that the cause of the downfall of a particular language is intolerance and narrow.

11(A). Gender refers to the socially constructed differences between men and women. It refers to the masculine and feminine qualities, behavior, roles, and responsibilities that society upholds. Gender can be changed / re-oriented.
- Gender is such a familiar part of life that it usually takes a deliberate disruption of our expectations of how women and men are supposed to act to pay attention to how it is produced.
- Transvestites and transsexuals construct their gender status of dressing, speaking, walking, gesturing in the way of prescribed for women or men whichever they want to be taken for and so does any normal person.
- Gendering is legitimated by religion, law, science, and society's entire set of values.

So, from the above-mentioned points, it becomes clear that Gender is a social construct.

12(D). Individual differences are characteristic of all living organisms. It refers to the difference which distinguishes an individual from another on the basis of psychological characteristics.

Effective strategies to cater to individual differences in the class:
- Recognize and respect differences: Teachers should recognize individual differences in their classroom, fulfill students' needs and respect the diversity and individual differences of learners.
- Use diverse pedagogical strategies: Teachers should use diverse pedagogical
- Reflect on one's verbal and non-verbal communication: While communicating with students teachers should pay attention to their verbal and non-verbal communication to provide required guidance.

So, we can conclude that identifying deficits in students and correcting them is not an effective strategy to cater to individual differences in the class.

13(B). Continuous and Comprehensive Evaluation (CCE) has been introduced as a school-based system of evaluation by the CBSE in 2009 with the enactment of the 'Right to Education Act.
- CCE refers to all-around development including both scholastic and co-scholastic aspects of a child's growth.
- It never assesses students according to their economic status rather it emphasizes the continuity of assessment.

The list of personal-social qualities (PSQ) that are assessed under Continuous and Comprehensive Evaluation:-
- Regularity and Punctuality
- Neatness (cleanliness)
- Discipline, Co-operation, and Responsibility
- Physical health
- Emotional stability and leadership qualities
- Consciousness with a spirit of social service
- Positive attitude towards school, teachers, peers, studies, and society
- Entrepreneurship, etc.

So, it becomes clear that painting is not a social-personal quality assessed under CCE.

14(A). In absolute grading, the reference point for an assessment of a student's performance is a pre-determined standard.
- Each point value is assigned a grade

represented by a letter with each grade assigned based on a predetermined or predefined standard that corresponds to the level of performance by a student

- The grades are associated with that fixed standard irrespective of the distribution of grades in the class
- For example, all students who score 95% and above are collectively grouped under outstanding category and awarded an A grade the categories like outstanding, excellent, very good etc are predetermined and each grade specifically assigned are associated only with that predetermined standard
- This system is used to evaluate students under scholastic areas.

So, we can conclude that in absolute grading, the reference point for an assessment of students' performance

- When the child meets other hearing-impaired children and realizes other people face similar challenges and manage fine, regardless of language or level of hearing, it supports identity development and increases confidence.

So, we can conclude that Hearing-impaired children exhibit barriers in communication by language.

17(D). Exceptional Children refer to deviated children as they are the ones:

- who deviate significantly from the normal children in respect to social, mental, physical, and emotional characteristics.
- who show deviations falling far above or extremely below from the average which limits their participation in normal activities.

"Specially designed instruction, to meet the unique needs of a child with special needs including instructions conducted in the classrooms.

- Inclusive education, as an approach, seeks to address the learning needs of all children (disabled and non-disabled) with a specific focus on those who are vulnerable to marginalization and exclusion.
- Inclusion emerged as a result of the social justice movement in the field of disability which emphasizes that schools should create an environment in which students with special needs are seen as valuable members of the social community.

Thus from above-mentioned points, it is clear that children with special needs should be included in 'regular' set-ups with

organizing a creational activity in the classroom related to the particular topic as:

- Inclusion of purposeful creational activities makes learning meaningful and fruitful. It is best for teaching students of class three.
- Creative expressions in learning ensure the active involvement of the child and develop the ability to assimilate the concept efficiently by building creative thinking skills.

Form of Creational Activities in Teaching-learning Process:

- Writing: Poetry, songs, dramas, etc.
- Graphic Arts: Designing posters, banners, etc.
- Music: Songs related to environmental messages.
- Movement and dance: Performing non-verbal arts.
- Puppetry: Transmitting environmental messages.

So, it could be concluded that organizing a creational activity in the classroom related to a particular topic will be the best way to enhance the readiness level of his students.

16(A). Hearing impairment refers to hearing loss that prevents a person from totally receiving sounds through the ear. If the loss is mild, the person has difficulty hearing faint or distant speech.

Language and Speech Development Barrier in Children with Hearing Impairment:

- Hearing impairment is a great barrier to the normal development of language; the child with such impairment is at a severe disadvantage in virtually all aspects of language development.
- A considerable number of educators of deaf individuals believe that many of the problems of people who are hearing-impaired related to social and intellectual development are primarily due to their deficiencies in language.

group. They are independent in their judgments as they possess advanced logical and creative thinking.

- Intelligent children: These categories of children have divergent thinking, curious in nature, and are able to find solutions for different problems on their own.
- Backward children: These are those children who are low in achieving academic skills. Backward learners not only lag behind other students in academics but in areas of social, emotional, and psychological well-being.
- Mentally Retarded children: The mentally retarded are those whose normal intellectual growth is arrested before birth, during the birth process, or in the early years of development.
- Physically handicapped learner: These categories of children can not participate in educational, social, and vocational activities on fairly equal terms with their peers due to physical disabilities.
- Disabled child: Disabled children are again divided into different groups based on types of disabilities. They can be learning, cognitive, developmental, intellectual, mental, physical, sensory, or some combination of these.

So, it could be concluded that in inclusive term, exceptional children means the gifted, intelligent, backward, mentally retarded children.

18(D). Children with special need are disabled ns any restriction or lack (resulting from an impairment) of ability to perform an activity in a manner or within the range considered normal for a human being.

- Special education is individualized education for children with special needs. Special education means,

associations or connections between seemingly unrelated or remote ideas They can rearrange elements of thought to create new ideas or products.

- Also, they pose many ideas or solutions to problems.
- They display intellectual playfulness, fantasize, imagine, and daydream. Also, a creative learner doesn't need to have a high IQ.
- They are good at lateral thinking and problem-solving. Creativity is associated with lateral thinking for the generation of new ideas.
- These children have divergent thinking and are very curious in nature that's why sometimes the classroom seems monotonous to them because they grab things fastly than their age-peers.
- Divergent thinking in creativity leads to a broadening of the definition and criteria of the problem to generate a wide variety of possible solutions.
- The creative learner has personality traits such as sensitivity to problems, fluency, flexibility, originality, ability to transform meaning, and ability to elaborate.

So, we can conclude that a creative learner refers to one who is good at lateral thinking and problem-solving.

20(C). Gifted children are those who show consistently remarkable performance in educational endeavours. They possess superior intellectual ability within the range of the upper two to three per cent of the population. Characteristics of Gifted Children:

- Learning commensurate with that expected of older students, often reading at an earlier than average age.
- Gifted child solve the problem quickly
- Knowing about things of which other students are unaware.

- They have a high ability for abstract and symbolic thinking.
- Curiosity indicated by asking serious questions.
- They have a large vocabulary and mature, expressive ability.
- They require limited exposure and fewer repetitions to learn. They have extra-ordinary memory.
- They can apply knowledge to unfamiliar situations.

So, from the above explanation, it can be concluded that gifted children solve the problem quickly.

21(B). 'Learning' means a relatively permanent change in behaviour that occurs as a result of experience with the environment.

Learning, in the case of all persons,

when 'Learner-centered instruction' and 'Interactive methods' are used which provides autonomy to students to control their own work.

- In these approaches, students work in flexible, cooperative groupings to solve problems and analyze texts to demonstrate an understanding of a task.

Characteristics of teaching:

- Teaching is a tripolar process. This process of education considers that the development of the child takes place in and through the society, in which the teacher and the child live together.
- Active engagement and student participation are fostered by the teachers through a series of interactive processes in the form of debate, group tasks, projects, etc.
- Teaching is a purposeful and effect-

overlook minor details and focus on bigger things.

- Whereas children may make a significantly big error as they may not have the experience of the concept.

Thus, it is concluded that errors made by children are indicative of children's thinking process which is qualitatively different from that of adults.

26(A). The term 'cognition' refers to all processes by which the sensory input is transformed, reduced, elaborated, stored, recovered, and used. Cognitive development refers to the development of the ability to think and reason.

- Cognition develops in the learners through the interaction of innate power (heredity), environment and maturation.

---

2. Fluency/Proficiency: During this stage, the person learns to perform the new task to a higher degree of accuracy.
3. Maintenance: During this stage, the person is able to perform the task independently, even after teaching has ended.
4. Generalization: During this stage, the person learns to generalize the learned skills/tasks to other situations or environments; in ' other words, he is able to perform the task in situations other than the ones in which he had learnt it.
5. Adaptation: During this stage, the learner applies a previously learnt skill in a new area of application without direct instruction or guidance.

So, we can conclude that the fifth and last stage is "Adaptation".

22(B). The teacher is a friend, philosopher, and guide to the students.

- If a new student is unable to adjust in the classroom, the teacher will make the classroom environment comfortable.
- The teacher will try to find out the reason by talking to her and try to resolve it.
- The teacher can introduce the new student to old students to make her comfortable.
- The teacher tells the other students to help her with all the work.

Thus, it is concluded that Rohini, a newly admitted student, is unable to adjust to the classroom, as a teacher, will try to find out the reason.

23(D). Teaching is a process related to the effective transmission of knowledge and skills in an individual. It limits or enhances the ways the learners learn and assimilate concepts and ideas.

- Teaching becomes much more effective

So, we can conclude that teaching is a process confined only to the classroom's statements about teaching is not correct.

24(D). Error: When a learner can't master a topic, he/she is vulnerable to make errors. Errors are nothing but incorrectness made by a child during learning.

Misconceptions: It takes place due to the mismatch in previously assimilated and the newly accommodated knowledge.

Children's errors and misconceptions:

- Are a significant step in the teaching-learning process.
- Are necessary in the learning process to give insight into children's thinking.
- Help the teacher to be aware of learners' learning styles, to cater them according to their needs.
- Are considered as a part of the teaching-learning process as it helps to understand the child.

So, it could be concluded that children's errors and misconceptions are a significant step in the teaching-learning process.

25(D). All learners make mistakes. As someone has said: "You can't learn without goofing". Whether you are learning how to ride a bicycle, how to fly a kite or learn a language, everyone does make mistakes.

- An error is an incorrect form and a sure indication that the learner has not mastered the core of the selective topic in a learning process.
- The qualitative difference in children's thinking as compared to adults is reflected in the type of errors made by the children.
- Errors can occur in adults as well as children. The qualitative effect of errors can be observed through the type of error.
- Adults tend to make silly mistakes that may not be serious as they tend to

human intelligence that we use to adapt to and make sense of the world and the emotional environment around him has an impact on his cognitive thinking.

- Cognitive skills are used to comprehend, process, remember, and apply incoming information.
- Cognition describes how mental processes i.e. learning, remembering, problem-solving, and thinking develop from birth until adulthood. Understanding cognitive development is useful in determining the kind of thinking children are capable of at different age levels.
- It develops the ability to solve problems, learn from experiences, and apply knowledge to deal with new situations. It is a mental process that facilitates obtaining, transform, store, retrieve, and use information.

So, it becomes clear that cognition is a process of acquiring and understanding knowledge through our thoughts, experience, and sense.

27(C). Motivation is something that makes the person to action and continues him in the course of action already initiated. There are two identifiable components of motivation. These are needed and drive.

Important principles of motivation in learning are as follows:

- All learning must have a purpose.
- Students need skills and knowledge.
- Specific directions empower students.
- Students want to have fun while they learn/work.
- Curiosity
- A blend of praise and Encouragement
- A combination of intrinsic and extrinsic rewards.
- Involvement in collaborative activities.

Thus from the above-mentioned points, it is clear that helps to get a higher position is not true about the principle of motivation.

28(D). Learning is the process by which skills, attitudes, knowledge, and concepts are acquired, understood, applied, and extended. All human beings, whether grown-ups or children engage in the process of learning, either consciously, or subconsciously.

Environmental factors that impact learning:

- Environmental factors refer to the combination of all external and environmental factors that affect the learning process.
- Some schools operate in dilapidated buildings with leaking roofs. They may not have a lab, library, toilets, or drinking water facilities which creates a barrier in the path of learning.
- On the other hand, a well-designed

children in achieving their objectives.

So, school is an environmental factor that impacts learning.

29(D). Learning is a process by which behavior is either modified or changed through experience or training. Learning is thus a relatively permanent change in response potentiality which occurs as a function of reinforced practice. There are many factors that influence learning.

Learning is influenced by:

Psychological factors:

- Psychological aspects are the elements of one's personality that limit or enhance the ways that one learns and thinks.
- Several psychological factors such as intelligence, personality, attitude, interest, and aptitude have considerable influence on the learning of a child.

Socio-Cultural factors:

- Socio-cultural factors refer to the combination of social and cultural factors. These factors play a vital role in shaping the abilities and behaviors of a child.
- The immediate environmental structure of social culture is where an individual has direct interaction with their significant others such as parents, siblings, teachers, and peers.

School-related factors:

- Overcrowding classrooms is another contributing factor. In some big cities, houses are converted into English medium schools. In small rooms, sixty to seventy children are made to sit and are unable to benefit from highly verbal instruction.
- The condition of the setting where the learning process takes place can also enhance or interfere with the intake of information.

Teacher-related factors:

- Learning problems may occur because of inadequate or inappropriate teaching. The child may have difficulty in learning because the teacher does not provide adequate or appropriate instruction.
- If the teacher is a poor communicator or uses monotonous and uninteresting methods, the children are put at a disadvantage.

So, it is clear that learning is influenced by all Psychological, Socio-Cultural, School-related, and Teacher related factors.

30(A). One of the major approaches to understand motivation is the behavioural approach.

- The behavioural approach considers the role of external rewards and punishment in motivation in the classroom. According to this approach, reinforcement is also considered important in teaching and learning. This approach promotes the use of grades, stars, rewards, certification, appreciation, etc., for enhancing the motivation of learners.
- Incentives motivate students to be more productive, as they create a sense of pride among students.
- The incentive is an amazing way to ensure that students stay motivated to do their work and learning.

Thus from the above-mentioned points, it is clear that teachers should promote motivation to learn among their students by using incentives to help students learn.

31(B). According to the passage, "According to the IWT, India is permitted to construct water storage on western rivers -Indus, Jhelum, and Chenab -up to 3.6 million acre-feet for various purposes, including domestic use."

So, it is concluded that Beas is not included according to the Indus Water Treaty for the construction of water storage for India.

32(D). According to the passage, "According to this agreement, control over the three "eastern" rivers — the Beas, the Ravi, and the Sutlej — was given to India, while control over the three "western" rivers — the Indus, the Chenab, and the Jhelum — to Pakistan. In aftermath of the 2016 Uri attack, India reviewed the treaty and its provisions and proposed several changes. The treaty was reviewed by India to explore possible ways to use its share of water from rivers, including the Jhelum, flowing into Pakistan."

So, it can be concluded that Chenab, Jhelum is not the correct pair of the eastern and western rivers.

33(D). According to the passage, "India refused to countenance any change of design of the Miyar dam in J&K, as asked by Pakistan, and plans to continue utilization of its allocation under the Indus Waters Treaty."

So, to countenance any change of design of the Miyar dam in J&K is refused by India as asked by Pakistan.

34(C). The meaning of the given words:

- Permit: to allow somebody to do something or something to happen, authorize, sanction, grant, license, and power.
- Ban: to officially say that something is not allowed, often by law, prohibition, forbid, veto, proscribe, outlaw, and embargo.

From the above meaning, it is evident that Ban is the opposite meaning of the word Permit.

recce.

- Investigate: trying to find out all facts about something, probe, scrutinize, look into, and explore.

From the above meaning, it is evident that Investigate is the same meaning as the word Explore.

36(C). 'Aftermath' is a noun.

- A noun is a part of speech that is a name of a thing, a place, or a person. Example: Slovakia.
- Here, "in" is the preposition that is used before the noun "aftermath" to show the time of happening of the Uri attack.
- Aftermath means the consequences or after-effects of a significant unpleasant event.

37(C). According to the passage, "The Indus Waters Treaty is a water-distribution treaty between India and Pakistan, brokered by the World Bank, then the International Bank for Reconstruction and Development. The treaty was signed in Karachi on September 19, 1960, by Prime Minister of India Jawaharlal Nehru and President of Pakistan Ayub Khan."

So, it can be concluded that the only option Indus Waters Treaty is the correct theme of the passage as it is mentioned in the passage and is also signed between the two countries in order to solve the issues related to water distribution and also the construction of the Dam and also the complete story of the passage revolves around the treaty between these two countries.

38(A). "One of" refers to a single entity of a group or subject.

A noun or pronoun or subject of such phrase will be in the plural form and the verb in such cases will always be singular as it refers to only a single subject.

The rule for such sentences:
- One/Every/Each/Neither/Either + of + Noun (Plural) + Verb (Singular).
- Example: One of the best students in the class is Manish.

Here, the error lies in "One of this" as the noun "projects" is in the plural form we need demonstrative adjectives "these" instead of "this" to define the plural noun "projects".

39(D). According to the passage, "The treaty was reviewed by India to explore possible ways to use its share of water from rivers, including the Jhelum, flowing into Pakistan."

So, it is concluded that Jhelum is included which is reviewed by India to use its share of water from rivers.

40(D). According to the given lines,

So, it is concluded that the school boy feels unhappy when he goes to school.

41(A). According to the given lines,
"How can the bird that is born for joy,
Sit in a cage and sing.
How can a child when fears annoy,
But droop his tender wing,"
So, it is concluded that the school boy is compared to a bird.

42(B). Alliteration: The repetition of an initial consonant sound in words that are in close proximity to each other.

Alliteration does not refer to the repetition of consonant letters that begin words, but rather the repetition of the consonant sound at the beginning of words. Ex: Piper picked a peck

Here, sky-lark sings. The sound of s represents Alliteration figure of speech in the above line.

43(D). Metaphor: An expression, often found in literature, that describes a person or object by referring to something that is considered to have similar characteristics to that person or object. Ex: I'm feeling red.

Here, 'Under a cruel eye outworn' represents the teacher who keeps a close eye on students. The child hates to be under scrutiny. He dislikes the fact that he had to spend his day in the supervision of an inconsiderate person.

44(D). According to the given lines,
"I love to rise in a summer morn,
When the birds sing on every tree;
The distant huntsman winds his horn,
And the skylark sings with me.
O! what sweet company."
So, it is concluded that sweet company refer skylark and huntsman horn.

45(C). According to the given lines,
"But to go to school in a summer morn,

O! it drives all joy away;"
So, it is concluded that going to school in the summer morning takes away all the happiness of the child.

46(D). Language acquisition: It refers to the subconscious process of learning a native or second language because of the innate capacity of the human brain.
- It is a natural process whereby children acquire language by observing and repeating what they hear in the natural setting of their native environment.
- Language acquisition does not require any formal instruction, children acquire the language without being taught. It is a natural process so, one does not forget one's native language.

So, it could be concluded that a child learns his/her first language in a natural setting.

- It refers to having a basic knowledge of grammatical rules and their use in communication.
- It is effectively done by providing comprehensible inputs to make the learners actively involved in real communication.
- It refers to the result of deliberate and conscious effort in a formal environment, for a better understanding of foundational skills of language learning.

So, it could be concluded that language learning is a conscious attempt by the learner.

48(B). Multiple Line of Approach:
- The term "multiple line" implies that one is to proceed simultaneously from many different points towards the one and the same end. In teaching a language, it implies attacking the problem from all fronts.
- It means a lesson that is to be taught by the teacher should be tackled from many sides. So, it reflects that the Multi-line approach consists of reaching the same target from different directions and means.
- For example, there is a lesson on 'Holidays' in the textbook. The teacher can have a number of language activities connected with the topic such as oral drill, reading, sentence writing, composition, grammar, translation, language exercises, etc.

So, we can conclude that Teaching a lesson, through a number of language activities connected with the topic, refers to Multiple Line of Approach.

49(C). Present Language in Basic Sentence Patterns:
- Present, and have the students' memories, basic sentence patterns used

in day-to-day conversation. From small utterances, the students can easily pass on to longer sentences.
- In the case of learning mother-tongue, the student's memory span can retain much longer sentences than those of a foreign language.
- The facility thus gained in a foreign language enables the learners to expand the grasp of the language material in respect of sounds and vocabulary items.

So, we can conclude that the 'Present Language in Basic Sentence Patterns' principle of second language could be associated with the above-mentioned statement.

50(D). 'Decorum' in spoken language pertains to appropriate gestures.

Decorum was a principle of classical of appropriate social behavior within set situations.

51(C). The teaching of grammar will help the learners to have good conversational skills as the ultimate aim of every language learner is to acquire the ability to speak and write the language correctly.
- In order to do this, he/she requires knowledge of grammar in some form or the other.
- So, any course in language teaching assigns an important role to grammar.
- The more we are aware of how it works, the more we can monitor the meaning and effectiveness of the way we and others use language.

From the above, we can conclude that Teaching of grammar will help the learners to have good conversational skills.

52(C). Grammar-translation method:
- The Grammar-Translation method of learning a language is through the detailed study of its grammar.
- In this method, the learner first learns grammatical rules and then applies those rules in translating sentences from the target language into the mother tongue.
- Primarily, the mother tongue or native language is used to teach the rule of grammar to the learners so that translations become easier.
- Vocabulary is built using bilingual word lists i.e., to teach the meaning of words in the mother tongue and in the target language.
- Rote learning or memorization plays a vital role when it comes to learning the rules of grammar.

So, the principle of the grammar-translation method is to memorize the rules of grammar.

53(D). The Main Challenges of Teaching

Language in a Diverse Classroom are:
- Issues and challenges to curriculum design.
- Challenge and issues of the teaching-learning process.
- Challenge of teaching-learning materials.
- Challenge of a mixed-ability group of learners.
- Challenge maintaining justice and democracy in the classroom.

So, we can conclude that all of the above are the main challenges of teaching language in a diverse classroom.

54(A). Language skills can be learned better in an integrated manner since it exploits all the skills. For example, when we speak, we also listen simultaneously, when we write we are also reading.

So, from the above-mentioned points, it becomes clear that language skills can be learned better if they are taught in an integrated manner.

55(D). Listening and Reading comes under the receptive category while speaking and writing comes under the productive category of language skills.
- Speaking and writing come under the productive category of language skills because these generate output in form of oral and written. This why these are known as productive skills.
- Listening and Reading comes under the receptive category because the learner receives the inputs given by the teacher. That is why these are known as receptive skills.

So, we can conclude that speaking and writing comes under the productive category of language skills.

56(D). Components in the evaluation of speaking:
- Articulation: While evaluating the speaking of students, the teacher must pay attention to their articulation of words i.e., how they join words including their way of speaking.
- Intonation, stress, and voice quality: The power of persuasion often depends on convincing voice quality. Intonations (Ups and downs in the voice), stressing on important words, and voice quality (change in sound as per the mood and requirement) are an important part of speaking. So, it is important for a teacher to assess the intonations and voice quality of students while they are speaking during their evaluation of speaking skills.
- Vocabulary and Pronunciation: While evaluating the speaking skills, it is important to note down the kind of vocabulary used by the speaker and how he is pronouncing the words. It reflects the proficiency of the speaker in the target language.
- Body language: Using hand and body movements while speaking helps the speaker to connect with the audience and to gain attention. Thus, the body language of students should also be evaluated along with the evaluation of speaking skills.
- Concentration: Children need to know that clear thought in an organized manner keeps the attention of the listener. So, they should speak by organizing their thoughts by concentrating on the main idea of the topic.

Thus, it is clear that evaluation of speaking consists of the evaluation of pronunciation students listening skills:
- Listen and Draw: this particular activity can be used with students who struggle to express themselves in English, Listen and Draw isolates listening from speaking. Simply have your students take out a blank piece of paper and give them instructions on what to draw.
- Dictations: with this activity, the teacher can easily evaluate students listening skills. The teacher just needs to select a couple of words and then call the words one by one and repeat at least once after calling the words. After calling all the words which the students have to write on a separate piece of paper. The teacher collects the papers and from there he can start evaluating each student based on their listening comprehension.
- Oral Presentations: It is more viewed in academic courses where the test takers have to talk about a given or selected topic, nevertheless, that doesn't mean that it cannot be used to assess other learners. Scoring is also easy because the test-taker speaks about a specific topic.

So, we can conclude that the vocabulary assessment task is not the activity of evaluating listening skills.

58(A). Flannel boards can be used in classrooms in a variety of situations.
- The advantage of using a flannel board is that it provides the flexibility of using a material to teach students.
- Flannel boards are used to display pictures, messages.
- In the English Language classroom, it can be used to teach picture composition.
- It allows children to explore stories, apply their imagination, boost fine motor skills, and enhance their creativity.
- The flannel board increases the child's learning abilities.

From the above, we can conclude that the flannel board is useful for teaching picture composition.

59(C). Realia refers to the objects associated with everyday life to be used in the classroom. Realia can be used as props for dialogues to teach new lexical or structural items as it is a tangible teaching-learning object.
- It includes coin, newspaper, map, tickets, fruits, vegetables, etc.
- It makes learning more interesting and enliven by bringing the class to life.
- It ensures the use of accurate and realistic materials in the teaching-learning process.
- It encourages healthy classroom structural items.

60(B). Remedial teaching: During learning, a child makes mistakes willingly-unwillingly or due to some alternative conceptions. It is the job of a teacher to help students to correct those mistakes after diagnosing them. The method so followed is known as remedial teaching. The following are its characteristics:
- It can be used for improving language skills
- To rectify a particular problem area, it can be used. For example, a student is confused among the pronunciation of 'no' and 'know', he can be taught the concept of silent letters.
- It is carried out after the identification of problems and challenges faced by students.
- A teacher should be well aware of students' strengths and weaknesses to apply this method.
- It is a systematic process as the teacher first diagnoses the problem of students and then applies appropriate remedial methods.

So, we conclude that remedial teaching is a systematic process.

61(B). Decimal values of the given numbers:
$$\sqrt{2} = 1.42 \quad \sqrt{3} = 1.73$$
So the number inserted must be between 1.42 and 1.73.
Now checking the options:
(A): $\frac{49}{28} = 1.75$
(B): $\frac{56}{35} = 1.6$
(C): $\frac{63}{45} = 1.4$
(D): $\frac{85}{66} = 1.28$
We can see that only $\frac{56}{35}$ can be put between $\sqrt{2}$ and $\sqrt{3}$.

62(A). Given,
$x, x + 2$ and $x + 4$ are all prime numbers.
As we know,
A number divisible by 1 and itself only is known as a prime number.
Checking the options:
Put $x = 3$, then the numbers are $3, 5, 7$
Put $x = 2$ then the numbers are $2, 4, 6$
Put $x = 11$ then the numbers are $11, 13, 15$
Put $x = 17$ then the numbers are $17, 19, 21$
After analyzing the options we can see that at $x = 3$ all numbers are coming prime.
$\therefore$ The value of $x = 3$

63(D). Given,
Sum of 5 consecutive integers is S.
Let the smallest of these 5 numbers be x.
5 consecutive numbers will be $x, x + 1, x + 2, x + 3, x + 4$.
According to the question,

Largest of these 5 number
$= x + 4 = \left[\dfrac{(S-10)}{5}\right] + 4$
$= \dfrac{(S+10)}{5}$

64(C). Given,
$(a - b) : (a + b) = 1 : 5$
As we know,
$(a + b) \times (a - b) = a^2 - b^2$
$(a + b)^2 + (a - b)^2 = 2\left(a^2 + b^2\right)$
Let $a - b = x$
$\Rightarrow a + b = 5x$
$\Rightarrow a^2 - b^2 = 5x^2$
$(a - b)^2 + (a + b)^2 = x^2 + (5x)^2$
$\Rightarrow 2\left(a^2 + b^2\right) = 26x^2$
$\Rightarrow a^2 + b^2 = 13x^2$
$\therefore \left(a^2 - b^2\right) : \left(a^2 + b^2\right) = 5 : 13$

65(D). As we know,
$(x + y + z)^2 = x^2 + y^2 + z^2 + 2(xy + yz + zx)$
$3^2 = 101 + 2(xy + yz + zx)$
$\Rightarrow 2(xy + yz + zx) = 9 - 101$
$\Rightarrow 2(xy + yz + zx) = -92$
$\Rightarrow (xy + yz + zx) = \dfrac{-92}{2}$
$\Rightarrow (xy + yz + zx) = -46$
Again, As we know,
$x^3 + y^3 + z^3 - 3xyz = (x + y + z)$
$\left[(x + y + z)^2 - 3(xy + yz + zx)\right]$
$\Rightarrow x^3 + y^3 + z^3 - 3xyz = 3$
$\left[3^2 - 3 \times (-46)\right]$
$= 3[9 + 138]$
$= 3 \times 147$
$= 441$
$\Rightarrow \sqrt{[x^3 + y^3 + z^3 - 3xyz]} = \sqrt{441}$
$\therefore \sqrt{[x^3 + y^3 + z^3 - 3xyz]} = 21$

66(C). Given:
$x = \sqrt{10} + 3$
We know that,
$a^2 - b^2 = (a + b)(a - b)$

$a^3 - b^3 = (a - b)\left(a^2 + ab + b^2\right)$
$\dfrac{1}{x} = \dfrac{1}{\sqrt{10}+3}$
$= \dfrac{\sqrt{10}-3}{(\sqrt{10}+3)(\sqrt{10}-3)}$
$= \dfrac{\sqrt{10}-3}{(\sqrt{10})^2-(3)^2}$
$\Rightarrow \dfrac{1}{x} = \sqrt{10} - 3$
$\Rightarrow x - \dfrac{1}{x} = \sqrt{10} + 3 - \sqrt{10} + 3 = 6 \quad \cdots$
(1)
Squaring both side of equation (1),
$\Rightarrow \left(x - \dfrac{1}{x}\right)^2 = (6)^2$
$\Rightarrow x^2 - 2x\dfrac{1}{x} + \dfrac{1}{x^2} = 36$
$\Rightarrow x^2 - 2 + \dfrac{1}{x^2} = 36$
$\Rightarrow x^2 + \dfrac{1}{x^2} = 38$
$\therefore x^3 - \dfrac{1}{x^3} = \left(x - \dfrac{1}{x}\right)\left(x^2 + x\dfrac{1}{x} + \dfrac{1}{x^2}\right)$

$x^3 - \dfrac{1}{x^3} = 254$

67(A). Given,
Ratio of two complementary angles is $1 : 5$.
As we know,
Sum of two complementary angles is $90°$.
Let the two angles be $1x$ and $5x$.
Sum of two complementary angles is $90°$.
$\Rightarrow (1x + 5x) = 90°$
$\Rightarrow x = 15°$
$\Rightarrow (5x - x) = 60°$
$\therefore$ The difference between two complementary angles is $60°$.

68(B). Given,
The length of a pendulum $= 60cm$ and an arc of length $= 16.5cm$
Length of arc $= \dfrac{\theta}{360°} \times 2\pi \times$ Radius
$\Rightarrow 16.5 \times 360° = 2 \times \dfrac{22}{7} \times 60 \times \theta$
$\Rightarrow \theta = \dfrac{63°}{4}$
$\Rightarrow \theta = 15°45'$
$\therefore$ The angle through which it swings $= 15°45'$

69(C). 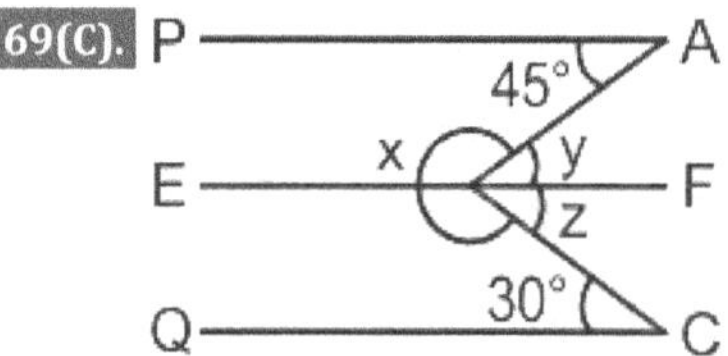

Draw a line segment EF which is parallel to PA and passes through the point making angle x and name the angles y and z.
$y = 45°$ (Alternate interior angles)
$z = 30°$ (Alternate interior angles)
$x + y + z = 360°$ (Complete angle)
$\Rightarrow x = 360° - z - y$
$\Rightarrow x = 360° - 30° - 45°$
$\Rightarrow x = 360° - 75°$
$\therefore x$ is $285°$.

70(B). Given,
A spherical ball of radius $R = 3cm$

Ball one radius $(r_1) = 1.5cm$
Ball two radius $(r_2) = 2cm$
Ball three radius $(r_3) = xcm$
As we know,
Volume of sphere $= \left(\dfrac{4}{3}\right)\pi R^3$
Volume of big spherical ball $=$ Volume of total spherical balls
$\Rightarrow \left(\dfrac{4}{3}\right)\pi R^3 = \left(\dfrac{4}{3}\right)\pi (r_1)^3 + \left(\dfrac{4}{3}\right)\pi (r_2)^3 + \left(\dfrac{4}{3}\right)\pi (r_3)^3$
$\Rightarrow 3^3 = 2^3 + (1.5)^3 + x^3$
$\Rightarrow 27 = 8 + 3.375 + x^3$
$\Rightarrow x^3 = 15.625$
$\Rightarrow x = 2.5cm$
$\therefore$ The value of x is $2.5cm$.

71(B). Given,
Circumference of the base $= 44m$
High conical tent $= 9m$
As we know,
$\Rightarrow r = 7m$
Volume of air contained
$= \left(\dfrac{1}{3}\right) \times \left(\dfrac{22}{7}\right) \times 7 \times 7 \times 9$
$= 462m^3$
$\therefore$ The volume of air contained $= 462m^3$

72(C). Given,
Total average marks of class $= 43$
Number of boys $= 25$
Average marks of boys $= 40$
Average marks of girls $= 48$
As we know,
Means of the marks $= \left(\dfrac{\text{Total marks}}{\text{number of students}}\right)$
Let, the number of girls $= x$
$\Rightarrow (25 \times 40) + (48 \times x) = 43 \times (25 + x)$
$\Rightarrow 1000 + 48x = 1075 + 43x$
$\Rightarrow 5x = 75$
$\Rightarrow x = 15$
$\therefore$ The number of girls is 15.

73(C). Given,
$x = 6 \times y \, ...(1)$
$(x + 4) = 4 \times (y + 4) \, ...(2)$
Put the value of eq. (1) in eq. (2), we get
$\Rightarrow 6y + 4 = 4y + 16$
$\Rightarrow 6y - 4y = 16 - 4$
$\Rightarrow 2y = 12$
$\Rightarrow y = 6$
$\therefore$ The present age of y is 6 years.

74(D). Given,
$18\dfrac{1}{3} + 9\dfrac{2}{3} - 10\dfrac{1}{3} = 1\dfrac{2}{3} + ?$
$\Rightarrow 18 + 9 + \dfrac{1}{3} + \dfrac{2}{3} - \left(10 + 1 + \dfrac{1}{3} + \dfrac{2}{3}\right) = ?$
$\Rightarrow 28 - 12 = ?$
$\Rightarrow ? = 16$
$\therefore$ The value of (?) is 16.

75(C). Given,
LCM $= 90 \times$ HCF
LCM + HCF $= 1456$
One of the Numbers $= 160$
As we know,

Product of two numbers = Product of their LCM and HCF

Let HCF be x and the other number be N.

$\Rightarrow$ LCM $= 90x$

The sum of LCM and HCF $= 91x$

$\Rightarrow 91x = 1456$

$\Rightarrow x = 16$

LCM $\times$ HCF $= 160 \times N$

$\Rightarrow 90 \times 16 \times 16 = 160 \times N$

$\Rightarrow N = 144$

$\therefore$ The other Number is 144.

76(D). Given,

A dishonest shopkeeper used to sell onions at Rs. $30/kg$.

Weight of onions bought by customer $= 2kg$

He gave $750g$ instead of $1kg$ to a customer.

Actual weight of onions received by customer $= 750 \times 2 = 1500g$

$= 1.5kg$

$= 60 - 45 = $ Rs. 15

$\therefore$ Profit percentage $= (\frac{15}{45}) \times 100 = 33.33\%$

77(B). Given,

$S = 16km/h$

$D = 40km$

Rest time $= 4$ min after every km

As we know,

Speed $= \dfrac{\text{Distance}}{\text{Time}}$

Time taken without break $= \frac{40}{16} = 2.5hrs$

Interval in distance of $40km = 39$

Resting time $= 39 \times 4 = 156$

$= 2hr\ 36min$

Total time $= 5hrs\ 6min$

$\therefore$ The time taken is $5hrs\ 6min$.

78(B). Given,

-6, - 8, - 2, 3, 2, 0, 5, 4, 8

As we know,

The range of a set of data is the difference between the highest and the lowest value.

Now,

The highest value in the data $= 8$

The lowest value in the data $= -8$

Difference between the highest and the lowest data $= 8 - (-8) = 16$

$\therefore$ The required temperature is 16 $^{\circ}$C.

79(A). Given,

The marks obtained by a student = 75, 75, 75, 75, 75

As we know,

If n is odd then, Median $= \dfrac{(n+1)}{2}$ th term

Arranging the given data in ascending order get,

75, 75, 75, 75, 75

Here,

The total number of data (n) = 5, which is an odd number

Then,

$\dfrac{(n+1)}{2}$ th term = 3th term = 75

Required median $= \dfrac{(n+1)}{2}$ th term = 3th term

$\Rightarrow 75$

$\therefore$ The median of the given numbers is 75.

80(B). Given,

There are some given central tendencies to find what will be affected by one or two extremely large or extremely small values.

The mean, median, and mode are the most popular metrics of central tendency.

The median and mode may or may not be changed by extreme values.

But the mean is the central tendency metric that is most likely to be influenced by an extremely small or large number. The only measure of central tendency that is independent of all values is the mean, which is calculated by dividing the total of

numbers, shape, quantity, and patterns. Mathematics is the 'queen of all sciences' and its presence is there in all the subjects. The Nature of Mathematics is Logical as it relies on:

- evaluation of truth or likelihood of statements.
- development of skills like speed, accuracy, estimation.
- improvement of reasoning power, analytical and, critical thinking.
- enhancement of scientific attitude like estimating, finding and verifying results.

So, it becomes clear that the nature of Mathematics is logical.

82(C). Mathematics: Mathematics is a systematized, organized, and exact branch of Science. It plays an important role in accelerating the social, economical, and technological growth of a nation. It helps in solving problems of life that need enumeration and calculation.

The nature of Mathematics can be made explicit by understanding the chief characteristics of Mathematics:

- Mathematics is a science of discovery.
- Mathematics is an intellectual game.
- It deals with the art of drawing conclusions.
- It is a tool subject.
- It involves an intuitive method.
- It is the science of exactness, precision, and accuracy.
- It is the subject of a logical and specific sequence.
- It requires the application of rules and concepts to new situations.
- It is a logical study structure and patterns.

So, ' expanded expression' is not related to the nature of Mathematics.

83(A). Role of Mathematics in School Curriculum: National Curriculum

framework, 2005 recommends that teaching of mathematics at the primary level should focus on:

- Children understand the basic structure of Mathematics like Arithmetic, algebra, geometry, and trigonometry, the basic content areas of school mathematics, all offer a methodology for abstraction, structuration, and generalization.
- Mathematics implies understanding of the appropriate use of learned mathematical techniques.
- Teachers engage every child in the class with the conviction that everyone can learn mathematics and enrich them with examples of achievements and contributions of mathematicians from different regions and different social groups.
- Helping students to connect classroom

problems.

So, from the above-mentioned points, it becomes clear that important Mathematics implies understanding the appropriate use of learned mathematical techniques.

84(A). Teaching-learning of mathematics takes account of well-defined objectives. Some Curricular Expectation of Teaching Mathematics at the Primary Level are as follows:

- To ensure a good start for the students in learning mathematics.
- To give clarity on the fundamental concepts and processes of the subject.
- To develop a connection between the logical functioning of daily life and that of mathematical thinking.
- To create love, faith and interest for learning mathematics.
- To develop in them a taste and confidence in mathematics.
- To develop language and symbolic notations with standard algorithms of performing number operations.
- Represent part of whole as a fraction and order simple fractions.
- To develop an appreciation for accuracy.
- To acquaint them with the relation of mathematics with their present as well as future life.
- To develop in them the habits like regularity, practice, patience, self-reliance and hard work.
- To link mathematics with other subjects.

So, we conclude that analysing and inferring from the representation of grouped data is not curriculum expectation at the primary level.

85(D). Algebra is generalized arithmetic where letters are used as symbols to represent numbers. Every number is a constant and every symbol can be assigned different values in different situations.

Algebraic expressions are formed using symbols and constants. Four fundamental operations on the symbols and constants to form expressions are used. Terms are parts of an expression which are separated by '+' or '_' sign. It may be a constant, a variable or combination of both. The algorithm (method) involved in solving real-life problems is to:

- Understand the situation expressed in the word problem
- Choose a symbol and substitute it for the unknown to be determined
- Write an equation from the given relation in the problem
- Solve the equation and find the value of the unknown
- Verify the correctness of the solution

So, it is concluded that algebra is best seen as a compact language and a means of

achievement will go up.

- The teacher should encourage the students to use a problem-solving approach to solve mathematical problems i.e., where teachers create a problematic situation for students and then assist them in perceiving, defining, and stating the problems.
- The teacher tries to raise a problem in the minds of students so that it can stimulate purposeful reflective thinking to arrive at a solution.
- Also, it is necessary to connect real-life problems with mathematics to make the students familiar with the use of mathematics in their daily life.
- The teaching of mathematics is mainly focused on the practical usability of mathematics i.e., to enable the children to apply mathematics in their daily life

understanding of algorithms which is correct, so the teacher assigns full marks to both the students.

- There is not a fixed pattern or method to solve a problem in mathematics. This enhances divergent thinking.
- Mathematics increases logical thinking.
- The students should be taught in a way so that they will think mathematically and use their logical thinking in their daily life.
- The teaching-learning process should not focus on robotic learning of steps of solving any question.
- The questions which only check the procedural learning, rote memorization, and drill do not initiate the mathematical thinking of students.
- Another aim is to develop numeracy skills in the students.

commonly used to identify the cause of student errors when they make consistent mistakes. It is a process of reviewing a student's work and then looking for patterns of misunderstanding. Errors in mathematics can be factual, procedural, or conceptual, and may occur for a number of reasons.

The most probable reason for writing 0.50 is larger than 0.5 is a misconception regarding the significance of zero in ordering decimal.

- They would not have a clear concept about dealing with zero right to the decimal.
- The only time you would want to keep zeros is when dealing with money. Monetary amounts require two place values after the decimal to indicate cents to the Hundredth place.
- Writing .5 cents is not appropriate; it should be Rs0.50.
- The concrete experience of representation of decimal numbers on a number line is required for abstract problems.
- Such misconceptions can be cleared by several examples.

So, we can conclude that students often make a mistake in comparing decimal numbers. For example, 0.50 is larger than 0.5. The most probable reason for this error is a misconception regarding the significance of zero in ordering decimal.

87(C). Problems of Teacher's attitude in teaching and learning of mathematics:

- It is the responsibility of a teacher to develop a liking and positive attitude for mathematics among the students.
- The attitude of students towards mathematics plays a significant role in their achievement. If the students learn mathematics with a positive attitude, interest, and liking then their level of

learning mathematics.

88(C). Remedial teaching refers to the teaching which is intended to improve the ability of slow learners to learn something. It is an integral part of the teaching-learning program, also known as compensatory or corrective teaching.

The Most Effective Strategies of Remedial Teaching:

- Tutorial: In this strategy, the teacher conducts remedial tutorial sessions for the students who have learning difficulties.
- Supervised: By using this strategy, the teacher supervises the learning of the students and guides them in which they suffer in learning the concepts.
- Action research: It is an interactive method of collecting information that's used to explore topics of teaching, curriculum development, and student behavior in the classroom. It refers to the integration of practice-based experiences in the learning process to help learners with difficulties in developing a better understanding of the concept.
- Programmed test: It refers to a test in which the items are so presented that they depend upon the earlier response of the learners, thus helps to design a test suited to the learning ability of the learners.
- Individual Teaching: It is characterized by the teacher in the educational process with individual students works individually, based on their intellectual characteristics.

So, we can conclude that tutorial and supervision both are the main remedial teaching strategies.

89(B). In this question, both the students have solved the problems according to their

algorithms are integral to solving problems in mathematics.

90(A). Mathematics is commonly perceived as the most difficult subject at all stages in the school curriculum. Further, its abstractness is highlighted in the textbooks and classroom transactions, although all the concepts included in the mathematics curriculum are related to the real-life experiences of the child. It is a common belief that mathematics concepts cannot be learned without being taught.

- A teacher asked the students to collect leaves and to identify symmetry patterns. This task reflects the teacher's efforts to relate a real-life experience with mathematical concepts.
- We can connect mathematics in our daily life. There are many activities and maths exercises which are directly or indirectly connected with our daily routine life.
- Certain qualities that are nurtured by mathematics are the power of reasoning, creativity, abstract or spatial thinking, critical thinking, problem-solving ability, and even effective communication skills.
- Maths puzzles and riddles encourage and attract an alert and open-minded attitude among students and help them develop clarity in their thinking.
  Emphasis should be laid on the development of the clear concept in mathematics which reflects daily life experience in a child, right from the primary classes.

So, we can conclude that through the above activity or task, the teacher wants to relate a real-life experience with mathematical concepts.

91(C). The respiratory system of cockroaches:

- The respiratory system of the cockroach consists of a network of the trachea, that opens through 10 pairs of small holes called spiracles present on the lateral side of the body.
- Thin branching tubes (tracheal tubes subdivided into tracheoles) carry oxygen from the air to all the parts. air enters the body through spiracles.
- When air through external openings, enters into its respiratory system, spiracles serve as muscular valves paving the way to the internal respiratory system. The respiratory organ of the cockroach is referred to as the tracheae.
- The trachea is a dense array of a network of air tubes found in the internal system.
- Tracheae are known to balance the tissues and cells of the body. Here, oxygen is used up to liberate energy.
- Likewise, carbon-dioxide rich air passes into the trachea and moves outwards through the spiracles.
- Carbon dioxide is given out as a result of the respiratory process.

92(B). The dish is named Undhiya or upside down, in Gujrati.
- This dish is a regional speciality of Surat.
- A little-known fact is that the name Undhiyu comes from the Gujarati word Undhu, which means being upside down.
- The upside-down is here because the pot in which this food is made is placed upside down.
- There are a total of eight vegetables are stirred upside down and cooked over a wood fire in large earthen (clay) pots along with fresh spices to give Undhiyu its distinctive texture and flavour.
- The pot was sealed and kept between hot coals.
- Undhiya would be eaten with bajra rotis, freshly cooked on chulha.

93(A). Mammals have glandular skin with hairs.
- Mammals or Mammalia class of animal kingdom are found in a variety of habitats – polar ice caps, deserts, mountains, forests, grasslands and dark caves.
- Some of them have adapted to fly or live in water.
- The most unique mammalian characteristic is the presence of milk-producing glands (mammary glands) by which the young ones are nourished.
- They have two pairs of limbs, adapted for walking, running, climbing, burrowing, swimming or flying.
- The skin of mammals is unique in possessing hair. External ears or pinnae are present. Different types of teeth are present in the jaw. The heart is four-chambered. They are homoiothermous. Respiration is by lungs. Sexes are separate and fertilisation is internal.

94(C). The essential nutrients that the body required for normal growth and metabolism, apart from water, protein, carbohydrate, and fats, are Minerals and Vitamins.
- Vitamins are a group of heterogeneous substances that differ widely in their chemical nature and function.
- They are classified based on their solubility in water or fats as water-soluble and fat-soluble vitamins.
- The fat-soluble vitamins A, D, E, and K are found in foods in association with unrelated compounds, containing nitrogen as a part of their chemical structure.
- The different B vitamins are called vitamin B1, B2, and so on, or by their chemical names.

95(A). The device used for producing electric current is called a generator.
- Generator: The device used for producing electric current is called a generator, The generator converts mechanical energy into electrical energy.
- A galvanometer is an instrument used for detecting and indicating electric current.
- An ammeter is a measuring instrument used to measure the current in a circuit. Ampere is the SI unit of current.
- An electric motor is an electrical machine that converts electrical energy into mechanical energy.

96(A). As we know, some electrons are the free particles in the atoms. When we apply the electric potential across the conductor then these free electrons move and we call it electric current.
- The charge on the electron is Negative.
- So, we can say that Electric current is considered to be the flow of Negative Charge.

97(A). Earthquakes are able to initiate landslides over mountainous regions or wet regions.
- If the earthquakes are under the sea bed, this sudden shake can create extreme pressure outwards and might take a shape of a Tsunami.
- Sometimes the earthquakes can break the dams and overflows of water can create the situation of floods.
So, landslides, Tsunami, and Floods can be caused by earthquakes.

98(A). The major source of minerals in the soil is the parent rock from which soil is formed. Rock weathering is a process that forms soil. Rocks are naturally occurring soil aggregates that are rich in minerals.
So rock is the source of minerals in the soil.

99(A). Ferromagnetic substances are those which gets strongly magnetised when placed in an external magnetic field. They have strong tendency to move from a region of weak magnetic field to strong magnetic field, i.e., they get strongly attracted to a magnet.
The individual atoms (or ions or molecules) in a ferromagnetic material possess a dipole moment as in a paramagnetic material. However, they interact with one another in such a way that they spontaneously align themselves in a

Optical fibers use total internal reflection to transmit light. It has a solid core of dense glass surrounded by a less dense cladding. The light ray passing through the inner core is reflected back instead of being refracted to the rarer cladding.

101(A). When acid and base is mixed together, then salt is formed.
Acids are generally sour in taste and it turns blue litmus paper to red. Bases are bitter in taste and turn red litmus paper into red. If we mix equal amounts of an acid and a base then two chemicals essentially cancel out each other and produce salt and water. Mixing equal amounts of a strong acid with strong base results in a neutral solution whose pH value remains 7 and this type of reactions, which is also known as neutralization reactions. So when we mix an acid and a base together then salt formation takes place and water is also released.

102(A). The amplitude of a wave is its height.
The amplitude of the wave represents the maximum displacement of a particle from the resting position on the medium. In a sense, the amplitude is the distance from the rest to the crest. Similarly, the amplitude can be measured from the resting position to the trough position. Therefore, the amplitude of a wave is a measure of its height.

103(B). In a transverse wave, the motion of the particles is perpendicular to the wave's direction of propagation.
Transverse wave, the motion in which all points of a wave oscillate along the path at right angles to the direction of propagation of the wave. Surface waves on water, seismic S (secondary) waves, and electromagnetic (eg, radio and light) waves

are examples of transverse waves.

104(A). The deficiency of Vitamin K causes the failure of blood clotting.
- The process that prevents excessive bleeding both inside and outside the body is known as clotting. Vitamin K plays an important role in blood clotting.
- Vitamin K is generally of two types: Vitamin K_1 which comes from our food especially leafy vegetables and other is Vitamin K_2 which is produced by our body.
- The test which is to detect blood clotting and to check the deficiency of vitamin K is prothrombin time (PT).

105(C). The liver is the largest gland in the body.
- The liver mainly secretes 'Bile Juice'

the form of glycogen.
- Heparin, Urea, and Bile Juice are produced in the liver.
- The major supply of blood to the liver is by 'portal vein' (75%)& remaining (25%) by Hepatic artery.
- That is why the liver is known to have a 'Dual blood supply'.

106(D). F, Cl, Br, I all are present in the same group of halogens.
- F is at the top and I is at the bottom of the group.
- As we go down a group, the electropositivity increases, and hence Iodine (I) becomes the most electropositive element. As it is the least electronegative, it is the most electropositive.
- Iodine is the least reactive of the halogens as well as the most electropositive halogen.
- Iodine has a tendency to lose electrons and form positive ions during chemical reactions.
- It is also the heaviest and the least abundant of stable halogens.
- The value of electronegativity of Iodine is 2.5.

Order of electropositivity:
$I > Br > Cl > F$
So, Iodine is the most electropositive element among halogens.

107(C). Thrust is the force that makes the aircraft move in the air.
Thrust is used to overcome the drag of an airplane, and to overcome the weight of a rocket.

108(C). Phosphorus is a material on the matchstick.
- The striking surface of the matchbox contains red phosphorus and the top of the matchstick contains potassium

chlorate.
- Antimony sulfide, sulfur, potassium chlorate are the chemicals present in match stick. The head of safety matches is made of an oxidizing agent such as potassium chlorate, mixed with sulfur, fillers, and glass powder.
- The striking surface of the matchbox is made rough by adding some powdered glass. Red phosphorus is present on the striking surface of the matchbox.
- When you rub the head of the matchstick on the striking surface of the matchbox, some heat is generated due to the friction.
- This heat breaks a small part of the red phosphorus chain.
- After that, some red phosphorus transforms into white phosphorus.
- White phosphorus is a highly volatile
- The sulfur catches fire and ignites the wood..

109(D). Inside a pressure cooker,
- the pressure can increase by an additional 1.5 atm, to almost 2 atm.
- At that pressure, water boils at 121°C.
- That means we are cooking food at a much higher temperature than the normal of 100°C.

And since the cooking process speeds up at higher temperatures,
- our food cooks faster.
- It also remains juicy and doesn't dry out, since the water stays in liquid form.

Cooking food in a cooker increases vapour pressure which increases the boiling point of water and hence makes the cooking food faster.

110(D). Magnetic materials are classified into three categories, based on the behavior of materials in the magnetic field. The three types of materials are diamagnetic, paramagnetic, and ferromagnetic.
- Diamagnetic substances when placed in an external magnetic field produce negative magnetization. Therefore, diamagnetic substances are repelled by magnets.
- Paramagnetic substances acquire a small net magnetic moment in the direction of the applied field. Therefore, they are slightly attracted by the magnetic field.
- Ferromagnetic materials are strongly attracted by the magnetic field. These materials retain the magnetism even when the magnetic field is removed. This lagging of magnetization of a ferromagnetic substance behind the magnetic field is called Hysteresis.

So, magnetic material not always attracted to the Magnet.

111(B). The teacher should give clear instructions to all the students before going on field trips. These instructions should include what is expected from them in the trip and the things that they can and cannot bring along with them. They would not be expected to take the full schoolbag on field trips because it won't be required there.

112(C). The concept of 'seed germination' can be taught best by asking the students to sow seeds, notice their different stages, and draw them as learning by doing and experiencing the consequences of one's own actions helps learners in:
- retaining information and concepts for a longer period.
- enhancing skills and better understanding of the concept.
- nurturing their curiosity and interest in applying theoretical knowledge.

So, it could be concluded the concept of 'seed germination' can be taught best by asking the students to sow seeds, notice their different stages, and draw them.

113(D). Sound is one of the important topics which is compulsorily and included in the science curriculum. There are many subtopics in the topic of sound which are related to pitch, vibration, tone, etc. In the above question, the teacher wants to show students the relationship between vibrations and sound.

Feeling the vibrations in your throat while speaking will be most aligned with this lesson objective because
- When we speak both sound and vibrations occur in enough quantity so that they could be observed.
- Since speaking is an internal process the students relate sound with vibration correctly.
- The frequency of sound with the amount of vibration can be observed.
- While speaking both vibrations and sound occur at the same time which increases the chance of understanding the relationship.

114(B). Fibre to Fabric is a lesson included in the curriculum of science in class 7 NCERT. Here many concepts related to fibres have been discussed and the transformation of fibre to fabric is also given clearly in a step by step manner.

Here the students grasp the concepts like:
- Steps involved in the conversion of fibre to fabric.
- Separation of fibres from cotton seeds.
- Sources of various fibres like wool, silk and cotton.
- The life cycle of the caterpillars.
- Process of rearing silkworms under laboratory conditions.

- Processing of natural fibres into wool.
- the weaving process of silk thread into cloth by the weavers.

115(C). A plant is a living organism. Do plants respire? is best suited to develop deductive reasoning in students because:
- Here an established generalization is given that a " Plant is a living organism".
- Children are proceeding from general to specific which is a characteristic of the deductive method.
- Children are first given a fact that plants are living things then they are going to characteristics of plants.
- One of that characteristics is the respiration of plants.
- Food production, transpiration, and reproduction are more characteristics of plants.

- The same soil is now left for drying in the hot sun for some time till it loses its moisture.
- The same soil is weighed again after drying.
- The student compares the change in weight of the soil.
- His misconception that" soil does not contain any moisture" will be cleared.

So, comparing the weights of a soil sample before and after drying under sunlight would be best suited to clarify this misconception.

118(C). Making a protective solution that prevents rusting of iron is the best example of an 'authentic task' that he can use to assess students regarding the concept of chemical change because
- The process and reason for rusting of

- To rectify a particular problem area, it can be used. For example, a student is confused between the pronunciation of 'no' and 'know', he can be taught the concept of silent letters.
- It is carried out after the identification of problems and challenges faced by students.
- A teacher should be well aware of students' strengths and weaknesses to apply this method.
- It is a systematic process as the teacher first diagnoses the problem of students and then applies appropriate remedial methods.

Thus, we conclude that remedial teaching should be planned after diagnosing the learning difficulties of the students in science teaching.

most appropriate instructional aid for a teacher to introduce the concept of sedimentation because:
- A glass of water will be taken.
- Some mud which has many particles like dust, sand, and pebbles will be put in that glass of water.
- The glass will be left for some time.
- After some time students can observe all the mud particles settle down on the bottom of the glass due to the effect of gravity.
- Thus students get introduced to a new topic called sedimentation in an effective manner.

So, A Glass of muddy water is the most appropriate instructional aid for a teacher to introduce the concept of sedimentation.

117(B). Comparing the weights of a soil sample before and after drying under sunlight would be best suited to clarify this misconception because:
- One lump of soil will be taken from the ground.
- The soil will be weighed immediately after it is taken from the ground.

formed on the iron.
- They realize this as a chemical change.
- Now the students are asked to make a protective solution that prevents rusting of iron.
- Here they can be assessed through the substance they are using to make that protective solution.
- Because the substance they use shows their understanding level regarding the chemical change.

So, making a protective solution that prevents rusting of iron is the best example of an 'authentic task' that he can use to assess students regarding the concept of chemical change.

119(D). Remedial Teaching: During learning, a child makes mistakes willingly-unwillingly or due to some alternative conceptions. It is the job of a teacher to help students to correct those mistakes after diagnosing them. The method so followed is known as remedial teaching. The following are its characteristics:
- It can be used for improving language skills.

coordination and movement.
- It is a type of learning disability associated with motor skill development, especially fine motor skills. It is also known as Clumsy Child Syndrome or Motor Learning Disability.
- Children with dyspraxia tend to struggle with balance and posture.
- Most individuals with dyspraxia manifest a combination of both ideational or planning dyspraxia and ideomotor or executive dyspraxia wherein ideational or planning dyspraxia affects the planning and coordination, and ideomotor or executive dyspraxia affects the fluency and speed of motor activities.

So, as you can see from the above-mentioned points, a disorder characterised by problems with movement and coordination is dyspraxia whereas a disorder that affects higher verbal skills and the disorder that affects the ability to understand numbers is known as verbal learning disability and dyscalculia, respectively.

Child Development and Pedagogy

1. Whom of the following has not propounded the learning theory?
(a) Thorndike (b) Skinner
(c) Kohler (d) B.S. Bloom

2. Meaning of stagnation in education is:
(a) Retention of a child in a same class for more than one year
(b) Not going to school by the child
(c) Taking not admission in school by the child

(a) .... process and keep the children passive
(b) Development of cognitive, affective and psychomotor domain of children will take place
(c) Emphasis will be only on reading, writing and mathematical skills
(d) Teaching system will be autocratic

4. Human development starts from:
(a) Stage of infancy
(b) Pre-childhood stage
(c) Pre-natal stage
(d) Post-childhood stage

5. "Adolescence is the period of great stress, strain, storm and strike" is the statement of :
(a) Crow & Crow
(b) Stanley Hall
(c) Jersield
(d) Simpson

6. Which of the following stages of development is called as 'A unique stage of emotional development' by Cole and Bruce?
(a) Adolescence (b) Childhood
(c) Infancy (d) Adulthood

7. In cognitive development heredity establishes:
(a) The basic nature of physical structure such as the brain.
(b) The development of the physical structure.
(c) The existence of reflexes.
(d) All of these

8. According to Piaget's cognitive development theory, accommodation is referred to:
(a) A find of matching between the already existing cognitive structures and the environmental needs as they arise.
(b) Adjust to new ways of thinking and behaving by making modifications in one's existing cognitive structures.
(c) Disequilibrium between previous knowledge and new knowledge.
(d) Arrangement of perceptual and cognitive in formations in

.... that are covered by evaluation?
(a) Cognitive domain
(b) Affective domain
(c) Conative domain
(d) Psychomotor domain

10. Which type of learning mainly influences personality of the child?
(a) Trial and Error learning
(b) Imitation learning
(c) Insightful learning
(d) Instructional learning

11. Which of the following is considered a sign being gifted?
(a) Curiosity
(b) Creative ideas
(c) Fighting with other
(d) (A) and (B) both

12. In which stage, the child responds to inferred reality?
(a) Sensori-motor stage
(b) Pre-operational stage
(c) Concrete operational stage
(d) Formal operational stage

13. Growth in adolescence is reverse of that in childhood because:
(a) All part of the body grow simultaneously.
(b) The torso grows first.
(c) Legs accelerate first.
(d) Hands, legs and feet accelerate first.

14. What is the adverse effect of insisting on the same answers from all children?
(a) It will discourage children from listening to the teacher.

(b) It will stop children from speaking in the classroom.
(c) It will hinder the growth of the child's own understanding and imagination.
(d) It will encourage children to copy from others.

15. What is the responsibility of a teacher for proper social development of adolescents?
(a) Information about HIV and other sex-related diseases should be provided on a scientific manner by the teachers to the young adolescents. If necessary, teachers and parents must take

.... Hence, it is suggested that importance should be given on using new dynamic methods of teaching.
(c) The adolescent has to face a large number of problems at this stage. As such, proper guidance and counseling should be provided by teachers.
(d) Group games, debates, seminars, conferences may be organised. These will help the adolescents to participate in social activities,

16. After occurrence of a desirable behaviour, the teacher says 'very good' to the child. She has used:
(a) Primary reinforcer
(b) Secondary reinforcer
(c) Negative reinforcement
(d) None of the above

17. Which one of the following is NOT a type of learning according to Gagne's Theory of Learning?
(a) Verbal association
(b) Signal learning
(c) Proper Prerequisites
(d) Concept learning

18. Which sequence depicts the correct hierarchical order of learning outcomes of affective domain in Bloom's taxonomy?
(a) Receiving, responding, valuing, organizing, characterizing,
(b) Responding, valuing, organizing, receiving, characterizing
(c) Organizing, receiving, valuing, characterizing, responding
(d) Valuing, receiving, responding, characterizing, organizing

19. Which one of the following is the key principles of inclusive education for children?

(a) Principle of Equality

(b) Principle of Participation

(c) Principle of acceptance

(d) All of above

20. Which one of the following statement is related to inclusive education?

(a) No discrimination among students

(b) Equal educational opportunity for all

(c) Adapting to the needs of students, for example, making institutions disabled-friendly

(d) All of above

(a) Peace

(b) Childhood

(c) Adolescence

(d) None of these

22. To which of the following events does the child first start getting attracted?

(a) Light   (b) Mother

(c) Sound   (d) Meal

23. The socialization of a child is determined by which of the following techniques?

(a) Interview technique

(b) Sociometry Techniques

(c) Inspection techniques

(d) Biography study techniques

24. _____________ places the child at the centre of the learning, and can also be referred to as 'invisible pedagogy'.

(a) Constructivist pedagogy

(b) Social constructivism pedagogy

(c) Both (A) and (B)

(d) None of these

25. What should be the amendments in teacher preparation in classroom management?

(a) Teacher with instructional approach to classroom management To provide candidates with feedback through curriculum and guided exercises

(b) Addressing the challenges faced by teacher candidates and new teachers in creating a positive classroom context

(c) Both (A) and (B)

(d) None of the above

26. What role should parents play in a child's learning process?

(a) Forward-looking

(b) Sympathetic

(c) Neutral

(d) Negative

27. _________ aims to study a child's development, especially information processing, conceptual processing, perceptual skills, language learning and other aspects related to brain development.

(a) Cognitive development

(b) Psychodevelopment

learning can the feelings of fear, love and hate be easily generated in the child?

(a) Classical contract theory

(b) Psychology contract theory

(c) Educational contract theory

(d) All of the above

29. The theory of classical conditioning was propounded by I.V. Paulov in the year _________.

(a) 1904   (b) 1906

(c) 1930   (d) 1924

30. The _________ of learning in children, in which the learner perceives and responds to the whole situation, comes under Kohler's theory of understanding.

(a) field theory

(b) associative principle

(c) Both (A) and (B)

(d) none of the above

Language - I: English

Ques (31-39): Direction : Read the passage given below and answer the question that follow by selecting the most appropriate option.

One day in 1924, five men who were camping in the Cascade Mountains of Washington saw a group of huge apelike creatures coming out of the woods. They hurried back to their cabin and locked themselves inside. While they were in, the creatures attacked them by throwing rocks against the walls of the cabin. After several hours, these strange hairy giants went back into the woods. After this incident the men returned to the town and told the people of their adventure. However, only a few people accepted their story. These were the people who remembered hearing tales about footprints of an animal that walked like a human being. The five men, however, were not the first people to have seen these creatures called Bigfoot. Long before their experience, local Native Americans were certain that a race of apelike animals had been living in the **neighbouring** mountain for centuries. They called these creatures Sasquatch. In 1958, workmen, who were building a road through the jungles of Northern California often found huge footprints in the earth around their camp. Then in 1967, Roger Patterson, a man who was interested in finding Bigfoot went into the northern California jungles with a friend. While riding, they were suddenly thrown off from their horses. Patterson saw a tall

Patterson's film was shown to the public, not many people believed his story. In another incident, Richard Brown, a music teacher and also an experience hunter spotted a similar creature. He saw the animal clearly through the telescopic lens of his rifle. He said the creature looked more like a human than an animal. Later many other people also found deep footprints in the same area. In spite of regular reports of sightings and footprints, most experts still do not believe that Bigfoot really exists.

31. What did the five campers do when they saw a group of apelike creatures?

(a) They ran into the woods and hid there for several hours.

(b) They quickly ran back into their cabin and locked the cabin door.

(c) They threw rocks against the walls of their cabin to frighten the creatures away.

(d) They attacked the creatures by throwing rocks at them.

32. Did the town people believe the story of the five men about their meeting with Bigfoot ?

(a) No, not everyone believed their story.

(b) Only those who had heard the same tale the second time believed them.

(c) Some said the five men were making up their own story.

(d) All the people believed what they said..

33. Who were the first people to have seen these apelike creatures before the five campers?

(a) The workers who built the road in the jungles of Northern California.

(b) Roger Patterson and his friend.

(c) The local Native Americans

(d) Richard Brown, a music teacher and a hunter.

34. The word neighbouring would BEST be replaced with:

(a) Far-off   (b) Nearby

(c) Remote   (d) Far-away

35. Who gave the name 'Sasquatch' to the apelike creatures?

(a) The five campers

(b) Roger Patterson

(c) The local Native Americans

(d) Richard Brown

(b) Woods -- jungles

(c) Spotted -- saw

(d) Huge -- hairy

37. The BEST title for this passage would be

(a) The adventures of the five campers.

(b) The experts and the existence of Bigfoot.

(c) The creature called Bigfoot.

(d) The adventures of Bigfoot.

38. Who has seen the telescopic lens?

(a) Roger Patterson

(b) Richard Brown

(c) The five adventures men

(d) Robert Brown

39. How many photo shot had been taken by Roger Patterson of hairy creature?

(a) Four   (b) Five

(c) Six   (d) Seven

Ques (40-45): Direction : Read the given poetry and answer the question that follow by selecting the most appropriate option.

The sun descending in the west,
The evening star does shine,
The birds are silent in their nest.
And I must seek for mine.
The moon, like a flower
In heaven's high bower,
With silent delight
Sits and smiles on the night.
Farewell, green fields and happy grove,
Where flocks have took delight,
Where lambs have nibbled, silent move
The feet of angels bright;
Unseen they pour blessing

And joy without ceasing
On each bud and blossom,
And each sleeping bosom.
They look in every thoughtless nest
Where birds are covered warm;
They visit caves of every beast,
To keep them all from harm:
If they see any weeping
That should have been sleeping,
They pour sleep on their head,
And sit down by their bed.

40. The evening star rises when ___________.

(a) the birds leave their nests

(b) it is midnight

(c) it is dawn

(d) the sun descends in the west

41. Here, 'bower' represents:

(d) a flower vase

42. The poet compares the moon to:

(a) a flower

(b) a bird in the nest

(c) an evening star

(d) an angel

43. The angels come down on earth to _________.

(a) spread moonlight

(b) give blessing and joy

(c) make people, dance and have fun

(d) take blessing and joy

44. Birds' nest is described as 'thoughtless' because:

(a) the angels are blessing the birds to be happy

(b) the birds are covered in the warmth of their nest

(c) it is made without any thought

(d) the occupants are asleep without any care

45. The figure of speech used, in the line 'In heaven's high bower' is:

(a) Metaphor

(b) Personification

(c) Alliteration

(d) Simile

46. Which of the following should be the characteristic of the textbooks included in the curriculum?

(a) The introduction at the beginning and conclusion at the end of the chapter should be given in the textbook.

(b) It should be content oriented

(c) A standardized language should be used

(d) All of the above

47. Grammar-translation method of teaching English heavily relies on :

(a) Form-focussed teaching

(b) Meaning-focussed teaching

(c) Direct teaching as a strategy for learning

(d) Language use as the main focus

48. Which one of the following is not accepted in association with multimedia and its pedagogical strengths?

(a) It helps in problem solving by means of learning by doing.

(b) It facilitates individualized and

(d) It facilitates mastering basic skills of a student by means of drill and practice.

49. Which of the following programme helps students to reinforce their knowledge and develop their communication and co-operation skill as well as good interpersonal relation?

(a) Reward scheme

(b) Handling pupils language acquisition problems

(c) Peer support programme

(d) None of these

50. What are the things that as a teacher should follow before, during or after the parent teacher meeting?

(a) Start the meeting by showing that you care and know something positive about their child.

(b) Do use materials from the student's work folder.

(c) Do use clear and descriptive terms.

(d) All of these

51. When a child learns a language naturally, without much practice, it is called:

(a) Language adaptation

(b) Language learning

(c) Language acquisition

(d) Language generalization

52. The study of 'chunks of language' which are bigger than a single sentence is :

(a) Discourse   (b) Morphology

(c) Syntax   (d) Semantics

53. A teacher asks the questions in the class to:
(a) Keep students busy
(b) Attract student's attention
(c) Maintain discipline
(d) For curriculum

54. Micro teaching focuses on the competency over:
(a) Methods
(b) Skills
(c) Contents
(d) None of these

55. Why oral composition is useful in development of child?
(a) It provides fluency in language

56. What is the importance of reading?
(a) It increase vocabulary
(b) It makes pupil knowledge
(c) It helps in getting information
(d) All of the above

57. Which one of the following is the usage of language laboratory?
(a) It makes education child centered
(b) It reduce the burdon on the teacher
(c) It provides mass education
(d) The student can hear his own mistake for himself

58. The material on opaque sheet is projected with the help of ______ hardware.
(a) Episcope
(b) Audio player
(c) Video cassette player
(d) Board, charts and graphs

59. Direction : Answer the following question by selecting the most appropriate option.
__ is the backbone of learning a language.
(a) Listening skill
(b) Speaking skill
(c) Reading skill
(d) Writing skill

60. Evaluation covers _____ domains of behavior.
(a) four   (b) three
(c) two   (d) five

61. Which of the following is not a component of food?
(a) Fats
(b) Fibres
(c) Water
(d) None of the above

62. Potatoes, cereals, beans, pulses and oats are rich in ________.
(a) proteins
(b) vitamins
(c) minerals
(d) carbohydrates

63. Which is a set of transparent materials?
(a) Glass and air
(b) Water and glass

body is about the size of:
(a) The head of a pin
(b) A grain of rice
(c) An eyelash
(d) A grain of sand

65. Deficiency of Vitamin-D results in which of the following problems?
(a) Night blindness
(b) Rickets
(c) Scurvy
(d) Hair fall

66. Large amplitude of sound vibrations will produce:
(a) Loud sound
(b) Soft sound
(c) Shrill sound
(d) Feeble sound

67. An aqueous solution turns red litmus solution blue. Excess addition of which of the following solutions would reverse the change?
(a) Ammonium hydroxide solution
(b) Lime
(c) Hydrochloric acid
(d) Baking powder

68. The source of energy in the sun is due to:
(a) Conversion of uranium to krypton
(b) Conversion of carbon into carbon dioxide
(c) Conversion of hydrogen to helium
(d) Burning of hydrogen

69. When light passes through a glass slab, the property of light that changes is:
(a) Frequency
(b) Wavelength
(c) Both frequency and wavelength
(d) There is no change in the property of the light wave

70. Which of the following is most suit for the core of an electromagnet?
(a) Air
(b) Soft iron
(c) Steel
(d) None of these

71. If the current flowing through a circuit is $0.6\,A$ for 6mins , the amount of electric charge flowing through it is:

(a) Coal   (b) Solar
(c) Geothermal (d) Tidal

73. The element with atomic number 26 will be found in group :
(a) 2   (b) 8
(c) 6   (d) 10

74. Which of the following is not attracted by a magnet?
(a) Steel   (b) Cobalt
(c) Brass   (d) Nickel

75. A bus travels at a speed of 50 km/h for 12 minutes & then at a speed of 40 km/h for the next 18 minutes. Total distance covered by the bus during this time is:
(a) 20 km   (b) 22 km
(c) 24 km   (d) 28 km

76. If a particle travels a distance $'s'$ in time t_1 to t_2 , the average speed V_{av} is:
(a) $\dfrac{s}{t_2-t_1}$ (b) $s\,(t_2-t_1)$
(c) $\dfrac{2s}{t_2-t_1}$ (d) $\dfrac{s}{2(t_2-t_1)}$

77. Species found in different geographical locations are called:
(a) Sympatric species
(b) Allopatric species
(c) Sibling species
(d) Morphospecies

78. The defining characteristic of living beings is:
(a) They reproduce
(b) They can digest their food
(c) They respond to external stimuli
(d) They regenerate

79. Which force moves an aircraft through the air?
(a) Lift force   (b) Drag force
(c) Thrust force   (d) Gravity force

80. Natural fibers are :
(a) Cotton
(b) Wool
(c) Silk
(d) All of the above

81. In remedial teaching, the teacher is __________.
(a) required to prepare instructional material for quality learning and adopting different methodologies
(b) expected to devise some strategy to remove problems in learning class activities
(d) All of the above

82. As a teacher how can you facilitate problem solving abilities in your students?
(a) Generating fear amongst your students
(b) Encouraging a fixed way of solving problem
(c) Encouraging use of analysis
(d) Emphasizing on use of passive memorization strategies

83. What will be the mode of numbers: $5, 7, 9, 12, 10, 15, 7, 8, 7, 25$?
(a) 5   (b) 7
(c) 9   (d) 12

84. The mean, mode and median of $6, 15, 50, 120, 80, 100, 15, 10, 10, 8, 15$.
(a) $39, 15, 17$ (b) $15, 15, 39$
(c) $39, 15, 15$ (d) $37, 15, 15$

85. If $\frac{2x-y}{x+2y} = \frac{1}{2}$, then value of $\frac{3x-y}{3x+y}$ is:
(a) $\frac{1}{5}$ (b) $\frac{3}{5}$
(c) $\frac{4}{5}$ (d) 1

86. If $x + \frac{1}{x} = 5$, then $\frac{2x}{3x^2 - 5x + 3}$ is equal to:
(a) 5   (b) $\frac{1}{5}$
(c) 3   (d) $\frac{1}{3}$

87. If $\sqrt{1 - \frac{x^3}{100}} = \frac{3}{5}$, then x equals to:
(a) 2   (b) 4
(c) 16   (d) $(136)^{\frac{1}{3}}$

88. Consider the following pairs:
a. 5 and 105
b. 15 and 105
c. 15 and 35
Which of the above pairs have H.C.F. as 5 and L.C.M. as 105 ?
(a) Only a   (b) Only b
(c) Only c   (d) Both a and c

89. If the profit on selling an commodity for Rs. 1420 is equal to three times the loss on selling it for Rs. 860, then find the cost price a price of the article.
(a) Rs. 1000   (b) Rs. 1200
(c) Rs. 1100   (d) Rs. 1050

90. Direction: Simplify the given expression.

91. If three metallic spheres of radii $6cm, 8cm$, and $10cm$ are melted to form a single sphere, then the diameter of the new sphere will be:
(a) $12cm$ (b) $24cm$
(c) $30cm$ (d) $36cm$

92. Find the surface area of cuboid, if its diagonals is $4\sqrt{5}cm$, and the sum of depth, breadth and length is $20cm$.
(a) $400cm^2$ (b) $420cm^2$
(c) $300cm^2$ (d) $320cm^2$

93. The sum of the digits of a two-digit number is 15 and the difference between the digits is 3. What is the two-digit number? (tens digit is greater than the unit digit)
(a) 96   (b) 78
(c) 128   (d) 69

94. In the examination a student scores 4 marks for every correct answer and loses 1 mark for every wrong answer. A student attempted all 200 questions and got 200 marks. How many questions did he answer correctly?
(a) 82   (b) 80
(c) 68   (d) 60

95. Which of the following number is divisible by 18?
(a) 444444   (b) 555555
(c) 666660   (d) 666666

96. In the given figure, l m and 't' is the transversal. Find the value of (x - y).

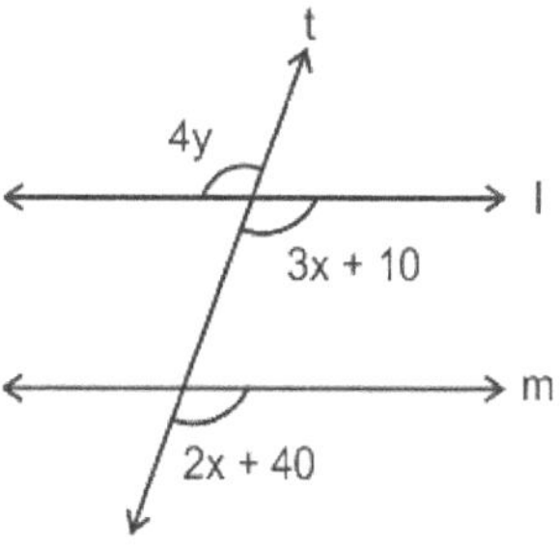

(a) $20°$ (b) $5°$
(c) $10°$ (d) $15°$

97. In the given figure, Line PQ and line RS intersect at a point O. If ∠POT = 90° and ∠SOQ = 130°, then find the ratio of x and y.

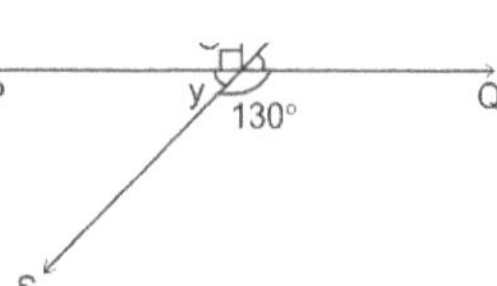

(a) $5 : 4$ (b) $4 : 5$
(c) $5 : 7$ (d) $7 : 5$

98. The ages of Manu and Bharat are in the ratio of $6 : 5$ and the sum of their ages is 44 years. What will be the ratio of their ages after 8 years?
(a) $1 : 2$ (b) $9 : 7$
(c) $8 : 7$ (d) $11 : 10$

99. Raman travelled 80 km partly by train and by bus and the fare of train and bus are Rs. 8 per km and Rs. 10 per km. Find the distance travelled by bus if the total fare is Rs.700.
(a) 30 km   (b) 50 km
(c) 25 km   (d) 55 km

100. Find the value of k if the median of data 3, 3, 4, 5, k, 11, 17, and 18 is 6?(Data is arranged in increasing order)
(a) 7   (b) 8
(c) 11   (d) 9

101. In 35 litres mixture of alcohol and water the quantity of alcohol is 5 litres more than that of water. Find the ratio of water to alcohol.
(a) $3 : 4$ (b) $4 : 3$
(c) $3 : 5$ (d) $5 : 3$

102. The sum of two numbers is 528 and their H.C.F. is 33. The number of such pairs is:
(a) 3   (b) 4

(c) 5   (d) 1

103. **A 7 year old boy recognizes all four sided regular figures as squares. According to Van Hiele's, he is at which stage of geometrical thinking?**
(a) Level 4-Deduction
(b) Level 3-Informal deduction
(c) Level 2-Analysis
(d) Level 1-Visualization

104. **A teacher makes a teaching method more effective by using devices known as ________.**
(a) Technique of teaching
(b) Principle of teaching
(c) Methodology of teaching
(d) Aim of teaching

Mathematics?
(a) Devise various learning activities related to mathematics
(b) Design meaningful learning situations
(c) Teacher provides home tuitions in mathematics
(d) Teaching preparations

109. **What can not be a perfect step to conduct error analysis?**
(a) Interview the students by asking him/her to explain how he/she solved the problem.
(b) Record all the responses made by the students.
(c) Always analyse the responses made by the learners

content, process, language, and pedagogical practices of the curriculum are age-appropriate, and within the cognitive reach of the child.
(a) Cognitive validity
(b) Content validity
(c) Process validity
(d) Environmental validity

115. **__________ is also known as the subject approach or the traditional approach.**
(a) Disciplinary approach
(b) Integrated approach
(c) Both (A) and (B)
(d) None of above

116. **Which one of the following is the**

lists.

	List- 1		List- 2
P.	Deductive method	1.	B.F Skinner
Q.	Inductive method	2.	Aristotle
R.	Project method	3.	David Hume
S.	Auto-instructional teaching	4.	William Heard Kilpatrick

(a) P-3; Q-2; R-4; S-1
(b) P-2; Q-3; R-4; S-1
(c) P-4; Q-3; R-2; S-1
(d) P-2; Q-4; R-1; S-3

106. **To decide whether a two digit number is divisible by 3, add the two digit number. If the sum of the digit is multiple of 3. This is an example of a/an:**
(a) Rational   (b) Relational
(c) Algorithm   (d) Prototype

107. **In Diagnostic test in Mathematics, both background and performance of the students is needed for helping them in:**
(a) Getting first position in the class
(b) Crack competitive exam like JEE, NEET etc
(c) Acquisition of intellectual habits and enhances learning
(d) Become a politician

108. **Which one of the following is not a principle of helping pupils with learning difficulties in**

mathematics in the curriculum prominent?
(a) To prepare for the future vocation or occupation.
(b) To develop their intellectual powers and discipline.
(c) Both (A) and (B)
(d) None of these

111. **Sequence the following tasks as they are taken up while developing the concept of measurement:**
a. Learners use standard units to measure length.
b. Learners use non-standard units to measure length.
c. Learners verify objects using simple observation.
d. Learners understand the relationship between metric units.
(a) a, b, d, c   (b) b, a, c, d
(c) c, b, a, d   (d) d, a, c, b

112. **Which of the following is the organization of Remedial teaching in Mathematics?**
(a) Tutorial teaching
(b) Auto-instructional teaching
(c) Informal teaching
(d) All of these

113. **Which one of the following is the aim for teaching science in our school?**
(a) Utilitarian Aim
(b) Intellectual Aim
(c) Disciplinary Aim
(d) All of above

114. **__________ requires that the**

(b) It is convenient and comfortable, and a teacher is free to develop his/ her style of teaching.
(c) The number of students can listen and prepare notes. It saves time and energy.
(d) All of above

117. **The best statement describes the relationship between science and technology, is:**
(a) Scientific principles are discovered first and technological application happen later.
(b) Science is an open - ended exploration whereas technology is usually goal oriented.
(c) Technology implies the use of advanced equipments and whereas science is largely theoretical.
(d) Science was part of ancient human civilisation but technology is relatively recent

118. **The learning materials are in the form of real objects or ideals that make the concepts very clear, are:**
(a) Visual material
(b) Surrounding environment
(c) Information and Communication Technology
(d) Tactile material

119. **__________ is a set of three hierarchical models used to classify educational learning objectives into levels of complexity and specificity.**

(a) Bloom's taxonomy
(b) Cognitive domain
(c) Both (A) and (B)
(d) None of above

120. **Which one of the following is the problem of science teaching?**

(a) Safety
(b) Dealing with Controversial Topics
(c) Time Consuming Planning Requirements
(d) All of above

// Hints and Solutions //

1(D). There are many learning theories in psychology that are related to different kinds of work, human and... behavior.

Some of the famous learning theories include:

Theory	Propounder	Main Idea
Trial and Error Theory	Thorndike	The theory emphasizes that learning is the result of associations forming between stimulus and responses.
Instrumental Learning Theory/ Theory of Operant Conditioning	B.F. Skinner	Theory implies the idea that learning takes place through rewarding a certain behavior or withholding reward for undesirable behavior.
Insight Theory of Learning	Kohler	The theory emphasizes that a sudden solution to the problem as insight doesn't rely on behavior or observation.
Socio-cultural Theory	Lev Vygotsky	Theory implies the idea that interaction with society and environment plays a vital role in shaping the behaviour, action, and abilities of a child.
Classical Conditioning Theory	Ivan Pavlov	The theory emphasizes that behaviour is learnt by a repetitive association between the response and the stimulus.

B.S. Bloom has not propounded any learning theory rather he has proposed a taxonomy which is a set of three hierarchical models that refers to the classification of educational learning objectives.

Bloom's Taxonomy Identified Three Domains of Learning:

- Cognitive Domain: It involves knowledge Comprehension, Application, Analysis, Synthesis, and Evaluation
- Affective Domain: It includes how we deal with things emotionally, such as feelings, values, appreciation, enthusiasms, motivations, and attitudes.
- Psychomotor Domain: It includes physical movement, coordination, and use of the motor-skill areas.

So, it could be concluded that B.S. Bloom has not propounded any learning theory.

2(A). Stagnation stands for the retention of a child in a class for a period of more than one year. Gradually when a student takes more than one year to pass a class it is considered a case of stagnation.

- Stagnation is one of the most acute problems of tribal education. Absenteeism leads to stagnation and both naturally lead to wastage.
- Formerly stagnation used to occur due to lower achievement in the examinations. It means those who fail to secure minimum marks in the class tests will not be sent for the terminal examination and such candidates will have to remain in the same standard for one more year.
- But this practice is now stopped, whether a student secures minimum marks in the class tests or not he/she is eligible to sit for terminal examinations. At present minimum attendance is prescribed for students for promotion.

So, it could be concluded that retention of a child in a same class for more than one year is the meaning of stagnation in education.

3(B). Learning refers to the modification of behavioral patterns. It is a comprehensive process which refers to a change in behavior, knowledge, and skill as a result of practice and experience.

- Learning of children will be most effective when development of cognitive, affective, and psychomotor domains of children will take place.
- These domains are proposed by Benjamin Bloom's in his taxonomy. It is a set of three hierarchical models that refers to the classification of educational learning objectives.

Let's Understand these domains in the context of child's learning:

- Cognitive domains: In this domain, a child deals with knowledge and hence, learns to create, evaluate, analyze, etc.
- Affective domains: This domain comes into play when child grows in emotional areas such as feelings, attitudes, etc.
- Psychomotor domains: It is concerned with acquiring skills that require the integration of mental and physical movements.

4(C). Development refers to an increase in structure for better and enhanced functioning of organs. It is a wide and continuous process that starts from the pre-natal stage.

In the pre-natal stage, baby develops inside the mother's womb and becomes a mature one by passing through three different stages of prenatal development.

The three stages of pre-natal development include:

- Germinal period: First 2 weeks after conception.
- Embryonic period: 8 weeks from conception.
- Fetal Period: 9 weeks until birth or 38 to 40 weeks.

Hence it could be concluded that development starts from the pre-natal stage.

Additional Information

Stage of infancy	• It refers to the first year or the early period of a child's development in which the child grows rapidly after birth. • It is a crucial period of development in which the child learns to sit, crawl, stand, etc.
Pre-childhood stage	• It refers to the time period from the age of 'Two to Seven years'. It is a very crucial period for child's overall development. • It is also known as the toy age, pregang age, and exploratory age, etc.
Post-childhood stage	• It refers to the time period from the age of 'seven to twelve years'. The signs of puberty usually begin to appear in this stage. • It is also known as troublesome age, gang age, play age, etc.

5(B). Childhood refers to the period of the human lifespan, ranging from birth to puberty. It consists of many developmental stages and 'adolescence' is one of them. 'Adolescence' comes from the Latin word 'Adolescere' which means 'to grow to become mature'. It a stage which lies between the age of '12 to 19 years'.
According to Stanley Hall:
- Adolescence is a turbulent time charged with conflict and mood swings.
- The time period of transition from childhood and adolescence is of great stress.
- Adolescence fails to think clearly and it creates great frustration and stress in their lives.

So, it could be concluded that "Adolescence is the period of great stress, strain, storm and strike" is the statement of Stanley Hall.

8(B). The Piaget theory of cognitive development has used the following two stages or activities, namely, organization and adaptation as described below:
Adaptation: According to Piaget, children have an innate tendency to adjust to their environment. This trend has been termed 'adaptation'. According to him, the child starts adapting to the environment from the beginning
Organization: When a child encounters an aggravating situation, their individual mental activities do not work separately, but they work together and collectively help them to acquire knowledge. At the mental level, this activity happens continuously. Adaptation to the development and cognitive psychology compared to an adult's point of view.

are much less egocentric in the concrete operational stage. It falls between the ages of 7 to 11 years old and is marked by more logical and methodical manipulation of symbols. The main goal at this stage is for a child to start working things out inside their head.

13(D). In childhood, physiological development follows the cephalocaudal sequence. their growth occurs from head to extreme parts.
In adolescents, their body size will increase, with the feet, arms, legs, and hands sometimes growing "faster" than the rest of the body. it does not follow the cephalocaudal sequence.
So, growth in adolescents is reverse of that in childhood because in adolescents hands feet and legs accelerate first than other

changes lead to the enhancement of various abilities and enable one to function effectively.
- Emotions: These are the feelings generated as an effect of experiences, or relationships of an individual with others. They are instinctive reactions that come naturally to all and contribute to personal and social adjustments of an individual.

According to Cole and Bruce, childhood is a unique stage of emotional development.
- Emotional development relies heavily on the process of socialization and proceeds in a stepwise manner.
- Basic emotions such as fear, disgust, happiness, sadness, surprise, anger, and interest, are present since birth.
- During childhood, mood tantrums are pretty common.
- Toddlers have a tendency to have fast temper swings. While their emotions may be very intense, these emotions additionally have a tendency to be pretty short-lived.
- One might be stunned at how an infant can go from screaming hysterically about a toy at one second to sitting in the front of the TV quietly looking at a favorite show simply moments later.
- Children at this age are very possessive and have difficulty in sharing.

So, it could be concluded that 'Childhood' is called as 'A unique stage of emotional development' by Cole and Bruce.

7(A). In cognitive development, heredity establishes the basic nature of physical structure such as the brain.
Cognitive development is a field of study in neuroscience and psychology focusing on a child's development in terms of information processing, conceptual resources, perceptual skill, language learning, and other aspects of brain

by the evaluation.
The cognitive domain is focused on intellectual skills such as critical thinking, problem solving, and creating a knowledge base. For evaluating cognitive development oral, written, essay type, objective type questions examinations are used.
The affective domain includes the manner in which we deal with things emotionally, such as feelings, values, appreciation, enthusiasms, motivations, and attitudes. For evaluating affective domain interest inventory, practical examinations, and observation techniques are used.
For evaluating psychomotor domain performance tests, practical examination, and observation techniques are used.

10(B). Imitation learning mainly influences the personality of the child. Imitation is an advanced behavior whereby an individual observes and replicates another's behavior. An imitation is also a form of social learning that leads to the "development of traditions, and ultimately our culture.

11(D). Curiosity and Creative ideas are considered a sign of being gifted. Fighting is a confrontation in which two or more people compete for dominance and respect to satisfy their own egos. Thus, it cannot be regarded as a sign of being gifted. Curiosity is a valuable agent in education when it is rightly valued and employed. Curiosity is highly important because it is a starting point of interest. Creative ideas are concerned with a holistic approach to education, focusing upon the learner becoming part of a professional community, involving the dimensions of knowledge, performance and identity formation.

12(C). In concrete operational stage, the child responds to inferred reality. Children

understanding and imagination. Cognitive powers of a child, like imagination power, intelligence, ability to make a decision, etc. are related to the child's 'mental development' as mental development refers to the development of the ability to understand, learn, reason, think, perceive, and solve a problem.
Hence, the correct option is (C).

15(D). Teachers can identify children who take part in all school activities and those children who are always left out. so he should organize group games, debates, seminars, conferences, etc. so that students can take part in these activities.
Teachers can make use of sociometric devices to identify isolates and cliquish in a given group.
The disliked or rejected can be helped by making them aware of the reasons and also planning and implementing some remedial programmes such as making groups consisting of disliked or rejected ad popular children for various work, such as assignment during school day programmes, Child's hostility, tension, nervousness, rebellion. temper tantrums, withdrawal, indifference and other undesirable reactions. Hence. parents and teachers should try to understand the probable causes for their children's aggressive behaviour.
Teachers and parents should help the children to release their emotions by playing with dolls. Children need many opportunities at school and home to sing, play outdoor games, to tell a poem or painting to release their emotions.

16(B). Secondary or social rewards such as praise, smile, or money: A secondary reinforcer is a stimulus to which we have learned to respond because of past learning by the association of the stimulus with a primary reinforcer. An example is money, as it is associated with primary reinforcers like it is used to get food when we are hungry.

Hence, we can conclude that after the occurrence of desirable behavior, the teacher says 'very good to the child. She has used secondary reinforcers as she had praised the child.

17(C). Eight Intellectual Levels or Eight Conditions of Learning:

- Signal learning: The learner makes a general response to a signal.
- Stimulus-response learning: The learner makes a precise response to a signal.
- Chaining: The connection of a set of individual stimulus and responses in a sequence.
- Verbal association: The learner makes

- Concept learning: The learner develops the ability to make a generalized response based on a class of stimuli.
- Rule learning: A rule is a chain of concepts linked to demonstrated behaviour.
- Problem-solving: The learner discovers a combination of previously learned rules and applies them to solve a novel situation.

Thus from the above-mentioned points, it is clear that proper prerequisites are not a type of learning according to Gagne's Theory of Learning.

18(A). Bloom's Taxonomy: It is a hierarchical ordering of cognitive, affective, and psychomotor domains and each domain has some objectives that can help teachers teach and students learn. As per him, there are three Domains of Learning:

- Cognitive domains: In this domain, a child deals with knowledge and hence, learns to create, evaluate, analyze, apply, understand, remember.
- Affective domains: When it comes to growth in emotional areas, this domain comes into play.
1. Receiving: When a learner shows sensitivity to certain stimuli.
2. Responding: It is defined as the tendency to respond to an object or stimuli.
3. Valuing: It refers to the acceptance of a behaviour and commitment to it. One values certain behaviours not by desires but by commitment.
4. Organizing: It refers to organizing the value system which is attained when one develops one's code of conduct or standard of public life.
5. Characterizing: It deals with behaviour as per values or attitudes a child has imbibed; children show teamwork.
- Psychomotor domains: These domains

are nothing but manual or physical skills. It deals with physical coordination, movements, and motor skills. It includes imitation, manipulation, precision, articulation, and naturalization.

Therefore, we conclude that the correct order is Receiving, Responding, Valuing, Organizing, Characterizing.

19(D). The key principles of inclusive education for children:

Principle of Equality: Everyone has the right to access knowledge skill and information. Indian constitution guarantees some educational rights for the children. In spite of these provisions there are some group of people who are deprived of education because of some special causes or factor. But inclusive education includes

participation. Inclusive education includes all the children in common educational settings where they can learn together without any discrimination. It provides opportunities for the students with disabilities for the active participation equally. Thus inclusive education promotes the participation for all children or adults in teaching learning process.

Principle of acceptance: It is another principle of inclusive education. Every parents wants to their child to lean or educate with all other students in a regular classroom and become able to lead their life independently. And it is base on this principle of acceptance of all children in education process irrespective of their disabilities.

Principle of Togetherness: Inclusive education provides such learning environment that promotes all round development of all learners together in the same educational setting. Irrespective of their caste, color and gender. So it is an approach which brings all children together in a common educational community.

20(D). A classroom/institution that welcomes diversity of categories, abilities, cultures, disabilities, etc. is an inclusive education.

The principles of inclusive education include:

- No discrimination among students
- Equal educational opportunity for all
- Adapting to the needs of students, for example, making institutions disabled-friendly
- Equal educational benefits to all students
- Individual difference is promoted among students
- The needs of the students are taken seriously.

21(A). Speaking short sentences and riding a three-wheeled bicycle, this work is done in infancy. From the birth of a child to the age of 6 years is called infancy or infancy. In this stage the child is completely dependent. Of course, he is completely dependent on the other. Parents and family member have to depend for his developmental care.

22(A). The child first starts getting attracted towards the light. Child development refers to the biological and intellectual changes that occur in humans from birth to the end of adolescence, when they gradually move from dependence to more autonomy. Since these developmental changes can be largely influenced by genetic factors and events during prenatal life, genetics and prenatal development are

Sociometric techniques are methods that qualitatively measure aspects of social interactions, such as social acceptance (i.e., how well a person is liked by peers) and social status (i.e., a child's social status compared to peers).

24(A). Constructivist pedagogy places the child at the centre of the learning, and can also be referred to as 'invisible pedagogy'. It is an approach to learning in which learners are provided the opportunity to construct their own sense of what is being learned by building internal connection or relationship among the ideas and facts being taught."

25(C). If the teacher comes to know that a student is absent in the class, in such a case, instead of expelling/punishing/preventing him/her from attending the class, the teacher should know the reason for his/her negligence and find out the appropriate remedy.

Revision in Teacher Preparation in Classroom Management:

- Teacher with an instructional approach to classroom management, providing candidates with feedback through curriculum and guided exercises, and
- Addressing the challenges faced by teacher candidates and new teachers in creating a positive classroom context.

26(A). Parents should play a forward-looking role in the learning process of their children and encourage them to do better. As preschoolers grow into school-age children, parents become their children's learning coaches. Through guidance and reminders, parents help their children organize their time and support their desire to learn new things in and out of school.

27(A). Cognitive development aims to study a child's development, especially information processing, conceptual processing, perceptual skills, language learning, and other aspects related to brain development. The process of striking a balance between adjustment and assimilation. Whereas on the other hand adaptation (a relatively stable structure) occurs when the child strikes a balance between the two processes while trying to internalize the perceived processes.

28(A). On the basis of the classical contract theory of learning, feelings of fear, love and hatred can be easily generated in the child. In classical contract theory, an association is established between the stimulus response. Before understanding classical conditioning, it is necessary to know that there are other functions in human beings, some are innate like breathing, digestion etc and some are for

in 1904. According to this theory, a response to a natural stimulus that is similar to a natural stimulus is classical conditioning, that is, the establishment of an association between the stimulus and the response is conditioning. Before understanding classical conditioning, it is necessary to know that there are other functions in human beings, some are innate like breathing, digestion etc and some are for psychological reasons like blinking, salivation etc.

30(A). The field theory of learning in children, in which the learner perceives and responds to the whole situation, comes under Kohler's theory of understanding.
The associative theory of learning in children is described on the basis of stimulus response. In this, a relationship is established between the stimulus response. It is also called stimulus response or S-R principle.

31(B). According to the passage, five men who were camping in the Cascade Mountains of Washington saw a group of huge apelike creatures coming out of the woods. They hurried back to their cabin and locked themselves inside.

32(A). According to the passage, After the incident when five men saw the big foots they returned to the town and told the people of their adventure. However, only a few people accepted their story.

33(C). The local native Americans were the first people to have seen these apelike creatures before the five campers.
According to the passage, Then in 1967, Roger Patterson, a man who was interested in finding Bigfoot went into the northern California jungles with a friend. While riding, they were suddenly thrown off from their horses. Patterson saw a tall apelike

animal standing not far away. Therefore the first people to have seen these apelike creatures before the five campers was Roger Patterson and his friend.

34(B). According to the passage, neighbouring means: a person or place which is adjacent with the given person of place. Therefore nearby will be correct option which can replace the word 'neighbouring.'

35(C). According to the passage, The local Native Americans were certain that a race of apelike animals had been living in the neighboring mountain for centuries. They called these creatures Sasquatch.

36(D). According to the passage, Animals are the creatures, woods are found in jungles and after seeing the objects are

37(C). According to the passage, After carefully reading the passage the best title of the passage would be "The creature called Bigfoot."

38(B). According to the passage, Richard Brown, a music teacher and also an experience hunter spotted a similar creature. He saw the animal clearly through the telescopic lens of his rifle. He said the creature looked more like a human than an animal.

39(D). According to the passage, Roger Patterson managed to shoot seven rolls of film of the hairy creature before the animal disappeared in the hushes.

40(D). From the lines ' The sun descending in the west, The evening star does shine, The birds are silent in their nest. ' it is clear that t he evening star rises when the sun descends in the west.

41(C). From the lines 'The moon, like a flower, In heaven's high bower'. Here, 'bower' represents a bouquet of flowers.

42(A). From the lines, The moon, like a flower, In heaven's high bower. Then in the passage the poet compares the moon to an angel.

43(B). From the lines 'The feet of angels bright; Unseen they pour blessing, And joy without ceasing, On each bud and blossom,'. It is clear that the angels come down on earth to give blessing and joy.

44(D). From the lines 'They look in every thoughtless nest Where birds are covered warm; They visit caves of every beast, To keep them all from harm'. Therefore in the poem, birds' nest is described as 'thoughtless' because the occupants are asleep without any care.

45(A). The figure of speech used, in the

line 'In heaven's high bower' is Metaphor. A metaphor is a figure of speech that, for rhetorical effect, directly refers to one thing by mentioning another.

46(A). Textbook is the area in which the language material presented prescribed for teaching and learning. A good textbook not only teaches but it also tests. The content of the book should be very clear, a proper beginning is required to prepare the learners for the upcoming content and a perfect conclusion is required to assemble the entire learning.

47(A). Grammar-translation method of teaching English heavily relies on form-focussed teaching. The grammar–translation method is a method of teaching foreign languages derived from the classical (sometimes called traditional) between the target language and the native language.
Form-focused instruction (FFI) refers to any pedagogical practice aimed at drawing learners' attention to language form. The "form" may consist of phonological (sound), morphosyntactic (word form, word order), lexical, pragmatic, discourse, or orthographical aspects of language.

48(C). Multimedia provides a technology based constructivist learning environment where students are able to solve a problem by means of self exploration, collaboration and active participation. This approach provides various opportunities to the learners and provides a platform to the learners to be an avtive individual performer. It is helpful for each kind of learner.

49(C). In this type of programme teachers may teach and train students who perform better in a particular subject and also helps to maintain their teaching learning difficulties within group teaching and self study itself. This programme helps students to reinforce their knowledge and develop their communication and co-operation skill as well as good interpersonal relation.

50(D). Keeping in mind teachers has many children demanding their time and attention; a good conference can help a busy teacher to focus on what your child needs. Review reports and check your files from previous conferences to see if they remind you of important topics you may have missed. Be clear in your own mind about each child's strengths, weaknesses and appropriate goals.

51(C). When a child learns a language naturally, without much practice, it is called language acquisition. It is the process by which humans acquire the capacity to perceive and comprehend language, as well as to produce and use words and sentences to communicate. It is one of the quintessential human traits, because non-humans do not communicate by using language.

52(A). The study of 'chunks of language' which are bigger than a single sentence is Discourse. It denotes written and spoken communications. It is a conceptual generalization of conversation within each modality and context of communication.

53(B). Children need frequent changes of activity: they need activities which are exiting and stimulate the curiosity, they need to be involved in something active, and they need to be appreciated by the teacher, an important figure for them. Question answer activity is an example to

can give Wh-question. It is expected the students can give relevant and suitable answers based on real situation.

54(B). Interaction analysis based on practice teaching training in teaching skills using micro-teaching approach and simulated teaching exercise are some of innovative technologies through which effective training program can be transacted. The present mode also pointed out each one of these technologies, its major emphasis on the use of micro-teaching in Indian situation for developing the required skills of teaching at the mastery level.

55(D). Oral compositions have been very popular in English language teaching for some time. The idea is for the teacher and students working together to build up a narrative orally before writing it. The process of building up the composition with the whole class allows the teacher and students to focus in on a variety of language items from tense usage to cohesive elements, etc. Oral composition develop much influencing grammar, once a child communicate orally to other self confidence also develop on him. After making such practice he get fluency in language too.

56(D). Reading is important because it increases vocabulary, makes pupil to gain knowledge and helps them in getting information.
Reading affects our attitudes, beliefs, standards, morals, judgments, and general behavior. It shapes our thinking and our actions. The purpose of reading is to correlate the ideas on the text to what you have already known. The reader must understand about the subject that he/she read to connect the ideas. Learning to read is about listening and understanding as

well as working out what's printed on the page. Through hearing stories, children are exposed to a wide range of words. This helps them build their own vocabulary and improve their understanding when they listen, which is vital as they start to read. Reading is important because it makes you more empathetic, knowledgeable and stimulates your imagination. Reading allows one to develop a better understanding of the subject and gain conceptual clarity. It is one of the simplest entertainment entities for humans.

57(D). Language laboratory is the place where the learners have to listen on headphone. It is an audio or audio-visual installation used as an aid in modern language teaching. Here, the student can hear his own mistake for himself and also projected with the help of episcope hardware. The opaque projector, epidioscope, epidiascope or episcope is a device which displays opaque materials by shining a bright lamp onto the object from above. A system of mirrors, prisms and/or imaging lenses is used to focus an image of the material onto a viewing screen.

59(A). In any language, attending to and interpreting the oral rendition is termed as listening. The student imitates and memorizes linguistic items, such as words, idioms, phrases, tone, etc. and thus learns speaking the language. Listening skill forms the backbone of learning a language, irrespective of the fact that it is a first language or a second language.

60(B). Evaluation encompasses more aspects than measurement, but proper evaluation is not possible without the process of measurement. Evaluation covers all the three domains of behavior which are; cognitive domain, affective domain and psychomotor domain.

61(D). Fats, fibres and water are the components of food. Fats in food come in several forms, including saturated, monounsaturated, and polyunsaturated. Too much fat or too much of the wrong type of fat can be unhealthy. Some examples of foods that contain fats are butter, oil, nuts, meat, fish, and some dairy products. Fibre is found in wholegrain cereals and fruit and vegetables. Fibre is made up of the indigestible parts or compounds of plants, which pass relatively unchanged through our stomach and intestines. Water is a nutrient in food groups: grains, meats, dairy products, fruits, and vegetables.

62(D). Potatoes, cereals, beans, pulses and oats are rich in carbohydrates. Carbohydrates are found in a wide array of

both healthy and unhealthy foods: bread, beans, milk, popcorn, potatoes, cookies, spaghetti, soft drinks, corn, and cherry pie.

63(D). Materials like air, water, and clear glass are called transparent. When light encounters transparent materials, almost all of it passes directly through them. Glass, for example, is transparent to all visible light. Translucent objects allow some light to travel through them.

64(B). The smallest bone in the human body is about the size of a grain of rice. This bone is called the stapes bone. The stapes bone of the ear is the smallest bone in the body. It is a part of the middle ear and transmits vibrations from the other ossicles to the inner ear.

65(B). Deficiency of Vitamin-D results phosphorus levels in bones, which can cause rickets.

66(A). The large amplitude of sound vibrations will produce a loud sound.
The intensity of sound is identified by loudness. The loudness of sound is proportional to the square of the amplitude of the vibration producing the sound. If the amplitude of vibration is large, the sound produced is loud.

67(C). An aqueous solution turns red litmus solution blue. Excess addition of Hydrochloric acid solution would reverse the change. Acids are sour in taste and change the blue litmus to red. Examples: Hydrochloric acid, Nitric acid, Sulphuric acid, etc. Bases are bitter in taste and change the red litmus to blue. Examples: Ammonium hydroxide, Sodium hydroxide, Calcium hydroxide, Baking soda(Sodium bicarbonate), etc.

68(C). The source of energy in the sun is due to conversion of hydrogen to helium.
- The generation of energy in the Sun from a process known as nuclear fusion.
- During, this fusion, the temperature and high pressure in the sun's core area cause nuclei to separate from their electrons.
- In this process conversion of hydrogen to helium atom takes place. During the process of nuclear fusion, radiant energy is released.

69(B). When light passes through a glass slab, the property of light that changes is wavelength. The distance between two adjacent maxima or two adjacent minima of a wave is called the wavelength of that wave. It is denoted by λ.

70(B). Soft iron is selected for making the core of an electromagnet because the core is used in a solenoid for the production of the strongest magnetism.

71(B). Given that:
Current $(I) = 0.6A$
Time $(t) = 6$ mins $= 6 \times 60$ sec
Electric charge (Q) = Current (I) $\times$ Time (t)
$Q = 0.6 \times 6 \times 60$ C
$Q = 216$ C

72(A). Non-Renewable Resources: The sources that cannot be replaced or reused once they are destroyed are called the Non-renewable resources.
- These are limited resources. so these are used limitedly.
- These are not environmentally friendly because the amount of carbon emission is high.
- The cost of these resources is high.

phosphate are some examples.

73(B). The element with atomic number 26 will be found in group 8. The element of atomic number 26 is Fe. It belongs to the eighth group and fourth period.

74(C). Brass is not attracted by a magnet. A magnet is an object which attracts pieces of iron, steel, cobalt, and nickel. Hence, Brass is not attracted by a magnet.
In their natural states, metals such as aluminum, brass, copper, gold, lead, and silver don't attract magnets because they are weak metals.

75(B). Given:
Speed of bus is 50 km/h for 12 minutes or $\frac{12}{60}$ hour.
The speed of the bus is 40 km/h for 18 minutes or $\frac{18}{60}$ hour.
Let Distances D_1 and D_2 for different speeds.
$\therefore D_1 = 50 \times \frac{12}{60} = 10$ km
Similarly, $D_2 = 40 \times \frac{18}{60} = 12$ km
Total distance covered by the bus is $D_1 + D_2 = 10 + 12 = 22$ km

76(A). Given,
The distance travelled is s.
Time interval $t = t_2 - t_1$
Average speed V_{av}
Average speed $= \frac{\text{total distance}}{\text{total time}}$
So,
$V_{av} = \frac{s}{t_2 - t_1}$

77(B). Species found in different geographical locations are called allopatric species. It is a mode of speciation that occurs when the biological population of the same species become isolated from each other to an extent that prevents or interferes with gene flow.

78(C). The defining characteristic of living beings is they respond to external stimuli. Response to external stimuli or to the environment in which an organism lives, is the most important characteristic of any living organism, besides growth and reproduction.

79(C). Thrust is the force that moves an aircraft through the air. Thrust is used to overcome the drag of an airplane, and to overcome the weight of a rocket.
Drag Force: The air resistance that tends to slow the forward movement of an airplane.
Gravity Force: The force that pulls all objects towards the earth.
Lift Force: The upward force that is created by the movement of air above and below a wing. Air flows faster above the wing and slower below the wing, creating a

and synthetic.
Natural Fibres:
- Natural Fibres are obtained from plants, insects and worms.
- Cotton, wool and silk are examples of natural fibres.
- All fibres are stretched and twisted to form long threads called yarns. This is called spinning.
- The yarn is woven on a machine called loom to produce fabric.
  - Cotton fibres come from the fruit of a cotton plant called cotton boll.
  - Woollen fibres come from the fleece of sheep, rabbits and goats.
  - Silk fibres are obtained from the cocoon of silkworms.

Synthetic fibres:
- Fibres which are man-made are called synthetic fibres. Synthetic fibres are made in factories.
- Rayon, terrycot, terylene, nylon are some popular synthetic fibres.

81(D). In remedial teaching, the teacher is:
- Required to prepare instructional material for quality learning and adopting different methodologies.
- Expected to devise some strategy to remove problems in learning.
- Provide pupils clear instructions to avoid confusion, summarize the main points and encourage pupils' active participation in class activities.

The word 'remedial' means 'to rectify, improve or remedy something.' Remedial teaching is teaching which is designed to bring students who are lagging behind up to the level of achievement realized by their peers. Remedial teaching means necessary learning support will be provided to pupils who need pedagogical or didactic assistance. There are often children who

receive a lower grade because of certain learning or behavioral problems/disorder. The ultimate aim of remediation or remedial teaching is to help pupils who have fallen behind to learn to the best of their ability and to bring them back into the mainstream of the teaching-learning process as far as possible.
- Remedial teaching in which a teacher is required to prepare instructional material for quality learning and adopting different methodologies as per the needs of the learner or a particular group.
- During the process of remediation, a teacher is expected to devise some strategy to remove problems in learning and the causes due to which the learner has faced the difficulties.
- Teachers provide pupils clear

- Teachers should prepare a rich, pleasant and comfortable learning environment for pupils during remedial classes.

82(C). As a teacher encouraging the use of analysis can facilitate problem-solving abilities in students.
As a teacher, it is necessary to facilitate problem-solving to help the children in becoming successful in life. To do so, a teacher should encourage the students to develop a habit of analyzing things.
To solve a problem means to eliminate the source of problem generation. And this can only be done by analyzing each and every probable root cause of the problem, simulating the effect of the probable cause, and then concluding the solution by eliminating the source of the problem or by enforcing a regular check on the source of the problem so that the problem does not get out of control. Analysis helps a person predict the situations in advance and allows a person to take necessary action against the source of problem generation.

83(B). Given:
The given numbers are
$5, 7, 9, 12, 10, 15, 7, 8, 7, 25$
In the given numbers the frequency of occurrence of 7 is maximum i.e., 3 times, therefore the mode of the numbers is 7.

84(C). The given observations are:
$6, 15, 50, 120, 80, 100, 15, 10, 10, 8, 15$
Arranging the given observations in ascending order:
$6, 8, 10, 10, 15, 15, 15, 50, 80, 100, 120$
Number of observations $= 11$ (odd)
Mean $= \dfrac{\text{Sum of the observations}}{\text{Number of the observations}}$
$= \dfrac{6+8+10+10+15+15+15+50+80+100+120}{11}$
$\Rightarrow \frac{429}{11} = 39$

Median $= \frac{n+1}{2}$ th terms

$= \frac{11+1}{2}$ th terms

$= \frac{12}{2}$ th terms

$= 6$ th terms

$= 15$

Now, in the given observations, 15 repeated most frequently, that is 3 times. Therefore, mode of the given observations is 15 .

85(B). Given,

$\frac{2x-y}{x+2y} = \frac{1}{2}$

$\Rightarrow 4x - 2y = x + 2y$

$\Rightarrow 3x = 4y$

$\Rightarrow x : y = 4 : 3$

$\therefore \frac{3x-y}{3x+y}$

$\Rightarrow \frac{3\times4-3}{3\times4+3}$

86(B). $x + \frac{1}{x} = 5$

$\therefore \frac{2x}{3x^2-5x+3}$ (Divide by x)

$= \frac{\frac{2x}{x}}{\frac{3x^2}{x} - \frac{5x}{x} + \frac{3}{x}}$

$= \frac{2}{3x+\frac{3}{x}-5}$

$= \frac{2}{3\left(x+\frac{1}{x}\right)-5}$

$= \frac{2}{3\times5-5}$

$= \frac{2}{10}$

$= \frac{1}{5}$

87(B). solution:

$\sqrt{1 - \frac{x^3}{100}} = \frac{3}{5}$

$\Rightarrow 1 - \frac{x^3}{100} = \left(\frac{3}{5}\right)^2$

$\Rightarrow 1 - \frac{9}{25} = \frac{x^3}{100}$

$\Rightarrow \frac{16}{25} = \frac{x^3}{100}$

$\Rightarrow x^3 = \frac{16\times100}{25}$

$\Rightarrow x^3 = 16 \times 4$

$\Rightarrow x^3 = 64$

$\Rightarrow x = 4 .$

88(D). Consider 1st pair,

By prime factorisation:

$5 = 1 \times 5$

$105 = 3 \times 5 \times 7$

$\Rightarrow$ H.C.F. $= 5$

$\Rightarrow$ L.C.M. $= 105$

Consider 2nd pair,

By prime factorisation:

$15 = 3 \times 5$

$105 = 3 \times 5 \times 7$

$\Rightarrow$ H.C.F. $= 15$

$\Rightarrow$ L.C.M. $= 105$

Consider 3rd pair,

By prime factorisation:

$15 = 3 \times 5$

$35 = 5 \times 7$

$\Rightarrow$ H.C.F. $= 5$

$\Rightarrow$ L.C.M. $= 105$

Both $(5, 105)$ and $(15, 35)$ have H.C.F. $= 5$ and L.C.M. $= 105$

89(A). Given:

Selling price of commodity on which profit is earned = Rs. 1420

Selling price of commodity on which loss is incurred = Rs. 860

Formula:

Profit = Selling price − Cost price

Loss = Cost price - Selling price

Calculation:

Let the cost price of an commodity be Rs. x

According to the question,

Profit on selling an commodity for Rs. 1420 $= 3\times$ Loss on selling it for Rs. 860

$\Rightarrow 1420 - x = 3 \times (x - 860)$

$\therefore$ The cost price a price of the article is Rs. 1000.

90(B). Given,

$\sqrt[3]{(126 + 392 \div 7 - 35 + 14^2)} =?$

$\Rightarrow \sqrt[3]{(126 + 392 \div 7 - 35 + 196)} =?$

$\Rightarrow \sqrt[3]{(126 + 56 - 35 + 196)} =?$

$\Rightarrow \sqrt[3]{(378 - 35)} =?$

$\Rightarrow \sqrt[3]{343} =?$

$\Rightarrow ? = 7$

91(B). Given radii of three metallic spheres be r_1, r_2, r_3 are $6cm, 8cm$ and $10cm$ respectively.

Let the radius of the new sphere be R .

We know,

Volume of sphere $= \frac{4}{3}\pi r^3$

So,

$\frac{4}{3}\pi R^3 = \frac{4}{3}\pi \left(r_1^3 + r_2^3 + r_3^3\right)$

$\Rightarrow \frac{4}{3}\pi R^3 = \frac{4}{3}\pi \left(6^3 + 8^3 + 10^3\right)$

$\Rightarrow R^3 = (216 + 512 + 1000)$

$\Rightarrow R^3 = 1728$

$\Rightarrow R = \sqrt[3]{12 \times 12 \times 12}$

$\Rightarrow R = 12$

$\therefore$ Diameter $= 24cm$

92(D). Here, $l + b + h = 20cm$

Also, $\sqrt{l^2 + b^2 + h^2} = 4\sqrt{5}$

Since,

$(l + b + h)^2 = l^2 + b^2 + h^2 + 2(lb + bh + lh)$

Surface area $= 2(lb + bh + lh)$

$= (l + b + h)^2 - (l^2 + b^2 + h^2)$

$= 20^2 - (4\sqrt{5})^2 = 320cm^2$

93(A). Let two digits of a number are x and y .

Then, the number be $10x + y$.

According to the question,

$x + y = 15$ ....(i)

$x - y = 3$ ....(ii)

Add equation (i) and equation (ii), we get

$2x = 18$

$\Rightarrow x = 9$

From equation (i), we get

$\Rightarrow y = 15 - 9$

$\Rightarrow y = 6$

$\therefore$ Required number $= 10 \times 9 + 6 = 96$

94(B). Suppose he answered x question correctly.

Marks obtained by him in x questions $= 4$ x

Wrong answer will be $= 200 - x$

According to the question,

4 x $- (200 - $ x $) = 200$

$\Rightarrow 4$ x $- 200 + $ x $= 200$

$\Rightarrow 5$ x $= 200 + 200 = 400$

$\Rightarrow$ x $= 80$

Thus, he answered 80 questions correctly.

(ii) A number is divisible by 9 only when the sum of its digit is divisible by 9

Now, checking the option,

Option (A): 444444

Unit digit = 4 (divisible by 2)

Sum of digit = 24 (not divisible by 9)

Option (B): 555555

Unit digit = 5(not divisible by 2)

Option (C): 666660

Unit digit = 0 (divisible by 2)

Sum of digit = 30(not divisible by 9)

Option (D): 666666

Unit digit = 6 (divisible by 2)

Sum of digit = 36(divisible by 9)

$\therefore$ 666666 is divisible by 18

96(B). Given:

line l II m

t is the transversal.

Concept Used:

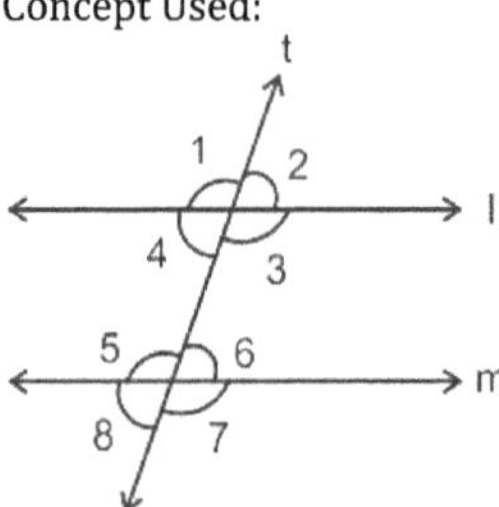

If l and m are two parallel lines and t is the transversal which intersects these parallel lines, then

The pairs of corresponding angles are equal.

$\angle 2 = \angle 6, \angle 3 = \angle 7, \angle 1 = \angle 5, \angle 4 = \angle 8$

The pairs of vertically opposite angles are also equal.

$\angle 1 = \angle 3, \angle 2 = \angle 4, \angle 5 = \angle 7, \angle 6 = \angle 8$

According to Question,

If the corresponding angles are equal, then

$3x + 10° = 2x + 40°$

$\Rightarrow x = 30°$

Vertically opposite angles are equal, then

$\Rightarrow 4y = 3x + 10°$
$\Rightarrow 4y = 3 \times 30° + 10°$
$\Rightarrow 4y = 100°$
$\Rightarrow y = 25°$
Now, $(x - y) = 30° - 25° \Rightarrow 5°$
The value of $\therefore$ x − y is 5°.

97(B). Line PQ and line RS intersect at a point O
∠POT = 90° and ∠SOQ = 130°
Calculations:
According to the question, we have

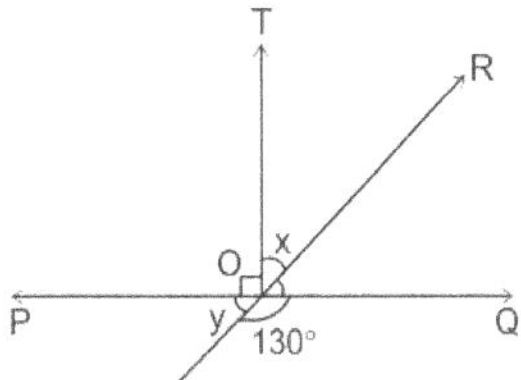

forms a total angle of 180°
$\angle POS + \angle SOQ = 180°$
$\Rightarrow y + \angle SOQ = 180°$
$\Rightarrow y + 130° = 180°$
$\Rightarrow y = 180° - 130°$
$\Rightarrow y = 50°$
Now, $\angle POS$ and $\angle ROQ$ are vertically opposite to each other
So, $\angle POS = \angle ROQ = 50°$
And, $\angle QOR$ and $\angle ROT$ are the complementary angles which makes a sum of angle of 90°
$\angle TOR + \angle ROQ = 90°$
$\Rightarrow x + 50° = 90°$
$\Rightarrow x = 90° - 50°$
$\Rightarrow x = 40°$
The Ratio of x and y is
$\Rightarrow x : y = 40° : 50°$
$\Rightarrow x : y = 4 : 5$
$\therefore$ The ratio of angle of x and y is 4 : 5.

98(C). Given,
The ages of Manu and Bharat are in the ratio = 6 : 5
Total age = 44 years
Let the ratio be x.
$6x + 5x = 44$
$\Rightarrow x = 4$
Manu's age after 8 years $= 6x + 8 = 6 \times 4 + 8 = 32$
Bharat's age after 8 years $= 5x + 8 = 5 \times 4 + 8 = 28$
Required ratio = 32 : 28
$= 8 : 7$
$\therefore$ The required answer is 8 : 7

99(A). Given:
Total distance = 80 km
Fare of train = Rs. 8/km
Fare of bus = Rs. 10/km
Total fare = Rs. 700
Calculation:
Let the distance travelled by bus be x km
$\Rightarrow$ Distance traveled by train = (80 - x) km

According to the question:
10x + (80 - x)8 = 700
$\Rightarrow$ 10x + 640 - 8x = 700
$\Rightarrow$ 2x = 60
$\Rightarrow$ x = 30
$\therefore$ Distance traveled by bus = 30 km

100(A). Given:
The given data is $3, 3, 4, 5, k, 11, 17$ and 18
Median of data = 6
Concept used:
If the number of terms is even
Median $= \dfrac{\left(\frac{n}{2}\right)^{th} + \left(\frac{n}{2}+1\right)^{th}}{2}$
Where n is the number of terms
Calculation:
In the given data the total number of the term is 8
$\therefore 6 = \dfrac{(4^{th} + 5^{th})}{2}$

⋯ The value of k is 7

101(A). Given:
In 35 litres mixture of alcohol and water the quantity of alcohol is 5 litres more than that of water
Calculation:
Let the amount of alcohol in the mixture be x
Then, mount of water = x - 5
According to the question:
x + x - 5 = 35
$\Rightarrow$ 2x = 40
$\Rightarrow$ x = 20
$\Rightarrow$ x - 5 = 15
x: (x-5) = 15 : 20 = 3 : 4
$\therefore$ Ratio of water to alcohol = 3 : 4

102(B). Given:
Sum of two numbers = 528
H.C.F. = 33
Let two numbers be 33x and 33y where x and y are prime to each other.
Accordingly,
33x + 33y = 528
$\Rightarrow$ 33(x + y) = 528
$\Rightarrow$ x + y = 16
So, The number of such pairs is (1, 15) (3, 13) (5, 11) (7, 9) where x and y are prime to each other.
$\therefore$ The number of such pairs is 4.

103(D). A 7 year old boy recognizes all four sided regular figures as squares. According to Van Hiele's, he is at Level 1-Visualization stage of geometrical thinking.
According to Van Hiele's, at this level, the focus of a child's thinking is on individual shapes, which the child is learning to classify by judging their holistic appearance. Children simply say, "That is a circle," usually without further description. Children identify prototypes of basic geometrical figures. According to this theory, if students do not teach at the

proper Hiele level that they will face difficulties and they cannot understand geometry. According to Van Hiele's theory, the development of student's geometrical thinking considered regarding the increasingly sophisticated level of thinking. These levels are hierarchies and able to predict future students' enactment in geometry. This model consists of five levels of understanding, which numbered from 0 to 4.

104(C). A teacher makes a teaching method more effective by using devices known as methodology of teaching. They are determined partly on subject matter to be taught and partly by the nature of the learner. For making particular teaching method to be appropriate and efficient it should to be in relation with the

R-4; S-1.
Deductive method is discovered by Aristotle. Inductive method is discovered by David Hume. Project method is discovered by William Heard Kilpatrick. Auto-instructional teaching is discovered by B.F Skinner.
Deductive method: It is a logical process in which a conclusion is based on the concordance of multiple premises that are generally assumed to be true. Deductive reasoning is sometimes referred to as top-down logic. Deductive reasoning relies on making logical premises and basing a conclusion around those premises.
Inductive reasoning: It is a method of drawing conclusions by going from the specific to the general. It's usually contrasted with deductive reasoning, where you go from general information to specific conclusions. Inductive reasoning is also called inductive logic or bottom-up reasoning.
Project method: It is a medium of instruction which was introduced during the 18th century into the schools of architecture and engineering in Europe when graduating students had to apply the skills and knowledge they had learned in the course of their studies to problems they had to solve as practicians of their trade.
Auto-instructional teaching: With auto-instructional methods, a student is allowed to go on to the next phase only after he has mastered the preceding phase. Thus, a grade shows how far a student has progressed. An A might indicate that he has mastered the whole course; a B, the first three-quarters of the course; a C, half of the course.

106(C). This is an example of an algorithm. In mathematics and computer science, an algorithm is an unambiguous specification of how to solve a class of problems. Algorithms can perform calculation, data processing and automated reasoning tasks.

107(C). In Diagnostic test, both background and performance of the students is needed for helping them in acquisition of intellectual habits and various powers as discipline. Diagnostic test in Mathematics are used by the teachers to detect the errors committed by the student during mathematical operations like addition, subtraction, multiplication, division. These tests are qualitative in nature not quantitative. These tests find the errors made by students and correct the so that help in their learning.

108(C). "Teacher provides home tuitions in mathematics" is not a principle of understanding, knowledge, and skills that students should acquire from lower primary section to upper primary section. It also provides proper guidance for teacher as well as students in making their decisions. Therefore, providing home tuitions in mathematics is not a principle of helping pupils with learning difficulties in Mathematics.

109(D). Identification of student's specific error is especially important for students with learning disabilities and low performances. The teacher plays a crucial role in the process of identification, and for that a close check is highly required of the performances of the learners.

Four steps for the analysis of error:
- Collecting samples of learner language
- Identifying the errors
- Describing the errors
- Explaining the errors
- Evaluating/correcting the errors

110(C). The objectives that makes the inclusion of mathematics in the curriculum prominent are "To prepare for the future vocation or occupation" and "To develop their intellectual powers and discipline". Mathematics provides an effective way of building mental discipline and encourages logical reasoning and mental rigor. In addition, mathematical knowledge plays a crucial role in understanding the contents of other school subjects such as science, social studies, and even music and art.

111(C). According to the National Council of Teachers of Mathematics (2000), "Measurement is the assignment of a numerical value to an attribute of an object, such as the length of a pencil.

The correct sequence of developing the concept of measurement is as:
c. Learners verify objects using simple observation.
b. Learners use non-standard units to measure length.
a. Learners use standard units to measure length.
d. Learners understand the relationship between metric units.

112(D). Tutorial teaching, Auto-instructional teachingn, Informal teaching are the organization of remedial teaching in Mathematics.

Tutorial teaching is a remedial teaching session given to one student or a small group of students.

Auto-instructional programs are educational material from which students learn by themselves. The teaching technique based on auto-instructional programs. Its purpose is to enable the interests within a curriculum in a regular classroom but is not limited to that setting. It works through conversation and the exploration and enlargement of experience.

113(D). The various aims for teaching science in our school are as follows:
1. Utilitarian Aim
2. Intellectual Aim
3. Disciplinary Aim
4. Cultural Aim
5. Moral Aim
6. Aesthetic Aim
7. Psychological Aim
8. Social Aim
9. Vocational aim

114(A). Cognitive validity requires that the content, process, language, and pedagogical practices of the curriculum are age-appropriate, and within the cognitive reach of the child. Simply, at this stage learners know the facts and principles of science and its applications, consistent with the stage of cognitive development. Thus the concept of Shadow formation at the upper primary level fulfilled by the concept of cognitive validity.

115(A). Disciplinary approach is also known as the subject approach or the traditional approach. As each subject is separately taught by the teacher in the area of the particular subject in question. For Example, example science was traditionally taught as a subject with different compartments such as physics, biology, and chemistry as separate components of the science subject.

116(D). Lecture method is one of the most popular and oldest methods of teaching in our schools. A lecture means teaching a lesson in the form of speech or talk. Merits of the lecture method:
- It is highly efficient if a teacher has a systematic and logical manner.
- It is convenient and comfortable, and a teacher is free to develop his/ her style of teaching.
- The number of students can listen and prepare notes. It saves time and energy.

117(B). Science is defined as the pursuit and application of knowledge and understanding of the natural and social world that follows a systematic methodology based on evidence. Technology is defined as the application of scientific knowledge for practical purposes. Science is an open-ended exploration-
Science exists since the day when the universe was created. scientific knowledge is never at a standstill. It is a dynamic, and ongoing process. It is an ever-growing enterprise that will never end. This is knowledge is that it is never complete. It is open to change."The soul of the learning of science is exploration. The learners should explore the facts and principles themselves."
Science is investigated but technology is created. In the words of Albert Einstein, "Scientists investigate that which already is; engineers create that which has never been.
Technology is usually goal-oriented-
"Technology refers to methods, systems, and devices which are the result of scientific knowledge being used for practical purposes".
Technology has a critical role in advancing the capabilities of Customer Success.
So, the application of science to develop new devices for goal-specific purposes, systems, or methods is called technology.
Therefore, We can say that technology is applied science. From now onward, we can say that science and technology became deeply intertwined in the sense that technology raises new problems to be solved by science in a kind of spiral that never ends and hence Science is an open-ended exploration whereas technology is usually goal-oriented.

118(D). As a teacher, you will be used to a class having over 35 children and you transact the lesson with considerable ease. This is because the children of a given age and class generally have ability levels and potentials within a certain range. When you have a CWSN in your class, he/she is likely to have certain needs that have to be addressed. The needs will vary from child to child depending on the disability he has. For example,
- A child with hearing impairment may need to have sufficient light to see the board or visuals and the teacher should talk clearly allowing him to look at her face so that he can lip read.

- A blind child will need along with verbal instructions, tactile material that he can touch and learn when the teacher uses visuals.
- A child with mental retardation will need concrete material and repeated instructions to understand a concept.
- A child with motor disabilities will need physical support depending on the need.

119(A). Bloom's taxonomy is a set of three hierarchical models used to classify educational learning objectives into levels of complexity and specificity. Bloom's taxonomy was named after psychologist Benjamin Bloom. He developed a set of three hierarchical models for the classification of learning objectives.

120(D). The problem of science teaching are follows:

- Safety
- Dealing with Controversial Topics
- Time Consuming Planning Requirements
- In Class Time Constraints
- Cost Limitations
- Facilities Limitations
- Prerequisite Information
- Collaboration vs. Individual Grades
- Missed Lab Work

Child Development and Pedagogy

1. Training before normal maturation is generally:
(a) highly beneficial with respect to the performance of the common skills
(b) beneficial from the point of view of long term
(c) harmful from all points of view
(d) beneficial or harmful depending on the method used in training

2. Which of the sequence is appropriate when development

(c) Locomotion Sequence
(d) Bilateral Sequence

3. A 6-year-old girl shows exceptional sporting ability. Her parents are sportspersons, send her for coaching daily and train her on weekends. Her capabilities are most likely to be the result of an interaction between:
(a) Health and training
(b) Discipline and nutrition
(c) Heredity and environment
(d) Growth and development

4. Peer groups are the agent of ______.
(a) Secondary Socialization
(b) Anticipatory Socialization
(c) Primary Socialization
(d) Developmental Socialization

5. During a task, Saina is talking to herself about ways she could proceed on the task. According to Lev Vygotsky's ideas on language and thought; this kind of 'private speech' is a sign of:
(a) Self-regulation
(b) Ego-centricism
(c) Psychological disorder
(d) Cognitive immaturity

6. The teacher observed that Ravi is not able to solve a problem alone while he solves it easily when individualized support is provided to him by his teacher. In Vygotsky's view, this kind of support is called:
(a) Generalization
(b) Abstract thinking
(c) Peer tutoring

(d) Scaffolding

7. Which of the following is central to the concept of progressive education?
(a) Belief in the capability and potential of every child
(b) Standard instruction and assessment
(c) Extrinsic motivation and uniform assessment parameters
(d) Textbook centric learning

8. According to Howard Gardner, ______ is not a type of intelligence.
(a) Musical
(b) Skeptical

emphasize that:
(a) Intelligence in one domain ensures intelligence in all other domains
(b) There are several forms of intelligence
(c) There are no individual differences in intelligence
(d) Intelligence Quotient (IQ) can b measured only by objective tests

10. Which of the following psychologists is associated with 'language development'?
(a) Binet   (b) Chomsky
(c) Pavlov   (d) Maslow

11. During classroom discussions, a teacher often pays more attention to boys than girls. This is an example of:
(a) Gender bias
(b) Gender identity
(c) Gender relevance
(d) Gender constancy

12. Which of the following may not be expected from a teacher to keep in mind while respecting individual differences?
(a) Ability grouping
(b) Adjusting the curriculum
(c) Leaving Children for self-study
(d) Adjusting the methods of teaching

13. Continuous and Comprehensive Evaluation mainly aims at promoting:
(a) Competition among children
(b) Competition among teachers

(c) Academic excellence among children
(d) Inclusive education

14. Continuous and comprehensive evaluation includes:
(a) only formative assessment
(b) only summative assessment
(c) neither formation nor summative assessment
(d) both formative and summative assessments using a wide variety of strategies

15. A self-guided, self-disciplined thinking which attempts to reason at the highest level of quality in a

(d) abstract thinking

16. A child 'who is in the middle of his school (about ten and half years) is unable to do the work of the class below that which is normal for his age" is known as which types of children?
(a) Mentally retarded
(b) Educationally retarded
(c) Moron
(d) Idiot

17. Which of the following is not a trait (ability) of a creative child?
(a) Originality   (b) Elaboration
(c) Novelty   (d) Accuracy

18. A child's notebook shows errors in writing like reverse images, mirror imaging, etc. Such a child is showing signs of:
(a) Learning disability
(b) Learning difficulty
(c) Learning problem
(d) Learning disadvantage

19. What effort will you make for bringing change in the behaviour of a problematic child?
(a) Make effort to bring change in the child's environment and attitude
(b) Try to improve by punishing the child
(c) Will not pay attention to him/her
(d) Will seat him in the front row in the class

20. What instructional adaptations should a teacher make while

working with students who are 'Visually Challenged'?

(a) Use a variety of visual presentations

(b) Orient herself so that the students can watch her closely

(c) Focus on a variety of written tasks, especially worksheets.

(d) Speak clearly and use a lot of touches and feel materials

21. Children's errors and misconceptions:

(a) Are a hindrance and obstacle to the teaching-learning process

(b) Should be ignored in the teaching-learning process

(c) Signify that children's capabilities are far inferior to

22. Which of the following is not the curve of learning?

(a) Convex

(b) Combination type

(c) Concave

(d) Longitudinal

23. 'Learning is any change in behaviour, resulting from behaviour' who said it?

(a) Crow & Crow

(b) Guilford

(c) Woodworth

(d) Skinner

24. Which of the following statements about children are correct?
A. Children are passive recipients of knowledge.
B. Children are problem solvers.
C. Children are scientific investigators.
D. Children are active explorers of the environment.

(a) A, B, C, and D   (b) A, B, and C

(c) A, B, and D   (d) B, C, and D

25. Knowing the naive conceptions that students bring to the classroom:

(a) hampers the teacher's planning and teaching

(b) pulls down the teacher's morale since it increases his work

(c) does not serve any purpose of the teacher

(d) helps the teacher to plan teaching more meaningfully

26. Which of the following is a constructive approach for dealing with the 'misconceptions' carried by students?

(a) Assign a lot of content to memorize and remember

(b) Create circumstances where misconceptions are not allowed to be expressed

(c) Give opportunities for experimentation and observation to counter misconceptions

(d) Ignore prior beliefs and alternative conceptions of students

27. The relationship between cognition and emotions is:

(a) independent of each other

(b) uni-directional - emotions influence cognition

(c) uni-directional - cognition

28. Ashok is very fond of playing cricket and is very good at it. He is the captain of his college team. He spends long hours playing or watching cricket and never gets tired or bored. Which personal factor is affecting learning in this example?

(a) Maturation

(b) Motivation

(c) Self-concept

(d) Levels of Aspiration

29. Which of the following is a teacher-related factor affecting learning?

(a) Maturation & Motivation

(b) The socio-emotional climate of the class

(c) Structure of the discipline

(d) Leadership style of teacher

30. Identify the factor that does not influence student difficulty in learning.

(a) Intellectual factor

(b) Social factor

(c) Economic factor

(d) All of the above

Language - I: English

Ques (31-39): Direction: Read the passage given below and answer the questions by choosing the correct/most appropriate options.

1. Today when we pick up a daily newspaper, we invariably find an increased incidence of vandalism, fraud, theft, robbery, rape, child spouse, battered spouses, murders, hate crimes, genocide (now termed as "ethnic cleansing") along with a multitude of other senseless violent acts that have become disturbingly common. These are not the actions of people who like themselves.

2. The solution to a great many problems, whether personal, national or global, lies in improving our feelings about ourselves both as individuals and members of society. When the significance of good self-esteem is well understood and it achieves the prominence it deserves, a transformation will begin, for as the people will learn they are deserving of self-respect, their respect for others will automatically increase.

3. Most of our behaviour has been shaped by our parent's caregivers and authority figures who played an important part in our early springing and were responsible for crystallizing our ideas about ourselves and the world. While everyone has self- as a human being. When, on the other hand, we have low self-esteem, we believe that we have little intrinsic worth.

4. We believe our personal value is in direct proportion to the value of our accomplishments. If we cannot accomplish certain results, we tend to feel low about ourselves. Some of us try too hard and become workaholics and over-achievers. With a few genuine feelings of self-worth, we try to create some and prove that we are somebody by our successes and achievements. Because our desire for perfection is so great, we tend to set unrealistic goals and place unreasonable demands on ourselves. Failing, rather than encouraging us to have realistic aspirations, only leads to a mere punishing round of self-blame and a resolve to drive ourselves harder next time. If we do finally achieve our goals we are disappointed; despite everything we have done, we still feel empty inside.

5. Vulnerable to the opinions of others, we desperately try to gain their recognition and approval sometimes through risky and dangerous behaviour. Thus, we are at the mercy of our emotions, instead of controlling them, we permit them to control us. Since we allow circumstances to influence our feelings, we are inclined to be moody. The insecurity we feel as a result of devaluing ourselves makes us react with jealousy, envy and possessiveness. Fear makes us greedy and acquisitive, and feelings of self-hate alternate with those of futility, unhappiness, and depression.

31. Which of the following are the things the newspapers are full of these days?

(a) News about the development of the country

(b) News about politics

(c) News about acts of crime and violence

(d) News about educational matters and employment

32. **Identify the parts of speech of the underlined segment in the given sentence.**
     When the <u>significance</u> of good self-esteem is well understood.
     (a) Adverb   (b) Pronoun
     (c) Noun   (d) Conjunction

33. **Find the word from the passage which is the antonym of the word, 'futility' as used in the passage(para 5)?**
     (a) Pointlessness

34. **Why is good self-esteem stressed?**
     (a) It is essential in solving many problems.
     (b) It builds up self-confidence.
     (c) It increases one's reputation.
     (d) It helps one respect others.

35. **Find the word from the passage which means the same as the word, 'vandalism' as used in the passage(para 1)?**
     (a) Construct   (b) Destruction
     (c) Build   (d) Mend

36. **Find the error in a part of the sentence:**
     The solution to a great many problems(A)/, whether personal, national, and global(B)/, lies in improving our feelings(C)/ No error. (D)
     (a) (A)   (b) (B)
     (c) (C)   (d) (D)

37. **Which of the following statements is true?**
     A. We need to accept ourselves unconditionally exactly as we are.
     B. We give permission to others to control our emotions.
     C. All non-violent acts are the actions of those who like themselves.
     (a) Only A
     (b) Only B
     (c) Both A and B
     (d) All of the above

38. **According to the passage, when does a person start feeling empty inside?**
     (a) When we get involved in crimes.

(b) When we push ourselves towards achieving goals and prove that we are somebody by our successes and achievements.

(c) When others start influencing our behaviour.

(d) None of the above

39. **Identify the part of speech of the underlined word:**
     We tend to set <u>unrealistic</u> goals and place unreasonable demands.
     (a) Noun   (b) Adverb
     (c) Adjective   (d) Pronoun

Ques (40-45): Direction: Read the extract given below and answer the questions.
There is a Reaper, whose name is Death,

Though the breath of these flowers is sweet to me,
I will give them all back again."
He gazed at the flowers with tearful eyes,
He kissed their drooping leaves;
It was for the Lord of Paradise
He bound them in his sheaves.
"My Lord has need of these flowerets gay,"
The Reaper said, and smiled;
"Dear tokens of the earth are they,
Where He was once a child.
"They shall all bloom in fields of light,
Transplanted by my care,
And saints, upon their garments white,
These sacred blossoms wear."
And the mother gave, in tears and pain,
The flowers she most did love;
She knew she should find them all again
In the fields of light above.
Oh, not in cruelty, not in wrath,
The Reaper came that day;
'T was an angel visited the green earth,
And took the flowers away.

40. **The poem presents death in a:**
     (a) gloomy light
     (b) positive light
     (c) fearful light
     (d) negative light

41. **According to the poet, the mother will meet her flowers in ____.**
     (a) Garden   (b) Playground
     (c) Home   (d) Paradise

42. **Who were the flowers for?**
     (a) Death   (b) Satan
     (c) God   (d) Mother

43. **Identify the figure of speech in the line:**
     She knew she should find them all again

(a) Alliteration
(b) Personification
(c) Metaphor
(d) Simile

44. **Who wears the flowers in the new world?**
     (a) Angels   (b) Cherubs
     (c) Saints   (d) God

45. **How did Death gaze at the flowers?**
     (a) Happy eyes   (b) Fearful eyes
     (c) Angry eyes   (d) Tearful eyes

46. **Ravi, an English teacher, is planning remedial teaching for his student who faces problems in expressing his view while talking with someone. Remedial work for**
     reviewing
     (c) Going through situational practice
     (d) Revision and practice

47. **A teacher divides the class in small groups and asks them to discuss and present their views on "Save Environment".**
     Students are free to plan and present their choice and creativity. The teacher is facilitating them as and when required. Which approach/method is followed in the class?
     (a) Structural Approach
     (b) Natural Approach
     (c) Deductive Approach
     (d) Constructivist Approach

48. **A Hindi - speaking teacher gets posted in a primary school which is situated in a remote area of Rajasthan. Since she doesn't know the local language, she faces lots of problems. She should:**
     (a) focus on the textbook as a source of standard Hindi.
     (b) use the child's language as a resource while teaching.
     (c) encourage the community to learn standard Hindi.
     (d) try to get a posting to a Hindi-speaking area.

49. **Direction: Answer the following questions by selecting the most appropriate option.**
     Students of Class IV can recognize flawed usage or sentence construction when the teacher:
     (a) tells them something is wrong

(b) gives alternatives as possible corrections

(c) lets them find the corrections

(d) focuses on certain surface errors

50. **'Pedagogical Grammar' means that:**
    (a) Begin from form and move on to use
    (b) Teaching through immersion
    (c) All grammar teaching should be rule focussed
    (d) Teaching grammar in context

51. **A teacher found an advertisement pamphlet for the sale of biscuits. She uses it for reading and speaking activities in her class. What do you call the pamphlet?**
    (a) Realia

52. **Choose the most appropriate option for the question given below:**
    At the end of each semester, a teacher tests the students in listening, comprehension, speaking, reading, and writing.
    The purpose of this approach is most likely to:
    (a) Measure the student's proficiency
    (b) Measure the student's aptitude for language learning
    (c) Help the teacher to define the curricular objective
    (d) Determine the student's attitudes toward language classes

53. **'The material should be according to the child's mental age, mental ability, grade, and level'.**
    Which principle of teaching is involved in this statement?
    (a) Concreteness
    (b) Accuracy and correctness
    (c) Selection and Gradation
    (d) Proportion

54. **The multilingual nature of the Indian classroom must be used as a resource so that ______.**
    (a) every child feels secure and accepted
    (b) every child learns at the same pace
    (c) children can learn many languages
    (d) the teacher develops language proficiency

55. **Damage to this area in the brain**

causes problems in speech production:
(a) Frontal cortex
(b) Occipital cortex
(c) Broca's area
(d) Wernicke's area

56. **Which of the following statements is correct?**
    (a) Receptive vocabulary are words we speak and productive vocabulary are words we hear.
    (b) Receptive vocabulary are words we recognize when we hear or see and productive vocabulary are words we speak or write.
    (c) Receptive vocabulary are words we discourse with people and productive vocabulary are words

productive vocabulary.

57. **According to the National Curriculum Framework 2005, which one of the following is NOT an objective of language teaching-learning?**
    (a) The competence to understand what one hears
    (b) Ability to read with comprehension
    (c) Effortless expression
    (d) To know the history of languages

58. **The term 'Comprehensible input' is associated with ____.**
    (a) Lev Vygotsky
    (b) Stephen Krashan
    (c) Noam Chomsky
    (d) James Asher

59. **While reading a text, which one among the following can help students understand the relations between the parts of a sentence?**
    (a) Adverbs   (b) Pronouns
    (c) Nouns   (d) Verbs

60. **Using 'realia' in the language class means bringing ____.**
    (a) real life situations to communicate
    (b) real objects as teaching aids
    (c) realistic objectives and targets for the learners
    (d) the real level of a child's learning to the knowledge of parents

Mathematics and Science

61. **x is a whole number which gives the**

same result when either added to or multiplied by itself. Which of these statements might be correct regarding x?
(a) x has only one possible value
(b) The multiplication of all possible values of x gives one of the values of x
(c) The number of possible values of x is a composite number
(d) One of the values of x is 1

62. **If the sum of two positive numbers is 65 and the square root of their product is 26, then the sum of their reciprocals is:**
    (a) $\dfrac{5}{52}$ (b) $\dfrac{7}{52}$
    (c) $\dfrac{1}{52}$ (d) $\dfrac{3}{52}$

(a) 0.027   (b) 0.27
(c) 2.7   (d) 27

64. $a^3 + b^3 = 26$ **and** $a + b = 2$**, then find the value of 6ab.**
    (a) 17   (b) -3
    (c) 7   (d) -18

65. **If** $x^2 + 9x - 22 = 0$ **and** $2y^2 - 7y + 6 = 0$ **then one of the value of** $\dfrac{x}{y}$ **is:**
    (a) 7   (b) 0
    (c) $\dfrac{-11}{2}$ (d) $\dfrac{3}{5}$

66. $p + \dfrac{1}{p} = 2$ **find the value of** $p \times p \times p$
    (a) 4   (b) 1
    (c) 6   (d) 8

67. **The number of sides of a regular polygon is 24 what is the interior angle of the polygon?**
    (a) 145°   (b) 155°
    (c) 165°   (d) 175°

68. **All sides of a quadrilateral ABCD touch a circle. If BC is 6.5 cm, CD is 4 cm, DA is 8 cm, then AB is?**
    (a) 11 cm   (b) 12.75 cm
    (c) 10.5 cm   (d) 9.75 cm

69. **All the sides of a cube are 8 units if it is cut into smaller cubes of side 2 units. What will be the total surface area of all the smaller cubes?**
    (a) 1536 square unit
    (b) 1632 square unit
    (c) 800 square unit
    (d) 64 square unit

70. **A piece of wire, bent in the shape of a square having 44 cm as its side, is subsequently bent to form a circle.**

What will be the radius of the circle?

(a) 108 cm   (b) 56 cm
(c) 14 cm   (d) 28 cm

71. In the adjoining figure $\angle BAD = a$, $\angle ABG = b$ and $\angle BGD = c$ and $\angle ADG = d$, find the value of $\angle ABG$ in terms of a, c and d:

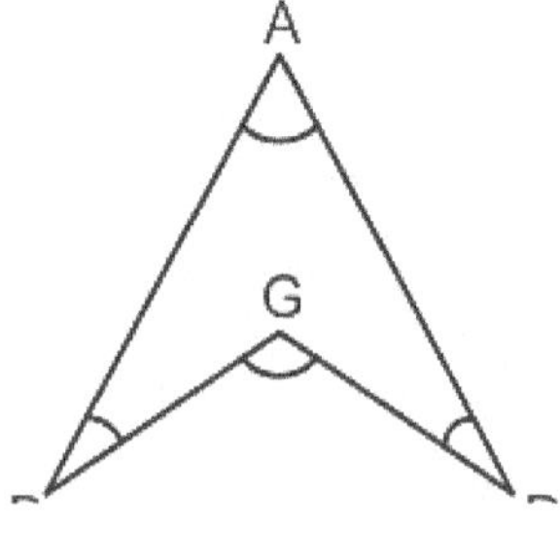

(d) None of the above

72. After allowing a discount of 34%, the shopkeeper still gained 10%. What is the % of marked price over the cost price?

(a) 15.23%   (b) 56.67%
(c) 33.34%   (d) 66.67%

73. What must be added to each term of the ratio 5 : 11, so as to make it equal to 3 : 4?

(a) 12   (b) 13
(c) 10   (d) 11

74. A worker covers a distance of 81 km in 11 hours. He travels partly on foot at 4.5 km/h and partly on bicycle at 15 km/h. What is the distance covered on the cycle?

(a) 45 km   (b) 37.5 km
(c) 52.5 km   (d) 30 km

75. My cousin is twice my age. If the difference between our ages is 20 years, then what is my age?

(a) 19   (b) 20
(c) 21   (d) 22

76. What is the least number that should be added to 2480 so that the sum is exactly divisible by 3, 4, 5 and 6?

(a) 40   (b) 60
(c) 20   (d) 50

77. Solve:
$(?)^3 \times 10 = 13230 \div (9.261 \div 7)$

(a) 10   (b) 25
(c) 125   (d) 0.5

78. The mean of the prime numbers between 20 and 45 is:

(a) 36   (b) 34
(c) 24   (d) 32

79. If the difference of the mode and median of a data is 38, then the difference of the median and mean is:

(a) 19   (b) 18
(c) 22   (d) 24

80. What is the difference in the mode and the mean of the observations?
4, 5, 6, 7, 8, 12, 9, 12, 5, 12

(a) 4   (b) 4.2
(c) 5.1   (d) 4.6

81. In the textbook of mathematics the content should be developed:

(a) In the order of exercise

82. Which among the following is correct about spatial thinking?

(a) It is an ability to discern shapes
(b) It is based on the idea of exposure to geometrical concepts
(c) It is one of the qualities of a teacher
(d) It is the ability to get directions

83. According to N.C.F, which of the following is not the aim of teaching Mathematics?

(a) Mathematics should bring mathematization of thoughts
(b) Learner should focus on building logical and abstract thinking
(c) Mathematics should be connected to the practical life of learners as well
(d) Learner should focus on solving as many problems as he can

84. Rajiv, a teacher of class 5th gives a newspaper to his students and tells them to find how math's is involved in the newspaper as well. A student begins to solve a sudoku puzzle given in the newspaper. This shows:

(a) Student doesn't care about teacher's instructions
(b) He is very much interested in numbers
(c) Sudoku helps logical and reasoning skills of a child
(d) Both (B) and (C)

85. Mathematics is itself a language with its own symbols, words, and rules of syntax. Which of the following is not a part of mathematical language?

(a) >, <   (b) *, !
(c) #, &   (d) [ ], { }

86. A students is asked to draw a cube in the class or to show the example of it from among the classroom after the chapter on shapes has been completed. Which type of evaluation is represented by the above example?

(a) Summative Assessment
(b) Formative Assessment
(c) Both (A) and (B)
(d) None of these

87. Permanent difficulties in learning are investigated in:

(a) Placement Assessment
(b) Formative Assessment

analysis process is/are:

(a) Collect a sample
(b) Record all responses
(c) Interview the student
(d) All of these

89. Why error analysis is important?

(a) Encompasses many branches and components
(b) For students with learning disabilities and low performing students
(c) Explain the key processes in mathematical reasoning
(d) Formally organized subject of study

90. Mathematics is that language in which the God has written the whole world or universe. "Who said these statement"?

(a) Galileo   (b) Russell
(c) Plato   (d) Hamilton

91. A food item X turns violet in solution of caustic soda and copper sulphate. When same food item gone through iodine test no change was observed. Identify the correct option based on the given information.

(a) The food contains carbohydrate, but not protein
(b) The food contains protein as well as starch
(c) The food contains protein but not carbohydrate
(d) The food contains fat but not protein

92. Which of the following foods can be eaten both raw and cooked?

(a) Cabbage and Carrot
(b) Broccoli and Rajma
(c) Spinach and Potato
(d) Chilly and Brinjal

93. When taken out of water, fishes die because:
(a) their body temperature rises too high
(b) they get too much carbon di oxide
(c) they are unable to drink water
(d) they are unable to respire

94. Which of the following is an aquatic pteridophyte?
(a) Lycopodium   (b) Azolla
(c) Equisetum   (d) Pteris

    nature
(b) Sound waves can propagate through water
(c) Speed of sound waves in steel is more than its speed in air
(d) Sound waves can propagate through vacuum

96. Which disease is caused by deficiency of Vitamin C in humans?
(a) Rickets
(b) Scurvy
(c) Beri-Beri
(d) Night Blindness

97. Salivation is controlled by __________.
(a) medulla   (b) cerebellum
(c) spinal cord   (d) cerebrum

98. Which of the following property is generally found in non-metals?
(a) Ductility   (b) Ductility
(c) Conductivity   (d) Brittleness

99. The weakest acid among the following is _____.
(a) Formic Acid
(b) Benzoic Acid
(c) Oxalic acid
(d) Hydrofluoric Acid

100. Which of the following has the highest velocity?
(a) Cosmic rays
(b) Light
(c) Electron
(d) Supersonic wave

101. The study of the earth's magnetic field is known as _________.

(a) Terrestrial magnetism
(b) Ferromagnetism
(c) Paramagnetism
(d) Diamagnetism

102. If equal and opposite forces applied to a body tend to elongate it, the stress so produced is called:
(a) Tensile stress
(b) Compressive stress
(c) Tangential stress
(d) Working stress

103. Water is renewable natural resource because:
(a) It can be reused again
(b) It is being recycled by human being

104. The centre of a cyclone is a calm area, it is called the ____ of the storm.
(a) point   (b) needle
(c) eye   (d) limit

105. A device used for converting AC into DC is called:
(a) Transformer
(b) Rectifier
(c) Induction coil
(d) Dynamo

106. A dynamo converts ______.
(a) electrical energy to mechanical energy
(b) electrical energy to magnetic energy
(c) chemical energy to electrical energy
(d) mechanical energy to electrical energy

107. There are four below-average students in a class. Which one of the following strategies will be most effective to bring them at par with the other students?
(a) Make them sit in a front row and supervise their work
(b) Identify their weak areas of learning and provide remedial measures
(c) Ensure that they attend the school regularly
(d) Give them additional assignments for homework

108. The point of primary concern to the teacher in handling disciplinary problems is:

(a) The nature of student behavior
(b) The cause of the misbehavior
(c) The type of punishment indicated
(d) The amount of punishment apparently necessary

109. The advantage(s) of project work is/are
(i) Students develop independent thinking
(ii) It develops fellow-feeling and democratic spirit
(a) Only (i)
(b) Only (ii)
(c) Both (i) and (ii)
(d) Neither (i) nor (ii)

110. One essential feature of a good

(c) involving participation of maximum senses
(d) Easy to handle

111. To showcase the creative ideas of students and to inculcate the value of appreciation for innovation done by their peers, which of the following activities should be organized by the science teacher?
(a) A debate competition
(b) Speech during assembly time
(c) Unit test
(d) Organize exhibitions

112. ____ method of teaching is also known as 'Inquiry method'.
(a) Inductive and Deductive method
(b) Discovery method
(c) Problem solving method
(d) Lecture method

113. Which one of the following approaches adopted by a Science teacher reflects scientific temper on their part?
(a) Maintaining perfect discipline in the class
(b) Covering the prescribed syllabus as quickly as possible
(c) Encouraging students to ask questions in the classroom
(d) Preparing difficult question papers to enhance learning

114. Which of the following is a challenge for a teacher while teaching science?
(a) Removing alternative concepts which they see while growing

up

(b) Translating the understanding of Science into a knowledge generation opportunity

(c) Removing superstitions from their mind

(d) All of the above

115. The role of a science teacher should be to ______.

(a) provide rich variety of learning experiences to learners

(b) provide product based teaching learning environment to learners

(c) guide learners to practice the memorization of the creative ideas

(d) encourage all learners to frame

least describes the nature of science?

(a) Science is both a body of knowledge and a process

(b) Science is a community enterprise

(c) Science is a global human endeavor

(d) The knowledge generated by science is not reliable

117. Bronze is an alloy of ______.

(a) Copper and Zinc

(b) Copper and Tin

(c) Copper and Iron

(d) Copper and Aluminium

118. Which chemical is used for ripening of fruits?

(a) Methane

(b) Ethylene

(c) Sulphuric acid

(d) Glucose

119. The major reason for using Bakelite for handles of pressure cooker is that:

(a) it is bad conductor of heat

(b) it is bad conductor of electricity

(c) it is unbreakable

(d) it is light in weight

120. Which of the following is NOT an example of neutralization in daily life?

(a) Taking milk of magnesia for acidity

(b) Rubbing baking soda in case of ant bite

(c) Treating soil with quick time

(d) Depositing a layer of zinc on

iron

//Hints and Solutions//

1(D). Every child has his own set of qualities. Also, there is the right time to learn a skill. The time at which a child becomes ready to learn is called maturation.

Maturation is interpreted as a relatively permanent change in an individual, such as cognitive, emotional, or physical, that occurs as a result of biological aging, regardless of personal experience.

Things to remember during training:

- A child can learn a new skill prematurely or late.

- Training of a child to learn a new skill is worth appreciating but it should be remembered that the child is mature

trainer in the training process.

- For example, for a primary school child to multiply 895 and 568 is rugged, explaining to him to multiply this may be troublesome and a burden for him. But there are instances when a child learns to multiply numbers of this extent using an abacus it becomes easy for him/her.

So, it could be concluded that training before normal maturation is generally beneficial or harmful depending on the method used in training.

2(B). The term development" is generally used to refer to the dynamic process by which an individual grows and changes throughout its lifespan. It is often thought of as the process of qualitative change taking place from conception to death. In this way, development is a broad term and deals with all areas including physical, motor, cognitive, physiological, social, emotional, and personality. It should be noted that developments in all these areas are interrelated.

- Cephalo - Caudal Sequence: The direction of development is from head to limbs i.e, in a longitudinal axis called 'cephalocaudal.

- Proximo distal Sequence: The spinal cord develops before the outer parts of the body. The child's arms develop before the hands and the hands and feet develop before the fingers and toes. The development direction is from the center to the periphery called 'proximodistal'.

- Locomotion Sequence: Various kinds of motions such as walking, running, jumping, swimming, etc. by the body are known as locomotion. Movement is one of the characteristic features of all living organisms. Locomotion helps us to move from one place to another.

- Bilateral Sequence: The human body plan is bilateral with symmetrical sense organs, a fast responding brain, half the body weight in muscles, a powerful heart, miles of arteries and veins, and a brain that coordinates it all.

So, we can conclude that the Proximo distal Sequence is appropriate when development proceeds from the center to the peripheral areas of the body.

3(C). According to the question girl's parents are sportspersons and she obtained training from coaching. Both of her parents are sportspersons. So, we can say that her capabilities depend on heredity and the environment.

- The individual's personality is the product of both heredity and environment.

Role of Heredity and Environment:

Heredity	Environment
• Heredity or "Nature" • Strong Influence on Physical Development. • Physical Makeup, that a child Inherits from parents.	• Environment or "Nature" • Everything surrounds and influences a child. • Family, School, Neighbours, Media, etc.

So, from the points, as mentioned above, it becomes clear that the girl's capabilities are most likely to be the result of an interaction between heredity and the environment.

4(A). Socialization is a process of internalizing the norms, culture, values, and customs of society to be socially acceptable. Peer groups are the agents of 'Secondary Socialization' throughout one's life.

Peer groups help children to be socialized by making them learn to behave in a way that is socially acceptable with age-peers. At this age, children learn appropriate social attitudes such as how to like and enjoy social life and group activities.

5 TYPES OF SOCIALIZATION	
1. Primary Socialization	• It happens during infancy and childhood. It refers to the process where the child becomes socialized through the family in the early childhood years. • This highlights that the key agent in the process of primary socization is the family. • For example, a very young child in a family has little knowledge of his culture. Through the family, the child learns what is accepted and what is not in a particular society.
2. Seco	• It occurs once the infant passes into the childhood phase and con

nd ary Soc iali zat ion	• tinues into maturity. It refers to t he process that begins in the late r years through agencies such as neighborhoods, schools, and pee r groups. • During this phase more than the family, some other agents of soc ialization like the neighborhood, school, and peers' group begin to play a role in socializing the chil d. • For example, Schools help childr en in learning the importance of social cohesion and unity and inc ulcating the informal cues about social roles through interaction.
3.D eve lop me ...	• It is the process of learning beha ...
ion	
4. Ant ici pat ory Soc iali zat ion	• It refers to the mental rehearsal s, concrete plans, and subtle cha nges in values and perceptions t hat a significant difference in soc ial roles is about to occur.
5. Re- soc iali zat ion	• It refers to the process of discard ing former behavior patterns an d accepting new ones as part of a transition in one's life. This occu rs throughout human life. • (Schaefer & Lamn, 1992)

5(A). Lev Vygotsky was a Russian psychologist and a social constructivist. He has propounded 'Socio-cultural Theory' which emphasizes the role of social interaction in cognitive development.
• Lev Vygotsky emphasized that the acquisition of speech is the major activity in cognitive development.
• Vygotsky embedded in this theory, the concept of 'private speech' which is a kind of speech directed to the self with no communicative function.
• Children use private speech to guide their actions by speaking to themselves.
Private Speech:
• It refers to the speech produced aloud by young children that seem to be addressed either to the self or others, which sometimes cannot be easily conceived by a listener.
• It has a significant role in the augmentation of the self and self-consciousness. It is the main aspect in the development of self and subjectivity.
• This phenomenon starts in the early years of life and proceeds to the end of adolescence and even later.

So, from the points, as mentioned above, it becomes clear that the above-mentioned kind of 'private speech' is a sign of Self-regulation.

6(D). 'Lev Vygotsky', a Soviet psychologist, has propounded the "Socio-cultural Theory". This theory implies the idea that social interaction plays a crucial role in the development of learners' cognitive ability.
In Vygotsky's view, the above-mentioned kind of support is called 'scaffolding' as it refers to a process through which:
• required assistance is given to children according to their individual needs.
• temporary support is imparted to the children to enhance their learning skills.
• individualized support is provided to children to increase their learning

• Abstract thinking is the ability to think about objects, principles, and ideas that are not physically present. It is a great way to generate new ideas and gain new insights during any problem-solving process.
• Peer tutoring refers to the learning process where fellow students teach each other. In this strategy, a higher-performing student is paired with a lower-performing student to teach specific skills.
• Generalization refers to the tendency to have conditioned responses caused by related stimuli.

7(A). John Dewey, an American philosopher has proposed the concept of 'P **rogressive Education' which emphasizes that learning takes place only through 'hands-on' approach so the students must interact with their environment to adapt and learn.**
Belief in the capability and potential of every child is central to the concept of progressive education as it promotes:
• emphasizes to enhance skills and understanding of the learners by engaging with the contents and experiences.
• promotes 'learning by doing' to make children self-reliant and productive to use their knowledge and talents effectively.
• ensures the active participation of students by working in a group and applying practical knowledge to complete an activity.
So, it could be concluded that belief in the capability and potential of every child is central to the concept of progressive education.

8(B). Intelligence refers to a set of different cognitive abilities to think

rationally, act purposefully, resolve problems and deal with the demands of the environment.
The Theory of Multiple Intelligence:
Howard Gardner proposed this theory wherein he formulated eight categories of intelligence. He defined intelligence as "Intelligence is a bio-psychological potential to process information that can be activated in a cultural setting to solve problems or create products that are of value in a culture".
To define intelligence more broadly, Gardner established several criteria for defining intelligence:
• the potential for brain isolation by brain damage
• its place in evolutionary history
• the presence of core operations
• susceptibility to encoding
• support from psychometric findings
From the criteria mentioned above he formulated the following types of intelligence:

Type of Int ellige nce	Description
Lingui stic	ability to effectively use language to express oneself
Logic al-ma thema tical	ability to analyse problems logica lly, perform mathematical operat ions and scientific investigation
Spatia l	ability to recognise and manipula te wide spaces such as navigation
Music al	ability to recognise and compose musical patterns
Bodil y-kine stheti c	ability to use mental abilities to c oordinate bodily movements
Interp erson al	ability to understand the intentio ns, motivations & desires of peop le
Intrap erson al	ability to understand oneself, ap preciate one's feelings, fears, and motivations
Natur alistic	nature, nurturing, and relating in formation to one's natural surrou ndings

From the above table, it becomes clear that 'skeptical' is not a type of intelligence formulated by Howard Gardner.

9(B). The 'Theory of Multiple Intelligence' or 'Multidimensional Intelligence Theory' was propounded by an American psychologist 'Howard Gardner' in his book 'Frames of Mind'.
This theory describes eight different kinds of intelligence and emphasizes that:
• intelligence is of several kinds.

- intelligence can't be tied to a single domain.
- each individual has his/her own unique abilities.
- intelligence is not dominated by a general factor.

So, it could be concluded that the Theory of multiple intelligence emphasize that there are several forms of intelligence.

10(B). Noam Chomsky, known as the father of modern linguistics, has made a crucial contribution in the field of linguistics.

Let's understand Chomsky's view about language in brief:

- Innate ability: He strongly believes that children are born with an innate knowledge of grammar that serves as the basis for all language acquisition.

language.

- Universal grammar: Chomsky's universal grammar suggests that all children have an innate ability to acquire, understand and develop grammar.
- Language Acquisition Device: Chomsky proposed that humans are equipped with a language acquisition device that enables a child to acquire and produce language.

A brief description of other psychologists:

Alfred Binet	A French psychologist, is known for developing the first intelligence test and the concept of mental age.
Ivan Pavlov	The Russian Psychologist propounded 'The Theory of Classical Conditioning' which emphasizes that behaviour is learnt by a repetitive association between the response and the stimulus.
Abraham Maslow	An American psychologist, best known for creating "Maslow's Hierarchy of Needs", in which he proposed a series of needs.

So, Noam Chomsky is associated with 'language development'.

11(A). Classroom Discussions play a vital role in shaping or constructing the overall personality of a child. The discussions help the child to not only presents his or her

point of view but to get an idea of other's perception as well and this helps in shaping the all-round thinking of a child.

Gender Bias:

- It refers to the belief that someone prioritizes one gender more than another.
- It is a form of unconscious bias, or implicit bias, which occurs when one individual attributes certain attitudes and stereotypes to another person or group of people.
- It is a preference or prejudice toward one gender over the other for example preferring boys over girls during an activity. Bias can be conscious or unconscious and may manifest in many ways, both subtle and obvious.

Examples of Gender Bias in Teaching and at school:

- Girls being given lesser opportunities to participate in school and classroom events.

Gender Constancy: The concept of gender constancy refers to a cognitive stage of development of children at which they come to understand that their gender (meaning their biological sex) is fixed and cannot change over time.

Gender Relevance: It is an important consideration in development. It is a way of looking at how social norms and power structures impact on the lives and opportunities available to different groups of men and women.

Gender Identity: It is a personal conception of oneself as male or female. This concept is intimately related to the concept of gender role, which is defined as the outward manifestations of personality that reflect gender identity.

So, during a classroom discussion if a teacher pays more attention to boys than girls then it will be regarded as an example of Gender Bias.

12(C). Individual difference: Every child is unique and different from others. It should be kept in mind that learners possess different abilities, and personalities, and belong to different backgrounds. The stimulus needs of every learner will be different. Teaching has to be done keeping in mind the individual differences and problems arising out of it.

The teacher should take care of the below points:

- As per the need of the students, the teaching method can vary.
- Generally confused with discrimination, ability grouping is a measure in which students of similar traits are grouped so that the teacher can choose a compatible teaching method.
- Keeping in mind the child-centered

education as proposed by the NCF, adjusting the curriculum is no exception because it is the child who has the freedom to choose what he wants to learn.

- The pace of learning should not be a matter of concern for a teacher as every child has his pace and more than results, the attempt to learn is important.

It should be noted that, though self-study improves knowledge, it should not be done simultaneously when the teacher's responsibility is to teach children.

So, we conclude that for a teacher, leaving children for self-study is not recommended

13(D). Continuous and Comprehensive Evaluation, commonly known as 'CCE', was introduced as a school-based evaluation system by the CBSE in 2009 with the

- CCE can be incorporated in the inclusive classroom while engaging in teaching through a variety of activities.
- Incorporating strategies for attending to diverse needs in classrooms would be particularly useful in developing CCE processes for the classroom.

Aims of CCE:

- Emphasizing continuity and regularity of assessment.
- Assessing both scholastic and co-scholastic aspects of a child's growth.
- Emphasize the thought process and de-emphasize memorization as CCE includes all aspects of students' development.
- Recording the methods of learning to make the required improvements.
- Making evaluation an integral part of learning through diagnostic and remedial teaching.
- Evaluating children comprehensively rather than focus only on cognitive or intellectual functioning.
- Ensuring all-around development of students including cognitive, psychomotor, and affective domains.
- Evaluate every aspect of the child during their presence at the school.
- Developing a student's cognitive, psychomotor, and affective domains.
- Assessing both scholastic and co-scholastic aspects of a child's growth.
- Evaluation of the interest of the child during their presence at the school.
- Observing and recording the methods of learning to make improvements.

So, we can conclude that Continuous and Comprehensive Evaluation mainly aims at promoting Inclusive education.

14(D). Continuous and Comprehensive Evaluation (CCE) refers to a system of school-based evaluation of students that covers all aspects of students' development.

- CCE was introduced by the Central Board of Secondary Education (CBSE) in India to evaluate the student's development in all aspects throughout the academic year on a continuous basis.
- The objective of CCE is to make evaluation an integral part of learning through diagnostic and remedial teaching.
- CCE helps improve student's performance by identifying his/her learning difficulties at regular intervals right from the beginning of the academic session and employing suitable remedial measures for enhancing their learning performance.

CCE describes two different types of evaluations which include summative and formative assessment/evaluation.

- "Summative Evaluation" commonly assessing them at the end of the term.
  - produces an accurate description of students' potential and achievement to promote them to the next grades.
- "Formative evaluation", commonly known as "Assessment for Learning" is a type of evaluation which:
  - monitor the child's progress throughout the teaching-learning process and improve students' academic achievements.
  - diagnoses and removes the learning difficulties of students with appropriate strategies.

So, it becomes clear that Continuous and Comprehensive Evaluation includes both formative and summative assessments using a wide variety of strategies.

15(A). According to Ross, "Thinking is a mental activity in its cognitive aspect of mental ability with regard to the psychological object."

According to Garrett, "Thinking is behaviour which is often implicit and hidden and in which symbols (images, ideas, and concepts) are ordinarily employed."

Critical Thinking: The ability to apply reasoning and logic to new or unfamiliar situations, ideas, and opinions. It refers to the process of judging or analyzing facts, events, etc. It requires proper analysis, evaluation, inference, and explanation.

- Critical thinking is self-guided, self-disciplined thinking which attempts to reason at the highest level of quality in a fair-minded way. People who think critically consistently attempt to live rationally, reasonably, and empathically.
- People use the intellectual tools that critical thinking offers – concepts and principles that enable them to analyze, assess, and improve their thinking.
- Thinking critically involves seeing and observing things in an open-minded way and examining an idea or concept in a way to form as many angles as possible.
- It can be enhanced by asking children to discuss among themselves in groups followed by sharing in a large group.

Abstract thinking is the ability to understand real concepts, such as freedom or vulnerability, but not directly tied to concrete physical objects and experiences.

So, self-guided, self-disciplined thinking which attempts to reason at the highest level of quality in a fair-minded way is called critical thinking.

16(B). Exceptional children are those who deviate from the normal population and need special education services to meet their needs. It includes children who are gifted, backward, creative, learning abilities as some learn fast and some learn slowly.

'Educationally retarded children':

- An educationally retarded child is not mentally retarded or physically disabled.
- He may have a neurological handicap or emotional disorder which hinders their abilities.
- Appropriate training is required to make educationally retarded children learn some self-care and communication skills.
- Educationally retarded children show the inability to do the work of the class below that which is normal for their age.

So, it could be concluded that if a child 'who is in the middle of his school (that is about ten and half years) is unable to do the work of the class below that which is normal for his age" is known as 'Educationally retarded children'.

Mental retardation: It refers to an intellectual disability characterized by low Intelligence Quotient (IQ) and impairments in adaptive daily life skills.

Moron: A child with mild intellectual disability and an IQ of (51-70).

Idiot: A child with the least intelligence on the IQ scale (0-25).

17(B). Creativity is a cognitive ability to produce something original by offering a fresh perspective. It is the ability possessed by people who are creative, persistent, and imaginative.

Creativity is related to divergent thinking which refers to a way of solving problems by more than one approach. It is goal-directed thinking which is unusual, novel, and useful and includes brainstorming and out-of-the-box thinking in it

- Creative children are those who show high-performance capability in several areas such as artistic and creative work, leadership quality, keen power of observation, etc.
- These children have divergent thinking and are very curious in nature that's why sometimes the classroom seems monotonous to them because they grab things fastly than of their age-peers.

Trait (ability) of a creative child:

- Elaboration
- Abstracting ability
- Fluency & Flexibility
- Originality & Novelty
- Sensitivity of problems

Characteristics of Creative Children:

- Perceive relation between impossible things.
- Curious, extrovert, and ambitious in nature.
- Think quickly and solve problems in a novel way.
- Try new things and risk failure in executing innovative ideas.

Accuracy refers to the ability to do anything without making any mistakes. it is the state of being precise and accurate. It is not necessary that every time the creative child will be accurate as it is natural for them also to make mistakes.

So, it could be concluded that 'Accuracy' is not a trait (ability) of a creative child.

18(A). Learning disability includes distinguished from the things related to a logical arrangement like unable to write, read or sturring, etc. Children with learning disabilities experience difficulty in learning and using certain skills namely reading, writing, listening, and reasoning.

Errors in writing like reverse images, mirror imaging, etc represent learning disabilities. Dyslexia is the most common learning disability which results in reverse or mirror images of the alphabet.

Dyslexia is a learning disability that makes learners:

- unable to read and interpret letters and words.
- confuse with the same shapes and sounds of the alphabet.
- bewilder in identifying and relating speech sounds with letters and words.

Types of Learning Disability: It is categorized either by the type of information processing that is affected or by the specific difficulties caused by a processing deficit.

Learning Disabilities	Related to
Dys	Writing disability, inability to write

graphia	properly, illegible handwriting
Dysphasia	Speech and language disorders
Dyscalculia	Mathematics disability, difficulty in learning mathematical concepts and organizing numbers besides, subtraction, multiplication, division
Dyspraxia	Difficulty with motor skills, non-verbal learning disability, motor clumsiness, and poor visual-spatial skills
Dysnomia	Inability to retrieve or recall appropriate words for oral or return language

Learning disability constitutes a condition that affects learning and intelligence across an individual.

So, we can conclude that child is showing signs of a learning disability.

19(A). Children are divided into different categories based on their interests, behavior, nature, I.Q level, understanding, grasping abilities, etc. Children live through critical phases of development, which influence their behavior.

- Most children learn to adapt well to this changing nature of skill demand, but some of these children find it difficult to do so.
- Further, much problematic behaviour which goes unnoticed or even tolerated in a home setting becomes more conspicuous in the school environment due to competition and frequent evaluation.
- Common problematic behaviours are attention deficit hyperactivity disorder, learning disability, bullying, and delinquent behaviour.

Problematic children are particularly those who are difficult to teach, due to a lack of self-control and disruptive and antisocial behavior.

Making an effort to bring change in a child's environment and attitude will be the best way for bringing change in the behavior of a problematic child as:

- A good learning environment helps in building a culture of mutual trust and respect that engages the learners meaningfully in the task of learning.
- Besides that, it also supports a relationship between teaching and learning that helps in improving childhood mental health and academic performance.
- By bringing a change in attitude child's thinking, feeling and behavior could be influenced towards a place, people, or situation.

So, it could be concluded that making effort to bring change in a child's environment and attitude will be the best way for bringing change in the behavior of a problematic child.

20(D). In the teaching-learning process, visually challenged learners suffer from an issue with sight or vision but when they are facilitated with the right training and tools, they develop a good literacy ability.

Instructional adaptations that a teacher should make while working with visually challenged learners include:

- using a lot of touches and feel materials.
- giving verbal clues to create opportunities to imagine.
- introducing tactile materials during classroom discussions.
- speaking clearly and loudly with
- using the braille system to make them read-write as its raised dots will help the child to study the words through the pattern.

A teacher should not use a variety of visual presentations and written tasks especially worksheets for visually challenged learners as it could lead to low self-esteem and feeling of failure in them.

So, it could be concluded that a teacher should speak clearly and use a lot of touches and feel materials while working with visually challenged learners.

Tactile materials: It refers to the inputs which children receive through the receptive sensors of their skins.

Braille system: It refers to a pattern of raised dots called "Braille" to represent letters, numbers, and punctuation marks, that can be felt with a finger.

21(D). Error: When a learner can't master a topic, he/she is vulnerable to make errors. Errors are nothing but incorrectness made by a child during learning.

Misconceptions: It takes place due to the mismatch in previously assimilated and newly accommodated knowledge.

Children's errors and misconceptions:

- are significant steps in the teaching-learning process.
- are necessary in the learning process to give insight into children's thinking.
- help the teacher to be aware of learners' learning styles, to cater them according to their needs.
- are considered as a part of the teaching-learning process as it helps to understand the child.

So, it could be concluded that children's errors and misconceptions are a significant step in the teaching-learning process.

22(D). A learning curve visualizes changes in pupil overall performance over time. The line graph displays opportunities across the x-axis, and a measure of student performance along the y-axis. A good learning curve which is also known as the 'experience curve', reveals improvement in pupils' performance as opportunity count (i.e., exercise practice with a given knowledge component) increases.

- Learning curve was first defined by Hermann Ebbinghaus in 1885.
- By learning curve, learners can relate his/her development through the method visually presented in the graph.
- There are 3 varieties of the curve of learning i.e. concave curve, convex curve, and concave and convex curve/ Combination type curve.

Let's Understand in Brief:

Co... ve	
Convex curve	It depicts rapid initial improvement in learning that slows down with time. When the task is simple and the learner has previous practice on a similar task, we get this type of learning curve.
Combination type curve	It is the combination of the convex-concave curve that looks like the capital letter 'S'. The curve takes a concave or convex shape, in the beginning, depending upon the nature of the task.

So, it could be concluded that longitudinal is not the curve of learning.

23(B). Learning is a comprehensive process that refers to a change in behavior, knowledge, and skills as a result of practice and experience. It is difficult to give a precise definition of learning so every psychologist has different beliefs about the derivation of the word 'learning' and they have defined it in different ways.

Some well-known definitions of learning are as follows:

Psychologist	Definition of learning
J.P. Guilford	"Learning is any change in behaviour, resulting from behaviour."
Woodworth	"Learning is the process of acquiring new knowledge and new responses."
B.F.	"Learning is a process of progressiv

Skinner	e behaviour adaptation."
Crow & Crow	"Learning is the acquisition of know ledge, habits, and attitudes. It involv es new ways of doing things and it o perates in an individual's attempts t o overcome obstacles or to readjust to new situations. It represents a pr ogressive change in behaviour.

So, it could be concluded that the above-mentioned definition of learning is given by J.P. Guilford.

24(D). The active participation and involvement of children play a very vital role in learning and shaping the personality of a child.

A child-centered method is one that gives

often found that children break the problem into parts and analyze it, then they try solving the parts logically, this critical thinking shapes the child to be Scientific Investigators.
- When a child is encouraged to be self-dependent, it helps in developing thoughts and rationality in them and they try multiple ways to find a solution, and doing this multiple times helps them evolve as a Problem Solver.
- Children are Active Explorers of the environment as they are excited to learn about what is this, why it is here, how it is working, etc. They ask many questions about objects and situations in their surroundings.

So, the statements about children emphasizing to be Scientific Investigators, Problem Solver, and Active Explorers of the environment are correct.

25(D). Naive Conceptions (also referred to as commonsense theory or folk theory) is a coherent set of knowledge and beliefs about a specific content domain (such as physics or psychology), which entails ontological commitments, attention to domain-specific causal principles, and appeal to unobservable entities.
- Teaching and learning are complements of each other.
- Changes in teaching methods and techniques are required to make learning more effective.
- As a teacher, it is very important to understand children's needs, curiosities, and problems.

By knowing the naive conceptions, the teacher can plan to make his teaching work more meaningful.

For example , if the child is comfortable reading and learning in the mother tongue if his concept is taught, then teaching can be made more meaningful for the teacher.

So, knowing the naive conceptions that students bring to the classroom, helps the teacher to plan to teach more meaningfully.

26(C). The constructivist approach to learning is based on the idea that meaningful learning takes place when learners actively construct their own knowledge . It allows learners to foster their own strategies of learning to perform a task.
- In order to follow a constructivist approach to deal with the misconceptions carried by students, a teacher should give opportunities for experimentation and observation to counter misconceptions.
- It will help the student to search for the truth and they can test their misconceptions whether they are true

their misconceptions.

Thus, it is concluded that Give opportunities for experimentation and observation to counter misconceptions is a constructive approach for dealing with the 'misconceptions' carried by students.

27(D). Emotion is a mental state associated with fear, anger, love, etc. Cognition is the process of acquiring knowledge through experiences and senses.

Cognition describes how mental processes i.e. learning, remembering, problem-solving, and thinking develop from birth until adulthood . Understanding cognitive development is useful in determining the kind of thinking children are capable of at different age levels.
- The relationship between cognition and emotion has fascinated important thinkers within the intellectual tradition. Physical, cognitive, emotional, and social development in a child is the development of an integrated and holistic fashion.
- Cognition is closely intertwined with emotions and language. Mind states are powerful determinants of one's current judgments and decision-making, which often effect once performance outcome in a task both in social and non-social contexts.
- Emotions or emotional approach is a psychological construct that involves the use of emotional processing and emotional expression in response to a different situation.
- The relationship between cognition and emotions is bi-directional - a dynamic interplay .
- Emotions are experienced as positive feelings, negative feelings, and undesired reactions to any stressful situation, these often impact decision

making i.e. cognition.
- The Emotional Approach involves the conscious use of emotional expression and processing to better deal with stressful situations.

So, the relationship between cognition and emotions is bi-directional i.e. a dynamic interplay between both cognition and emotions.

28(B). Learning is a process by which the individual acquires various habits, knowledge, and attitude that are necessary to meet the demands of life in general. There are different factors that affect learning.

These include learner-centered factors like motivation, needs, self-concept, interests, goals, level of aspiration, etc., teacher and task-related factors such as teaching style,

occurs.

Ashok is very fond of playing cricket and he is very good at it too. He is the captain of his college team. He spends long hours playing or watching cricket and never gets tired or bored. Motivation and personal factors is affecting learning in this example.
- Ashok is intrinsically motivated i.e. he derives internal satisfaction from the game. Intrinsic motivation is closely related to one's need for self-fulfillment, and achievement.
- These needs impel us to become better by learning more, interacting with our environment, and developing ourselves.
- Learning is most effective when there is intrinsic motivation - a desire to learn from within, which finds satisfaction in the achievement itself and does not bother about other factors.

Thus, it is concluded motivation is the personal factor that affects learning in the given an example.

Maturation: A one-year-old cannot be made to write and a three months old child cannot walk. Unless the learner has 'matured' optimally, he cannot learn. In order for learning to take place, physical, intellectual, and socio-emotional maturation is essential. Also, individual variations in the process of maturation should be acknowledged and appropriately dealt with.

Self-concept: Self-concept is very important in matters of learning because it influences individual differences in learners, in their, learning orientations, cognitive styles, and the self-learning strategies which they use.

Level of aspiration: This refers to the extent to which an individual wish to strive to achieve. It emanates from the targets, goals, and ambitions that individuals construct for themselves.

29(D). Learning is a process by which

behaviour is either modified or changed through experience or training. Learning is thus a relatively permanent change in response potentiality which occurs as a function of reinforced practice.

Teacher-related factors affecting learning:

- Teacher's Knowledge over the subject matter : Teachers who are firmly rooted in their subject knowledge make clearer presentations and recognize students' difficulties readily. He/she should be able to undertake application-oriented teaching as well.
- The leadership style adopted by the teacher in terms of whether it is authoritarian, democratic, benevolent, or indifferent greatly influences how the students will respond and involve themselves in the learning tasks.
- The relationship which teachers have

have a great bearing on students learning. They have the power to motivate and encourage or stifle and discourage.

- Apart from expectations, there are many other characteristics related to teachers that influence their learners and the teaching-learning process. The most significant among these are modeling, enthusiasm, caring, and positive expectations .
- Research indicates that teachers who present information enthusiastically , increase learners' self-efficacy, attributions of effort and ability, self-confidence, and achievement.
- The caring attitude of a teacher and how he/she communicates it is another important factor, Caring refers to a teacher's ability to emphasize and invest in the protection and development of her learners.

From the above, we can conclude that mastery over the subject matter is a teacher-related factor affecting learning.

30(D). Learning is an active process, transferable, measurable and goal-oriented. It is the desired change or modification of behaviour attained through experience and environment. It is both a formal and informal process, it is universal and continuous. From birth, every child should have access to high-quality learning opportunities for language, literacy and mathematics. These should be available in all early years settings, including the home, and facilitated by parents.

- Psychological Factors: Psychological factors are unique or specific to the individuals engaged in the process of learning. Thorough knowledge and understanding of these factors are very essential for the teachers and parents in providing and guiding learning among

the children.
  ◦ Intelligence
  ◦ Motivation
  ◦ Maturation for Readiness to Learn
  ◦ Emotions
  ◦ Interests
  ◦ Attitudes
  ◦ Self-Concept
  ◦ Learning Styles

- Socio-Cultural (Environmental) Factors Influencing Learning: The socio-cultural environment, within which a child grows, has a significant impact on his/her learning. In fact, all learning occurs with special reference to the cultural context of an individual. The social constructivist view of psychology holds that all learning is culturally oriented and guided. For our own understanding, we can subdivide socio-cultural factors

factors are affecting learning, so does economic factor, because, suppose, a poor boy may not have access to online learning while a rich boy may have.

- School-Related Factors Influencing Learning: Learning is also assumed to be greatly influenced by the school and the school environment in which students are imparted with different types of learning experiences. The term 'school environment' encompasses the terms 'school culture' and 'school climate' that affect the behaviour of teachers and students.
- Teaching-Learning Processes Related Factors Influencing Learning: It includes methods of learning and the influence of media on learning.

So, we conclude that all the facts influence student difficulty in learning.

31(C). As we can see in the first paragraph of the passage, it is clearly mentioned that "when we pick up a daily newspaper, we invariably find an increased incidence of vandalism, fraud, theft, robbery, rape, child spouse, battered spouses, murders, hate crimes, genocide (now termed as "ethnic cleansing") along with a multitude of other senseless violent acts that have become disturbingly common".

Thus, it is concluded that newspapers are full of news about acts of crime and violence these days.

32(C). The underlined word significance is a noun that means a word (other than a pronoun) used to identify any of a class of people, places, or things (common noun), or to name a particular one of these (proper noun).

It can be defined as any member of a class of words that typically can be combined with determiners to serve as the subject of a verb, can be interpreted as singular or

plural, can be replaced with a pronoun, and refer to an entity, quality, state, action, or concept.

Significance can be defined as the quality of being important.

33(C). Futility means the quality or state of being futile; uselessness.

Usefulness means the quality or fact of being useful.

From the above meanings, it is evident that usefulness is the correct antonym of the word futility.

The meaning of the other given words are as follows:

- Pointlessness - The fact of having no purpose or of being a waste of time.
- Vanity - excessive pride in or admiration of one's own appearance or achievements.

good self-esteem is well understood and it achieves the prominence it deserves, a transformation will begin, for as the people will learn they are deserving of self-respect, their respect for others will automatically increase".

Thus, it is concluded that good self-esteem is stressed because it helps one to respect others.

35(B). Vandalism means an action involving deliberate destruction of or damage to public or private property.

Destruction means the action or process of causing so much damage to something that it no longer exists or cannot be repaired.

From the above meanings, it is evident that destruction is the correct synonym of the word vandalism.

The meaning of the other given words are as follows:

- Construct - build or make (something, typically a building, road, or machine).
- Build - construct (something) by putting parts or materials together.
- Mend - repair (something that is broken or damaged).

36(B). The error is in part (B).

Whether- "or" is correlative conjunction.

Example: I didn't know whether you'd want the cheesecake or the chocolate cake, so I got both.

So, in part (B), and should be replaced by or.

Correct part: whether personal, national, or global

Correct sentence: The solution to a great many problems, whether personal, national, or global, lies in improving our feelings

37(C). Let's refer to the lines:

- High self-esteem denotes that we accept ourselves unconditionally exactly as we are , and we appreciate our value as human beings.

- Vulnerable to the opinions of others, we desperately try to gain their recognition and approval sometimes through risky and dangerous behaviour. Thus, we are at the mercy of our emotions, instead of controlling them, we permit them to control us.
- Today when we pick up a daily newspaper, we invariably find an increased incidence of vandalism, fraud, theft, robbery, rape, child spouse, battered spouses, murders, hate crimes, genocide (now termed as "ethnic cleansing") along with a multitude of other senseless violent acts that have become disturbingly common. These are not the actions of people who like themselves.

Upon the perusal of the above lines, it can

41(D). Let us take a look at the line, 'And the mother gave, in tears and pain,/_The flowers she most did love;/She knew she should find them all again/_In the fields of light above.'

- It says the mother will meet her flowers in fields of light .
- 'Fields of light' is an allegory for Paradise .
- Paradise is the garden of Eden .
- Thus the mother will meet her flower in Paradise.

42(C). Let us take a look at the line, 'It was for the Lord of Paradise'.
The lines state that the flowers are for the 'Lord of Paradise'.
'Lord of Paradise' refers to God.
Thus, the flowers are for God.

43(C). The figure of speech is

- The method is known as remedial teaching. It helps the teacher to provide learners with the necessary help and guidance to overcome the problems.

The following are its characteristics:

- It can be used for improving language skills by revision, drill, situation communicative practice, and reviewing.
- For example, if a student is confused about the pronunciation of 'no' and 'know', he can be taught the concept of silent letters.
- It also helps teachers to know which areas are left during regular teaching. It is used by teachers to remove the weakness of the learner.
- It is carried out after the identification of problems and challenges faced by students. It is a systematic process as the teacher first diagnoses the problem of

---

- If we cannot accomplish certain results, we tend to feel low about ourselves. Some of us try too hard and become workaholics and over-achievers. With a few genuine feelings of self-worth, we try to create some and prove that we are somebody by our successes and achievements.
- If we do finally achieve our goals we are disappointed; despite everything we have done, we still feel empty inside.

Upon the perusal of the above lines, it can be concluded that a person starts feeling empty inside when he pushes himself towards achieving goals and proving that he is somebody by his successes and achievements.

39(C). Adjectives are words that are used to describe or modify nouns or pronouns.
Goals is a noun. Unrealistic is a word that is modifying the word 'goals'. Thus, unrealistic is an adjective.
So, the part of speech of the underlined word is an adjective, making option (C) the correct answer choice.
Adjective modifies a noun while an adverb modifies a verb, adjective, adverb, or phrase.

40(B). Look at the lines:
There is a Reaper, whose name is Death,
_And, with his sickle keen

- The poem subverts the meaning of death.
- Death is a character in the poem .
- Death may seem merciless on the surface but it takes loved ones to a new world .
- Therefore, death is not gloomy or fearful.
- Gloomy means dark or poorly lit, especially so as to appear depressing or frightening.
- Thus, death is shown in a positive light.

'Alliteration' is a literary device that reflects repetition in two or more nearby words of initial consonant sounds.
For example:

- rocky road.
- big business.

Similarly in the expression 'She knew she should find them all again', the figure of speech 'Alliteration' is used as consonant sound 's' is being repeated in she, she, and should.

44(C). Let us take a look at the line, 'And saints, upon their garments white, _These sacred blossoms wear.'
It is stated that saints wear the blossoms.
Blossoms are a kind of flower.
Thus, saints wear flowers over their white garments.

45(D). Let us take a look at the line, 'He gazed at the flowers with tearful eyes'.
It is stated that Death gazed at the flowers with tearful eyes.
Thus, Death gazed at the flowers with tearful eyes.

46(B). A great teacher is warm, accessible, enthusiastic, and caring. This is the teacher to whom students know they can go with any problems or concerns.

- Effective teachers strive to motivate and engage all their students in learning rather than simply accepting that some students cannot be engaged and are destined to do poorly.
- They believe every student is capable of achieving success at school and they do all they can to find ways of making each student successful.

Remedial teaching:

- During learning, a child makes mistakes. It is the job of a teacher to help students to correct those mistakes after diagnosing them.

---

situation communicative practice, and reviewing.

47(D). Approach: The practices in language teaching are based on theories concerning the nature of language and language learning. These theories together form the first component of a method.

- Constructive approach: One of the most essential principles in the constructivist approach to language teaching is action-orientedness. Another principle of constructive approach refers to content-oriented language teaching and usually takes place in bilingual classes. A constructive approach to language teaching is based on the foundation that knowledge is constructed. Students are given the freedom to plan their choice and to be creative.
- Structural Approaches: Structural approach is a scientific study of the fundamental structures of the English language, their analysis, and logical arrangement. Every structure expresses an important grammatical point. A sentence needs a grammatical background. The different formats or patterns of words are called structures.
- Natural approaches: The theory is based on the notion that we learn the language the same way as we acquire our first language. It doesn't force to utter words or phrases, much less pronounce them correctly. There are no endless drills on correct usage and no mentions of grammar rules or long lists of vocabulary to wrap the head around.
- Deductive approaches refer to developing a Hypothesis. It is a testing of the Existing theory.

So, we conclude that the above situation

48(B). Different teachers would face different challenges in their regular teaching– in terms of the curriculum, classroom transactions, time and resource management, as well as dealing with individual students. These may change from time to time.

- A teacher should overcome the language barrier to go through the process of teaching-learning.
- The basis of the communication of ideas and information to the learners is the responsibility of the teacher.
- A teacher should use the child's language as a resource and start teaching.
- As mentioned in the question above, a teacher should not apply for transfer since it shows that he wants to run away from his duty.
- Communicating in English is not the correct choice in such situations because language as a resource while teaching.

The Three-Language Formula as Stated in the 1968 Policy is:

- The First language: It has to be studied must be the mother tongue or the regional language.
- The Second language: In Hindi-speaking States, the second language will be English or some other modern Indian language.
- In non-Hindi-speaking States, the second language will be Hindi or English.
- The Third language: The third language is taught at a later stage in school, and that too for a shorter time, as it is needed only in a limited context i.e. in a social situation where neither first nor second language could help the child to communicate.

49(B). Children learn various lessons of learning the English language throughout their school life. At various stages/standards, children learn different difficulty levels of English. For the students of class IV learning English, their learning outcomes include, reciting poems correctly, being responsive to simple announcements, they having a simple knowledge of correct punctuations in writing. The teacher can provide possible alternative corrections for the sentence as the students can get better insight about the words, and their usage and also learn about the flaws in the wrong sentence.

- The teacher does not have to tell them something is wrong as it will not help them in learning the correct usage.
- The teacher has to guide a little to the students and cannot just let them find the corrections on their own as it is not their level yet, they need guidance.
- Students of Class IV cannot recognize flawed usage or sentence construction when the teacher focuses on certain surface errors such as grammatical errors as they are learning only to know the basics of sentences and their usage in daily life and thus do not have that knowledge.

Thus, it is concluded that Students of Class IV can recognize flawed usage or sentence construction when the teacher gives alternatives as possible corrections.

50(D). Pedagogical grammar means that teaching grammar in context.

Pedagogical Grammar:

- It is a grammatical analysis and instruction designed for language students.
- It is a description of how to use the grammar of a language to communicate, for people wanting to learn the target
- It focuses on how grammatical items may be made more learnable and teachable for meaningful learning.
- It is the study of the grammatical problems of learners or a combination of approaches.
- Pedagogical grammar is the learning of grammar in context through use.
- Pedagogic grammars contain assumptions about how learners learn, follow certain linguistic theories in their descriptions, and are written for a specific target audience.

51(B). Teaching aids or teaching-learning material is used by teachers to help learners to learn concepts with ease and efficiency. It can be an artificial or real object which makes learning more effective.

- A teacher found an advertisement pamphlet for the sale of biscuits. She uses it for reading and speaking activities in her class.
- He is using authentic text as the advertisement pamphlet is the authentic pamphlet that a shopkeeper is using to increase his sale of biscuits.
- Whereas Realia refers to the objects associated with everyday life to be used in the classroom. Using realia in the language class means bringing real objects as teaching aids.
- The advertisement pamphlet is a type of realia but if we have to say it more accurately, we will say it is an authentic text.
- The newspaper clipping and extra materials can be a type of realia also. But here as per the given question, the authentic text is best suited.

52(A). The five parts of language learning are:

- Listening
- Comprehension
- Speaking
- Reading
- Writing

If the student is able to perform successfully in all these skills, it shows that: He or she is proficient in the language.

Thus the correct answer is: "Measure the students' proficiency".

53(C). English is a global language spoken by 700 hundred million people in the world. It is officially recognized all over the world. It is the link language in India.

- It is a language of the library, language of media, language of trade, internet, commerce, business, international negotiations, and higher education.
- Since English is a language of international communication, learning the English Language is a common goal along with its characteristics:

Concreteness	This principle implies the idea that the language used by the speaker must be concrete, specific, definite, concise, and considerable for a better understanding of the listener.
Selection and gradation	It deals with selecting age-appropriate teaching materials and placing the language materials properly in order or sequence. The material should be according to the child's mental age, mental ability, grade, and level.
Accuracy and Correctness	This principle implies the idea that a language learner must be accurate and correct in spelling, pronunciation, structure, expression, etc.
Proportion	Equal attention should be paid to all the aspects and skills of language learning along with equal balance should be maintained among all the elements of language teaching.
Purpose Related	If the purpose is decided in the beginning it becomes a simple affair to design a course suitable for that purpose. In the absence of any specific purpose they simply dragon.
Habit formation	A habit of listening to the sounds of English words, speaking English with proper accent and intonation, and spelling.
Motivation	The ways of arousing interest are linguistic games, use of gramophone records, use of flashcards and other audiovisual aids, conversational approach, pictures, models, etc.
Multiple lines	The teacher has to proceed simultaneously from many different

of App roach	points of view toward the goals to be realized by him. He has to select and reject judiciously without favor or prejudice, the material to be presented and the method of its presentation.
Interest	Children learn easily and quickly things in which they are interested.
Linking with Life	The job of an English teacher should be to encourage his students to use the learned structures of the English language in their daily life situations.

So, we conclude that the above statement deals with the Principle of Selection and gradation.

54(A). A multilingual classroom refers to

hemisphere. It is responsible for the processing of the visual information that is received from the eyes. Any damage to the occipital lobe leads to problems in vision when flashes of light are seen, a visual hallucination or visual agnosia.

- Frontal lobes(left and right) are present in front of the brain. They are responsible for motor movements and fine movements, such as moving of a finger at a point of time, etc. Since it is connected to the limbic system, it also controls emotions. They are also involved in language functions (in most cases, the left frontal lobe). If there is any damage or lesion to the Broca's area, then it causes difficulties in producing and fluency in speech and sound, also called Broca's aphasia.

So, we conclude that Damage to Broca's

the competence to understand what one says and what one hears.

- Verbal clues can be one/two-word phrases, etc. and non-verbal clues can be silence, facial expressions, hand movements, etc.

Ability to read with comprehension, and not merely decode:

- The ultimate test of reading ability is a critical appreciation of an unseen text that is at least one stage above the cognitive level of the reader.
- The child must be able to construct meaning by drawing inferences and relating to the text with his previous knowledge.
- He must also develop confidence in reading the text by critically analyzing it.

Ability to express effortlessly in a variety of situations

classroom must be used as a resource so that every child could:

- feel secure and accepted.
- learn various language skills.
- connect the classroom with real life.
- express their thought in multiple ways.

So, we conclude that the multilingual nature of the Indian classroom must be used as a resource so that every child feels secure and accepted.

55(C). Aphasia is an impairment of language functioning caused by damage to the left hemisphere of the brain. There are different types of aphasias, for example; Broca's aphasia and Wernicke's aphasia.

Broca's aphasia is caused by damage to the brain's left frontal lobe area, responsible, in part, for controlling motor commands used in speech production. A person suffering from Broca's aphasia exhibits speech containing excess pauses and 52 slips of the tongue, and he has trouble finding words when talking. The person also fails to make use of function words such as a, the, and, of. For this reason, Broca's aphasics also produce ungrammatical sentences. Furthermore, they have a problem using syntactic information when understanding sentences. For example, while a Broca's aphasic has no trouble understanding a sentence such as "The bicycle that the man is holding is blue", but he has trouble comprehending a sentence such as "the dog that the woman is biting is grey."

Wernicke's aphasia is caused by damage to the left temporal lobe of the brain. It is characterized by notable impairment in the understanding of spoken words and sentences. People with Wernicke's aphasia have generally fluent phonetic and syntactic but semantically coherent speech. Some other notable terms:

- The occipital cortex is located at the back and base of each cerebral

words a person knows, uses or want to learn.

Types of Vocabulary:

Receptive Vocabulary: It refers to a word which an individual:

- recognises when he/she hears or sees it.
- understands and comprehends when others use it.
- perceives and retrieves while listening and reading the word.

Productive Vocabulary: It refers to a word which an individual:

- uses when he/she speaks or writes.
- frequently uses while writing or speaking.
- regularly uses to express his/her thoughts appropriately.

So, we conclude that Receptive Vocabulary are words we recognize when we hear or see and Productive Vocabulary are words we speak or write.

57(D). NCF (National Curriculum Framework) 2005 is one of the four NCFs published in India by NCERT. It seeks to provide a framework for the betterment of educational purposes and experiences.

- Language is a medium through which human beings tend to communicate with each other by using various attributes of a language that are symbols, gestures, words, etc.
- The main purpose of teaching a language is to enable the children to use it practically while communicating with others.

The objectives defined by NCF 2005 regarding language teaching-learning include:

Ability to understand various verbal and non-verbal clues

- A child must be able to understand various verbal and non-verbal clues coming from the speaker for comprehending what has been said i.e.,

ideas and thoughts in different kinds of situations smoothly.

- He must be able to engage in a discussion in a logical, analytical and creative manner.

The ability to write coherently by a proper organization of thoughts

- Writing involves a rich control on grammar, vocabulary, content, and punctuation as well as abilities to organize thoughts coherently often using a variety of cohesive devices such as linkers.
- A child should develop the confidence to express her thoughts effortlessly and in an organized manner.

Use of creativity

- In a language classroom, a child should get ample space to develop her imagination and creativity.
- Classroom ethos and healthy teacher-student relationships build confidence to enable the children to use their creativity.

So, it is clear that knowing the history of language is not an objective of language teaching-learning as per the objectives given by NCF-2005.

58(B). Language Acquisition is the process in which a child acquires the capacity to comprehend language. Language acquisition is the process in which a child learns his mother tongue. When language is learned without any practice and with the help of surroundings, it is known as language acquisition.

Theory of Second Language Acquisition: Stephen Krashen proposed the five main hypotheses, the input hypothesis is one of them. According to the Input hypothesis, comprehensible input refers to the input slightly above the learner's current level. It helps learners in language learning by making them able to:

- communicate efficiently.
- acquire language naturally.
- understand the text effectively.

The other hypotheses are given below:

Psychology	Theory	Main Idea
Vygotsky	Socio-cultural Theory	Three stages of language that a child progresses through while developing language functions are social, private, and silent inner speech.
Noam Chomsky	Theory of language acquisition	Children are borns with an innate knowledge of grammar that serves as the basis for all language acquisition.
James Asher	Total Physical Response	Coordination of speech and student's physical movement is a good tool to be used in language learning.

So, we conclude that the term 'Comprehensible input' is associated with Stephen Krashen.

59(D). Reading texts typically implies a wide range of structures and vocabulary, registers and styles, formats, and patterns of organization. The type of reading activity we, engage in with such 'real' reading texts is also very different from the traditional classroom approach to a specially written text.

Verbs determine the relations between the different words in the sentence according to the grammar of the language. It treats the structure of sentences and their structural relationships with one another.

- A verb is a word or a combination of words that indicate an action or a state of being or condition. A verb is the part of a sentence that tells us the relationship between different parts of sentences like an affirmative sentence, negative sentence, complex sentences, etc.
- That verb may be a single word or a word made up of more than one word.
  - Examples:
  - Jacob walks in the morning.
  - Mike is going to school.
  - Albert likes to walk.
  - Anna is a good girl.

Nouns	Nouns are used to identify people, places, and things. For eg: cat.
	he, etc.
Adverbs	Adverbs are used to give us more information and are used to modify verbs, clauses, and other adverbs. Example: Quickly, Gently, etc.

So, we can conclude that While reading a text, a Verb can help students understand the relations between the parts of a sentence.

60(B). Realia refers to the objects associated with everyday life to be used in the classroom. Using realia in the language class means bringing real objects as teaching aids as it is a tangible teaching-learning aid that:

- includes coins, newspapers, maps, tickets, fruits, vegetables, etc.
- makes learning more interesting by bringing the class to real life.
- ensures the use of accurate and realistic teaching-learning materials.
- Encourages classroom interaction and helps in meeting individual differences.

Realia has also been included as part of CLT (communicative language technique), i.e. posters, advertisements, maps, train schedules, and graphs. The tasks set have a specific communicative purpose and train the learners to be fluent as well as accurate, although CLT has tended to emphasize fluency over accuracy.

So, we conclude that u sing 'realia' in the language class means bringing real objects as teaching aids.

61(B). Given:
x is a whole number.
x gives the same result when either added to or multiplied by itself.
Calculation:
x × x = x + x (given)
$\Rightarrow x^2 = 2x$
$\Rightarrow x^2 - 2x = 0$
$\Rightarrow x(x - 2) = 0$
$\Rightarrow x = 0$ or $x = 2$
On checking options:
Option (A) False, because x has 2 possible values.
Option (B) True, because $0 \times 2 = 0$
Option (C) False, because no. of possible values of x is 2 which is not a composite number.
Option (D) False, because no value of x is 1.

62(A). Given:
The sum of two positive numbers = 65
The square root of their product = 26
Let the two numbers be a and b respectively.
$\Rightarrow ab = (26 \times 26) = 676$
Now,
The sum of the reciprocals $= \frac{1}{a} + \frac{1}{b}$
$= \frac{a+b}{ab}$
$= \frac{65}{676}$
$= \frac{5}{52}$
$\therefore$ The sum of their reciprocals $\frac{5}{52}$.

63(B). Given:
The product of the two numbers is 0.432.
One of them is 1.6
Calculation:
Let the other number be P.
According to the question,
1.6 × P = 0.432
$\Rightarrow$ P = 0.27
$\therefore$ The other number is 0.27.

64(D). Given:
$a^3 + b^3 = 26$ and $a + b = 2$
Concept:
$a^3 + b^3 = (a + b)^3 - 3ab(a + b)$
Calculation:
$a^3 + b^3 = (a + b)^3 - 3ab(a + b)$
$\Rightarrow 26 = 2^3 - 3ab(2)$
$\Rightarrow 26 = 8 - 6ab$
$\Rightarrow 18 = -6ab$
$\Rightarrow -18 = 6ab$
So, 6ab = -18

65(C). Given:
$x^2 + 9x - 22 = 0$
$2y^2 - 7y + 6 = 0$
Solution:
$x^2 + 9x - 22 = 0$ ----(1)
$\Rightarrow x^2 + 11x - 2x - 22 = 0$
$\Rightarrow x(x + 11) - 2(x + 11) = 0$
$\Rightarrow (x - 2)(x + 11) = 0$
x = 2, -11
$2y^2 - 7y + 6 = 0$ ----(2)

$\Rightarrow 2y^2 - 4y - 3y + 6 = 0$
$\Rightarrow 2y(y-2) - 3(y - 2) = 0$
$\Rightarrow (2y - 3)(y - 2) = 0$
$y = \frac{3}{2}, 2$

∴ The following values of $\frac{x}{y}$ are

$1, \frac{-11}{2}, \frac{4}{3}, \frac{-22}{3}$

So, $\frac{x}{y} = \frac{-11}{2}$

66(B). Given:
$p + \frac{1}{p} = 2$
Solution:
$p + \frac{1}{p} = 2$
$\Rightarrow p^2 + 1 = 2p$
$\Rightarrow p^2 + 1 - 2p = 0$
$\Rightarrow (p - 1)^2 = 0$
$\Rightarrow p = 1$

The sum of the interior angle and the exterior angle in 180°
Formula:
The exterior angle of regular polygon
$= \frac{360°}{n}$ Where n = The number of sides of the polygon
Calculation:
Let us assume the interior angle of the polygon be X
$\Rightarrow$ The exterior angle of the polygon
$= \frac{360}{24} = 15°$
$\Rightarrow X = 180° - 15° = 165°$
∴ The required result will be 165°.

68(C). Given:
BC = 6.5 cm
CD = 4 cm
DA = 8 cm

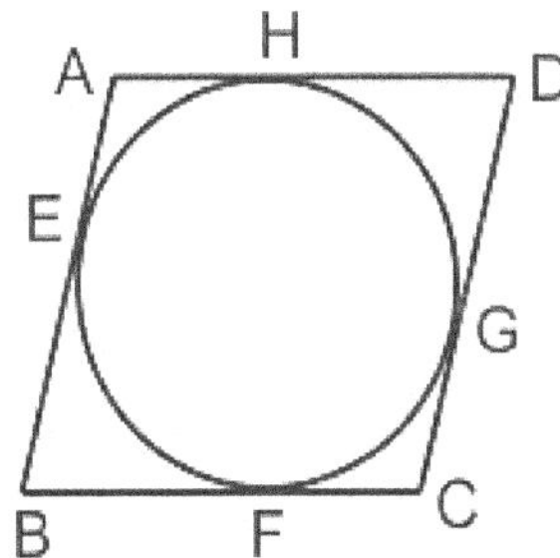

$\Rightarrow$ AE = AH
$\Rightarrow$ BE = BF
$\Rightarrow$ GC = FC
$\Rightarrow$ GD = HD
Add all the terms
$\Rightarrow$ AE + BE + GC + GD = AH + BE + FC + HD
$\Rightarrow$ AB + CD = AD + BC
$\Rightarrow$ AB + 4 = 8 + 6.5
$\Rightarrow$ AB = 14.5 – 4
$\Rightarrow$ AB = 10.5 cm
∴ AB will be 10.5 cm.

69(A). Given:
All the sides of a cube are 8 units if it is cut into smaller cubes of side 2 units.

Concept used:
Volume of a cube = (Side)^3
Surface area of a cube = 6 × (Side)^2
Calculation:
Volume of the bigger cube = 8^3 = 512 cube units
Volume of the smaller cubes = 2^3 = 8 cube units
Surface area of each smaller cube = 6 × 2^2 = 24 square units
Let the number of smaller cubes made be Q. Since the bigger cube is cut into smaller cubes, the volume of the bigger cube has to be equal to the total volume of the smaller cubes.
So
Q × 2^3 = 512
$\Rightarrow$ Q = 64

70(D). Given:
A piece of wire, bent in the shape of a square having 44 cm as its side, is subsequently bent to form a circle.
Formula:
The perimeter of a Square = 4 × Side
The perimeter of a Circle = 2πr
Let the radius of the circle be r cm
According to the question,
Perimeter of Square = Perimeter of Circle
$\Rightarrow 4 \times 44 = 2 \times \frac{22}{7} \times r$
$\Rightarrow r = 28$ cm
∴ The radius of the circle is 28 cm.

71(A). Given:
∠BAD = a, ∠ABG = b and ∠BGD = c and ∠ADG = d
Calculation:
We know that,
Sum of all angles of a quadrilateral = 360°
∠A + ∠B + ∠G + ∠D = 360° ----- (1)
but, from the figure,

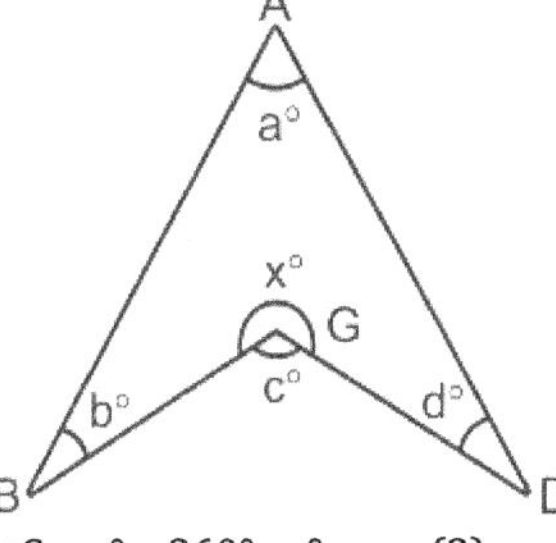

∠G = x° = 360° - c° ------ (2)
Using equation (1) and (2), we get
$\Rightarrow$ a° + b° + 360° - c° + d = 360°
$\Rightarrow$ a° + b° - c° + d° = 0
$\Rightarrow$ b° = c° - (a° + d°)
∴ The value of ∠ABG is c° - (a° + d°).

72(D). Let the marked price be x.
$\Rightarrow$ SP = x - 0.34x = 0.66x
Gain % = 10
So, 0.66x = C.P × 110%
$\Rightarrow$ 0.66x = 1.1 C.P

$\Rightarrow$ C.P = 0.6x
So, The required % $= \frac{x - 0.6x}{0.6x} \times 100$
$\Rightarrow$ The required % $= \frac{0.4x}{0.6x} \times 100$
∴ The required % = 66.67%

73(B). Let the term to be added be x.
$\Rightarrow \frac{5+x}{11+x} = \frac{3}{4}$
$\Rightarrow$ 4 (5 + x) = 3 (11 + x)
$\Rightarrow$ 20 + 4x = 33 + 3x
$\Rightarrow$ 4x - 3x = 33 - 20
$\Rightarrow$ x = 13
So, the correct answer is "13".

74(A). Given:
The total distance = 81 km
The total time = 11 hours
Formula:
Speed $= \frac{\text{Distance}}{\text{Time}}$

The distance covered by foot = 81 - X
$\Rightarrow \frac{81-X}{4.5} + \frac{X}{15} = 11$
$\Rightarrow 1215 - 15X + 4.5X = 742.5$
$\Rightarrow -10.5X = -472.5$
$\Rightarrow X = 45$
The distance covered on cycle X = 45 km
∴ The required result will be 45 km.

75(B). Given:
My cousin is twice my age.
Calculation:
Let my age be 'x' years
$\Rightarrow$ age of my cousin = 2x years
$\Rightarrow$ 2x - x = 20
$\Rightarrow$ x = 20 years
∴ Required age = 20 years

76(A). Given:
The numbers = 3, 4, 5 and 6
Calculation:
Let us assume the number be X.
The LCM of (3, 4, 5, 6) = 60
When 2480 divides by 60 $= \frac{2480}{60} = 41.3$
Remainder = 20
Subtracting 20 from 60 = 60 - 20 = 40
The number should be added to 2480 = 40
∴ The required result will be 40.

77(A). Given expression is:
$\Rightarrow (?)^3 \times 10 = 13230 \div (9.261 \div 7)$
$\Rightarrow (?)^3 \times 10 = 13230 \div (1.323)$
$\Rightarrow (?)^3 \times 10 = 10000$
$\Rightarrow (?)^3 = 1000$
$\Rightarrow (?)^3 = (10)^3$
$\Rightarrow ? = 10$

78(B). Given:
20 and 45
Formula:
Mean $= \frac{\text{Sum of all observation}}{\text{Number of observation}}$
Calculation:
Prime numbers between 20 and 45 are 23, 29, 31, 37, 41 and 43

$$\text{Mean} = \frac{23+29+31+37+41+43}{6}$$
$$= \frac{204}{6}$$
$$= 34$$

∴ The mean of the prime numbers between 20 and 45 is 34.

79(A). Given:
The difference between the mode and median of a data is 38
Concept:
Mode = 3 Median – 2 Mean
Calculation:
According to the question,
Mode - Median = 38
We know,
Mode = 3 Median – 2 Mean
⇒ 3 Median - Mode = 2 Mean
⇒ 2 Median + (Median - Mode) = 2 Mean
⇒ 2 Median - 38 = 2 Mean

80(A). Given:
4, 5, 6, 7, 8, 12, 9, 12, 5, 12
Concept:
The mode is the most frequently occurring value on the list.
$$\text{Mean (Average)} = \frac{\text{Number of entities}}{\text{Total}}$$
Calculation:
Given series is:
4, 5, 6, 7, 8, 12, 9, 12, 5, 12
Mean of the series
$$= \frac{4+5+6+7+8+12+9+12+5+12}{10}$$
Mean of the series $= \frac{80}{10} = 8$
Mode of the series = 12
Difference in the mode and the mean of the observations = 12 - 8 = 4
∴ 4 is the difference in the mode and the mean of the observations.

81(B). In the textbook of mathematics the content should be developed in a logical order.
Textbooks are predominantly textual with some images. Normally, content in a textbook is organized under chapters, units, and lessons. Most textbooks are written in factual or information giving style with little or no interactivity inbuilt in the text. Thus, most of them do not serve the purpose of self-learning materials for learners.
Organization of content in Mathematics Textbook:
- The textbook should provide authentic content knowledge;
- Contents in the textbook should be logical, coherent, and sequential;
- The language used in the textbook needs to be simple, and comprehensible by elementary students;
- Presentation of contents needs to be conversational and based on sound pedagogic principles;
- Concepts and propositions need to be explained with examples and illustration;
- There need to be a lot of activities, cases built into the textbook;
- Presentation of contents needs to motivate the learners throughout the process of learning.

82(A). Spatial thinking the ability to discern shapes.
Spatial thinking is an ability to discern shapes, to mentally visualize objects, their orientations, and their relationships. It is used in reading maps, charts, drawing images, puzzles, imaging things, visualization.
Spatial thinking in Mathematics:
- It uses to recognize or detect particular shapes in mathematics concepts like numbers, geometry, algebra, etc.
- areas of mathematics to learn not only in geometry concepts.
- Students use spatial reasoning and use blocks to represent each number on the number line in mathematics.
- The learning is best through working with pictures and colors, visualizing, modem drawing.
- It is used to understand the relations between figures in mathematics.
- It cannot be considered as the quality of a teacher.

83(D). N.C.F 2005, f ocusing on solving as many problems as a learner can , is not the aim of Mathematics teaching.
According to NCF-2005, aims of Mathematics teaching includes:
- Developing the basic abilities of a child to do mathematics and to bring mathematization of thoughts is the main goal of mathematics education.
- The narrow aim of school mathematics is to develop 'useful' capabilities, particularly those relating to numeracy- numbers, number operations, measurements, decimals, etc.
- The higher aim is to pursue assumptions to their logical conclusion, and to handle abstraction by developing the logical and abstract thinking of learners.
- NCF-2005 states that mathematics should be taught in a way that children learn to enjoy mathematics rather than fear it.
- The teaching of mathematics should be done in a way so that mathematics can be easily connected to the practical life of the students.
- The teaching of mathematics should be done in the way, in which a student learns the best by engaging students actively in the learning process.
- The teacher should provide students more opportunities to experience typical processes of mathematical activity like looking for patterns, making quizzes, puzzles, etc.

84(D). Rajiv, a teacher of class 5th gives a newspaper to his students and tells them to find how math is involved in the newspaper as well. A student begins to solve a sudoku puzzle given in the newspaper. This shows the student is very much interested in numbers and game-like sudoku helps the logical and reasoning skills of a child.
- The teacher needs to provide the students with varied types of experience in a Mathematics classroom, like group discussion, problem-solving exercises, mathematical games, puzzles, etc.
- It enhances the logical and reasoning skills of a child.
- During the Upper primary stage, slowly care must be taken to provide various mathematical games, puzzles, shortcuts, and recreational activities. This is the stage at which algebra needs to be introduced.
- It should be introduced by connecting it to real-life situations and through its use in solving various life problems. This is the stage at which the concepts like percentage, ratio, proportions, interest, etc. are to be introduced.
So, both statements (B) and (C) are correct regarding the above situation.

85(C). #, & are not a part of mathematical language.
(#) This symbol is known as the hashtag that is not a mathematical symbol but is used in the language before relevant or important terms like people usually hashtag in social media while blogging or writing anything important or to give tags.
(&) It is the ampersand symbol that is used to denote the "and" in short form in the English language.

86(B). A students is asked to draw a cube in the class or to show the example of it from among the classroom after the chapter on shapes has been completed. The evaluation of formative assessment is represented by the above example.
Assessment is the process of collecting, reviewing and using data for improvement in the learning process. One of the ways of collecting data about student's learning is by taking test.
Evaluation is described as the process of passing judgement based on some set standards. It is the decision making process.
Formative assessment: Assessment during instruction, immediate assessment or feedback during instruction or on-going programme. In this situation, a student is

asked to draw a cube which is recently taught (this can be understood from the question) to test the understanding of the student and to make sure if diagnosing of problem or re-teaching is required hence it is a formative assessment which is done time to time to assess the understanding of the students.

87(D). Permanent difficulties in learning are investigated in diagnostic assessment.
Diagnostic Assessment: It is the assessment that is conducted along with formative assessment during the instructional process.
- It is carried out based on the data obtained from the formative assessment. Diagnostic assessment is specially conducted for investigating and removing the learning permanent understand these concepts, diagnostic assessment is conducted and remediation is provided.
- This is conducted by diagnostic remedial test. The keyword in diagnostic assessment is an assessment of learning difficulties.

88(D). Error analysis is a method commonly used to identify the cause of student errors when they make consistent mistakes. It is a process of reviewing a student's work and then looking for patterns of misunderstanding. Errors in mathematics can be factual, procedural, or conceptual, and may occur for a number of reasons.
The following steps describe the error analysis process, applied to mathematics:
- Collect a sample of student work for each type of problem.
- Have the student verbalize or think aloud as he solves the problems without providing any type of cues or prompting.
- Record all student responses in written and verbal format.
- Analyze the responses and look for patterns among common problem types.
- Look for examples of "exceptions" to an apparent pattern.
- Describe the patterns observed in simple language and the possible reasons for the student's problems.
- Interview the student by asking him/her to explain how s/he solved the problem to confirm suspected error patterns.

89(B). Error analysis is important for students with learning disabilities and low performing students.
Why is error analysis important:
- Identification of students' specific errors is especially important for students with learning disabilities and low performing students.

- By pinpointing student errors, the teacher can provide instruction targeted to the student's area of need.
- In general, students who have difficulty learning math typically lack important conceptual knowledge for several reasons, including an inability to process information at the rate of the instructional pace, a lack of adequate opportunities to respond (i.e., practice), a lack of specific feedback from teachers regarding misunderstanding or non-understanding, anxiety about mathematics, and difficulties in visual and/or auditory processing.

90(A). The above-mentioned statement is stated by an Italian astronomer and mathematician 'Galileo Galilei' who made major contributions to the field of assimilate mathematical terms.
- express mathematical thoughts and ideas.
- recognize and employ patterns of mathematical thought.
So, it could be concluded that the above-mentioned statement is stated by 'Galileo Galilei'.

91(C). The food X is tested for presence of protein first using the solution of caustic soda and copper sulphate. The colour turns violet that shows the presence of protein. No changes happened when food is tested with iodine. This shows carbohydrate is not present.
So, the correct option is 'The food contains protein but not carbohydrate'.

92(A). Cabbage and carrots both can be eaten both raw and cooked.

Food Item	Eating method
Cabbage	Can be **eaten raw** in salads. Can be **cooked** as a vegetable.
Carrot	Can be **eaten raw** in salads. Can be **cooked** as a vegetable.
Broccoli	Can be **eaten raw** in salads. Can be **cooked** as a vegetable.
Spinach	Can be **eaten raw** in salads. Can be **cooked** as a vegetable.
Chilly	Can be **eaten raw** as a condiment. Can be **cooked** along with vegetables.
Rajma	Can be **only eaten after cooking.** Can be boiled and baked.
Potato	Can be **only eaten after cooking.** Can be boiled, roasted, baked, fried etc.
Brinjal	Can be **only eaten after cooking.** Can be boiled, roasted, baked, fried etc.

93(D). Gills are functional only in water so when fishes are taken out of the they die as they are unable to respire
Respiratory System of Fish:
- Most fishes absorbed dissolved oxygen in water by means of the gills.
- Water taken in continuously through the mouth passes backward between the gill bars and over the gill filaments where feathery structures called gill filaments that provide a large surface area for gas exchange.

94(B). Azolla is a free-floating aquatic fern (pteridophyte). There are six species of Azolla – Azolla Carolina, Azolla nilotica, Azolla filiculoids, Azolla Mexicana, Azolla microphylla and Azolla pinnata.
- They are extremely reduced in form and specialized, looking nothing like the typical fern but more resembling duckweed or some mosses.
- It can be used as animal feed, human food, medicine, and water purifier.
- It is also used as a bio-fertilizer which improves soil fertility and boosting crop yields.
Pteridophyta: Plants from this group have well-developed roots, stem and leaves, and separate tissues for conduction of food and water. But, they do not bear flowers and fruits.

95(D). Sound waves need a medium to travel. Hence, it can propagate through the water. The speed of sound waves in steel is more than its speed in the air since the molecules in solid material are closely packed together and can transfer the energy faster than molecules in liquid which are loosely packed. A sound wave is an example of an elastic wave and longitudinal wave and due to the elastic wave nature of the sound wave, it can't travel in a vacuum.
Mechanical waves:
- The oscillation of matter which is responsible for the transfer of energy through a medium is called a mechanical wave.
- The mechanical wave always needs a medium to travel.
- It can't travel through a vacuum.
- The wave which propagates in a solid,

liquid, or gaseous medium is called an elastic wave.

There are two types of mechanical waves:

Transverse waves:

- The wave in which the movement of the particles is at right angles to the motion of the energy is called a transverse wave.
- Light is an example of a transverse wave.

Longitudinal wave:

- The wave in which the movement of the particles is parallel to the motion of the energy is called a longitudinal wave.
- A sound wave is an example of a longitudinal wave.

96(B). Scurvy is caused by vitamin C deficiency or ascorbic acid. It can lead to anemia, exhaustion, spontaneous bleeding, pain in the limbs, swelling in some parts of the body such as legs and ulceration of alcohol or substance abuse.

97(A). Salivation is controlled by Medulla.
- The medulla is the lowermost part of the brain.
- It is conical in form and encloses a cavity.
- It controls involuntary activities such as heartbeat, salivation, respiration, swallowing, coughing, sneezing, urinating, vomiting, etc.
- At its lower end, the medulla oblongata joins the spinal cord.
- A special neural center in the medulla oblongata can moderate the cardiac function through autonomic nervous system.

98(D). Metals are malleable and ductile in nature whereas non-metals are neither malleable nor ductile; they are brittle.

The property of metals by which they can be drawn into thin wires is known as ductility, e.g. gold, silver.

The property of metals by which they can be beaten into thin sheets is known as malleability, e.g. copper, aluminium.

Metals are malleable and ductile in nature whereas non-metals are neither malleable nor ductile; they are brittle.

99(B). The weakest acid among the following is benzoic acid.
- Benzoic acid is an aromatic carboxylic acid with the chemical formula C_6H_5COOH.
- This compound is a weak acid that is known to naturally occur in many plants and also in gum benzoin.
- Salts of this weak acid are widely used in the food industry as preservatives.
- It can be noted that benzoic acid is also referred to as benzene carboxylic acid and carboxy benzene.
- Due to the presence of an aromatic system in the compound, benzoic acid is known to possess a faintly pleasant odour.

100(B). The speed of light in the air is 3×10^8 m/s.
- The speed of light in a vacuum is 186,282 miles per second (299,792 kilometres per second).
- In theory, nothing can travel faster than light.

101(A). The study of the earth's magnetic field is known as terrestrial magnetism.

Terrestrial magnetism: The science of Terrestrial Magnetism is based on the fact that a magnet, free to move around its center of gravity, tends to assume a position of relative rest in an approximately definite direction in relation to the geographical meridian and the vertical position at the observation site.

object is such that it tends to increase the length of an object then it is called tensile stress.

Compressive stress: If the applied force on the object is such that it tends to decrease the length of an object then it is called compressive stress.

Tangential stress: When the direction of the deforming force or external force is parallel to the cross-sectional area, the stress experienced by the object is called shearing stress or tangential stress.

Working stress: Working stress is known as the maximum allowable stress that material or object will be subjected to when in service.

103(D). Water is a renewable natural resource because it is renewed and recharged through the hydrological cycle.

Renewable resource:
- Renewable resources are replenished naturally and over relatively short periods of time.
- The five major renewable energy resources are solar, wind, water (hydro), biomass, and geothermal.

Hydrological Cycle:
- The process of circulation of water within the hydrosphere of Earth in different forms such as liquid, solid and gaseous states are called the Hydrological Cycle of water.
- It starts with the Evaporation of water from the surface of the water bodies and further, it includes Transpiration, Sublimation, Condensation and Precipitation.
- The water cycle is essentially a closed system.
- Although the volume of water that is in the hydrosphere today is the same amount of water that has always been present in the Earth system.

- The water in the biosphere is continuously recycled and renewed.

104(C). The Eye of the storm is at the centre of strong cyclones. It is a region of mostly calm weather.
- The eye region is usually between 20-50 km in diameter.
- The eye is the focal point of the hurricane around which the rest of the storm rotates.

105(B). A device used for converting AC into DC is called rectifier. Rectifiers can take a wide variety of physical forms, from vacuum tube diodes and crystal radio receivers to modern silicon-based diode.

There are two types of rectifiers: Half wave rectifier and full-wave rectifier.
1. Half-wave rectifiers
2. Full-wave rectifier

Induction.
- The stator provides a magnetic field and armature (rotating windings) turns in a magnetic field. This magnetic field produces an electromotive force that pushes electrons thus generating current.
- Earlier Dynamos were equipped with permanent magnets for magnetic field generation but later replaced by electromagnets.
- They were the first generators to supply power to the industries.

107(B). Remedial measures: While diagnosis is the process of investigating the learner's difficulties and the reasons for this, its follow-up leads to actions that may help children make up for their deficiencies. This step is generally termed Remedial measures or Remedial teaching. It is generally prepared by observing students' behaviour. Objectives of Remedial Teaching:
- To timely solve doubts of the students
- To solve the problems that arise during teaching
- To develop good tendencies among the students
- To correct the emotional difficulties of students
- To overcome deficiencies in work, study, and skill.

108(B). The primary concern to the teacher in handling disciplinary problems is the cause of the misbehavior.

How should a teacher deal with disciplinary problems:
- First of all, the teacher has to create such a friendly environment where every student feels comfortable, joyful, and feel encouraged to use his potentials in a maximum way for learning.
- If a student does not cooperate or misbehave then the teacher should try

to know the cause of his misbehavior which sometimes becomes very difficult to know.

- As the teacher can only observe and analyze the behavior of a student in school and classroom learning activities but what he does at home, with his friends, and neighbors, etc. are completely out of sight of a teacher.
- So, the primary concern to a teacher in handling disciplinary problems is the cause of misbehavior of students.
- As it is not necessary that the root of the misbehavior of a student lies in the classroom only, it can be due to the quarrel between family members, disturbances in the neighborhood, etc. which is difficult for a teacher to recognize until and unless he consults his parents or guardians.

so that the learning outcomes of students should be optimized. ("To involve participation of maximum senses" is the most essential one, even more than the other three features which are mentioned in the question)

- Learning outcomes are highly dependent on the learning experience given in the classroom using teaching-learning materials.
- A teacher uses it to make teaching-learning effective. It also helps learners achieve learning outcomes after classroom teaching and learning.
- It should be easy to handle and easy to use.
- It should be cost-effective.
- The direct experience is always a more effective process of learning than other processes.

where the student draws on his/her own experience and prior knowledge.

113(C). Encouraging students to ask questions in the classroom is correct in the context of the question.

The teacher has to create and sustain an intellectually stimulating classroom environment and encourage students to participate actively. S/he has to:

- Choose a topic suitable for being taught by this method
- Plan significant questions that direct the teaching-learning process and challenge students
- Ask probing questions to stimulate critical and deep thinking
- Ensure that the questions are specific and challenging
- Ensure that the discussion is focused

choice of these methods and techniques depends on the nature of the contents to be taught to students. These methods and techniques may be teacher-centred, learner-centred or group-centred. In teacher-centred methods, the teacher plays a pivotal role in comparison to learners in the transaction of learning experiences. In learner-centred methods, learners play a significant role in comparison to the teacher in the transaction of learning experiences. Similarly, a group of learners plays a major role in learning experiences in group-centred methods.

Advantages of project work:

- Working on a project enables the learner to develop knowledge of his/her topic and various techniques used in his/her area of study.
- Students develop independent thinking and working habits while working on a project.
- Project work develops fellow-feeling and democratic spirit among members of a group.
- Project work develops the learner's communication skills through a variety of activities.

Thus, from the above-mentioned points, it is clear that both (i) and (ii) are true.

110(C). One essential feature of good teaching aid is Involving the participation of maximum senses.

Teaching Aids help in teaching-learning programs. It helps the teacher to present the lesson effectively and students to learn and retain the concepts better and for a longer duration.

- Effective teaching aid is direct experience, as the use of this type of teaching aids create a good impact on knowledge understanding.
- The most essential feature of teaching aid is to involve all the senses of students

111(D). To showcase the creative ideas of students the teacher should organize exhibitions.

- All activities in science are done with a specific purpose, evidence is collected with reliable and valid methods, and they are examined critically by controlling different variables.
- Exhibitions are organized to present the scientific innovations, ideas, and projects made by the students. These exhibitions are generally hosted and managed by the school authorities.
- The people from surrounding locality, members of school management authorities, parents and guardians of students, siblings and peers of students, etc. are invited to visit the science exhibitions.
- The main purpose is to bring the creative ideas of students to lime-light so that their creativity can be nurtured well.
- Also, their peers will be able to appreciate the innovation done by their classmates that will also inspire them to do the same in some manner.
- The different types of science projects and models are exhibited and the students who innovated them stood beside their models and projects to explain the relevancy of their innovation to the coming audience.

112(B). The discovery method of teaching is also known as the 'Inquiry method'.

Discovery learning is a method of inquiry-based instruction. Jerome Bruner is often credited with originating discovery learning in the 1960s. He argues that "practice in discovery for oneself teaches one to acquire information in a way that makes that information more readily viable in problem-solving". Discovery learning takes place in a problem-solving situation

interesting and challenging for a teacher. Interesting because it lets explore new ideas and opportunities not only for students but also for a teacher. It is a challenge because of the following reasons:

- Superstitions are generated since the day gained consciousness. India is a country which follows several rituals. Some of them are a representation of our culture, but many of them rely on some sort of myth. So, for a teacher, it's not a cakewalk to remove them.
- Alternative concepts are those concepts which seem to be true but they are not. For example, a child believes the moon also walks with him when he walks. So, it's necessary for a teacher to explain the concept of rotation and revolution.
- It is a challenging task for a teacher to translate the understanding of Science into a knowledge generation opportunity for learners. A broad understanding can help a teacher in designing meaningful situations and in selecting appropriate tools for classroom transition.

So, we conclude that all are challenges for a teacher while teaching science.

115(A). Science aims at enabling students to develop their communication skills to be able to understand scientific information, such as data, ideas, arguments, and investigations, and communicate it using appropriate scientific language in a variety of communication modes. Science Teachers help middle and high school learners understand scientific phenomena.

The Role of a Science Teacher:

- Design curriculum as per the needs of the students.
- Instruct students on the proper use of equipment, materials, aids, and textbooks.

- Provide a rich variety of learning experiences to learners.
- Establishing classroom, lab, and field trip rules and regulations and ensuring that all students understand what is expected of them.
- Grading papers, updating records, and handling various administrative tasks.
- Creating an environment where students feel comfortable asking questions.
- Participating in other school activities and regularly communicating with parents.
- Drawing up suitable assessments and delivering helpful feedback to students, parents, and other teachers.

So, from the above-mentioned points, it becomes clear that the role of a science teacher should be to provide rich variety of nature of science.

Nature of science:

- Science is both a body of knowledge and a process as science provides us the knowledge about the natural world and natural phenomena and also it has its own unique process of discovering the truth about facts, ideas, and theories.
- It is a global human endeavor as it originates from the curiosity of the individuals who want to know the cause and effect of all the natural phenomena going around them using their imagination, creativity, thinking, and logical skills.

- It is a community enterprise as it includes the members of a community as specialized individuals who can be students, researchers, professors, and scientists, etc. These members of the community use science to solve the problems of the community and works for the betterment of society.
- For example, using robots to do daily life tasks to provide comfort to human beings such as cleaning or driving and use of scientific knowledge to predict the upcoming natural disasters.

117(B). Bronze is the mixture of the metals tin and copper.

The bronze alloy was made as early as the Harappan age. An alloy is considered a homogeneous mixture because, by definition, a homogeneous mixture has the mixtures are uniform throughout, they fit the definition of being homogeneous.

118(B). The chemical used for the ripening of fruits is Ethylene.

Ripening of fruits:

- Most fruits produce a gaseous compound called ethylene that starts the ripening process.
- Its level in under-ripe fruit is very low, but as the fruits develop, they produce larger amounts of the chemical that speeds up the ripening process or the stage of ripening known as the "climacteric."

- The most commonly used chemical is called ethephon (2-chloroethyl phosphonic acid).
- It penetrates into the fruit and decomposes ethylene.
- Another chemical that is regularly used is calcium carbide, which produces acetylene, which is an analog of ethylene.

119(A). The major reason for using Bakelite for handles of pressure cooker is that it is bad conductor of heat.

Bakelite:

- Bakelite is a thermosetting plastic used to make different articles.
- It is made from a synthetic component.
- It is a resin made of phenol-formaldehyde.
- It cannot be moulded again.

life.

Acid: The substances which can turn blue litmus paper red. Acids are donors which give away hydrogen ions easily.

Base: The substances which can turn red litmus paper blue. Bases are received that give away hydroxide ions easily.

Salt: The neutral substances which are neither acidic nor basic in nature. Mostly, they have 7 as their pH value.

Neutralization Reaction: A reaction in which acids and bases react in fixed quantities to neutralize one another.

Practice Test 08

1. Jean Piaget has presented his thoughts about the preoperation stage, how the child starts doing his own work like wearing clothes, eating food, keeping a copybook, etc. Which of the following is not a limitation of pre-operative thought?
   (a) Development of symbolic thought
   (b) Conservation
   (c) Decentralization
   (d) Seriation

   (a) Knowledge is generated through direct experience and collaboration.
   (b) Examination is norm centered and external.
   (c) Teachers are the originator of information and authority.
   (d) Education is teacher centered.

3. If Rachna learns from her family about how to be a good daughter, sister, friend, wife and mother. This learning results from the process of:
   (a) Adaptability (b) Change
   (c) Maturity (d) Socialisation

4. There are lot of debates all around whether girls and boys have specific set of abilities due to their genetic materials. In this context which among below option is most agreeable?
   (a) All girls have inherent talent for arts, while boys genetically programmed to be better at aggressive sports.
   (b) Girls are socialised to be caring, while boys are discouraged to show emotions such as crying.
   (c) Boys cannot be caring since they are born this way.
   (d) After puberty, boys and girls cannot play with each other since their interest are completely opposite.

5. In a class individual learners differ from each other in terms of:
   (a) Sequence of development
   (b) Principles of growth and development

6. Which among the following are the parameters for measuring the validity of a test?
   (A) Construct
   (B) Stability
   (C) Criterion
   (D) Content
   (a) A, B only
   (b) A, B, C
   (c) A, C, D
   (d) All of the above

7. According to Piaget's cognitive

   (a) Perception
   (b) Assimilation
   (c) Schema
   (d) Accommodation

8. According to Vygotsky, 'the relationship between development and learning' summarizes best by which among the following option given below:
   (a) Development is synonymous with learning
   (b) Development is independent of learning
   (c) Development process lags behind learning process
   (d) Learning and development are parallel process

9. Which among the following is correct regarding ability grouping?
   (a) Ability grouping of student should be encouraged as it promotes competition among students.
   (b) Ability grouping of students should be discouraged as it gives the message that ability is valued more than effort.
   (c) Ability grouping of student should be encouraged as it maximizes learning using special methods.
   (d) Both (A) and (C)

10. If a child fails to perform well in the class test leads us to believe that-
    (a) There is no need to reflect upon the syllabus, pedagogy and assessment process
    (b) Children are born with certain capabilities and deficits

(c) General capacity for development
(d) Rate of development

(c) There is a need to reflect upon the syllabus, pedagogy and assessment processes
(d) Some children are deemed to fail irrespective of how hard the system tries

11. In which factor children's language development is depended?
    (a) Freedom of expression
    (b) Better schooling
    (c) Co-education
    (d) Technical education

12. According to Piaget's stages of cognitive development, with whom the 'sensory-motor state' is

    (c) Logically problem-solving ability
    (d) Ability to interpret and analyze options

13. The best measure of identifying mildly mentally retarded is:
    (a) Administration of standardized intelligence test
    (b) Administration of behavior test
    (c) Administration of adjustment test
    (d) A combination of all

14. A child in school is called a problem child when:
    (a) He is able to solve the problems of other children
    (b) He suggests useful approaches to teachers when they are explaining any problem
    (c) He behaves in such a way that becomes a problem for the teacher to understand him
    (d) He is very resourceful in suggesting good problems for the class to workout

15. Visual-spatial dysfunction is a _______ disability.
    (a) mental (b) learning
    (c) physical (d) social

16. In a heterogeneous and mixed ability class, a teacher should:
    (a) employ one type of teaching for all
    (b) use a variety of teaching-learning methods
    (c) conduct many tests
    (d) employ teacher-directed teaching

17. What does SEN mean?

(a) Social Education Standard

(b) Special Education Needs

(c) Social Education Needs

(d) Social Exception Needs

18. Special education is a branch of education that deals with ______.

(a) Educating children in special schools

(b) To provide opportunity of special education to students

(c) Instructions designing for students with special needs

(d) Education for preparation of students for special jobs

19. Repeatedly asking children to engage in learning activities either

(b) increases intrinsic motivation

(c) would encourage children to focus on mastery rather than performance goals

(d) decreases children's natural interest and curiosity involved in learning

20. Learner-centred teaching means that:

(a) learners are considered passive recipients and teacher has the 'right' knowledge.

(b) learners are slow in learning and teacher stresses completion of syllabus.

(c) learners are given an opportunity to construct knowledge and teacher is a guide in the learning process.

(d) learners know little and teaching involves transmission of facts to them.

21. In most schools today the primary consideration for homogeneous grouping is based on:

(a) grade levels

(b) age levels

(c) ability levels

(d) pupil preferences

22. Psychosocial theory emphasises on which of the following?

(a) Stimuli and Response

(b) Ophallic and Latency stages

(c) Industry versus Inferiority stage

(d) Operant Conditioning

23. Micro-teaching is:

(a) Scaled down teaching

(b) Effective teaching

(c) Evaluation teaching

(d) Real teaching

24. According to Aristotle Emotional catharsis is:

(a) Feeling highly depressed

(b) Bringing out emotional repression

(c) Increasing the ability to tolerate emotional repression

(d) Suppression of emotions

25. How a teacher can enhance the learning as per the context of motivation theories?

(a) By setting uniform standards of expectation

(b) By not having any expectation from students

26. Which among the following is not a personal factor influencing learning?

(a) Sensation or perception

(b) Needs

(c) Cultural demands

(d) Emotional conditions

27. Which among the following is an autocratic strategy of teaching?

(a) Heuristic method

(b) Discovery method

(c) Brain storming method

(d) Demonstration method

28. Errors made by children are indicative of-

(a) poor intelligence

(b) low ability

(c) their inability to reproduce knowledge

(d) children's thinking process which is qualitatively different from that of adults

29. The cephalocaudal principle of development explains how development proceeds from:

(a) General to specific functions

(b) Differentiated to integrated functions

(c) Head to toe

(d) Rural to urban areas

30. According to Piaget, which one of the following factors plays an important role in influencing development?

(a) Reinforcement

(b) Language

(c) Experience with the physical world

(d) Imitation

Ques (31-39): Direction: Read the passage given below and then answer the questions given below the passage. Some words may be highlighted for your attention. Pay careful attention.

In the UK, roughly a third of the food grown in the field never actually makes into anybody's mouth. For every three pigs raised on a farm, the equivalent of one will ultimately be sent to landfill. A third of all apples, perfectly good for consumption, will somehow be discarded. The message is simple: we waste food, and we waste a food waste that occurs at these early stages is largely unavoidable (meat bones, eggshells, banana peel, and the like).

Conversely, in UK homes – where 7m of the 13m tonnes of food waste comes from each year – 77% of waste is either avoidable (at some point, it has been perfectly good food) or possibly avoidable (food that some people eat, but others don't, such as potato skins and meat fat). This is akin to throwing away one shopping bag in five as you leave the supermarket – with an annual cost to a family of four of more than £740.

Clearly, not all food waste is equal. The cost and environmental impact of a kilo of beef are much higher than that of a kilo of potatoes, as would be expected. And so with short **shelf-life** food categories. Fresh produce, bakery, meats, and dairy top the most wasted list – and have the largest energy, CO_2, and water footprints – and so should be the main focus for reducing waste.

It seems too easy to say that it is the responsibility of consumers to reduce these **ridiculous** levels of waste. And it is too easy. A couple of years ago, Professor Tim Lang wrote here about food waste being a symptom of a much bigger problem, explaining that the relatively low cost of food almost forces a consumer society to buy more food than it can eat. It is arguably the economic powerhouses (in this case, the food giants) that drive this through brand advertising, store layouts, and clever pricing strategies. So the question is now: isn't it the food providers' responsibility to reduce food waste?

Well, the answer is that both providers and consumers have a part to play. For the consumers, the argument for this is easy: wasting less food equals saving more money, and you feel good for doing less harm to the environment. For the providers (manufacturers and retailers), the drive is less clear: selling less food equals less profit.

So how can food providers help consumers reduce food waste, but still remain profitable? There are a few options, but some of them are not easy to **swallow**. The price of food seems a pretty obvious place to start. Consumers currently spend around 11% of their income on food and drink. Five decades ago, the proportion was three times higher, so naturally, people wasted less. In sub-Saharan Africa, where consumers spend half of their income on food, it would be difficult to envisage high levels of waste. But increasing the price of food such that consumers "value" it more is likely to be very unpopular – and such a move would

products with short shelf-lives not being used in time. Consequently, there is potential for improvements in food processing or packaging and storage to increase the useable life of such products and reduce the potential for spoilage before use.

But given that leading supermarkets demand 90% of product life at the point of store entry, and goods already have extended lifetimes due to already excessive packaging and protective atmospheres, significant increases in shelf-life are unlikely.

A brave move might be to abolish "use-by" and "best-before" dates (we didn't have them before the 1970s), but this would open up a legislative **can of worms.** Until somebody invents a device that can reliably tell whether a leg of lamb has gone off, I suspect these dates are likely to stay. You could just make sure you eat the food before it goes bad, but the nation's already bulging waistline might struggle with this extra consumption. Food waste via overconsumption is yet another issue.

Perhaps the greatest improvement would be to completely change the food provision market. Consumers are like micro-manufacturers: they buy stock (ingredients) and use processes (cook) to meet demand (their family's hunger). But unlike manufacturers, consumers aren't very good at managing their inventory, using their processes efficiently, or predicting demand accurately. This leads to food waste.

There is therefore an argument for food providers to help consumers meet their families' needs by selling meals, not food. It's not inconceivable to imagine in the future people planning meals and then ordering them off the internet for home delivery – it might build better

relationships between providers and consumers, too. Even if consumers pay more for food which is delivered when wanted and actually gets eaten, it would be more convenient and could well end up being cheaper overall.

31. **Which of the following is a correct inference that can be drawn from the facts given in the passage?**

(a) Wastage of left over food only contributes to what is called food wastage

(b) Only households contribute to food wastage

(c) There are other factors besides wastage of left over food that contribute to 'wastage of food

(d) Agriculture based industries are the real culprits when it comes to

(a) Fresh produce, bakery, meats and dairy

(b) Vegetables, agriculture produce and dairy

(c) Bakery, fruits and dairy

(d) Perishable goods and food grains

33. **Which of the following is most similar in meaning to term 'shelf life' as used in the passage?**

(a) The life a product after preservatives have been added

(b) The life of a product when kept in the worst kind of environment

(c) The length of time for which an item remains fit for consumption without the addition of preservatives

(d) The length of time for which an item remains fit for consumption with or without the addition of preservatives

34. **What role does the market play in food wastage in the UK?**

(a) The agriculture industry in the US is so prosperous that the markets gets flooded with food products which are wasted as the demand is not as much

(b) Relatively lower food prices encourage people to buy more food products than they require and the extra food ultimately ends up getting wasted

(c) The price of food being exceptionally high leads to wastage of food as people are incapable of buying them

(d) The online shopping websites in the race of providing the best end

up wasting a lot of food

35. **Which of the following is most similar in meaning to the word 'ridiculous' as used in the passage?**

(a) Reasonable   (b) Amusing

(c) Evil   (d) High

36. **What is the major roadblock in the face of the food providers to control wastage of food?**

(a) They cannot compromise with the supply as they never want to run short in case of sudden excessive demands

(b) The idea of selling less food products is not congrous to the profit they intend to make

(c) The providers cannot control the

(d) All the above

37. **Which of the following is most similar in meaning to the word 'swallow' as used in the passage?**

(a) Eat   (b) Understand

(c) Believe   (d) Memorise

38. **Which of the following comes closest in meaning to the phrase (to)'open a can of worms' as given in the passage?**

(a) A dark secret

(b) To reveal a secret

(c) To make obvious while trying to hide something

(d) To make things even more complicated while attempting to solve a problem.

39. **Which one of the following constitute the possible solutions to reduce food wastage from the end of 'providers' as mentioned in the passage?**

(a) Increase the price of the food products

(b) To do away with the approximate expiry dates mentioned in packaged products

(c) To keep consuming edible items even after the mentioned expiry dates have passedA

(d) Both (A) and (B)

Ques (40-45): Direction: Read the following poem and answer the questions by choosing the correct/most appropriate options:

A thing of beauty is a joy for ever:
Its loveliness increases; it will never
Pass into nothingness; but still will keep
A bower quiet for us, and a sleep

Full of sweet dreams, and health, and quiet breathing.
Therefore, on every morrow, are we wreathing
A flowery band to bind us to the earth,
Spite of despondence, of the inhuman dearth
Of noble natures, of the gloomy days,
Of all the unhealthy and o'er-darkened ways
Made for our searching: yes, in spite of all,
Some shape of beauty moves away the pall
From our dark spirits.
Such the sun, the moon,
Trees old and young, sprouting a shady boon
For simple sheep; and such are daffodils
With the green world they live in; and clear rills
That for themselves a cooling covert make

And such too is the grandeur of the dooms
We have imagined for the mighty dead;
All lovely tales that we have heard or read:
An endless fountain of immortal drink,
Pouring unto us from the heaven's brink.

40. **The overall tone of the poem is:**
   (a) Optimistic   (b) Gloomy
   (c) Bitter   (d) Challenging

41. **Which figure of speech has been used in the line?**
   "For simple sheep; and such are daffodils"
   (a) Metaphor
   (b) Simile
   (c) Alliteration
   (d) Personification

42. **The poem underlines that:**
   (a) We need not preserve things of beauty as they wane some day.
   (b) We should preserve and take care of the things of beauty.
   (c) We should preserve only beautiful things.
   (d) Beauty diminishes with the time and disappeared.

43. **The poem tells us about:**
   (a) Beauty is mortal
   (b) Love with nature wanes with time
   (c) The beauty of nature degrades with time
   (d) Beauty never diminishes or fades

44. **Which figure of speech has been used in the line 'we wreathing, A flowery band to bind us to the earth'?**

   (a) Alliteration
   (b) Metaphor
   (c) Personification
   (d) Simile

45. **Identify the part of speech of the underlined word in the following line:**
   A flowery band to bind us to the earth
   (a) Noun   (b) Pronoun
   (c) Adjective   (d) Conjunction

46. **Language Acquisition stands for:**
   (a) learning a language with a deliberate and conscious effort.
   (b) learning a language without making any deliberate or conscious effort.
   (c) learning a language by taking recourse to one's mother tongue.

47. **Grammar-Translation method is:**
   (a) costly method
   (b) economical method
   (c) consume more time
   (d) None of the above

48. **While evaluating writing skill of a learner which of these will be the most important criteria?**
   (a) The Learner is able to take dictation
   (b) The Learner is able to express ideas coherently and systematically
   (c) The Learner is able to write about a character
   (d) The Learner is able to comprehend the questions and write their answers.

49. **The teacher informs the children about the 'adjective' and asks them to give at least one feature and definition of the adjective. What is such a method called?**
   (a) Inductive Method
   (b) Deductive Method
   (c) TPR
   (d) Immersion Method

50. **Which of the following are receptive skills ?**
   (a) Writing and reading
   (b) Speaking and listening
   (c) Speaking and writing
   (d) Listening and reading

51. **A good language textbook should include:**

   (a) extracts from British and American literature
   (b) more grammar exercises
   (c) interesting stories
   (d) attractive fonts, illustrations and learner-friendly texts

52. **Which is an effective way of teaching-learning grammar?**
   (a) Teaching the rules first followed by examples.
   (b) Presenting grammar form in a natural discourse, then explaining how the form is made and used.
   (c) Presenting single sentence examples in plenty of ways and then explaining the form.
   (d) Teaching through a typical

   (b) Lack of graded materials
   (c) Deficiency in associating phoneme and grapheme
   (d) All of the above

54. **Remedial teaching in language learning is____**
   (a) one to one approach
   (b) group approach
   (c) multiple approach
   (d) Both 1 & 2

55. **Which one of the following is not a language component?**
   (a) Structure   (b) Script
   (c) Vocabulary   (d) Sound

56. **Complete the following statement: Language tests are designed to measure ______ at a particular moment in the teaching programme.**
   (a) the learner's liking for the language
   (b) the learner's knowledge of the language
   (c) the teacher's knowledge of the language
   (d) the learner's attitude towards the language

57. **Teena, a 5 years old girl, begins to speak language structures that she has not heard before because when children are exposed to speech, certain general principles for discovering or structuring language automatically begin to operate. This function of the human brain is called:**
   (a) Innate ability

(b) Generative grammar

(c) Language Acquisition Device

(d) Universal grammar

58. When we want to test speaking skills, we test the ability of the students :

(a) to use proper punctuation marks

(b) to narrate incidents or events

(c) to make conclusions from the given extract

(d) to understand the main thought

59. Deficiency in the ability to write associated with impaired handwriting is a symptom of

(a) Dyscalculia   (b) Dysgraphia

(c) Dysphasia   (d) Aphasia

language

(b) Help the learners acquire a language

(c) Facilitate the teaching-learning process

(d) Be a source of entertainment

Mathematics and Science

61. $x^3 + x^2 + 16$ is exactly divisible by x, where x is a positive integer. The number of all such possible values of x is:

(a) 3   (b) 4

(c) 5   (d) 6

62. What is the digit in the unit place of 3^{99} ?

(a) 1   (b) 3

(c) 7   (d) 9

63. If the 5 -digit number $535ab$ is divisible by 3,7 and 11 then what is the value of $\left(a^2 - b^2 + ab\right)$?

(a) 83   (b) 89

(c) 95   (d) 77

64. If $x = 7 - 4\sqrt{3}$, then $\sqrt{x} + \dfrac{1}{\sqrt{x}}$ is equal to:

(a) 1   (b) 2

(c) 3   (d) 4

65. If $A + B\sqrt{6} = \dfrac{(4 - 3\sqrt{6})}{(5 + 2\sqrt{6})}$, then find the value of $(A + B)^2$

(a) 1024   (b) 1225

(c) 1156   (d) 1089

66. If $(7x - 10y) = 8$ and $xy = 5$, then what is the value of $49x^2 + 100y^2$?

(a) 623   (b) 764

(c) 632   (d) 746

67. The length of the diagonal BD of the parallelogram $ABCD$ is $18\,\text{cm}$. If P and Q are the centroids of $\triangle ADC$ and $\triangle ABC$ respectively, then the length of PQ is?

(a) 9 cm   (b) 5 cm

(c) 8 cm   (d) 6 cm

68. How many diagonals are there in a polygon of 12 sides?

(a) 78   (b) 66

(c) 54   (d) 48

69. The chord of a circle is equal to its radius. The angle subtended by the chord at the minor arc of the circles

70. The base of a pyramid is a square of side $10\,\text{cm}$. If its height is $10\,\text{cm}$, then the area (in cm^2) of its lateral suface is:

(a) $50\sqrt{5}$ (b) $100\sqrt{5}$

(c) 100   (d) $100(\sqrt{5} + 1)$

71. The area of the region bounded externally by a square of side $2a$ cm and internally by the circle touching the four sides of the square is:

(a) $(4 - \pi)a^2$ (b) $(\pi - 2)a^2$

(c) $\dfrac{(8 - \pi)a^2}{2}$ (d) $\dfrac{(\pi - 2)a^2}{2}$

72. Mr. Mahesh buys a toy for Rs. 25 and sells it for Rs. 30 . Find the gain percentage.

(a) 20%   (b) 22%

(c) 25%   (d) 21%

73. The average of five consecutive odd numbers is 51. What is the difference between the highest and lowest number?

(a) 3   (b) 7

(c) 8   (d) 11

74. A person crosses a 455-meter long distance in 35 minutes. What is his speed in km/hr?

(a) 0.52   (b) 0.95

(c) 0.62   (d) 0.78

75. LCM of two numbers is 28 times their HCF. The sum of the HCF and the LCM is 1740 . If one of these numbers is 240 , then what is the other number?

(a) 420   (b) 640

(c) 820   (d) 1040

76. **Simplify:** $16 - 2 \div 14 + 6 \times 2$

(a) $27\frac{6}{7}$ (b) $29\frac{5}{7}$

(c) $26\frac{5}{7}$ (d) $27\frac{5}{8}$

77. Which of the following statements is NOT correct with regard to nature of mathematics?

(a) Mathematical concepts are hierarchical in nature

(b) Primary level mathematics is concrete and does not require abstraction

(c) Mathematics uses special vocabulary to communicate ideas precisely

(d) Argumentation skill is important in construction of mathematical knowledge

mathematics-

(a) It is based on objective facts

(b) It is a study of logic

(c) It is a system of rigour, purity and beauty

(d) It is a tool for solving problems

79. Which of the following is most suitable for teaching children the concept of fractions?

(a) Geoboards

(b) Number charts

(c) Cuisenaire rods

(d) Abacus

80. Identify the correct statement with respect to the mathematics curriculum.

(a) The concept of fractions should be introduced only at upper primary level

(b) The concept of negative numbers should be introduced at the primary level for better understanding

(c) The concept of area-measurement should be introduced only at upper primary level

(d) The foundation of algebraic thinking can be laid at primary level

81. Identify the symbol that is unique to the mathematics language.

(a) %   (b) ?

(c) &   (d) /

82. A teacher gives the following task to the students of class-IV:

"Arrange 25 tiles in all possible rectangular arrays."

Which of the following mathematical concepts can be addressed through this task?
(a) Area, factors, perimeter
(b) Area, perimeter, volume
(c) Area, volume, length
(d) Volume, Area, Width

83. Which of the following is not a dimension of assessment of mathematical learning?
(a) Communication
(b) Patterns and procedures
(c) Disposition towards mathematics
(d) Mathematical reasoning

84. The purpose of remedial teaching is to

not properly learnt
(d) teach again the language items already learnt

85. Which of the following is the major problem of teaching Mathematics?
(a) Teaching methods of Mathematics teacher
(b) Ability to use Mathematical tools.
(c) Class Room operations
(d) Knowledge of teaching methods

86. Which of the following could be a contributing factor towards underachievement in mathematics?
(a) Gender
(b) Socio-Cultural background
(c) Nature of Mathematics
(d) Innate ability of person

87. Most of animal fats are:
(a) Saturated fats
(b) Unsaturated fats
(c) Monounsaturated fats
(d) Monosaturated fats

88. Fruits taste sweet because they contain ______.
(a) Maltose   (b) Ribose
(c) Lactose   (d) Fructose

89. Which of the following factors exclusively affects reproduction in seasonal breeders, both plants and animals?
(a) Water   (b) Temperature
(c) Photoperiod   (d) All of these

90. Growth by cell division occurs __ in plants and __ in animals.

(a) Continuously, only up to a certain age
(b) Only up to a certain age, continuously
(c) Continuously, continuously
(d) Never, continuously

91. The specific resistance of a rod of copper as compared to that of thin wire of copper is ________.
(a) Less
(b) More
(c) Same
(d) Depends upon the length and area of cross-section of the wire

92. At what temperature, a ferromagnetic material becomes paramagnetic material?

(d) None of the above

93. Wool is obtained from:
(a) Hair of Sheep, Camel and Yak
(b) Hair of Sheep, Lion and Camel
(c) Hair of Camel, Elephant and Rabbit
(d) Hair of Cow, Goat and Sheep

94. which of the following is a thermosetting polymer?
(a) Terylene   (b) Polystyrene
(c) Bakelite   (d) Neoprene

95. A passenger in a moving bus is thrown forward when the bus suddenly stops. This is explained by :
(a) Newton's first law
(b) Newton's second law
(c) Newton's third law
(d) Principle of conservation of momentum

96. Why are the soles of the shoes treaded?
(a) To give the shoes more protection
(b) To decrease friction
(c) To increase friction
(d) To increase life of the shoes

97. Which is not a natural phenomenon?
(a) Earthquakes
(b) Cyclones
(c) Lightning
(d) Nuclear explosion

98. Which of the following minerals is known as brown diamond?
(a) Manganese   (b) Mica

(c) Iron   (d) Lignite

99. Which force moves an aircraft through the air?
(a) Lift Force
(b) Drag Force
(c) Thrust Force
(d) Gravity Force

100. Earth's magnetism is due to:
(a) Dynamo effect
(b) Doppler effect
(c) Solar effect
(d) Magnus effect

101. The speed of light is maximum in which of the following mediums?
(a) Air   (b) Glass
(c) Vacuum   (d) Water

(b) Bridge element
(c) Transitional element
(d) Normal element

103. The hepatic portal vein drains blood to the liver from:
(a) Heart   (b) Stomach
(c) Kidneys   (d) Intestine

104. Deficiency of which vitamin causes failure of blood clotting?
(a) K   (b) B
(c) D   (d) A

105. Sound wave is a _____.
(a) Radio wave
(b) Longitudinal wave
(c) Transverse wave
(d) Electromagnetic wave

106. Which one of the following is not true of the nature of science?
(a) Science is always tentative.
(b) Science promotes scepticism.
(c) Science is a process of constructing knowledge.
(d) Science is static in nature.

107. Which one among the following is not a desirable aim of science education at upper primary level?
(a) To know the facts and principles of science and its applications
(b) To gain the knowledge available through memorising the content and process of science
(c) To imbibe the values of honesty, integrity and cooperation
(d) To nurture the natural curiosity, aesthetic sense and creativity in

science and technology

108. Which one is most important to promote the quality in teaching learning of science in schools ?
(a) Teacher-Taught Ratio
(b) Trained Resource Teacher
(c) Required Apparatus
(d) Regular Teaching

109. Which of the following approaches to teaching science in the classroom is completely teacher-centred?
(a) Hands-on experiment approach
(b) Inquiry approach
(c) Expository transmission approach

approach for teaching science in the teaching-learning process?
I. Open Discovery Method
II. Guided Discovery Method
III. Deductive Discovery Method
(a) Both II and III
(b) I, II and III
(c) Both I and III
(d) Both I and II

111. Which of the following types of question require the students to design and redesign which involve good deal of innovation?
(a) Diverged questions
(b) Questions challenging assumptions
(c) Future problem solving questions
(d) Questions seeking new relationships

112. As a teacher of Class V, which of the following resources would you find best to use while dealing with a topic on 'conservation of fuels'?
(a) Reference books
(b) Posters
(c) Newspapers
(d) Textbooks

113. The continuous and comprehensive evaluation in science means—
(a) summative and formative assessment
(b) more frequent test and examination
(c) routine activities and exercises to assess learning
(d) evaluation of all aspects of

science

114. Which type of teaching should be planned after diagnosing the learning difficulties of the students in science teaching?
(a) Microteaching
(b) Team teaching
(c) Diagnostic teaching
(d) Remedial teaching

115. If most of the students of the class are unable to learn then what should the teacher do ?
(a) Answers of the questions should be written on the blackboard.
(b) Extra class should be taken.
(c) Should bring modification in his

116. What is the chemical name of 'oil of vitriol'?
(a) Methyl alcohol
(b) Calcium hydroxide
(c) Sodium chloride
(d) Sulphuric acid

Ques (117-119): Direction : Study the following graph carefully and answer the question based on the information given below.

Percentage distribution of teachers who teach six different subjects

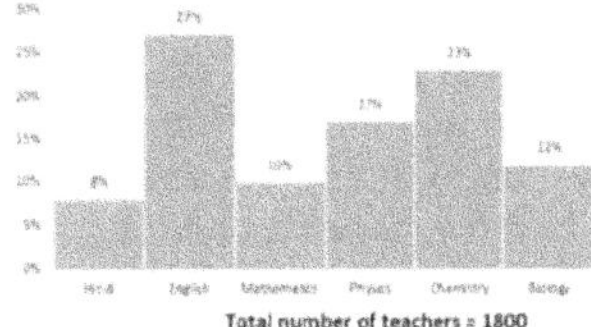

117. If two-ninths of the teachers who teach Physics are females, then the number of male Physics teachers is approximately what per cent of the total number of teachers who teach Chemistry?
(a) 57%   (b) 42%
(c) 63%   (d) 69%

118. What is the total numbers of teachers who teach Chemistry, English and Biology?
(a) 1226   (b) 1116
(c) 1176   (d) 998

119. What is difference between the total number of employees teacher who teach English and Physics together and total number of teacher who teach Mathematics and Biology together?
(a) 352   (b) 342

(c) 332   (d) 322

120. 5 years ago, my sister's age was 5 times my age. Now it is 3 times only. What is my sister's present age (in years)?
(a) 30   (b) 25
(c) 20   (d) 15

1(A). Jean Piaget, a Swiss psychologist, has made a systematic study of cognitive development in his theory that is categorized into four stages.
Preoperational stage:
• The preoperational stage is the second stage in Piaget's theory of cognitive development.

engage in symbolic play and learn to manipulate symbols.
• Three main characteristics of pre-operational thinking are centration, static reasoning, and irreversibility.
• In this stage, children can verbalize thoughts but think intuitively rather than logically.
• The key development of this stage is learning to form internal representations.
• During this period, children are thinking at a symbolic level but are not yet using cognitive operations.
Limitation of Pre-operational stage:
• Inability to decenter, conserve, understand seriation (the inability to understand that objects can be organized into a logical series or order) and to carry out inclusion tasks.
• Children in the preoperational stage are able to focus on only one aspect or dimension of problems.
Thus, it can be concluded that the Development of symbolic thought is not the limitation of the pre-operational stage.

2(A). Progressive education focuses on learning that is both experiential and collaborative.
Some of the progressive educations qualities are:-
• Emphasis on learning by doing
• Integrated curriculum focused on thematic units
• Strong emphasis on problem solving and critical thinking
• Group work and development of social skills
• Collaborative and cooperative learning projects
• Education for social responsibility and democracy
• Emphasis of lifelong process and social skills

3(D). If Rachna learns from her family about how to be a good daughter, sister, friend, wife and mother. This learning results from the process of socialisation.

Socialisation is a life long process of inheriting norms, customs and philosophies from prevailing environment. It provides an individual with the necessary skills and habits that help him/her get accustomed to the given social environment.

4(B). Girls are socialised to be caring while boys are discouraged to show emotions such as crying, is a gender-biased thought of the society. Girls are considered to be more caring as they are quick in showing emotions than boys who are not expected to act emotionally in front of others.

learning as proposed by Vygotsky.

According to Vygotsky, learning is a process that occurs anytime in everyday life and that isn't just an external phenomenon. His theory of Zone of Proximal Development (ZPD) expanded learning and development, which posits that learning precedes development processes.

- Development: It refers to a progressive and systematic series of changes that occur in the life of an individual he/she grows from infancy to old age.
- Learning: The process by which a person alters his responses and behavior in order to adjust himself to the changing environment is called learning.

9(B). Sorting of students according to their talents in a classroom is ability grouping. It should be discouraged as it

identify a mentally retarded person:

- The Management document of the standardized intelligence test presents intellectual performance significantly.
- Management of behavior and adjustment testing should document deficits in at least two adaptive behavioral areas.
- Management document of emotion that mental retardation affects school performance.

Following are the symptoms of mentally retarded person:

- IQ (IQ) score of 50-69.
- cannot be easily diagnosed.
- More likely to be guilty than easily.

Therefore, it can be concluded that a combination of standardized intelligence tests, behavioral and management of adjustment tests is the best approach to

child is different from that of another child. This principle is known as the 'principle of individual differences'. For instance, some children may learn to walk in 8 months, while some may take more than a year to start walking.

It is important for teachers to know variables such as physical characteristics, intelligence, perception, gender, ability, learning styles, which are individual differences of learners. An effective and productive learning-teaching process can be planned by considering these individual differences of students.

6(C). To have confidence that a test is valid, and thus the inferences we make based on the test scores are valid, three kinds of validity evidence are:

Construct - It is the extent to which the content of the test matches the instructional objectives.

Criterion - It is the extent to which scores on the test are in agreement with or predict an external criterion.

Content - It is the extent to which an assessment corresponds to other variables, as predicted by some rationale or theory.

7(D). According to Piaget's cognitive theory of learning, identify the process among the following by "Accommodation" the cognitive structure is modified.

There is accommodation when a child either modifies an existing schema or forms an entirely new schema to deal with a new object or event. This concept was developed by Jean Piaget, a Swiss developmental psychologist who is best known for this theory of cognitive development in children.

8(C). "Development process lags behind learning process" best summarizes the relationship between development and

within the same age group for instruction as opposed to placement on age and grade level. Ability grouping can be implemented in regular and special education classrooms. Groups are typically small, consisting of ten and fewer students.

10(C). If a child fails to perform well in the class test leads us to believe that there is a need to reflect upon the syllabus, pedagogy and assessment processes.

The failure of a child is also the failure of the syllabus pedagogy and assessment. So we need to reflect upon all these points before making any judgment about the students.

To avoid failure or to tackle it when it looks likely, both parents and teachers must get involved. They can do this by involvement of parents, skill development, increase in the motivation.

11(A). Language development is even more impressive when we consider the nature of what is learned. It may seem that children merely need to remember what they hear and repeat it at some later time. But as Chomsky pointed out so many years ago, if this were the essence of language learning, we would not be successful communicators. Verbal communication requires productivity, i.e. the ability to create an infinite number of utterances we have never heard before. Therefore Freedom of expression is a must for children's language development.

12(B). According to Piaget's theory of cognitive development, our thoughts and logic are part of adaptation. Cognitive development takes place in a certain order of steps. Sensory motivational state is simulation. It is based on memory and mental representation.

Hence, the correct option is (B)

13(D). The following are good ways to

child when he behaves in such a way that becomes a problem for the teacher to understand him.

A child in school is called a problem child who:

- Demonstrate aggressiveness.
- Dominate the discussion and demands attention.
- Are inattentive and unprepared.
- Behaves in such a way that becomes a problem for a teacher.
- Make excuses.

15(B). Visual-spatial disability is a non-verbal learning disability. The children have problems with visual-spatial information. It includes:

- Difficulties with visual-spatial orientation.
- Difficulties in interpreting graphs, charts, maps.
- Difficulties in judging rotate figures because of the direction and position concepts.
- Difficulties with a sense of direction, estimation of size, shape, distance, time.

Thus, it is concluded that Visual-spatial dysfunction is a learning disability.

16(B). To deal with a mixed-ability class a teacher should use a variety of teaching-learning methods.

- Make sure that there is a variation in the content i.e., using different types of content to develop contextual understanding.
- In addition to a common supply of learning materials and learning activities that contains the basic learning material, provide opportunities for students to obtain additional explanation and revision, or more in-depth analysis and extension. Make it clear to the students what the core of the material is and what involves extension

or broadening.
- Give examples from different settings. This way, students with different interests and prior knowledge feel included. Teachers can also ask students to present their own case studies or examples from their own experience or reference framework.
- Provide sufficient variety in teaching methods and teaching strategies during your teaching-learning process.
- Teachers can create variety by asking questions, creating interaction, providing room for discussion, in addition to theory also paying attention to applications and exercises, telling a small anecdote, or giving examples.

Therefore, to make sure that the teacher is effectively dealing with heterogeneous and mixed classrooms, they should use a variety

- Give your child curiosity tools: Give your kids the ability to pursue their curiosity on their own. Try to build a good stock of books at your home as well as getting them membership in the local library.
- Let your child make mistakes: As parents, our tendency is to prevent our kids from feeling disappointed, hurt, discouraged, or rejected. But making mistakes and pulling themselves up again keeps your child curious and resilient.
- Fight boredom: Your child learns from you. When you label any activity or situation as "boring" they too will learn that only.
- Teach them how to observe: When you are with them encourage them to look around themselves and notice things that seem interesting mysterious

microteaching is scaled-down teaching in which the teacher teaches a short lesson to a small group of students for a short period. One teaching skill is practiced at a time. Thus microteaching is a miniature form of teaching in which teaching is scaled down in terms of class size, time, complexity, and activities with a focus on developing a specific teaching skill.

"Microteaching is a real teaching" this is an assumption in microteaching because it has nothing to do with students' learning. It totally focuses on teachers' teaching skills.

24(B). According to Aristotle Emotional catharsis is bringing out emotional repression.

Aristotle describes the catharsis as the purging of the emotions of pity and fear that are aroused in the viewer of a tragedy.

children with the above-mentioned challenges in all settings such as classrooms, homes, workplaces, public places, the street, and rehabilitation homes. Special Educational Needs (SEN) refer to learners with learning, physical, and developmental disabilities; behavioural, emotional, and communication disorders; and learning deficiencies. Children's Special Educational Needs (SEN) are met through certain methodologies of special education.

18(C). Special education is the practice of educating students in a way that provides accommodations that address their individual differences, disabilities, and special needs. Ideally, this process involves the individually planned and systematically monitored arrangement of teaching procedures, adapted equipment and materials, and accessible settings. Special education refers to a range of educational and social services provided by the public school system and other educational institutions to individuals with disabilities who are between three and 21 years of age. Special education is designed to ensure that students with disabilities are provided with an environment that allows them to be educated effectively.

19(D). Repeatedly asking children to engage in learning activities either to avoid punishment or to gain a reward decreases children's natural interest and curiosity involved in learning.

Tips to Encourage Curiosity in Children:
- Be a good role model: Your child does everything he or she sees you doing. So take advantage of this behaviour to increase their curiosity.
- Encourage your child's interest: Your child's curiosity will lead him or her naturally towards subjects and topics that are of interest to them.

curiosity: Explain to your child how so many of the things that are staples in our lives are born out of someone's curiosity about that subject.
- Give open-ended materials to play: Along with toys that have specific ways to be played with give your child open-ended materials like sand, arts and craft supplies, empty boxes, blocks that can be used in any way they want.

20(C). The learner-centred approach of teaching puts learners in the centre and gives primacy to children's experiences and needs. It strongly believes that when children are given the freedom to work at their own pace, they develop the ability to assimilate the concepts efficiently.

21(C). Grouping based on Ability: Grouping based on ability levels alone is attempted if the primary learning goal is the enhancement of students' attainments. In the context of ability levels, the groups can be homogeneous and heterogeneous.

22(C). Erikson's theory describes the impact of social experience across the whole lifespan. He felt the course of development is determined by the interaction of the body (genetic biological programming), mind (psychological), and cultural (ethos) influences. the psychosocial theory basically asserts that people experience eight 'psychosocial crisis stages' which significantly affect each person's development and personality. Each crisis stage relates to a corresponding life stage and its inherent challenges. Erikson used the words 'syntonic' for the first listed 'positive' disposition in each crisis (example trust) and 'dystonic' for the second listed 'negative' disposition (example, Mistrust).

23(A). As the term itself indicates,

terms.

25(D). According to the theories of motivation, a teacher can enhance learning by setting realistic expectation from students. This is because a teacher's expectation have a strong effect on the performance of his/her students. The expectation of a teacher from his/her students works as a motivational force for them which in turns results of better performance.

26(C). Cultural demand is an environmental factor influencing the learning.

Learning-centred education focuses on the learning process. Although its primary concern is on the learning of the students, all those involved in the education of students such as teachers are also co-learners with the students in the learning-centred education. It is basically learner-centred but includes teachers in the process of learning in a classroom situation.

Learner-related factors affecting learning are:

Following are the factors affecting individual learning:
- Physical health
- Sensation or perception
- Needs
- Emotional conditions
- Mental health
- Willingness to learn
- Learning time
- Readiness to learn
- Student's basic ability
- Intelligence level
- Interest
- Motivation level

27(D). Demonstration method- it is the autocratic strategy of teaching. Teacher shows all the activities given in a lesson to the students as an action and explains the important points before them during demonstration. It is a teaching method used in technical and training colleges and in teacher education. This strategy focuses to achieve psychomotor and cognitive objectives.

Heuristic method- it is a democratic strategy of teaching. Students learn themselves as teachers raise problem before the students and ask them to discover the answer.

Discovery method- this method is used in social science to clarify the facts and concepts. This is democratic style of teaching.

Brain storming- a problem is given to the students and they are asked to put forward their views one by one, conclusion is drawn after evaluating their jumbled ideas.

all children.

30(C). **Swiss psychologist Jean Piaget** was the most well known and influential theorist for cognitive development. Piaget was interested in how children reacted to their **environments** .

- He envisioned a child's knowledge as composed of schemas, the basic unit of knowledge used to organize past experiences and serve as a basis for understanding new ones.
- Development is influence the most when a child's experiences interact with his physical environment.
- These processes are influenced by the child's experience and activity, social interactions, and biological process of becoming mature (maturation).
- They perform all activities and think

'Ridiculous' means 'laughable' or 'funny' but in the given context it means that the exceptionally high rate of food wastage must be reduced.

36(B). The passage discusses how both providers and consumers have a part to play in food wastage and only their combined effort can solve the problem. The consumers can be encouraged not to waste food as it would help them save more money and in this way, they can also do less harm to the environment. However, the incentive is not as strong for the food providers as selling less food will yield less profit. Thus major roadblock for the providers is that selling less (in order to reduce food wastage) is inversely proportional to the profit they make.

37(C). The passage mentions the

in children's thinking as compared to adults is reflected in the type of errors made by the children.

Errors can occur in adults as well as children. The qualitative effect of errors can be observed through the type of error. Adults tend to make silly mistakes that may not be serious as they tend to overlook minor details and focus on bigger things. Whereas children may make a significantly big error as they may not have the experience of the concept.

Thus, it is concluded that errors made by children are indicative of children's thinking process which is qualitatively different from that of adults.

29(C). The cephalocaudal principle states that development proceeds from head to toe. According to this principle, a child will gain physical control of their head first. After this, physical control will move downward to the arms and lastly to the legs.

- The Head region starts growth at first and followed by other organs.
- The child gains control of the head first, then the arms and the legs.
- Infancy develops control of the head and face movements at the first two months. In the next few months, they are able to lift themselves up by using their arms and then gain control over the toe and able to crawl, walk, jump, climb, day by day.
- The cephalocaudal principle applies to both physical and functional development.
- Development is seen in the earliest years of post-natal development specifically ranging from infancy into toddlerhood.

A child develops in an orderly sequence which is almost similar in all children. The rate and speed of development may vary in individual cases but the sequence of development patterns is almost the same in

people s) interactions with their culture.

- Interaction of physical factors such as temperature, humidity, pollution, and natural disasters on human behavior. The influence of the physical arrangement of the workplace on health, the emotional state, and interpersonal relations are also investigated.

Thus from the above-mentioned points, it is clear that according to Piaget, experience with the physical world plays an important role in influencing development.

31(C). The very first paragraph of the passage mentions that in the UK, roughly a third of the food grown in the field never actually makes into anybody's mouth. This means that food is wasted in the farms itself. Later the passage mentions that not only the consumers but also the providers have a hand in wasting a lot of food. So there are other factors besides wastage of leftover food that contribute to 'wastage of food'.

32(A). According to the fourth paragraph of the passage, 'Fresh produce, bakery, meats and dairy top the most wasted list'.

33(D). The term shelf life refers to 'the length of time that a commodity may be stored without becoming unfit for use, consumption, or sale.' This is independent of the fact whether preservatives are added or not.

Hence, the correct option is (D)

34(B). According to the fifth paragraph of the passage, 'the relatively low cost of food almost forces a consumer society to buy more food than it can eat.' This is the effect of the prevailing market dynamics.

The other options are irrelevant with reference to the passage.

35(D). According to the passage the ridiculous levels of waste need to reduced.

believe or accept.

38(D). 'Opening a can of worms' is an idiom which means 'to examine or attempt to solve some problem, only to complicate it and create even more trouble'.

39(D). The passage mentions both options (A) and (B) as possible solutions to reduce food wastage from the end of 'providers'.

Thus both the options are correct.

Note that the passage also suggests that the "use-by" and "best-before" dates must be abolished to reduce food wastage, but it nowhere says that edible items should be continued to be consumed even after the mentioned expiry dates have passed.

40(A). To find out the tone of the poem, we should focus on the words and devices used by the poet.

- From reading the poem we can clearly see that the tone of this poem is full of loving, peaceful and optimistic.
- In the second line "loveliness increases", These words just create a gentle yet vivid image in the reader's mind.
- "a bower quiet for us", "sweet dreams" these words describe pleasant mood of the poet.
- "Some shape of beauty moves away the pall, From our dark spirits" define that Some beautiful shapes or a thing of beauty removes the pall of sadness from our hearts or spirits.
- "An endless fountain of immortal drink" these lines tells us about that beautiful bounty of the earth, has bestowed us with sun, moon, flowers, rivers, greenery.

"inhuman dearth", "gloomy days", "unhealthy and o'er-darkened ways" in these lines the poet says that beauty fills us with the feeling of being alive. Without beauty the earth would be full of cruel people and sad moments and It is beauty that brings happiness to our hearts'.

Thus, we can clearly see that the tone of the poem is full of love, peaceful and optimistic.

41(C). Alteration figure of speech has been used in these word in the above line: simple sheep such.

Alliteration: a literary device that reflects repetition in two or more nearby words of initial consonant sounds. Alliteration does not refer to the repetition of consonant letters that begin words, but rather the repetition of the consonant sound at the beginning of words.

42(B). Beautiful things are a source of endless joy. It is the eternal beauty that never goes away.

A beautiful thing is like a shady shelter that

materialistic things and will get away from eternal happiness. Because this earth is full of hatred, greed and negativity. And because of this negativity we will be surrounded by sadness all around and get carried away with positive thoughts of beautiful things. That's why it is necessary that we should preserve and take care of beautiful things.

43(D). The poet describes that beauty is everywhere and it lies in the eye of the beholder.

In the first stanza 'The poet says that beauty lasts forever. It never ends but keeps on increasing with time'.

In the second stanza 'The poet says that beauty fills us with the feeling of being alive. Without beauty the earth would be full of cruel people and sad moments and It is beauty that brings happiness to our hearts'.

In the third stanza 'According to the poet, worldly things and material things keep us away from eternal happiness.

In the fourth stanza 'These are those beautiful things that are immortal and give us a reason to live on earth despite having so much suffering in our lives'.

Thus from all the points given above, we can conclude that the poem is about 'Beauty never diminishes or fades'.

44(B). Metaphor figure of speech has been used in the above lines: wreathing, A flowery band. The poet has used the phrase wreathing a flowery band to show how beautiful things bind humans to Earth.

Metaphor: An expression, often found in literature, that describes a person or object by referring to something that is considered to have similar characteristics to that person or object.

45(C). "Flowery" is an adjective.

Adjectives are words that describe the qualities or states of being of nouns. Here, band is a noun and flowery describes what kind of band the poet is talking about. A noun is always qualified by an adjective.

46(B). Language acquisition is the process by which humans acquire the capacity to perceive and comprehend language as well as to produce and use words and sentences to communicate.

- The acquisition is the process by which humans acquire the capacity to perceive and comprehend knowledge as well as to produce and use words and sentences to communicate.
- The major difference between language acquisition and learning is that language acquisition is natural and language learning is deliberate/instructed.

language use.

Hence, from the above-mentioned points, it becomes clear that Language Acquisition stands for learning a language without making any deliberate or conscious effort.

47(B). Principles of Grammar-Translation method: This method has its own basic principles that would justify the measures it advocates for the teaching of English. Apparently, the rules of the conduct of the method have their justification in their own way:

- It is easier to teach the foreign language through the medium of the mother tongue than through the foreign language itself as the former would smoothen all the complexities at a single stroke.
- Teaching through translation is a quick and economical process. A teaching procedure should economies on time, energy, and labor and should aim at quick results.
- Translation allows comparison and contrast between the language patterns of the mother tongue and those of English.
- Such a comparative study quickens the pace of learning and makes it firm in the minds of the learners.
- The liberal use of the mother tongue conforms with the well-known maxim of learning that going from the known to the unknown elements of knowledge.

Hence, we can conclude that the Grammar-Translation method is an economical method.

48(B). While evaluating writing skills it is most important to evaluate whether the learner is able to express their ideas systematically and coherently because:

- if the ideas are systematically expressed then we can conclude that the thoughts

are clear in the mind of the learner.

- it ensures that they are able to express their experiences and thoughts beautifully and can convey the information in the best way.
- it encourages learners to exercise their creative minds by using their imaginations. It improves their ability to come up with alternatives.

Thus, it is concluded that the most important criteria of evaluating writing skills is that the learner is able to express ideas coherently and systematically.

49(B). In this question, the teacher is teaching Adjectives and then asks to give them at least one feature and definition. This method is called Deductive method of teaching.

Deductive method:-

- This method is used mostly to teach grammar structures.
- For example- The teacher has taught the concept of adjectives and asked them to describe one feature.

Thus, it is concluded that The teacher informs the children about the 'adjective' and asks them to give at least one feature and definition of the adjective. This method is called deductive method.

50(D). Language skills are necessary for effective communication in any environment and to interact with others. It allows an individual to comprehend and produce language for proper and effective interpersonal communication. These foundational skills of language are divided into two categories which are receptive and productive skills.

Receptive skills:

- The receptive skills of language are listening and reading because these skills don't require the production of language.
- These skills focus on an individual's ability of understanding and comprehending language.

51(D). A textbook is a tool to be used in the teaching process to facilitate effective learning. Language textbooks primarily provide comprehensible inputs to develop a good understanding of the concept for better academic outcomes. A good language textbook should include:

- child-centered material,
- teacher-friendly instruction,
- content-related materials which have more syntactical items in its content,
- attractive fonts, illustrations, and learner-friendly texts.

52(B). Inductive method is a method which makes grammar learning an effective and productive process by:

- presenting grammar form in a natural discourse, then explaining how the form is made and used.
- promoting divergent and critical thinking and leading learners from known to unknown or example to formula.
- giving illustration in sentences or paragraph to help students to learn grammatical rules in context and integrated manner.

Hence, we conclude that presenting grammar form in a natural discourse, then explaining how the form is made and used is an effective way of teaching-learning grammar.

53(D). Problems Students often Encounter with Reading
- **Lack of concentration** is another

from reading with concentration. But students, in most cases, cannot or do not concentrate properly while reading, or they cannot hold their attention for a long time due to their lack of practice and patience.
- **The long and complex structure of sentences** often causes a reading barrier for most of the students. They cannot understand the proper subject-verb relationship in a long or complex sentence, which creates constant difficulties. Eventually, these difficulties result in poor and insufficient reading.
- **Lack of graded materials** is another important reason for the failure of reading. This inadequacy of proper texts or textual materials affects students' reading much. Sometimes students are not supplied with their texts according to their linguistic level.
- **Deficiency in associating phoneme and grapheme** is another reason for students' poor reading. Sometimes poor reading results from students' "inability to relate symbols, to associate the proper phoneme with the proper shape, or to match a visual sequence with an auditory sequence. The pupil has great difficulty acquiring phonic skills." And obviously, this lack of phonic skills results in their inability to associate experiences and meanings with symbols.

Hence, we can conclude that all of the above are the causes of poor reading skills.

54(A). **Remedial Teaching** is an integral part of the teaching-learning program, also known as compensatory or corrective teaching.
- The objective of remedial teaching is to give additional help to learners who have fallen behind the rest of the class in any topic or subject.

- It is one to one approach, in which teacher gives remedial measures as per the learning difficulties faced by a particular child.
- It is the process of identifying slow learners and providing them with the necessary help and guidance to overcome their problems.

Hence, we can conclude that remedial teaching in language learning is one to one approach.

55(B). **Language** is a medium through which one can express one's ideas, thoughts, and feelings. The script is not a part of the language component.
- **The script** is related to the return part of language every language can be written in many steps as well as the Hindi language written in Devnagri

points are:-
1. Phonemes
2. Morphemes
3. Lexemes
4. Syntax
5. Context

Hence, from the above-mentioned points, it becomes clear that the Script is not a language component.

56(B). Language tests are tests that play a significant role in the teaching-learning process of language. Language tests measure the learning, skills learnt by learners and also help in finding mistakes and weak areas of the ner in any subject.

Language Tests are designed to:
- Diagnose learners' strength and weakness in language learning
- Measure learner's knowledge of the language
- Test the level of learner's language skills to make them proficient in communication
- Evaluate how well an individual uses a particular language to communicate in daily life

There are many types of language tests which include proficiency test, achievement test, diagnostic test, placement test, etc.

Hence, it becomes clear that language tests are designed to measure the learner's knowledge of the language at a particular moment in the teaching programme.

57(C). The above-mentioned function of the human brain is called **Language Acquisition Device** as according to Chomsky, Language acquisition device is a **hypothetical tool** in a child's brain that makes learners able to:
- acquire and produce language.
- learn and assimilate language easily.
- analyze language and extract basic rules.
- encode the grammatical structure of

language.

Hence, it could be included that the above-mentioned function of the human brain is called Language Acquisition Device.

58(B). Before speaking we plan in our minds, as to what we should speak about such that the listener understands what we are saying.

We also make up our minds about 'what' and 'how' to speak depending upon who we are speaking to.

When a teacher wants to test the speaking skills of students, he needs to check how they speak which includes their way of pronouncing words and how correctly they are able to words in a well-structured form. And it can be best done by asking them to narrate incidents or events. As when the students will narrate incidents they will use

Thus, it is clear that to test the speaking ability of the students, a teacher should ask them to narrate incidents or events.

59(B). **Dysgraphia** refers to a learning disability which:
- affects learners' ability to write coherently.
- hinders in organizing letters, numbers, or words on papers.
- leads to problems with poor spelling, impaired handwriting, etc.

R emedies useful for treating students with **Dysgraphia** :
- giving extra time for writing assessment, will reduce the copying activity and will emphasize the importance of writing original answers.
- dividing tasks into small steps will enable the learners to assimilate the idea easily and will help them in putting their thoughts on paper.
- providing low-stress opportunities will allow the learners to learn and write at their own pace and to foster their own strategy of learning and writing.

Hence, we can conclude that deficiency in the ability to write associated with impaired handwriting is a symptom of dysgraphia .

60(C). A good teaching-learning material is very necessary for effective teaching and facilitates the teaching-learning process in a proper way.
- Advantages of TLM are as follows:
- Facilitates learning and teaching
- Helps students to grasp concepts easily
- Makes classroom activities interesting

When these points are integrated, it can be rightly said as the teaching-learning process as it includes all above pints.

Accurate and realistic teaching-learning materials encourage healthy classroom interaction and are helpful in meeting individual differences.

61(C). Given:
$x^3 + x^2 + 16$ is exactly divisible by x, where x is a positive integer.
Let a number N be equal to $x^3 + x^2 + 16$.
$N = x^3 + x^2 + 16$
Now divide $\frac{N}{x}$
$\frac{N}{x} = \frac{x^3 + x^2 + 16}{x}$
$\Rightarrow x^2 + x + \left(\frac{16}{x}\right)$
As N is divisible by x so 16 must be divisible by x.
Values of x that can divide 16 are $1, 2, 4, 8$ and 16.
So, there are total 5 values of x that can divide N without leaving the remainder.

62(C). Given:
3^{99}

3^0 unit digit $3 \ldots$
After 4 power unit digits repeat again.
Now,
$\Rightarrow 3^{99} = \left(3^4\right)^{24} \times \left(3^3\right)$
$\Rightarrow 3^{99} = (1)^{24} \times 7 = (1) \times 7$
Unit place $= 1 \times 7 = 7$
$\therefore$ The unit place of 3^{99} is 7.

63(C). If 5 digit number $535ab$ is divisible by 3,7 and 11, then we can say number also divisible by 231 because $= (3 \times 7 \times 11 = 231)$.
Let's assume the largest number be 53599.
Now on dividing 53599 by 231
We get approx 232.03
So, the actual number $= 231 \times 232 = 53592$
$\therefore a = 9$ and $b = 2$.
$\Rightarrow \left(a^2 - b^2 + ab\right) = \left(9^2 - 2^2 + 9 \times 2\right)$
$\Rightarrow \left(a^2 - b^2 + ab\right) = 81 - 4 + 18$
$\therefore \left(a^2 - b^2 + ab\right) = 95$

64(D). Given,
$x = 7 - 4\sqrt{3}$
$\Rightarrow x = 4 + 3 - 4\sqrt{3}$
$\Rightarrow x = (2)^2 + (\sqrt{3})^2 - 2 \times 2\sqrt{3}$
As we know,
$a^2 + b^2 - 2ab = (a - b)^2$
$\Rightarrow x = (2 - \sqrt{3})^2$
$\Rightarrow \sqrt{x} = 2 - \sqrt{3} \ldots (i)$
$\Rightarrow \frac{1}{\sqrt{x}} = \frac{1}{2 - \sqrt{3}} \times \frac{2 + \sqrt{3}}{2 + \sqrt{3}}$
$\Rightarrow \frac{1}{\sqrt{x}} = 2 + \sqrt{3} \ldots (ii)$
From equation (i) and (ii), we get
$\sqrt{x} + \frac{1}{\sqrt{x}}$
$= 2 - \sqrt{3} + 2 + \sqrt{3}$
$= 4$

65(D). Given:
$A + B\sqrt{6} = \frac{(4 - 3\sqrt{6})}{(5 + 2\sqrt{6})}$
Formula:

$(a - b)(a + b) = \left(a^2 - b^2\right)$
$A + B\sqrt{6} = \frac{(4 - 3\sqrt{6})}{(5 + 2\sqrt{6})}$
$\Rightarrow A + B\sqrt{6} = \frac{(4 - 3\sqrt{6})}{(5 + 2\sqrt{6})} \times \left[\frac{(5 - 2\sqrt{6})}{(5 - 2\sqrt{6})}\right]$
$\Rightarrow A + B\sqrt{6} = \frac{(4 - 3\sqrt{6})(5 - 2\sqrt{6})}{(25 - 24)}$
$\Rightarrow A + B\sqrt{6} = 20 - 8\sqrt{6} - 15\sqrt{6} + 36$
$\Rightarrow A + B\sqrt{6} = 56 - 23\sqrt{6}$
Compare on both side,
$A = 56$ and $B = -23$
$(A + B)^2 = (56 - 23)^2 = (33)^2 = 1089$

66(B). Given:
$(7x - 10y) = 8$ and $xy = 5$
Formula used:
$(a - b)^2 = a^2 + b^2 - 2ab$
$\Rightarrow (7x - 10y)^2 = 8^2$

$\Rightarrow 49x^2 + 100y^2 = 764$

67(D).

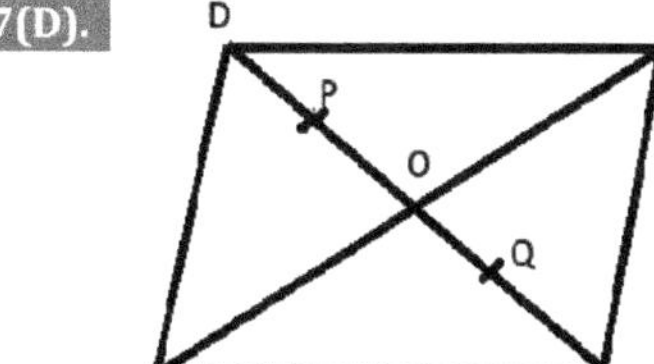

Since diagonal of a parallelogram bisect each other,
$\therefore BO = OD = \frac{18}{2} = 9 \text{ cm}$
P centroid of $\triangle ADC$
$OP = \frac{1}{3}OD = \frac{1}{3} \times 9 = 3 \text{ cm}$
Q centroid of $\triangle ABC$
$OQ = \frac{1}{3}OB = \frac{1}{3} \times 9 = 3 \text{ cm}$
$\therefore PQ = OP + OQ = 3 + 3 = 6 \text{ cm}$

68(C). A polygon of 12 sides has 12 vertices.
By joining any two of the vertices, we obtain either a side or a diagonal of the polygon.
Number of all straight lines obtained by joining 2 vertices at a time
$= {}^{12}C_2 = \frac{12 \times 11}{2 \times 1}$
$= 66$
These straight lines include 12 sides of the polygon.
$\therefore$ The number of diagonals of the polygon
$= 66 - 12$
$= 54$

69(D). Given,
The chord of a circle is equal to its radius.
As we know,
If all sides of a triangle are equal, then each angle of the triangle is $60°$.

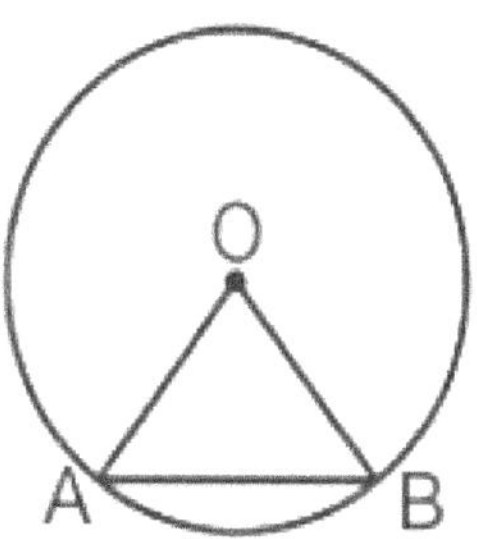

From the following figure AB is a chord and OA and OB are radius of the circle.
According to the question,
AB = OA = OB
Now, we can say ABC is an equilateral triangle, then
$\angle AOB = 60°$
$\therefore$ The angle subtended by the chord at the centre of the circle is 60°.

Height of pyramid $= 10 \text{ cm}$
As we know,
Lateral surface $= \left(\frac{1}{2}\right) \times$ Perimeter of the base $\times$ Slant height

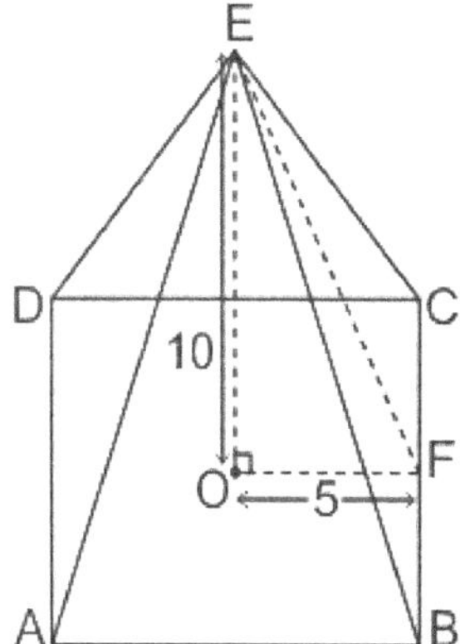

Slant height $= EF$
Height $= EO = 10 \text{ cm}$
$OF = \frac{10}{2} = 5 \text{ cm}$
In $\triangle EOF$,
$EF^2 = OE^2 + OF^2$
$= 10^2 + 5^2$
$\Rightarrow EF = \sqrt{125}$
$= 5\sqrt{5}$
Slant height $= EF = 5\sqrt{5} \text{ cm}$
Perimeter of the base $= 4 \times 10$
$= 40 \text{ cm}$
Lateral surface $= \left(\frac{1}{2}\right) \times$ Perimeter of the base $\times$ Slant height $= \left(\frac{1}{2}\right) \times 40 \times 5\sqrt{5}$
$= 100\sqrt{5} \text{ cm}$
$\therefore$ The lateral surface are of the pyramid is $100\sqrt{5} \text{ cm}^2$.

71(A). In the figure shown below, the shaded region is the region bounded externally by the square and internally by the circle,

Given:

Side of square = 2acm

Area of square = (side)^2 = 4a^2 cm^2

∵ The circle touches the four sides of the square,

Diameter of circle = 2a cm

Area of circle = $\left(\frac{\pi}{4}\right) \times$ (diameter)^2

= $(4 - \pi)$a^2 cm^2

72(A). Given,

Cost price of toy = Rs. 25

Selling price of toy = Rs. 30

As we know,

Profit = Selling price - Cost price

Profit = Rs. $(30 - 25)$ = Rs. 5

Profit percentage = $\left(\dfrac{\text{Profit}}{\text{Cost price}}\right) \times 100$

Profit percentage = $\left(\dfrac{5}{25}\right) \times 100 = 20\%$

So, the gain percentage is 20% .

73(C). Let the numbers be $x, x + 2, x + 4, x + 6$ and $x + 8$

According to question,

$\dfrac{[x+(x+2)+(x+4)+(x+6)+(x+8)]}{5} = 51$

$\Rightarrow 5x + 20 = 255$

$\Rightarrow x = 47$

So, required difference = $(47 + 8) - 47 = 8$

74(D). Given:

Covers 455 meters in 35 minutes

Speed = $\dfrac{\text{Distance}}{\text{Time}}$

Speed = 455 meters /35 minutes

But we need speed in km/hr

We know that,

1 km = 1000 meters

1 hour = 60 minutes

$\Rightarrow$ Speed = $\dfrac{\left(\frac{455}{10000}\right)}{\left(\frac{35}{60}\right)}$

$\Rightarrow$ Speed = $\dfrac{(455 \times 60)}{(1000 \times 35)}$

$\Rightarrow$ Speed = 0.78 km/hr

∴ Speed of a person is 0.78 km/hr .

75(A). Given:

LCM of two number = $28 \times HCF$

First number = 240

HCF + LCM = 1740

As we know,

LCM × HCF = first number × second number

Now,

Let HCF be x and the second number be y

HCF = x

LCM = $28x$

According to the question,

The Sum of the HCF and the LCM is 1740

HCF + LCM = 1740

$\Rightarrow x + 28x = 1740$

$\Rightarrow 29x = 1740$

$\Rightarrow x = 60$

∴ HCF = 60, LCM = $28 \times 60 = 1680$

By using formula,

LCM × HCF = first number × second number

$1680 \times 60 = 240 \times y$

$\Rightarrow y = 420$

∴ The other number is 420 .

76(A). Given,

$16 - 2 \div 14 + 6 \times 2$

= $\dfrac{392 \overset{14}{-2}}{14}$

= $\dfrac{390}{14}$

= $27\dfrac{12}{14}$

= $27\dfrac{6}{7}$

77(B). Nature of mathematics:

- Mathematics plays a very important role in education because it has universal applicability i.e., it is present everywhere in our life from buying vegetables to predicting the weather of different cities at a time. Therefore, it has a wide scope of generalization.
- The teaching of mathematics proceeds from the concrete to abstract concepts of mathematics. In primary classes, the mathematical concepts are concrete in nature which moves to abstract from one class to the next class.
- At the primary level, the teaching of concrete concepts helps in developing the basic mathematical skills that are required to handle abstractions in the later level of learning.
- And then in the upper primary and higher classes the abstract concepts of mathematics are taught like algebra, trigonometry, etc.

Thus it is clear that primary level mathematics is concrete and does not require abstraction is not correct with regard to the nature of mathematics.

78(D). The basic characteristic of pure mathematics are:

- Applicability and Effectiveness,
- Abstraction and Generality,
- Objectivity,
- Simplicity,
- Logical Derivation, Axiomatic Arrangement,
- Precision, Correctness, Evolution through Dialectic.
- Rigour, Purity, and Beauty.

Pure Mathematics solve mathematical problems and not all the problems. Therefore, It is a tool for solving problems does not express the view of pure mathematicians regarding mathematics.

79(C). Cuisenaire rods are the teaching aids for teaching and learning mathematics. A Cuisenaire rod is made up of squares equal to the number the rod represents, and the rods help us visualize math operations.

This aid is providing hands-on experience to students which helps to explore mathematics and learn mathematical concepts:

- Arithmetical operations
- Working with fractions

80(D). A good mathematics curriculum should present suitable learning experiences to foster common needs as citizens and special needs as an individual. The main consideration should be given to desirable pupil growth within the overall purposes of all levels of education.

- The negative numbers concept should be introduced at the upper primary level for better understanding.
- The concept of area measurement should be introduced at both levels as per the conceptual understanding and difficulty level.
- The foundation of algebraic thinking can be laid at the primary level.
- The concept of fractions should be introduced only at the primary level.

81(A). The mathematical expressions remain constant irrespective of the languages that are used to describe them i.e., to explain any of the mathematical theorems in different regional languages. /, ? and & are symbols used in all the subjects being learned.

Therefore, the symbol that is unique to the mathematics language is %.

82(A). Literal meaning of the verb 'mathematize' is 'to reduce to or as if to mathematical formulas.' In general, the term "mathematization" refers to the application of concepts, procedures and methods developed in mathematics to the objects of other disciplines or at least of other fields of knowledge. In the above situation:

- To arrange rectangular arrays, students need to have basic ideas about the properties of a rectangle.
- To arrange tiles students should have ideas of area, perimeter, and factors so that tiles can be adjusted on the required area according to size.

- Tiles are considered as 2D figures so volume has no role to play in this context.

Hence, in the above situation, the concepts of Area, Factors, and Perimeter are addressed.

83(B). At the elementary stage, all the mathematical concepts and procedures can be included in ten broad areas:
- Number (Real number system)
- Number operations (Four processes)
- Fractions (including decimals)
- Space and spatial thinking
- Measurement (both standard and non-standard measures)
- Problem-solving
- Patterns
- Data handling
- Basic algebraic processes (only in the

procedures are not a dimension of the assessment of mathematical learning.

84(C). Remedial Teaching is an integral part of the teaching-learning program, also known as compensatory or corrective teaching.

Purpose of Remedial Teaching:
- To eliminate ineffective habits
- To make learners learn better by giving additional help
- To teach again the language items not properly learned
- To arise learners' interest in learning with stimulating approaches
- To transmit practical experiences to learners according to their diverse needs

Hence, it becomes clear that the purpose of remedial teaching is to teach again the language items not properly learnt.

85(C). In a math class, a teacher follows a proper sequence in teaching which is usually practically followed in any classroom. This is known as classroom operations. It plays a major role in Mathematics learnings and one of the challenges that teacher face in a classroom depending on different factors i.e., nature of the content, the learning style of the students, knowledge of teaching methods and also depends on the ability to use mathematical tools. It should be noted that teaching methods, ability to use math tools comes under the vast category called classroom operations. So instead of choosing three different opinions, one single opinion is selected which covers all the three aspects.

Hence, 'Class Room operations' are the major problem of teaching Mathematics.

86(B). Underachievement is defined as a large discrepancy between the child's performance (at school) and his innate ability.
- When a child with a high I.Q. level is performing poorly, he is said to be an underachiever.
- A child who has average intelligence, but whose performance is below average is also said to be a low achiever.
- Factors are those related to the underachievement in mathematics, which surrounds the individual as well as to his unique persona (e.g., socio-economic level and educational background of the family, the school climate, the language background, and students' attitudes toward mathematics).
- Among social variables, the factors which were considered very widely are socio-economic status, parental involvement and parent's education

87(A). Most of animal fats are Saturated fats, A saturated fat is a type of fat in which the fatty acid chains have all or predominantly single bonds.Saturated fat is mainly found in animal foods, but a few plant foods are also high in saturated fats, such as coconut, coconut oil, palm oil, and palm kernel oil.

88(D). Fruits taste sweet because they contain fructose.

Fructose is a type of sugar known as a monosaccharide. Like other sugars, fructose provides four calories per gram. Fructose is also known as "fruit sugar" because it primarily occurs naturally in many fruits. It also occurs naturally in other plant foods such as honey, sugar beets, sugar cane and vegetables.

89(C). Photoperiod is the physiological reaction of organisms to the length of day or night. It occurs in plants and animals. It can also be defined as the developmental responses of plants to the relative lengths of light and dark periods. Photoperiod exclusively affects the reproduction in seasonal breeders, both plants and animals.

90(A). Growth by cell division occurs continuously in plants and only up to a certain age in animals.

A multicellular organism increased its mass by cell division. In plants, growth continues throughout life as they have meristematic areas where cell divisions occur continuously. In animals, growth occurs to a certain age after which cells divide only to replace worn out and lost cells.

91(C). The specific resistance of a rod of copper as compared to that of thin wire of copper is same.

Specific resistance of a conductor depends on the nature of material but is independent of the dimension of the conductor. Thus specific resistance of rod of copper as compared to that of thin wire of copper is same.

92(B). Curie temperature is the temperature above which a ferromagnetic material becomes paramagnetic material.

Curie Temperature is the temperature at which a magnetic material undergoes a sharp change in its magnetic properties. Above this temperature, some materials lose their magnetism. Above this temperature, ferromagnetic material becomes paramagnetic.

When a ferromagnetic material is heated to Curie temperature, it disrupts the arrangements of the molecules and a weak magnetic behaviour remains. This weak magnetic behaviour is called Paramagnetic.

skin of some animals. These follicles are located in the upper layer of the skin called the epidermis.

Thus, wool is obtained from the hair of Sheep, cashmere goats, camel, and yak.

94(C). The thermosetting polymer is a polymer that can be irreversibly hardened to the desired shape. It is hardened by the process of curing of a soft solid or viscous liquid prepolymer or resin. Curing is induced by heat or suitable radiation and may be promoted by high pressure, or mixing with a catalyst. Once hardened, a thermoset cannot be melted for reshaping. Some examples of a thermosetting polymer are Polyurethanes, Polyurea, Bakelite, Urea-formaldehyde, etc.

95(A). Newton's first law states that, if a body is at rest or moving at a constant speed in a straight line, it will remain at rest or keep moving in a straight line at constant speed unless it is acted upon by force. This postulate is known as the law of inertia. The law of inertia was first formulated by Galileo for horizontal motion on Earth.

96(C). The sole of the shoe is made to increase the grooved friction.

Friction is a contact force when two surfaces interact. Friction is a force that resists the sliding or rolling of one solid object over another.

97(D). A nuclear explosion is not a natural phenomenon. The natural phenomenon is referred to as a phenomenon where no human involvement is there. The reasons for the occurrence of such a phenomenon are completely natural.

Types of natural phenomena include Weather, fog, thunder, tornadoes; biological processes, decomposition, germination; physical processes, wave propagation, erosion; tidal flow and natural disasters such as electromagnetic pulses, volcanic eruptions, cyclones, lightning, earthquakes, midnight sun and polar night.

98(D). Lignite is a mineral known as brown diamond. is easily combustible with carbon content up to 60-70%. Lignite is the stone coal of the inferior class. Its color is brown or black-brown and the relative density is also less than stone coal. It exhibits the initial stage of conversion of vegetative tissue.

99(C). Thrust is the force that moves an aircraft through the air. Thrust is used to overcome the drag of an airplane, and to overcome the weight of a rocket.
- Drag Force: The air resistance that tends to slow the forward movement of an airplane.

the wing and slower below the wing, creating a difference in pressure that tends to keep an airplane flying.

100(A). Earth's magnetic field is due to the dynamo effect.
Dynamo Effect : The dynamo effect is a geophysical theory that explains the origin of the Earth's main magnetic field in terms of a self-exciting (or self-sustaining) dynamo. Electric currents are generated by the movement of convection currents of a mixture of molten iron and nickel in the Earth's outer core, and magnetic fields are generated from those electric currents as the Earth rotates on its axis.

101(C). The speed of light is dependent on the refractive index of the medium it is travelling in. The higher the refractive index of the medium, the lower is the speed of light. Hence, the speed of light in a medium is inversely proportional to the refractive index of the medium in which it is travelling through.
The denser a medium is the more is its refractive index and thus, the lesser is the speed of light. The speed of light is thus minimum in solids as they are denser and will be maximum in a vacuum as a vacuum is the least dense medium.

102(B). Elements of the IInd period are known as Bridge elements. Bridge elements are the gap between the alkali and alkali earth metals (groups 1 & 2) on one side and the metalloids/nonmetals (groups 13 - 18) on the other side.

103(D). In the hepatic portal system, the hepatic portal vein drains blood from the intestine to the liver.
Hepatic portal system is the vascular connection between the digestive tract and the liver. The hepatic portal vein carries blood from the intestine to the liver before

it is delivered to the systemic circulation.

104(A). The deficiency of Vitamin K causes the failure of blood clotting. The process that prevents excessive bleeding both inside and outside the body is known as clotting. Vitamin K plays an important role in blood clotting.
Vitamin K is generally of two types: Vitamin K1 which comes from our food especially leafy vegetables and other is Vitamin K2 which is produced by our body. The test which is to detect blood clotting and to check the deficiency of vitamin K is prothrombin time (PT).

105(B). The sound wave is a longitudinal wave.
Longitudinal Wave:
- A wave in which the particles of the medium vibrate in the same direction of
- The waves which are produced in the air are always longitudinal waves.
- Example: The waves produced in spring when it is pushed and pulled at one end are longitudinal waves.

106(D). Science is not static, rather dynamic in nature because science is a field of new researches and inventions.
Nature of science:
- Science is always tentative.
- Science promotes scepticism.
- Science as an approach to investigation.
- Science is an interdisciplinary area of learning.
- Science is a particular way of looking at nature.
- Science is a process of constructing knowledge.
- Science demands perseverance from its practitioners.

107(B). Desirable Aims of Science Education at the Upper Primary Level:
- To provide practical knowledge of the subject matter content.
- To provide the latest knowledge to develop scientific knowledge scientific appreciation and scientific temper among the students.
- To know the facts and principles of science and its applications.
- To encourage them to learn about nature to develop the love for nature and to try to conserve natural resources and prevent pollution.
- To imbibe the values of honesty, integrity, and cooperation.
- To develop the scientific attitude and to use it for the development works to have the open-mindedness for objective decision making and critical thinking.
- Students should be aware of the global dimension of science, as a universal activity with consequences for our lives

and subject to social, economic, political, environmental, cultural, and ethical factors.
- To nurture the natural curiosity, aesthetic sense, and creativity in science and technology.
- Students should be able to understand how science and technology are interdependent and assist each other in the development of knowledge and technological applications.

Hence, it becomes clear that gaining the knowledge available through memorizing is not a desirable aim of science education at upper primary level.

108(C). A Science laboratory refers to a building equipped for scientific experiments to explore knowledge and the tools like laboratory apparatus used in
- These apparatuses provide hands-on experience to the learners.
- Application-based Learning is the best way to understand a concept.
- Clear understanding empowers a learner to think clearly and hence promotes innovation.

109(C). The expository transmission approach to teaching science in the classroom is completely teacher-centred.
Expository Approach:
- Expository Approach is also known as the Transmission Approach.
- In this approach, the teacher is communicating maximum information to the students in a minimum of time.
- This approach helps the teacher to cover the content to be taught to the students.
- This approach is widely used across all the subjects and different levels of education by the teacher.
- The main proponent of this method is David P. Ausubel.
- In the expository approach all the cues provided by the teacher while teaching, the deductive thinking wherein abstract content is differentiated by the teacher giving appropriate examples to the students.
- Teaching Learning process is totally controlled by the teacher.

110(B). The discovery approach is a type of teaching that encourages students to take a more active role in their learning process by answering a series of questions or solving problems designed to introduce a general concept. There are three types of methods that are included under discovery approach:
- Open Discovery Method: Based on inductive reasoning and followed by scientists.
- Guided Discovery Method: This too is

based on inductive reasoning and used by teachers. The pattern that is used in Guided Discovery method is Example-Rule.

- Deductive Discovery Method: It is used to discover by using the deductive method, that is, something can be discovered fro some general principle.

111(C). Teachers and researchers have developed a number of types of questions, which can be used to foster creativity.

- Future problem-solving questions: These questions require the students to design and redesign which involve a good deal of innovation. They make the students look differently at things and make them think in different ways. Ex: A machine to dig the tunnel without disturbing the traffic on the road.

and children learn to be aware of unusual characteristics and look beyond the obvious. Ex: Why is a fountain pen like a tap.

- Consequences questions: These questions pose situations or events that might not have happened or will never happen. Such questions make the children to imagine and write the consequences of such an event takes place. Ex: Suppose the petrol supply on earth vanishes all of a sudden.
- Hypothetical questions: In this type of questions students have to go beyond the available data (their learning) and synthesise them with their personality characteristics. Ex: If you were the manager of a bank?
- Provocative questions: The children may be taught a passage or they may be asked to go through a passage and proactive question may be put. They help the children to imagine and go beyond the information provided in the passage. Ex: What would have Gandhiji done had he lived today?
- Questions seeking new relationships: Sometimes theses questions look to be funny or crazy and may lead to frustration on the part of the students, but they will enjoy later. Ex: Is month a mile?
- Divergent questions: These questions require the students to break from the fixed pattern of one question one answer and develop many relevant responses. The cost or time need not be an inhibiting factor in such relevant responses. Ex: A town hidden beneath the mud has been found. What might have been the reasons as to why the town might have gone underground?
- Challenging assumptions questions: These questions help children develop a functional understanding of the world.

The assumptions are being questioned which have been accepted for a long time. These exercise the mind and children develop a new perspective. Ex: Why questions like why should be respecting our parents?

112(B). Poster is a symbolic representation of a single idea. As a single idea is depicted posters are usually bold, eye-catching to attract learners for giving a message. Posters have both visual and textual components.

- Posters acts as the resource to deal with the topic of 'conservation of fuels'.
- Posters convey information quickly and the drawings or relevant slogans catch the eye of almost all the students.
- Many posters can be read and understood in a short period as

v students and not every student might read up in that much depth about the topic.

113(C). Continuous and Comprehensive Evaluation (CCE) refers to a system of school-based evaluation of students that covers all aspects of students' development.

- The objective of CCE in science means routine activities and exercises to assess learning.
- CCE ensures to make evaluation an integral part of learning through diagnostic and remedial teaching.
- The comprehensive assessment of all-round development of the child's personality includes assessment in the scholastic and co-scholastic aspect in student's growth.

Hence, from the above-mentioned points, it becomes clear that continuous and comprehensive evaluation in science means routine activities and exercises to assess learning.

114(D). Remedial Teaching: During learning, a child makes mistakes willingly-unwillingly or due to some alternative conceptions. It is the job of a teacher to help students to correct those mistakes after diagnosing them. The method so followed is known as remedial teaching. The following are its characteristics:

- It can be used for improving language skills.
- To rectify a particular problem area, it can be used. For example, a student is confused between the pronunciation of 'no' and 'know', he can be taught the concept of silent letters.
- It is carried out after the identification of problems and challenges faced by students.
- A teacher should be well aware of students' strengths and weaknesses to apply this method.

- It is a systematic process as the teacher first diagnoses the problem of students and then applies appropriate remedial methods.

Hence, we conclude that remedial teaching should be planned after diagnosing the learning difficulties of the students in science teaching.

115(C). If most of the students of the class are unable to learn then the teacher should try to look for the possible reasons for this. He should bring modification in his method of teaching as may be due to his inaccurate teaching style, the students are not able learn properly.

He should use such teaching methodologies which gives opportunities to students to observe, explore, learn, and practice in a natural environment.

writing answers on the blackboard is not a good thing to do by a teacher as it will limit the responses of students and can make them inactive and uninterested in learning because the students will think that the teacher will eventually give them answers and they will not even try to give answers. Extra classes should be taken for specific students who are facing difficulties in learning some specific concepts but here most of the students are not able learn properly which is pointing out that there is a problem in teaching methodology. Sending complaints to the guardians of the students will not be beneficial in this situation as the students are having problem in learning which can be cured completely by the intervention of their teacher only.

116(D). Sulphuric acid is the chemical name of 'oil of vitriol'.

- Sulphuric acid is a dense, colourless, oily, corrosive liquid.
- It is one of the most commercially important of all chemicals.
- It is prepared industrially by the reaction of water with sulfur trioxide.
- Vitriol is any of certain hydrated sulfates or sulfuric acid.

Uses of Sulphuric acid (H_2SO_4):

- In lead storage battery.
- In the manufacturing of HCl.
- In the manufacturing of Alum.
- In the manufacturing of fertilisers, drugs, detergents and explosives.

117(A). Given,

Total number of teachers $= 1800$,

Physics $= 17\%$

Chemistry $= 23\%$

Now,

If $\dfrac{2}{9}$ th of physics are female teachers,

Then,

Male teachers $= 1 - \frac{2}{9} = \frac{7}{9}$ th of physics

Let's take $x\%$ of male physics teacher equal to Chemistry teachers,

Then,

$x\%$ of Chemistry teacher $= \frac{7}{9}$ th of physics

Let's take $x\%$ of male physics teacher equal to Chemistry teachers,

Then,

$x\%$ of Chemistry teacher $= \frac{7}{9}$ th of physics

$\Rightarrow x\%$ of $(23\%$ of 1800 $) = \frac{7}{9}$ th $(17\%$ of 1800 $)$

$\Rightarrow x\%$ of $23 = \frac{7}{9}$ th of 17

$\Rightarrow x = \frac{7}{9} \times \frac{17}{23} \times 100$

$\Rightarrow x = 57.4\% \approx 57\%$

118(B). Given,

Total number of teachers $= 1800$

Now,

(Chemistry + English + Biology) % of Total number of teachers

$= (23 + 27 + 12)\%$ of 1800

$= 62\%$ of 1800

$= \frac{62}{100} \times 1800$

$= 1116$

119(B). Given,

Total number of teachers $= 1800$

English $= 27\%$

Physics $= 17\%$

Mathematics $= 10\%$

Biology $= 12\%$

Now,

Required difference $= [($ English $+$ Physics $) - ($ Mathematics $+$ Biology$)] \%$ of 1800

$= [(27 + 17) - (13 + 12)]\%$ of 1800

$= (44 - 25)\%$ of 1800

$= 342$

120(A). Given:

5 years ago, my sister's age was 5 times my age.

Now, my sister's age is 3 times my age.

Calculation:

Let my present age be "x" years and my sister's age be "y" years.

According to the question,

y = 3x ----(1)

5 years ago, the relation between their age would be:

y - 5 = 5(x - 5) ----(2)

Putting the value of y from equation (1) in equation (2),

3x - 5 = 5(x – 5)

$\Rightarrow$ 3x – 5x = 5 – 25

$\Rightarrow$ -2x = -20

$\Rightarrow$ x = 10 years

Child Development and Pedagogy

1. **Which of the following statement is correct about the process of development of an individual?**
   (a) It is uni-dimensional in nature.
   (b) It is influenced only by heredity of an individual.
   (c) There is cultural diversity in the process of development.
   (d) Development is only based on environmental factors.

2. **The belief that children's behaviour can be modified by**
   (b) Both heredity and environment
   (c) Environment only
   (d) Neither heredity nor environment

3. **Most classrooms in India are multilingual and this needs to be seen as ____by the teacher.**
   (a) a problem   (b) a resource
   (c) an obstacle   (d) a bother

4. **Individuals who have the ability to understand the motives, feelings and behaviours of others to bond with them are high on____intelligence in Howard Gardner's theory.**
   (a) naturalistic
   (b) interpersonal
   (c) intrapersonal
   (d) spatial

5. **Monozygotic is to ____ twins as dizygotic is to ____ twins.**
   (a) Male, female
   (b) Female, male
   (c) Fraternal, identical
   (d) Identical, fraternal

6. **Who used the word IQ first?**
   (a) Thorndike
   (b) William stern
   (c) Alfred Binet
   (d) Terman

7. **Vygotsky's social development theory laid the foundations for:**
   (a) Behaviourism
   (b) Humanism
   (c) Constructivism
   (d) Operant Conditioning Theory

8. **Kohlberg's idea of moral development has levels.**
   (a) Three   (b) Four
   (c) Two   (d) Eight

9. **On the basis of child psychology which statement is appropriate?**
   (a) Every child is same.
   (b) Every child is special.
   (c) Some children are special.
   (d) Some children are same.

10. **A teacher wants her students to know about government schemes through primary sources. Which**
    (b) An interview with a Block Development Officer
    (c) A survey of schemes in the students' neighbourhood
    (d) A report on expenditure incurred, on various schemes in the student's neighbourhood.

11. **For which group of learners, sign-language method is the most appropriate?**
    (a) Visually impaired
    (b) Hearing impaired
    (c) Mentally retareded
    (d) Physically disabled

12. **The hyperactive children need:**
    (a) Special attention in the classroom
    (b) A separate classroom
    (c) Special teachers
    (d) Special curriculum

13. **The term used to describe 'reading disability' is:**
    (a) Dyslexia   (b) Dysgraphia
    (c) Dyscalculia   (d) Dysparaxia

14. **The stage of creative problem solving in which the individuals do not give attention to the problem is:**
    (a) Translation   (b) Illumination
    (c) Incubation   (d) Preparation

15. **Which IQ range is called trainable IQ level of mentally retarded children?**
    (a) 70 - 79
    (b) 50 - 69
    (c) 35 - 50
    (d) 35 and below

16. **Which of the following is not considered as a factor of cognition?**
    (a) Anger   (b) Hunger
    (c) Retreat   (d) Fear

17. **'Choice of challenge' is a characteristic of which of the following?**
    (a) Values
    (b) Motivation
    (c) Discipline
    (d) Inclusive education

18. **When a child gets bored while doing a task, it is a sign that:**
    (a) the task may have become mechanically repetitive.
    (d) the child needs to be disciplined.

19. **Which of the following factors affect learning?**
    A. Motivation of the learner
    B. Maturation of the learner
    C. Teaching strategies
    D. Physical and emotional health of the learner
    (a) A, B and C   (b) A, B C and D
    (c) A and D   (d) A and C

20. **____ exhibits a basic level of order, but the teacher still struggles to maintain it.**
    (a) Adequate classroom environment
    (b) Orderly restrictive learning environment
    (c) Orderly enabling learning environment
    (d) Dysfunctional classroom environment

21. **Primary objective of analysing errors in student's work is:**
    (a) to rank students and segregate them in ability-based groups.
    (b) to understand children's thinking.
    (c) to reprimand students for making any kind of mistakes.
    (d) to compare the efficiency of teachers at the school.

22. **Which one of the following is not one of the stages of learning?**
    (a) Acquisition
    (b) Maintenance
    (c) Generalization
    (d) Adoption

23. **If a previously learned task**

impedes a new task, which is being learnt. This transfer of learning will be:
(a) Positive Transfer
(b) Negative Transfer
(c) Zero Transfer
(d) Primary

24. Several research studies show that teachers have more overall interacting with boys than girls. What is the correct explanation for this?
(a) Boys need more attention than girls.
(b) This is an example of gender bias in teaching.
(c) Boys are easier to manage than girls in the classroom.

teaches students is:
(a) Internal   (b) External
(c) Diagnostic   (d) Placement

29. Which of the following are examples of secondary socializing agency?
(a) Family and neighbourhood
(b) Family and media
(c) School and media
(d) Media and neighbourhood

30. One of the basic principles of socializing individuals is:
(a) Religion   (b) Caste
(c) Education   (d) Imitation

Language - I: English

33. Which literary device is used in the following line:
"Blind eyes could blaze like meteors and be gay"
(a) Elegy
(b) Assonance
(c) Consonance
(d) None of the above

34. Which of the following statements is not true?
A) Men dislike the dark
B) One should not accept death gently
C) Even small actions could have had a great effect
D) One should rage against death
(a) A   (b) B
(c) C   (d) D

_____.
I. as concerning only girls and women (a biological category)
II. as an isolated category, not related to other issues
III. in terms of provision of equal facilities
(a) Only I   (b) I, II and III
(c) I and III   (d) II and III

26. The knowledge of individual differences helps teachers in:
(a) understanding the futility of working hard with backward students as they can never be at par with the class
(b) accepting and attributing the failure of students to their individual differences
(c) making their presentation style uniform to benefit all students equally
(d) assessing the individual needs of all students and teaching them accordingly

27. School-based assessment was introduced to:
(a) decentralize the power of Boards of school education in the country
(b) ensure the holistic development of all the students
(c) motivate teachers to punctiliously record all the activities of students for better interpretation of their progress
(d) encourage schools to excel by competing with the other schools in their area

28. The evaluation in which the evaluation is done by the one who

options:
Do not go gentle into that good night,
Old age should burn and rave at close of day;
Rage, rage against the dying of the light.
Though wise men at their end know dark is right,
Because their words had forked no lightning they
Do not go gentle into that good night.
Good men, the last wave by, crying how bright
Their frail deeds might have danced in a green bay,
Rage, rage against the dying of the light.
Wild men who caught and sang the sun in flight,
And learn, too late, they grieved it on its way,
Do not go gentle into that good night.
Grave men, near death, who see with blinding sight.
Blind eyes could blaze like meteors and be gay,
Rage, rage against the dying of the light.

31. What does light symbolize in the following expression:
"Rage, rage against the dying of the light".
(a) Life   (b) Heaven
(c) Inspiration   (d) Morning

32. What does this expression "Because their words had forked no lightning" mean?
(a) They haven't seen the lightning yet
(b) They haven't said anything about the lightning yet
(c) They were not smart enough to say anything
(d) They haven't said anything revolutionary to make a mark

(c) Imagery   (d) Alliteration

36. The word 'frail' in the line 'Good men, the last wave by, crying how bright/Their frail deeds might have danced in a green bay,' means:
(a) Good   (b) Cry
(c) Weak   (d) Lonely

Ques (37-45): Direction: After reading the passage given below, choose the best answer to each question that follows.

What advice would I give to new entrepreneurs who need funding? Forget about your business plan and buy a lottery ticket — your chances are better. My point is that when you need venture funding no one will give any money until you already have a marketable product. In other words, funding comes just when you do not need it. A myth is that the way to start a venture is to create a great business plan, perfect your pitch, and then present this to investors, starting with venture capitalists. If that does not work, you knock on the door of angel investors. But ask any entrepreneur who has called on venture capitalists and they will probably tell you that it is almost impossible to even get calls returned. If venture capitalists do respond and you are invited to present your idea, the process will drag on for many months while you borrow more and survive on hope. If you do hit the jackpot, you are required to let the investors make many of the business decisions in exchange for an investment. To be fair, most business plans do not deserve funding. Venture capitalists receive hundreds of plans every week, and few are worth the paper they are printed on. Everyone jumps on the same new trend, or the ideas are so far out that they have no chance of success. And great ideas are not enough: it takes experienced management, excellent execution, and a receptive market. It is hard for even the best venture capitals to identify the potential successes. So what should an entrepreneur do? What all new entrepreneurs should understand is that, even if you have a realistic business plan for a great idea that can change the world, you need to develop it yourself until you can prove it. Focus on validating your idea and building it up. Raise money to get started by begging and borrowing from family and friends. And be prepared to dip into your savings and credit cards, obtain second mortgages, and perhaps look for consulting work or customer advances. There is no single recipe for developing your business idea yourself, but there are some essential ingredients. Here are some pointers: Consult widely. Share your ideas

If you cannot find anyone who is excited about your idea, the chances are it is not worth being excited about. This may be time to reflect deeply and come up with another. Identify markets. Speak to anyone who can help you understand your target customers. If you can sell your concept, some customers may help you find it or agree to be a test site or a valuable reference. Customers do not usually know what they want, but they always know what they do not need. Make sure that there is a real need for your product. Start small. Your idea may be grand and have the potential to change the world, but you are only going to do this one step at a time. Look for simple solutions, test them and learn from the feedback. If you are starting a restaurant, work for someone else first. If you are creating a software product, learn by doing some consulting assignments or create some utilities. You do not have to start with the ultimate product. Watch every penny. Focus on revenue and profitability from the start. Find creative ways to earn cash by selling tactical products, prepaid licenses, or royalties. Pay employees partially in stock. Look for access to free hardware or premises. And sweep the floors yourself. In short, use any methods to avoid costs. Prepare for the worst. It is going to take longer than you think. There will likely be product problems, unhappy customers, employee turnover, and lots of financial challenges. You may even fail a number of times before you achieve your goals. By learning from each success and failure alike, you increase the odds that you eventually make it. Keep your integrity. Never forget the importance of business ethics and your own values. Ethics need to be carefully sewn into the fabric of any start-up. And the only way to reach long-

term success is by achieving outstanding customer satisfaction. With a lot of luck and hard work, you may build a successful company that markets products customers really want. It is very likely that by this stage, you receive phone calls from venture capitalists. This is the time to think of exit strategies and decide if you want to own a small piece of a big pie or a large piece of a small pie. (The passage taken from Book/News/Open source)

37. Which of the following statements is true as per the given passage?

(a) Investors always respond promptly to funding applications

(b) Venture Capitalist is a sure source of funding for new businesses

38. Which of the following advices are given by the writer in this passage?

(a) Make sure that you have enough money before you start your business

(b) Make sure you have secured an educational degree before you start your business

(c) Make sure that there is a real need for your product. Start small

(d) Make sure that you have approached an angel investor before you start your business

39. What are the two business ideas that are shared in the passage as examples?

(a) Starting a school and creating a web portal for selling grocery

(b) Starting a clothing store and creating a web portal for house hold services

(c) Starting a hospital and manufacturing a product

(d) Starting a restaurant and creating a software product

40. A. It is hard for even the best venture capitals to identify the potential successes.
B. Focus on validating your idea and building it up.

(a) According to the above passage, both A and B are true

(b) According to the above passage, both A and B are false

(c) According to the above passage A is true and is false

(d) According to the above passage is false and B is true

41. According to the given passage which of the following is NOT a correct statement?

(a) Ethics need to be carefully sewn into the fabric of any start-up

(b) Share your ideas with those who have done it before

(c) It also shows that the phenomenon is heterogeneous

(d) In other words, funding comes just when you do not need it

42. According to the passage which are the essential ingredients for developing a business idea?

(a) Identify market but hide the idea from others

(b) Consult widely. Share your ideas with entrepreneurs. Identify first even before you develop your idea

43. "Exit strategies", as mentioned in the passage, signifies:

(a) An entrepreneur's strategic plan to sell his or her ownership in a company to investors or another company

(b) An entrepreneur's strategic plan to execute the daily plan for his/her business

(c) An entrepreneur's strategic plan to conduct exit interviews for employees who plan to leave

(d) An entrepreneur's strategic plan to analyse market and exit from one product to another

44. The phrase "and few are worth the paper they are printed on" as exists in the above passage means:

(a) The ideas are good

(b) Hardly any idea is good

(c) Some ideas are good

(d) The few ideas that are good can get others to invest in it

45. "a marketable product" as mentioned in the passage signifies:

(a) A product that appeals to buyers and sell at a certain price range to generate profit

(b) A product that appeals to investors and help them get their money back

(c) A product whose market value is increasing continuously and becoming difficult for buyers to buy the same

(d) A product that is appreciated by the media houses and earn revenue from advertisements

46. Pick the option that includes the correct matches of column A with column B.

Column 'A'	Column 'B'
a. The Structural Approach	(i) patterns or structures of the language
b. The Humanistic Approach	(ii) oral/aural work and pronunciation taught through drills
c. Communicational Teaching	(iii) emphasized the importance of creating environments
d. The Au	(iv) a five-year project of exploratory teach

(a) a-(ii), b-(iii), c-(iv), d-(i)

(b) a-(iv), b-(ii), c-(i), d-(iii)

(c) a-(i), b-(iii), c-(iv), d-(ii)

(d) a-(i), b-(ii), c-(iii), d-(iv)

47. According to National Curriculum Framework 2005, which one of the following is NOT an objective of language teaching-learning?

(a) The competence to understand what one hears.

(b) Ability to read with comprehension.

(c) Effortless expression.

(d) To know the history of languages.

48. Anshu is teaching English to class VI students and her class seems to be noisy. She is probably:

(a) teaching a crowded class.

(b) not able to manage a class.

(c) not bothered about the noise.

(d) having group work.

49. When a test item expects the learners to use tense forms, voice, connectors, prepositions, and articles accurately, such an approach can be called:

(a) integrated grammar testing

(b) asserted grammar practice

(c) mixed grammar task

(d) improper grammar testing

50. Students learning a language often lack confidence when speaking due to the language's unique pronunciation rules. One way to overcome this problem is:

(a) children reading aloud in class

(b) using game-like activities which require verbal interactions in the classroom

(c) conducting special speech therapy with a counsellor

(d) correcting errors whenever they happen

51. Children substitute sounds made in the back of the mouth (g, k) for sounds made in the front of the mouth (d, t) so that tab becomes cab and dot becomes got. This type of error is known as:

(a) Reading error

(b) Phonological error

(c) Both (A) and (B)

(d) None of the above

52. In_______approach a teacher

(a) Guided reading

(b) Read aloud

(c) Free reading

(d) Formal reading

53. Teaching aids are used for making a lesson
A. interesting
B. effective
C. stimulating
D. exciting

(a) A, B and C   (b) A, B, C and D

(c) B and C   (d) A and D

54. Directions: In the question below is given a statement you have to decide which of them logically follows beyond a reasonable doubt from the information given in the statement. Give the answer.
(a) Thorough diagnosis with a pretest.
(b) Frequent planned remedial lessons.
(c) Co-operation with the parents.
Which of the above are general principles of remedial teaching?

(a) (a) and (b)

(b) (a) and (c)

(c) (b) and (c)

(d) All of the above

55. "Children deserve most of the credit for the language that they acquire." 'This observation implies that in modern classrooms:

(a) students pursue their own lines of inquiry.

(b) students need not attend L2 classes.

(c) students may choose L2 on their own.

(d) the teacher established the task support or facilitates learning.

56. Which is not a correct parameter of reading skill assessment?

(a) Recognition of words in a text

(b) Reading aloud

(c) Comprehension questions

(d) Enriched vocabulary

57. Which of the following is least important to you as a language teacher?

(a) Development of the abilities to use a language

(b) Knowledge of grammatical rules

(c) Knowledge of language skills

(d) Knowledge of constitutional values

(a) It should be easily available in nearby market

(b) It should not be very expensive

(c) The student should make them themselves

(d) It should be contextualised and fit to be used in an integrated manner

59. The intonation of question-tags is often quoted as a case of a difference in meaning being falling and rising tone. Thus the question tag 'aren't they' in "They are coming on Tuesday, aren't they" means:

(a) The speaker is comparatively certain that the information is correct

(b) The speaker is not certain that the information is correct

(c) Both of the above are correct

(d) None of the above is correct

60. What could be the reason to ask questions from listeners in story-based lessons?
I. To check pupil' s understanding and learning.
II. To encourage pupil' s to think about and express their reactions to a story or character.

(a) Only I

(b) Only II

(c) Neither I nor II

(d) Both I and II

Mathematics and Science

61. What is the sum of a rational number and its additive inverse?

(a) 0   (b) 1
(c) 2   (d) 3

62. What will be the sum of the different prime factors of the number 27720?
(a) 28   (b) 17
(c) 40   (d) 30

63. Which of the following statement is true in the context of nature of mathematics?
(a) Mathematics is consistent
(b) Mathematics is not procedural
(c) Mathematics is rigid
(d) Mathematics is different from other science

64. Which of the following problems

symmetry in the flag
(b) Draw the mirror image of a given figure
(c) How many lines of symmetry are there in a given figure?
(d) To draw a line of symmetry in a given geometrical figure

65. Which of the following statement is incorrect?
(a) Mathematics learning helps to apply mathematical concepts and theorems to new situations.
(b) Mathematics provides a clear understanding of laws of nature.
(c) Mathematics learning helps to think alternative methods of solving problems.
(d) None of the above

66. The section, 'Practice Time' included in different topics in mathematics textbook aims at:
(a) providing fun and enjoyment to students
(b) having a change in daily routine
(c) ensuring better utilization of time
(d) providing extended learning opportunities

67. The teacher is teaching arithmetic in the class. She continues to repeat a particular concept until it gets fixed in the mind of the students. The approach the teacher is following in the class is called:
(a) Meaningful approach
(b) Drill approach
(c) Incidental approach
(d) Social approach

68. A number consists of two digits. If the digits interchange places and the new number is added to the original number, then the resulting number will be divisible by which of the following:
(a) 3   (b) 5
(c) 9   (d) 11

69. In $\triangle ABC$, $\angle B$ is 25° more than $\angle A$ and $\angle C$ is 5° more than four time $\angle A$. The biggest angle is ____.
(a) 25°   (b) 50°
(c) 95°   (d) 105°

70. AB = 8 cm and CD = 6 cm are two parallel chords on the same side of the centre of a circle. The distance between them is 1 cm. The radius of

71. The values in x and y in the given figure are measure of angles. The value of x + y is equal to:

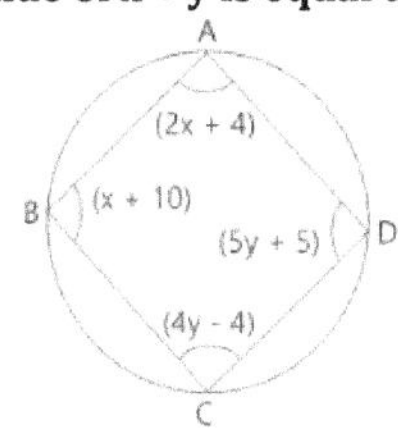

(a) 90°   (b) 85°
(c) 75°   (d) 65°

72. A semi-circular plate is rolled up to form a conical surface. The angle between the generator and the axis of the cone is:
(a) 60°   (b) 45°
(c) 30°   (d) 15°

73. A rectangular block of length 20 cm , breadth 15 cm and height 10 cm are cut up into an exact number of equal cubes. The least possible number of cubes will be:
(a) 12   (b) 16
(c) 20   (d) 24

74. If the roots of the equation $a(b-c)x^2 + b(c-a)x + c(a-b) = 0$ are equal, then which one of the following is correct?
(a) a, b and c are in AP
(b) a, b and c are in GP
(c) a, b and c are in HP
(d) a, b and c do not follow any regular pattern

75. If $a - b = 3$ and $a^3 - b^3 = 279$, then what is the value of $a^3 + b^3$?

(a) 317   (b) 407
(c) 297   (d) 502

76. If $a^3 + 3a^2 + 9a = 1$, then what is the value of $a^3 + \left(\frac{3}{a}\right)$?
(a) 31   (b) 26
(c) 28   (d) 24

77. Simplify the following expression.
$$\frac{3\frac{2}{3} - 5\frac{7}{9} \div \frac{1}{3} \times 1\frac{2}{13}}{\frac{2}{3} \text{ of } 1\frac{1}{3} \div \frac{1}{3}}$$
(a) $-6\frac{1}{8}$ (b) $-29\frac{2}{5}$
(c) $-2\frac{77}{104}$ (d) $-14\frac{1}{4}$

78. A milkman purchases 25 litres of milk from a diary for Rs. 800 and sells it at the rate of 33.50 per litre.

79. Gautam's present age is equal to 20% of his father's age 15 years ago and Gaurav's present age(brother of Gautam), is 60% of his father's age ten years ago. If the sum of Gautam's present age and Gaurav's present age is 31, then find their father's present age?
(a) 45 years   (b) 50 years
(c) 35 years   (d) 40 years

80. The average of nine numbers is 60, that of the first five numbers is 55 and the next three is 65. The ninth number is 10 less than the tenth number. Then, tenth number is:
(a) 80   (b) 70
(c) 75   (d) 85

81. Time taken to travel a certain distance of ' x ' km at speed of 40 kmph is 2 hours more than the time taken to travel $(x + 20)$ km at a speed of 60 kmph. Find the time is taken to travel $(x + 40)$ km at the speed of 40 kmph.
(a) 8 hours   (b) 6 hours
(c) 7.5 hours   (d) 4 hours

82. Which of the component helpful in translating verbal language to the language of mathematics?
(a) Mode-Building
(b) Word-Building
(c) Concept-Building
(d) None of the above

83. Activity-Centred Curriculum is based on:
(a) the premise that child loves to play and activity will help to create motivation

(b) help the child to enjoy Mathematics, to make him realize its beauty, and to remove the fear of difficulty of the subject

(c) the premise that whenever a child encounters a new experience, he/she can either easily connect it

(d) The role of students in this approach is to repeat what teacher transacted in the classroom

84. Acrylic is preferred over wool because of _______.
(a) arcrylic provide more warmth
(b) low cost of acrylic
(c) durability of acrylic

(a) They dry up quickly.
(b) They are durable.
(c) They are less expensive.
(d) They are very hard to maintain.

86. A teacher begins the class by demonstrating the chemical test of starch in a given sample of food. The cognitive process associated with the underlined word in the above statement is.
(a) Creating
(b) Analysing
(c) Applying
(d) Understanding

87. Which of the following best explains the concept of cognitive validity of a science curriculum:
(a) Focus on hands - on activities in curriculum
(b) Age - appropriateness of curricular materials
(c) Focus on continuous assessment
(d) Respect for constitutional value in curriculum

88. In which method of teaching science at school level emphasis is given on 'seeing' and 'doing' ?
(a) Demonstration
(b) Observation
(c) Excursion
(d) Experimentation

89. Remedial teaching is helpful for-
(a) Teaching the whole class
(b) Recapitulating the lesson
(c) Teaching in play-way method
(d) Removing learning difficulties of weak students

90. Geeta is preparing a lesson - plan for teaching the topic on 'Human eye' to Class VIII students. Inclusion of which of the following activities in the lesson - plan is likely to be most effective in helping the students understand related concepts better?
(a) Preparing a good home assignment
(b) Dictating notes to students in the classroom
(c) Using student activities and interactive classroom questioning
(d) Demonstration using model of human eye

91. A teacher has to teach grade 4

(b) Custard
(c) Dosa
(d) Bhelpuri

92. If you go to Ahmedabad (Gujarat) by train, then at Ahmedabad railway station you will find that most of the vendors are selling _________.
(a) Dhokla with chutney and lemon rice
(b) Chholay-bhature and lassi
(c) Idli-chutney and Vada-chutney
(d) Puri-Saak and thanda doodh

93. Positive pollution of soil is due to:
(a) Excessive use of fertilizers
(b) Addition of wastes on soil
(c) Reduction in soil productivity
(d) All of the these

94. The table below matches three human diseases with their causative microorganisms and mode of transmission.

Human Disease	Causative Microorganism	Mode of transmission
Polio	X	water,milk
Chicken pox	virus	y
Tubrculosis	z	direct and indirect

Replacing X, Y, Z respectively with which of the following terms would correctly fill the table?
(a) Virus, Direct contact, bacteria
(b) Virus, air, Virus
(c) Protozoa, contact, bacteria

(d) Bacteria, water, virus

95. Which property of metal is called mechanical property?
(a) conductivity
(b) tenacity
(c) fusibility
(d) specific gravity

96. Red colour appears during sunrise and sunset because of:
(a) Refraction   (b) Dispersion
(c) Scattering   (d) Reflection

97. The pitch of the sound is related to:
(a) Frequency   (b) Intensity
(c) Amplitude   (d) Loudness

98. Audible range for adult human

(d) 100 to 120 kHz

99. The magnetism of Earth is due to:
(a) Dynamo effect
(b) Doppler effect
(c) Solar effect
(d) Magnus effect

100. Direction: Read the following statements and choose the correct response.
Assertion (A) - Sound travels faster in water than in air
Reason (R) - Rigidity of medium impact the speed of sound.
(a) Both (A) and (R) are correct and (R) is correct explanation for (A)
(b) Both (A) and (R) are correct and (R) is not correct explanation for (A)
(c) (A) is correct and (R) is incorrect
(d) (R) is correct and (A) is incorrect

101. The part of human alimentary canal where complete digestion of fats takes place is:
(a) large intestine
(b) small intestine
(c) mouth
(d) stomach

102. The light energy escaping from the Sun can be spread by:
(a) a shower of raindrops
(b) a plane mirror
(c) a convex lens
(d) a combination of a convex lens and a concave lens

103. SI unit of pressure is:
(a) newton.meter
(b) newton meter^2
(c) newton/ meter
(d) newton/ meter^2

Ques (104-106): Direction : Following pie chart shows the percentage of students who participated in the CAT entrance test for MBA from different states.
Total Number of students is 8800.

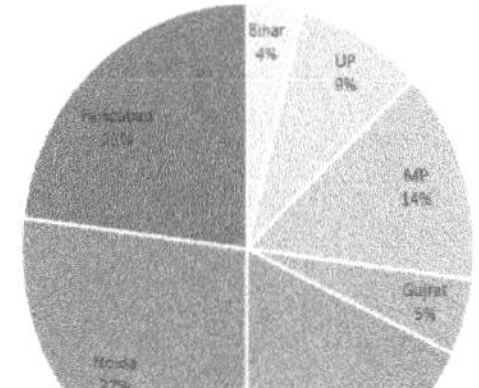

(a) $1:8$ (b) $9:14$
(c) $10:14$ (d) $2:5$

105. If the number of students passed from Bihar and UP are the same. If 50% of students passed from Bihar, then what % of students did not clear the test from UP?
(a) 77.7%   (b) 22.3%
(c) 70%   (d) 30%

106. If 20% passed from Delhi, then find the number of students passed from Faridabad.
(a) 2000
(b) 200
(c) 1000
(d) Cannot be determined

107. Which of the following is the most accurate description of scientific theories?
(a) Good scientific theories become scientific laws
(b) Scientific theories have a higher status than scientific laws
(c) Scientific theories are inferred explanations of observable phenomena
(d) Scientific theories become law only when enough supporting evidence is available

108. Systematic application of scientific knowledge to the practical tasks is termed as:
(a) Philosophy   (b) Science
(c) Education   (d) Technology

109. Which of the following forms part of the revised basic types of Learning in Tolman's system?
(a) Latent learning
(b) Field cognition modes
(c) Reward Expectancy
(d) Place learning

110. Out of the following which is not an example of Visual aids-
(a) Real objects   (b) Models
(c) Pictures   (d) Radio

111. The technique of 'classroom questioning' in teaching of Science can be more effectively used for Ensuring levels of learning:
(a) Ensuring levels of learning
(b) Developing problem solving skills
(c) Maintaining discipline in the class

assessment strategies is not suitable for formative assessment of learners in science?
(a) Journal writing
(b) Field trip
(c) Term-end achievement test
(d) Concept mapping

113. A teacher before beginning to teach 'digestion' to class VI students provides them with the outline diagram of a human body and asks them to draw all parts, through which they think the food would travel from mouth when they eat.
What could be the teacher's purpose of asking this question?
(a) To evaluate students' drawing skills as drawing diagrams is an important skill in life sciences
(b) To judge students' understanding of the digestive system and grade them accordingly.
(c) To investigate students' prior ideas related to human body and digestion so that future teaching learning sessions can be accordingly planned.
(d) To find out which students have read the topic in advance and come prepared for the class and grade them accordingly.

114. From which part of the plant is turmeric, a commonly-used colorant and antiseptic, obtained?
(a) Fruit   (b) Stem
(c) Flower   (d) Root

115. Which of the following statements related to magnetism is false?
(a) Magnetic field lines do not form closed loops.
(b) Magnetic monopoles do not exist.
(c) Ferromagnetic materials have large magnetic susceptibility
(d) Permeability of free space is a scalar quantity.

116. Which of the following statements is/are correct regarding Cockroaches?
1. A cockroach belongs to the class Insecta of phylum Arthropoda.
2. The cockroach has a 13-chambered tubular heart.
3. They do not have an abdomen and thorax.
(a) 1 only   (b) 2 and 3 only

following levels:
(a) Primary
(b) Upper primary
(c) Secondary
(d) Senior secondary

118. Which of the following is the usual sequence in a scientific investigation?
(a) Observation → Experiment → Hypothesis → Analysis → Conclusions
(b) Experiment → Observation → Hypothesis → Analysis → Conclusions
(c) Hypothesis → Experiment → Observation → Conclusion → Analysis
(d) Observation → Hypothesis → Experimentation → Analysis → Conclusion

119. Which is not a characteristic of objective type questions?
(a) Validity   (b) Subjectivity
(c) Reliability   (d) Objectivity

120. The HCF and LCM of two numbers are 24 and 168 and the numbers are in the ratio $1:7$. Find the greater of the two numbers.
(a) 168   (b) 144
(c) 108   (d) 72

⎰ **// Hints and Solutions //**

1(C). Development refers to qualitative changes in an individual such as a change in personality or other mental and emotional aspects.
- The term individual development is the process of maturation of a child up to a stage where he\she can independently

make their own decisions about their life.

- Individual development caters to the overall development of the child in terms of its physical, mental, emotional, and psychological growth.

As we live in a society, we come across persons who are followers of different cultures which allows us the opportunity to understand and expose our minds to the different customs and cultures of the society.

When individual experiences and interacts with different persons he is influenced by them and this influence plays an important role in the psychological development of a person.

It not only affects psychological development, but it also affects the other factors of development as the kind of

and influenced to participate in sports which will impact his physical and mental development.

Thus, it is concluded that there is cultural diversity in the process of development is correct for the process of development of an individual.

2(C). Development refers to an increase in structure for better and enhanced functioning of organs. It is a product of the interaction of hereditary and the environment.

Development takes place when environmental forces interact with the hereditary forces in an organism as they are the elements that play a vital role in determining the development of an individual.

The belief that children's behavior can be modified by reinforcers and punishers is based on the idea that development is primarily influenced by the environment only.

A reinforcer increases the probability of a behavior it is contingent on; a punisher decreases the probability.

Behavior modification involves assessing and modifying the current environmental events that are functionally related to the behavior.

Human behavior is controlled by events in the immediate environment, and the goal of behavior modification is to identify those events.

Environment refers to the circumstances in which an individual lives. Child's immediate environment strongly influenced their behavior, development, personality, and intelligence.

All mental and social traits depend on the environment. Environment determines the numeric position of IQ within these limits.

So, it could be concluded that the belief that children's behaviour can be modified by

reinforcers and punishers is based on the idea that development is primarily influenced by environment only.

3(B). Multilingualism is the ability to use more than two languages. Multilingualism is constitutive of the identity of a child and a typical feature of the Indian linguistic landscape, must be used as a resource, classroom strategy, and a goal by a teacher.
Benefits of Multilingual Classroom:

- It emphasizes on the significance of a smooth transition between the home and school language.
- Multilingualism encourages children to believe in themselves.
- It shows a greater number of independent cognitive strategies at their disposal and exhibits greater flexibility in the use of these strategies to solve her linguistic background.
- Multilingual children are capable of greater cognitive flexibility and creativity and perform better academically than monolinguals.

Thus, it could be concluded that most classrooms in India are multilingual and this needs to be seen as a resource by the teacher.

4(B). Individuals who have the ability to understand the motives, feelings and behaviours of others to bond with them are high on interpersonal Intelligence in Howard Gardner's theory.

Interpersonal intelligence: In this type of intelligence people have the ability to understand others' feelings, wishes, expectations, and needs & others' behavior. These people have better social communication skills and have the ability to relate well with others and manage relationships.

Thus, people having interpersonal intelligence have the ability to interact with others in society.

5(D). Monozygotic is to Identical twins as dizygotic is to fraternal twins.

Twins refer to two children produced by the same pregnancy. There are two types of twins including identical and fraternal twins.

Monozygotic twins are also known as identical twins. They are reproduced from one fertilized egg(ovum) that splits, resulting in the birth of two babies with the same genetic conditions.

On the other hand, reproduction of dizygotic twins which are also known as fraternal twins occurs during the fertilization of two eggs (ova) by two sperm resulting in the production of two genetically unique babies.

Thus, we conclude that Monozygotic is to

identical twins as dizygotic is to fraternal twins.

6(B). William stern used the word IQ first.
Assessment of Intelligence:

- In 1905, Alfred Binet and Theodore Simon made the first successful attempt to formally measure intelligence.
- In 1908, when the scale was revised, they gave the concept of Mental Age (MA), which is a measure of a person's intellectual development relative to people of her/his age group.

7(C). Vygotsky's social development theory laid the foundations for Constructivism.
Constructivism: It is the theory which backs the idea that child construct their knowledge by themselves when they explore, Lev Vygotsky who idealized the intermingling of culture, social interaction (which has three components explained below), and language.

Zone of Proximal Development (ZPD): It is the zone a child wants to master in. For example, if he wants to learn chess, it would be ZPD for him.

More knowledgable other (MKO): To learn chess, when he needs a person who is good at chess, that person is more knowledgable other.

Scaffolding: It is the help or motivation that is provided by MKO to that child.

Thus, it can be concluded that Vygotsky's social development theory laid the foundations for Constructivism.

8(A). Kohlberg's idea of moral development has three levels.

- Lawrence Kohlberg, an American psychologist, has propounded the 'Theory of Moral Development'.
- He has made a systematic study of moral development in his theory that is categorized in three levels and six stages.
- He has studied moral development by posing moral dilemmas to groups of children as well as adolescents and adults.

9(B). The basis of child psychology, 'Every child is special' is an appropriate statement. The study of child psychology helps the teacher to teach students in the most appropriate manner as it helps to be familiar with children's progressive developmental stages.

On the basis of child psychology, 'Every child is special' is an appropriate statement as the study of psychology helps:

- To know the child's views about the world.
- To understand how a child's brain functions.

- To know and meet children's diverse needs.
- To be aware of individual differences of children.
- To be familiar with children's progressive developmental stages, etc.
- To observe how a child interacts with their parents, themselves, and the world.

10(A). A review of a book on government schemes is not appropriate to take knowledge of primary sources.

Primary Sources: A source will be considered as a primary source in case it carries newly generated information, original work of research, or a new interpretation of already known facts. The document is the first and often the only published record of original research. The information contained in primary sources

they appear unable to stop moving or talking.
- They have poor attention to details and distractibility. Their activities are often disorganised. They are often forgetful and leave many activities incomplete, make many silly mistakes in school work.
- Due to poor attention, they fail to comprehend long instructions, even avoid activities that require sustained attention. Thus, they require special attention in the classroom.

13(A). The term used to describe 'reading disability' is dyslexia.

Dyslexia is the most common learning disability(Reading disorder) which makes learners:
- Confuse with the same shapes and

retardation. They are medical, psychological, and educational. The psychological and educational classifications are more commonly and widely used than medical classifications.

16(C). Retreat is not considered as a factor of cognition.

Cognitive factors refer to characteristics of the person that affect performance and learning. These factors serve to modulate performance such that it may improve or decline. These factors involve cognitive functions like attention, memory, and reasoning.
- Most psychologists today believe that our cognitions, i.e. our perceptions, memories, interpretations are essential ingredients of emotions.
- Stanley Schachter and Jerome Singer

has difficulty in hearing. For such people, sign languages are used to show them what one is saying. The first person credited with the creation of a formal sign language for the hearing impaired was Pedro Ponce de León, a 16th-century Spanish Benedictine monk.
- A language that employs signs made with the hands and other movements, including facial expressions and postures of the body is called sign language.
- But people with disabilities including Autism, Apraxia of speech, Cerebral Palsy, and Down Syndrome may also find sign language beneficial for communicating.
- Sign language may be as coarsely expressed as mere grimaces, shrugs, or pointings; or it may employ a delicately nuanced combination of coded manual signals reinforced by facial expression and perhaps augmented by words spelt out in a manual alphabet.

12(A). The hyperactive children need special attention in the classroom.

Attention Deficit Hyperactivity Disorder (ADHD) belongs to the group of externalising disorders of childhood. The term hyperactive is familiar to most people, especially parents and teachers. The child who is constantly in motion, tapping fingers, jiggling legs, poking others for no apparent reason, talking out of turn, and fidgeting is often called hyperactive. These children also have difficulty concentrating on the task at hand for an appropriate period of time.
- Children with ADHD seem to have particular difficulty controlling their activity in situations that call for sitting still, such as in the classroom or at mealtimes. When required to be quiet,

speech sounds with letters and words.

14(C). The stage of creative problem solving in which the individuals do not give attention to the problem is incubation.

Graham Wallas (1926) outlined the creative thinking process into four stages:
- Preparation: It involves collecting information regarding a problem in order to solve it through trial and error, recalling personal experiences, and investigating in all possible directions.
- Incubation: It is a slow process in which the individual sinks into the unconscious and reflects on the problem. In this stage, individuals forget irrelevant information or unsuccessful attempts and engage with the task effectively.
- Illumination: It is the stage the individual is most active and conscious. It is in this stage that an insight to the problem is experienced suddenly and a new idea or solution emerges.
- Verification: This stage might involve modifications to the solution reached in the previous stage by adding or subtracting, or making new connections. The final solution achieved is tested in reality. If the solution does not apply to the problem then the whole process is repeated.

15(C). The 35 – 50 IQ range is called a trainable IQ level of mentally retarded children.

Mental retardation, as a developmental disability, has attracted considerable public attention. Its general debilitating character has made it a distinct category of disability. Individuals with mental retardation, face considerable difficulty in their lives in adapting to the demands of day-to-day life.

Based On IQ: There are mainly three methods of classification of mental

emotion grows from our awareness of our present arousal. They also believed that emotions are physiologically similar.
- Therefore, Anger, Hunger, and fear are factors of cognition.

17(B). 'Choice of challenge' is a characteristic of motivation.

Motivation is the drive to achieve something in life that satisfies one's needs. There are two primary types of motivation namely, intrinsic motivation and extrinsic motivation. A number of behavioural characteristics are indicators of high motivation. Here are some of the important factors and some ways to help a child develop these characteristics:
- Persistence is the ability to stay with a task for a reasonably long period of time. While very young children cannot concentrate on one activity for an hour, there are still measurable differences in the length of time that young children will engage in an activity. A highly motivated child will stay involved for a long period of time, whereas an unmotivated child will give up very easily when not instantly successful. Children learn persistence when they are successful at a challenging task.
- Choice of challenge is another characteristic of motivation. Children who experience success in meeting one challenge will become motivated, welcoming another. These motivated learners will choose an activity that is slightly difficult for them but provides an appropriate challenge. Unmotivated children (those who have not experienced early success) will pick something that is very easy and ensures instant success.
- The amount of dependency on adults is another indicator of motivation.

Children with strong intrinsic motivation do not need an adult constantly watching and helping with activities. Children who have a lower level of motivation or are extrinsically motivated need constant attention from adults and cannot function independently.

- The last indicator of motivational level is emotion. Children who are clearly motivated will have a positive display of emotion. They are satisfied with their work and show more enjoyment in the activity. Children without appropriate motivation will appear quiet, sullen and bored.

18(A). When a child gets bored while doing a task, it is a sign that the task may have become mechanically repetitive.

children are energetic. Keeping this in mind, plan play activities involving running, jumping, climbing, catching and throwing.

- During the day there should be some indoor and some outdoor play activities. Outdoor play is generally vigorous and indoor activities are usually quieter.
- There must be a balance between structured activities initiated by you and free play initiated by the children. For example, taking the children out on a trip or organizing activities around a particular theme are structured activities.
- During the day you must organize both group and individual activities. The group activities will foster a spirit of cooperation and social skills, while the individual activities will give the child a chance to be alone and do something on her own, hence children are intelligent enough to do things by their own, and are capable of learning.
- The schedule of activities should be at a reasonable pace throughout the day. This means that you should allow enough time to children. But it should not be too slow that children begin to repeat it after completing it, else it will make children bored.

19(B). Learning is the acquisition of new behaviour or the strengthening or weakening of old behaviour as a result of experience. It represents progressive changes in behaviour. It also involves the acquisition of knowledge, habits, and attitude.

Factors Affect Learning:
The main factors affecting learning are Motivation of the learner, Maturation of the learner, Teaching strategies, and Physical and emotional health of the learner.

- The Interest of the Student - The factor of interest is very closely related in nature to that of symbolic drive and reward. A favourable mental attitude facilitates learning.
- Teaching Strategies - The strategies or steps taken by the teacher to make the class environment interactive and that also engrave interest among students regarding the topic.
- Physical and Emotional Health of the Learner: Concentration needs emotional and mental poise and absence of mental conflict or complexity. Some children find it difficult to prepare for the examinations, simply because of fear of the examination and anxiety neurosis.
- Giving motivation to the learner can increase their interest in learning.
- Maturation of the learner affects learning because maturation is related

So, from the above-mentioned points, it becomes clear that all the given factors affect learning.

20(A). Adequate classroom environment exhibits a basic level of order, but the teacher still struggles to maintain it.
There are four categories of classroom environment including dysfunctional, adequate, orderly restrictive and orderly enabling/flexible environment, in which adequate classroom environment exhibits the basic level of order for meaningful learning, but the teacher still struggles to maintain it.

21(B). Primary objective of analysing errors in student's work is to understand children's thinking.
All learners make mistakes. As someone has said: "You can't learn without goofing". Whether you are learning how to ride a bicycle, how to fly a kite or learn a language, everyone does make mistakes.

- An error is an incorrect form and a sure indication that the learner has not mastered the core of the selective topic in a learning process.
- The primary objective of analyzing errors in students' work is to understand children's thinking or thought processes since they are a window to children's thinking.
- Errors are necessary for the learning process to give insight into children's thinking. It helps the teacher to be aware of learners' learning styles and to cater to them according to their needs.
- Making an error cannot be just due to negligence and carelessness. It may be so that students are thinking about it in a different manner other than what is the right process.
- To understand this, a teacher should analyze what mistake the students are

doing, how the mistake is generated, and where exactly they tend to make mistakes.

22(D). Adoptation is not the stage of learning.
'Learning' means a relatively permanent change in behavior that occurs as a result of experience with the environment.

- For example, a child touches a hot pan placed near the gas stove in the kitchen because he is unaware that it can burn his fingers.
- Once he has had such an experience, he becomes careful in the future. He has 'learned' that hot objects can burn his fingers.

23(B). If a previously learned task impedes a new task, which is being learnt. This transfer of learning will be negative from one learning situation, in which they were initially acquired, to a different learning situation.

Negative Transfer-
- There are cases in which the previous learning interferes with subsequent learning.
- In such cases, the carryover of knowledge or experience in one task interferes with further learning.
- As a result of negative transfer, performance on one task may block performance on the subsequent task.
- For example, a child's experience in learning the plural of 'house' may inhibit his/her learning the plural of the word 'mouse'. He/She may spell the plural of the word 'mouse' as 'mouses', instead of 'mice'.

24(B). Teachers interacting more with boys than girls is an example of gender bias in teaching.
Gender refers to the socially and culturally constructed system that attributes meaning to what it means to be a male or a female in a particular society.
Gender bias in teaching leads to differential learning experiences, even though the girls and boys of a class sit in the same classroom and attended by the same teacher.

- It refers to the belief when someone prioritize one gender more than the other one.
- The result of the research studies about teachers interacting more with boys than girls is an example of gender bias in teaching.

25(B). Gender:
- Gender is what we make of boys and girls.
- It is about the opportunities we give them to develop.
- It has got to do with their upbringing,

socialization, culture and the role models we present for them.

- Gender is what a society and culture make of boys and girls.

Sex:

- Sex of a person indicates a boy or girl, a male or female, a man or woman.
- This distinction is based on the natural differences that exist in the body of males and females.
- These differences are biological and do not generally change.

However, if we talk about it in the Indian context, For three decades gender has been accepted as a category in the formulation of policy and curricula frameworks in India. "Gender", "Equality" and "Empowerment" of girls have also been used as keywords in educational documents for a long as it is evident from the policy review section

terms of learning outcomes in a holistic manner during the teaching-learning process.

- Assessment embedded in the teaching and learning process within the broader educational philosophy of 'assessment for learning'.
- Assessment of school students by school teachers in the schools.

28(A). The evaluation in which the evaluation is done by the one who teaches students is internal.

An internal evaluation is done by someone who knows the subject taught. It is usually the class teacher. The criterion is that the evaluator knows what has been taught and how it has been taught. All other types of evaluation are external evaluations.

29(C). School and media are secondary

This poem was written by Dylan Thomas and was published in 1951.

Given line is in the second stanza of the poem,

Because their words had forked no lightning they

Do not go gentle into that good night.

Poet expresses that wise people are aware that death is inevitable.

However, their words were not like lighting i.e revolutionary or startling to leave a mark.

That's why they resist and refuse to accept death peacefully.

So, the given expression means They haven't said anything revolutionary to make a mark.

33(B). The correct answer is Assonance.

Assonance is a literary device where the

---

other issues

- In terms of provision of equal facilities

So, we conclude that all the above-mentioned statements are correct.

26(D). The knowledge of individual differences helps teachers in assessing the individual needs of all students and teaching them accordingly.

Individual differences, as the term suggests, refer to how individuals differ from each other.

- Different people have different interests; and their behavior is influenced by these interests, likings, dislikings, values and beliefs, etc.
- Understanding of individual differences helps in planning course material and training programmes.
- Understanding of individual differences of the teachers and the taught can help in matching teaching and learning styles for better- academic results.
- To take care of individual differences you should design your instructional activities to suit the mental level of each student.

27(B). School-based assessment was introduced to ensure the holistic development of all the students.

In order to overcome the maladies and shortcomings that had crept in during the implementation of CCE causing serious malfunctioning, school-based assessment has been proposed as next-generation assessment.

It may be fourth in the sequence of one-time external (board) examination to a combination of external and internal examination to CCE and now SBA.

School-Based Assessment (SBA) may be defined as-

- Assessment that facilitates the attainment of competencies specified in

a quite helpless human infant into a self-aware, knowledgeable person who is skilled in the ways of their society's culture.

30(C). One of the basic principles of socializing individuals is education.

Socialization is a process by which an individual becomes a member of society through a mechanism of interaction. Its purpose is to prepare individuals for future roles.

Principles of Socialization:

- To make new members of society familiar with social traditions, manners, customs, etc.
- To prepare the members of the society to adapt to the constantly changing environment
- To lead to education through a process of social interaction
- To study the various types of social relationships and their impact on individual development.
- To control the teaching-learning process to achieve the personality development of every single child.

31(A). The correct answer is 'Life'.

Symbols in literature are a 'stand-in' for bigger ideas.

It can be a motif, location, character, image or so on.

Poet Dylan Thomas dedicated this poem to his ailing father.

The poem encourages the dying people to bravely and valiantly fight the death.

Death and life are in contrast in the poem.

If life is light then death is night or dying of light.

Therefore, in the given expression, light refers to life.

32(D). The correct answer is 'They haven't said anything revolutionary to make a mark'.

For example:

She seems to beam rays of sunshine.

In the given line, the sound "i" is getting repeated.

Blind eyes could blaze like meteors and be gay.

Therefore, from all the points given above, we can infer that the literary device used is Assonance.

34(A). The correct answer is Men dislike the dark.

The whole poem is about the brave resistance to death by smart and wise men.

The poet in every stanza describes a different type of person who wants to live more or do more in life.

He explains how these men know about death and its inevitability but at the same time, they don't want to die and are fighting death bravely.

It is mentioned in the first line of the second stanza:

Though wise men at their end know dark is right.

Thus, the men know that dark i.e. death is right.

Therefore, the incorrect statement will be men dislike the dark.

35(B). The poem is about the brave efforts of people to resist death even when it's inevitable.

Poet wrote this for his ailing father who was also fighting for his life.

Metaphors are figures of speech that create comparisons between different notions or entities.

For example, day and light in the poem refer to life.

Thus, dying of the light stands for the end of life i.e. death.

These phrases appear in the following lines:

Rage, rage against the dying of the light.

Therefore, the literary device used in the

given phrases is a 'metaphor'.

36(C). This line is given in the third stanza and describes when good people resist death.

Frail in the given lines means weak.

Thus, the line describes the emotions of men when they realise even a small deed could have meant something.

So, the word 'frail' means weak.

37(C). The given passage is about different aspects that should be considered while opting for Entrepreneurship or starting a new business:

Let's refer to the passage: Never forget the importance of business ethics and your own values. Ethics need to be carefully sewn into the fabric of any start-up. And the only way to reach long-term success is

38(C). The given passage is about different aspects that should be considered while opting for Entrepreneurship or starting a new business:

Let's refer to the passage: "Customers do not usually know what they want, but they always know what they do not need. Make sure that there is a real need for your product. Start small. Your idea may be grand and have the potential to change the world, but you are only going to do this one step at a time."

On perusal of the above statement, we can state that entrepreneurs should go for products that are useful for the customers and appeals to them.

Option (B), is nowhere stated in the passage.

Option (A) and Option (D) are incorrect as it is clearly mentioned that in the passage go for borrowing for money from family and friends instead of going for investors and waiting for their response.

39(D). The given passage is about different aspects that should be considered while opting for Entrepreneurship or starting a new business:

Let's refer to the passage: If you are starting a restaurant, work for someone else first. If you are creating a software product, learn by doing some consulting assignments or create some utilities.

By stating the above examples the author is stating that before going for a bigger step, we need to consider the product from the ground up and understand its usability from users' point of view.

Seeking advice from the experienced entrepreneur and understanding it from the users' point of view are the basic aspects that need to be considered.

40(A). The given passage is about

different aspects that should be considered while opting for Entrepreneurship or starting a new business:

Let's refer to the passage:

- Everyone jumps on the same new trend, or the ideas are so far out that they have no chance of success. And great ideas are not enough: it takes experienced management, excellent execution, and a receptive market. It is hard for even the best venture capitals to identify the potential successes.
- The above statement means that having ideas is not enough for a business to be successful. It needs management with great experience, proper execution, and market with users that accept the product that is being sold out.
- What all new entrepreneurs should understand is that, even if you have a

building it up.

- The above statement means that, for a business to be successful it requires the ideas to be properly substantiated with usability. Without proper planning and proof for your ideas, it becomes difficult to determine their success in the future.

41(C). Let's check each of the given options:

- Ethics need to be carefully sewn into the fabric of any start-up.
- Never forget the importance of business ethics and your own values. Ethics need to be carefully sewn into the fabric of any start-up. And the only way to reach long-term success is by achieving outstanding customer satisfaction.
- Share your ideas with those who have done it before.
- Share your ideas with those who have done it before. You can learn a lot from the experience of seasoned entrepreneurs, and they are much more approachable than you think.
- In other words, funding comes just when you do not need it
- My point is that when you need venture funding no one will give any money until you already have a marketable product. In other words, funding comes just when you do not need it.

Option (C) is nowhere postulated in the passage. Thus, it not the correct statement.

42(B). The given passage is about different aspects that should be considered while opting for Entrepreneurship or starting a new business

Let's refer to the passage: "There is no single recipe for developing your business idea yourself, but there are some essential ingredients. Here are some pointers: Consult widely. Share your ideas with those who have done it before. You can learn a

lot from the experience of seasoned entrepreneurs, and they are much more approachable than you think. If you cannot find anyone who is excited about your idea, the chances are it is not worth being excited about. This may be time to reflect deeply and come up with another. Identify markets. Speak to anyone who can help you understand your target customers. "

On the perusal of the above statement, we can understand sharing ideas with experienced entrepreneurs, taking advice and understanding the market and buyers' needs are some of the points that need to be considered while going for entrepreneurship.

43(A). "Exit strategies", as mentioned in the passage, signifies an entrepreneur's strategic plan to sell his or her ownership Entrepreneurship or starting a new business:

Let's refer to the passage: " With a lot of luck and hard work, you may build a successful company that markets products customers really want. It is very likely that by this stage, you receive phone calls from venture capitalists. This is the time to think of exit strategies and decide if you want to own a small piece of a big pie or a large piece of a small pie."

On the perusal of the above statement, we can say the author is asking for contriving a plan in such manner that is useful to customers and that lures the investors to put their investment in the company.

44(B). The phrase "and few are worth the paper they are printed on" as exists in the above passage means hardly any idea is good.

On perusal of the following statement given in the passage: "Venture capitalists receive hundreds of plans every week, and few are worth the paper they are printed on. Everyone jumps on the same new trend, or the ideas are so far out that they have no chance of success"

Investors receive hundreds of propositions and there are rarely any in which investors like to invest their money.

'Hardly any idea' means 'rarely any idea'.

45(A). "a marketable product" as mentioned in the passage signifies a product that appeals to buyers and sell at a certain price range to generate profit.

Across the passage, the author presents certain constraints/ aspects that need to be considered when one opts for entrepreneurship.

Let us inspect the individual options:

According to the lines given in the passage:

- You do not have to start with the ultimate product. Watch every penny.

Focus on revenue and profitability from the start.

- Customers do not usually know what they want, but they always know what they do not need. Make sure that there is a real need for your product.

Thus, option (A) is correct as the production that generates profit and pleases the buyers will be considered as a marketable product.

Option (B) is incorrect. From the lines given in the passage:

- "If you do hit the jackpot, you are required to let the investors make many of the business decisions in exchange for an investment. To be fair, most business plans do not deserve funding."
- "Raise money to get started by begging and borrowing from family and friends."

Upon the perusal of the given statements

Bangalore and the British Council in Madras.

Audio-Lingual Method: This method focused on oral/aural work and pronunciation taught through drills as well as dialogue practice in small groups of motivated learners and native language teachers. Dialogues were the main aspect of the audio-lingual approach as they provided the learners an opportunity to mimic/imitate, practice, and memorize bits of language considered to be relevant to their situations.

Thus, from the above-mentioned points, it is clear that option (C) is correct.

47(D). NCF (National Curriculum Framework) 2005 is one of the four NCFs published in India by NCERT. It seeks to provide a framework for the betterment of

- The teaching rules at the initial stage do not lend much to language learning. Grammar teaching should move from meaning to form.
- While teaching grammar, the activities should be designed in a way that requires the Inductive and creative reasoning of the child.
- Inductive approach, rules learners discover for themselves are more likely to fit their existing mental structures than rules they have been presented with.
- By teaching grammar, we not only give our students the means to express themselves, but we also fulfill their expectations of what learning a foreign language involves.

So, we conclude that when a test item expects the learners to use tense forms

and 'media houses' in the given passage.

46(C). Language educators have sought to solve the problem of language teaching by focusing attention almost exclusively on method'.In other words, they have assumed that if a teacher teaches using the right method, learning will automatically take place.

Teaching method: Different teaching methods are used by teachers as per the requirements of students. For choosing the one, the teacher may classify students based on their abilities (ability grouping) or he can choose it based on the compatibility of the topic.

Following are the methods of language teaching:-

Structural Approach: A structural approach is a language tool that helps the learner to master the structure or pattern of sentences. It is the descriptive approach that gives more importance to speech only without reference to meaning.

Humanistic Approach: The Humanistic movement in language teaching emerged, as did some of the other approaches, from developments that occurred in education and psychology. This approach argued even more strongly against the authoritarian teacher-centered classroom and emphasized the importance of creating environments that minimized anxiety, enhanced personal security, and promoted genuine interest through a deeper engagement of the learner's whole self.

Communicational Teaching: Communicational teaching refers to a five-year project of exploratory teaching of English as a second language which was 'planned, carried out and reviewed regularly by a group of interested teacher trainers and teachers of English as a part-time activity but with institutional support from the Regional Institute of English,

language that are symbols, gestures, words, etc.

The main purpose of teaching a language is to enable the children to use it practically while communicating with others.

48(D). One of the main advantages of the group-learning approach is that it can be used to achieve an extremely wide range of educational objectives, especially higher-cognitive objectives of all types like problem-solving, decision-making and other complex life skills. It is also an approach for developing creative thinking and other divergent thought processes. Some general features of group learning are:

- Several learners can provide more time/effort/resources available than one;
- A wider range of knowledge/skills/experience can be acquired through sharing knowledge and experience;
- More and a variety of ideas can be generated through brainstorming in the groups, hence class can be noisy sometimes.
- Errors can be identified and corrected more easily;
- Participation increases the commitment of the students to the activity

So, in the above situation, the teacher may have group work.

49(A). When a test item expects the learners to use tense forms, voice, connectors, prepositions, and articles accurately, such an approach can be called integrated grammar testing.

Grammar teaching:

- It should be done in an integrated manner, that is, learners should use tense forms, voice, connectors, prepositions and articles accurately, such an approach can be called integrated grammar testing.

50(B). Students learning a language often lack confidence when speaking due to the language's unique pronunciation rules. One way to overcome this problem is using game-like activities which require verbal interactions in the classroom.

- Using game-like activities which require verbal interactions in the classroom is the way to overcome the above-mentioned problem.
- A language game is a system of manipulating spoken words to render them incomprehensible to the untrained ear. Language games are effective in learning a language because they:
- allow students to practice language skills.
- encourage them to interact and communicate in a meaningful context.
- provide a stress-free and natural environment for all learners to enhance the usage of language.

So, it could be concluded that using game-like activities which require verbal interactions in the classroom is the way to overcome the above-mentioned problem.

51(B). Children substitute sounds made in the back of the mouth (g, k) for sounds made in the front of the mouth (d, t) so that tab becomes cab and dot becomes got. This type of error is known as Phonological error.

Phonological error: Children with phonological process disorders have difficulty learning the sound systems of the language, and may not understand that changing sounds can change meanings. They produce consistent error patterns (called phonological processes).

- These patterns may be normal in early childhood, but should not occur past a certain age.
- An example of a phonological process is substituting sounds made in the back of

the mouth (g, k) for sounds made in the front of the mouth (d, t) so that tab becomes cab and dot becomes got.
- Children may simplify consonant clusters (i.e., consecutive consonants in a word) so that string becomes sting or even sing.
- Another pattern is replacing sounds made without the voice (e.g., p, t, k) with voiced sounds (e.g., b, d, g), such that pie becomes bye and cat becomes gat.

52(A). In Guided reading approach a teacher working with a small group of students who demonstrate similar reading behaviors and can read similar levels of texts.
Guided reading is an instructional approach that involves a teacher working with a small group of students who demonstrate similar

- it offers challenges and opportunities for problem-solving but is easy enough for students to read with some fluency. You choose selections that help students expand their strategies.

53(B). Teaching aids are used for making a lesson interesting, effective, stimulating, and exciting.
Teaching Aids:
- These are sensory devices, they provide a sensory experience to the learner, and i.e. the learners can see and hear simultaneously using their senses.
- Teaching Aids are an integral part of teaching which are used by the teachers to teach in a classroom
- These are instructional devices that are used to communicate messages more effectively through sound and visuals.
- For example, LCD project, Film projector, TV, Computer, VCD player, Multimedia, etc.
- Teaching aids are used for making a lesson interesting, effective, stimulating, and exciting.
- They provide more clarity and detail to the teaching process.
- Motivate the learners to learn by providing the learning content in an attractive and interesting way rather than monotonous lectures by the teachers.
- Through the inclusion of audio and visual effects, teaching aids can and stimulate the learners and transform a learning process or environment
- Since it provides more detail and enhances learning through sensory perceptions, teaching outcomes can be more effective.
- Teaching aids include audio-visual aids like slideshows, charts, flashcards, animations, pictures, models, television, radio, online sources, etc.

54(A). In remedial teaching, the teacher manages students' records in a timely and appropriate way. A teacher works with the students who have difficulty in learning and retaining the information. Before preparing for their lessons, teachers should identify pupils' diverse learning needs as soon as possible so that they may design appropriate teaching plans to facilitate pupils' effective learning.

55(A). "Children deserve most of the credit for the language that they acquire." 'This observation implies that in modern classrooms students pursue their own lines of inquiry.
Acquiring a language refers to learning the basics of a language through the natural process of observation of the language.
- A child learns the language through his

the language that they acquire means that the students deserve all the appreciation for the efforts they have put together to acquire their language.
- It is not so easy to acquire a language other than one's mother tongue. It takes constant observation of the peer group, consistent efforts to grasp the accent, and parallelly understand and comprehend each and every word.
So, it should be noted that efforts pursued by the students deserve the credits for the language acquired.
Thus, it is concluded that "Children deserve most of the credit for the language that they acquire." 'This observation implies that in modern classrooms students pursue their own lines of inquiry.

56(D). Enriched vocabulary is not a correct parameter of reading skill assessment.
Parameters of reading skill assessment:-
- Reading assessment has to be done on the basis of recognition of words in a text because if the reader cannot read the words, it will be a failure of the reading exercise.
- Reading aloud has to be assessed during reading as while reading, a person has to be clear in his pronunciation so that listeners can listen well to what reader is trying to inform them.
- Comprehension directly means how much a person can comprehend or understand what they are reading. If they fail in this criteria, the purpose of reading will be zero because the person will not be able to understand the information.

57(D). Knowledge of constitutional values is least important to you as a language teacher.
A good language teacher has fluency in the

language, is enthusiastic about it, and is someone who can deliver well and in an interesting manner.
Knowledge of constitutional values does not require for a language teacher because these values are inculcated through teaching social studies by a social science teacher.

58(D). Important thing for the selection of teaching-learning material for students is that the teaching-learning material should be contextualized and fit to be used in an integrated manner.
The learning process is aimed to bring out the permanent desirable changes in the behavior of an individual. The teaching-learning process respects the diversity among students and the teacher follows different paths to achieve the goals of

learning and to keep them indulging actively in the teaching-learning process. These materials are known as "TLM" or "teaching-learning materials".

59(A). The intonation of question-tags is often quoted as a case of a difference in meaning being falling and rising tone. Thus the question tag 'aren't they' in "They are coming on Tuesday, aren't they" means the speaker is comparatively certain that the information is correct.
Intonation:-, Intonation is the use of changing vocal pitch to convey grammatical information or personal attitude. It describes how the voice rises and falls.
- When the speaker is adding a question-tag he/she might increase or decrease the volume tone at the end.
- If the volume is increasing, it is called rising intonation.
- If the volume is decreasing, it is called falling intonation.

60(D). Listening and telling stories helps children in learning language in primary classes. Listening to stories is of interest to children and also enhances their creativity. Often it is seen that children mould the stories they have heard as per their wishes while telling it to their friends. Through this children not only learn the meaning of the words but also develop an understanding of various incidents and this facilitates in enhancing their imagination. Another way in which stories are beneficial is that it enhances the ability of children to estimate. For example, whenever children are listening to a story, they are curious to know about what happens next.
- Discussing a story after listening to it, is a little difficult task but if the teacher is prepared with its objective then it can become a useful medium.
- Most of the teachers feel that after

telling the story, it is their right to ask the children, about the lesson they have learnt from it.

- Telling stories to children is as important as listening to stories from them.
- This helps the children in developing their ability to express themselves, makes them curious, and motivates them to learn.
- Instead of asking the children to repeat the story told by the teacher, it is more beneficial to ask them questions so as to check their understanding and learning and encourage them to think about and express their reactions to a story or character.
- While responding to the personality and the character of the story, the child includes her experiences in it.

imagination.

So, we conclude that both the points could be the reason to ask questions from listeners in story-based lessons.

61(A). Let assume that rational number = a

Additive inverse = -a

$\Rightarrow$ Sum = a + (-a) = 0

∴ The sum of a rational number and its additive inverse is '0'.

62(A). Prime factors of 27720 are 2, 3, 5, 7, 11

$\Rightarrow$ The sum of all prime factors = 2 + 3 + 5 + 7 + 11 = 28

∴ The sum of all prime factors of 27720 is 28.

63(A). Mathematics is a subject that finds application in every walk of our life. Knowingly or unknowingly, people use concepts of Mathematics in their daily life. Considering the relevance of Mathematics, it is treated as one of the basic and compulsory subjects in the school curriculum. In the elementary school curriculum, learning basic concepts of Mathematics is emphasised. As and when children reach higher classes, the complexity of mathematical concepts gets widened. It is commonly observed that many children have a belief that Mathematics is, in a way, difficult to learn and understand.

Mathematics is consistent:

- Consistency is defined as the absence of contradictions. In Mathematics, we know that there is a definite consistency of results. That is, the results of a defined problem will not show varying results.
- Most of the mathematical principles are consistent barring some exceptions in the area of pure mathematics. The consistency of mathematics makes it

universal and timeless. If it was not consistent and depended on time, location or any other variable then it would be difficult to teach mathematics efficiently. Given its universal usage, it is safe to say that mathematics is consistent, unlike literature.

Mathematics is procedural:

When students understand a concept in a meaningful way, they are more likely to be able to correctly apply it in various situations. The knowledge of procedures followed in solving mathematical problems is called procedural knowledge. For example, the procedure followed in drawing perpendicular bisector of a given line segment.

Mathematics is not rigid:

This subject is not rigid. On the other hand, Mathematics is a very flexible subject as we

thinking skills.

Here the conclusion is that Mathematics is consistent is true in the context of the nature of mathematics.

64(A). Mathematics is the study of numbers, shape, quantity, and patterns. Mathematics is the 'queen of all sciences' and its presence is there in all the subjects. It acts as the basis and structure of other subjects.

A multidisciplinary problem in mathematics refers to those problems which tests other skill set as well along with the ability to do math. For example, drawing a flag of India and counting a number of symmetrical lines. This question tests drawing skill, counting skill, meaning of symmetry. A good textbook contains many multidisciplinary problems.

Other Qualities of a Good Textbook of Mathematics are:

- It should be child-centred subject matter should be arranged from "simple to complex" and "concrete to abstract" method the subject matter should create interest in the pupil.
- The language used in the text would be simple and easily understandable.
- The books should be written in listed simple, precise, and practical language.
- At the end of the book, there should be given tables and appendices.
- The most important and general speciality is it should be free from mistakes.
- In the textbook, there should also solve examples so that the child can develop concept understanding and he can easily solve the practice questions based on it.
- Practice questions develop the child's ability to solve questions within the time limit and provide an opportunity to follow practice and error theory.

So, it becomes clear that 'Drawing the flag

of India and identifying the number of lines of symmetry in the flag' is an example of a multidisciplinary problem.

65(D). Mathematics can be referred to as the study of patterns, numbers, geometrical objects, data, and information. It deals with data analysis, integration of various fields of knowledge, involves proofs, deductive and inductive reasoning, and generalizations.

Needs and significance of learning mathematics:

- Mathematics learning helps to apply mathematical concepts and theorems to new situations.
- Mathematics provides a clear understanding of laws of nature.
- Mathematics helps in clear understanding of the culture and
- Mathematics provides a frame work for solving problems.
- Mathematics is a powerful tool in the hands of the learners.
- Mathematics learning helps in a better understanding of the world around us.

So, we can conclude that all of the above statement are correct, none of the above are incorrect.

66(D). Practice time is the time in which students practice the mathematical question and check their learning.

- It aims at extended learning opportunities
- The extended learning opportunity is the acquisition of knowledge through instruction or study.
- It helps in extending the knowledge and progress of students.
- Practicing mathematics gives students more learning opportunities.
- This will allow students to engage in experiences that teach them skills to solve a problem.

So, practice time included in the textbook will provide an extended learning opportunity.Providing fun and enjoyments, change in daily routine, and better utilization of time is not supported by providing the section 'Practice Time'.

67(B). The teaching of mathematics at the basic level helps in developing mental discipline and logical reasoning along with mental rigor. In addition, its knowledge plays a significant role in the understanding of other school subjects such as science, social studies, etc.

For better learning experiences, different methods of teaching and approaches are used. Whatever method a mathematics teacher may adopt for teaching, each lesson builds upon the lessons previously taught. Hence, reinforcement by adequate practice or drill of previously learned skills becomes an important task, therefore, oral recitation and written work both form vital components of any lesson.

In the above-mentioned situation, the teacher is following the Drill approach as drill includes the repetition of the content or the subject matter over a period of time to retain and internalize it in a better and effective way.

A learner who makes use of sufficient drill work, practice work, revision, and review of his learning can be expected to harvest a good yield in terms of its good retention, reproduction, and utilization at the proper time.

A good drill should follow the learning and understanding of basics as only the learned or the concepts that are taught in the classroom should be given for drill practice.

Each student should understand that practice will make them master in that specific content and they should do it on a regular basis.

The drill should be individualized and rewarding to each pupil as when they performed enough drills of addition and subtraction then they should be learning new concepts and getting new drill exercises.

Children also need to understand the utility and purpose of the drills such as when they had attained mastery in the basic mathematical operations then they can calculate and use those procedures in their daily life as well i.e., buying vegetables, stationery items from the market, and so on.

So, it is evident from the above points, that in the above-mentioned situation, the teacher is following the Drill approach.

68(D). In this question, we are given that a number consists of two digits. If the digits interchange places and the new number is added to the original number.

We need to find that the resulting number is divisible by which number in the options.

For the original number, let the digit in the units place be y and the digit in the tens place be x.

Using this, the original number is 10x + y.

Now, when we interchange the digits, for the new number, the digit in the units place is x and the digit in the tens place is y.

Using this, the new number is 10y + x.

Now, we will add these numbers to get the resultant number.

$(10x + y) + (10y + x) = 11(x + y)$

Clearly, the resultant number is divisible by 11 which is in the options.

69(D). Given,

$\angle B$ is more than $\angle A$ by $25°$.

$\angle C$ is $5°$ more than four time $\angle A$.

As we know,

Sum of all three angles of a triangle is $180°$.

Let $\angle A$ be x.

$\angle B = x + 25°$

$\angle C = 4x + 5°$

$\angle A + \angle B + \angle C = 180°$

$\Rightarrow x + x + 25° + 4x + 5° = 180°$

$\Rightarrow 6x + 30° = 180°$

$\Rightarrow 6x = 180° - 30°$

$\Rightarrow 6x = 150°$

$\Rightarrow x = \dfrac{150°}{6}$

$\Rightarrow x = 25°$

$\angle A = 25°$

$\angle B = 25° + 25° = 50°$

$\angle C = 4 \times 25° + 5° = 100° + 5° = 105°$

$\therefore$ The biggest angle is $105°$.

70(A).

Given,

Chords AB = 8 cm and CD = 6 cm

Then, AE = EB = 4 cm and CF = FD = 3 cm

EF = 1 cm

Let OE = x cm

Then, OF = (x + 1) cm

OA = OC = r cm ($\because$ radius)

From ΔOAE, By pythagoras theorem

$OA^2 = AE^2 + OE^2$

$\Rightarrow r^2 = 4^2 + x^2$

$\Rightarrow x^2 = r^2 - 16$ ...(i)

From ΔOCF, By pythagoras theorem

$OC^2 = CF^2 + OF^2$

$r^2 = 3^2 + (x + 1)^2$

$(x + 1)^2 = r^2 - 9$ ...(ii)

By equation (ii) – (i),

$(x + 1)^2 - x^2 = r^2 - 9 - r^2 + 16$

$\Rightarrow x^2 + 1 + 2x - x^2 = 7$

$\Rightarrow 2x = 7 - 1 = 6$

$\Rightarrow x = 3$ cm

$\therefore$ From equation (i),

$9 = r^2 - 16$

$\Rightarrow r^2 = 25$

$\Rightarrow r = 5$ cm

71(D). As $\angle B + \angle D = 180°$

(Since, the sum of opposite angles of a cyclic quadrilateral is $180°$)

and $\angle A + \angle C = 180°$

So, x + 10 + 5y + 5 = 180°

or, x + 5y = 165° ....(i)

And 2x + 4 + 4y – 4 = 180°

or, 2x + 4y = 180° ....(ii)

Solving (i) and (ii), we get

x = 40° and y = 25°

Therefore, x + y = 40° + 25° = 65°

72(C). Let the angle between the generator and the axis of the cone be 'θ', shown below,

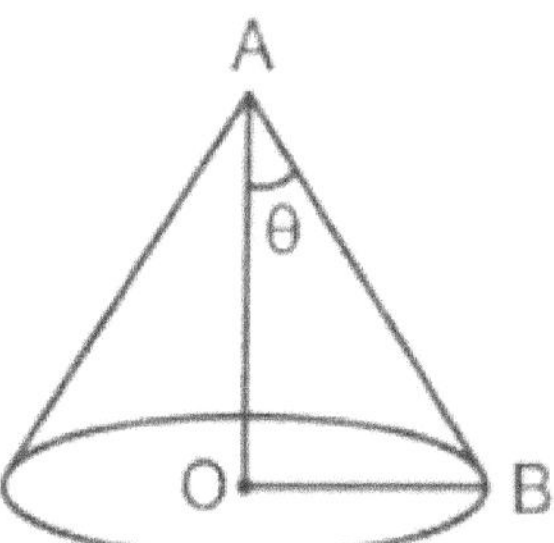

Radius of cone = OB = r (let)

When the semi-circle is rolled to form a cone, slant height of cone = Radius of semi-circle

AB = R (let)

Also, the circumference of the base of cone = Circumference of semi-circle

$2\pi r = \pi R$

$\Rightarrow \sin\theta = \frac{1}{2}$

$\Rightarrow \sin\theta = \sin 30°$

$\therefore \theta = 30°$

73(D). Given,

A rectangular block of length 20 cm, breadth 15 cm and height 10 cm are cut up into an exact number of equal cubes.

$\because$ Volume of cuboid = Length $\times$ Breadth $\times$ Height

$\Rightarrow$ Volume of rectangular block $= 20 \times 15 \times 10 = 3000$ cm^3

Now, the least possible number of cubes will be cut from the rectangular block, when a cube cut is of the maximum possible size.

Side of maximum possible cube = HCF of $(20, 15, 10) = 5$ cm

Volume of one cube cut $= (5)^3 = 125$ cm^3

$\therefore$ Least possible number of cubes $= \dfrac{3000}{125} = 24$

74(C). Given:

$a(b - c)x^2 + b(c - a)x + c(a - b) = 0$ has equal roots.

So, Discriminant, $D = 0$

$D = b^2 - 4ac = b^2 \times (c - a)^2 - 4 \times a(b - c) \times c(a - b) = 0$

$D = (bc + ab - 2ac)^2 = 0$

$bc + ab - 2ac = 0$

$b \times (a + c) = 2ac$

$b = \dfrac{2a}{a+c}$

So, a, b and c are in HP.

75(B). Given,

$(a - b)^3 = a^3 - b^3 - 3ab(a - b)$

$\Rightarrow 3^3 = 279 - 3ab \times 3$

$\Rightarrow 9ab = 279 - 27 = 252$

$\Rightarrow ab = 28$

Now,

$(a + b)^2 = (a - b)^2 + 4ab$

$\Rightarrow (a + b)^2 = 3^2 + 4 \times 28 = 121$

$\Rightarrow (a + b) = 11$

Now,
$$(a+b)^3 = a^3 + b^3 + 3ab(a+b)$$
$$\Rightarrow 11^3 = a^3 + b^3 + 3 \times 28 \times 11$$
$$\Rightarrow 1331 = a^3 + b^3 + 924$$
$$\Rightarrow a^3 + b^3 = 407$$

76(C). Given,
$$a^3 + 3a^2 + 9a = 1 \quad \ldots\ldots\ldots \text{(i)}$$
Multiplying equation (i) by a, we get
$$a^4 + 3a^3 + 9a^2 = a \quad \ldots\ldots \text{(ii)}$$
Multiplying equation (i) by 3, we get
$$3a^3 + 9a^2 + 27a = 3 \quad \ldots\ldots\ldots \text{(iii)}$$
Subtracting equation (iii) from equation (ii), we get
$$a^4 - 27a = a - 3$$
$$\Rightarrow a^4 = 28a - 3 \quad \ldots\ldots\ldots \text{(iv)}$$
Dividing the whole equation (iv) by a, we get
$$\Rightarrow a^3 = 28 - \frac{3}{a}$$

$$= \frac{\left[\frac{11}{3} - \frac{52}{9} \times 3 \times \frac{15}{13}\right]}{\frac{2}{3} \times \frac{4}{3} \times 3}$$
$$= \frac{\left[\frac{11}{3} - \frac{20}{1}\right]}{\frac{8}{9} \times 3}$$
$$= \frac{11 - 60}{3} \times \frac{3}{8}$$
$$= \frac{-49}{8}$$
$$= 6\frac{1}{8}$$

$\therefore$ The value of $\dfrac{3\frac{2}{3} - 5\frac{1}{9} \div \frac{1}{3} \times 1\frac{2}{13}}{\frac{2}{2} \text{ of } 1\frac{1}{\circ} \div \frac{1}{2}}$ is $-6\frac{1}{8}$.

78(A). Given,
C.P for 25 litres of milk = Rs. 800
S.P for 1 litre of milk = Rs. 33.5
We know that-
$$\text{Profit} = \text{S.P} - \text{C.P}$$
$$\text{Profit \%} = \frac{\text{Profit}}{\text{C.P}} \times 100$$
S.P for 25 litres of milk $= 25 \times 33.5 =$ Rs. 837.5
$\therefore$ Profit $= 837.5 - 800 =$ Rs. 37.5
$$\text{Profit \%} = \left(\frac{37.5}{800}\right) \times 100$$
$$\Rightarrow 4.6875\%$$
$\therefore$ Profit % (rounded off) $= 4.7\%$

79(B). Given,
Gautam's present age is equal to 20% of his father's age 15 years ago
Let the father's present age be x years
Father's age 15 years ago $= (x - 15)$ years
Gautam's present age = 20% of $(x - 15)$
$$= \frac{(x-15)}{5} \text{ years}$$
Gaurav's present age = 60% of $(x - 10)$
$$= \frac{3(x-10)}{5} \text{ years}$$
According to the question,
$$\frac{x-15}{5} + \frac{3(x-10)}{5} = 31$$
$$\Rightarrow x - 15 + 3x - 30 = 155$$
$$\Rightarrow x = 50$$

80(A). Given,

Average of nine numbers $= 60$
Average of first five numbers $= 55$ and average of next three numbers $= 65$
Tenth number = Ninth number $+10$
As we know,
$$\text{Average} = \frac{\text{Total sum of all numbers}}{\text{Count of the numbers}}$$
The sum of nine numbers $= 60 \times 9 = 540$
The sum of the first five numbers $= 55 \times 5 = 275$
The sum of the next three numbers $= 65 \times 3 = 195$
Ninth number $= (540 - 275 - 195) = (540 - 470) = 70$
$\therefore$ Tenth number $= 70 + 10 = 80$

81(A). Given,
Time taken to travel certain distance of 'x' km at speed of 40 kmph is 2 hours more than the time taken to travel $(x + 20)$ km at

$$40 \qquad 60$$
$$\Rightarrow \frac{x}{40} - \frac{(x+20)}{60} = 2$$
$$\Rightarrow \frac{(3x - 2x - 40)}{120} = 2$$
$$\Rightarrow x - 40 = 240$$
$$\Rightarrow x = 280 \text{ km}$$
Time taken to travel $(x + 40)$
$$= \frac{(280+40)}{40} = 8 \text{ hours}$$
$\therefore$ Required time $= 8$ hours

82(A). Mode-Building component helpful in translating verbal language to the language of mathematics.
Mode-Building: Translating verbal language to the language of mathematics, that is solving a word problem, involves three stages: (i) encoding, (ii) operations, (iii) decoding.

- Encoding is the process of building a mathematical model from a given verbal statement. Suppose we say that "a father's age is 5 years more than twice his son's age". If we assume the two ages to be x and y years respectively, then the corresponding mathematical model is: x=2y+5
- Operations: After a model has been set up, we operate on it according to given conditions, obtain a solution, and then translate it back into verbal language.
- The skill of model-building requires a clear understanding of the mathematical equivalent of words that have mathematical meanings.
- Words such as more, less, times, difference, is equal to, square, etc., have to be identified and used in the model for the verbal statement.

83(A). Activity-Centred Curriculum is based on the premise that child loves to play and activity will help to create motivation.
Activity-Centred Curriculum:

- This is also very similar to a learner-centred curriculum.
- The role of the learner is very important and should be very active.
- This is based on the premise that a child loves to play and activity will help to create motivation.
- When curricular material is presented in terms of activity, it is known as activity centred curriculum.
- Learning of the prescribed material included in the curriculum takes place through appropriate activities.
- Another benefit of this approach is that throughout the teaching period, the students should be active participants in the process of learning.
- A goal-directed activity should end in a productive experience. In an activity-centred curriculum, the content is

84(D). Acrylic is a synthetic fibre.
- Acrylic is commonly known as synthetic wool because it mimics wool.
- Acrylic is used to make sweaters, blankets, and a variety of other garments.
- They are also used to fill soft toys and pillows, in addition to producing garments.

Acrylic is preferred over wool because:
- Wool derived from natural sources is fairly costly, whereas acrylic clothing is reasonably inexpensive.
- It can be coloured in a wide range of colours.
- Acrylic fibres do not felt together, making it easier to wash garments made of them than wool fibres.
- Acrylic allergy is exceedingly uncommon, although wool or lanolin (a fatty component found in sheep wool) allergy is more frequent.
- They are more popular than natural fibres since they are more durable.
- They are of good quality for fashionable apparel.

As a result, acrylic is becoming increasingly popular and is increasingly replacing wool.

85(D). Fiber is a thin long threadlike substance. These can be obtained from either natural resources or can be synthesized in laboratories. Laboratory synthesized fibers are identified as synthetic fibers.
Synthetic fiber is a chain of small units joined together. Each small unit is actually a chemical substance. Many such small units combine to form a large single unit called a polymer.

86(C). Cognitive development of children is enhanced through social interaction with other people, particularly those who are more skilled.

Benjamin Bloom's taxonomy is a hierarchical organization of cognitive objectives. Bloom classifies learning objectives into three domains, cognitive, affective, and sensory domain.

1. Cognitive Domain: mental skills
2. Affective Domain: growth in feelings or emotional areas
3. Psychomotor Domain: manual or physical skills

The cognitive domain involves six categories of learning that serve in the development of intellectual skills.

87(B). Approaches are age-appropriate and within the learner's cognitive reach so that children can understand them.

The science curriculum refers to the entire subject matter of science that will be covered in a given class during a set length

necessitates that the curriculum content, process, language, and pedagogical approaches are age-appropriate and within the learner's cognitive reach so that children can understand them.

- For example, the basic concepts of electromagnetic induction have to be taught before should be taught before introducing the electric generator.

88(A). Demonstration at school level emphasis is given on 'seeing' and 'doing'

Demonstration Method:-

- The demonstration method is an activity-centered method that is being used frequently in a science classroom.
- There are several concepts and theories in science, which can be explained to learners only by demonstration.
- The basic principle of Demonstration is learning by seeing and doing.
- Demonstration helps learners to learn through observation.
- It is a visual approach for examining information, ideas, and processes.
- It involves various senses that make learning permanent.
- It is a method of learning by doing.

89(D). Remedial teaching refers to the teaching which is intended to improve the ability of slow learners to learn something.

- It is an integral part of the teaching-learning program, also known as compensatory or corrective teaching.
- The objective of remedial teaching is to give additional help to learners who have fallen behind the rest of the class in any topic or subject.
- It is the process of identifying slow learners and providing them with the necessary help and guidance to overcome their problems.

90(D). An approach may be explained as a comprehensive way of dealing with a

particular problem. It is a general plan of action, on the basis of which, various methods and models have evolved.

If Geeta is preparing a lesson - plan for teaching the topic on 'Human eye' to Class VIII students. Inclusion of demonstration activities in the lesson - plan is likely to be most effective in helping the students understand related concepts better.

91(D). The word "classroom activity" refers to a variety of skill-based games, techniques, and interactive activities that aid in the educational growth of students.

- Getting involved in this activity will also help the children to build other important life skills like teamwork, meal planning, organization clean up and basics of food safety.
- The dish which can be prepared quickly

- Gujrat lies in the western part of India.
- It is surrounded by Pakistan in the northwest.
- In the south, it is surrounded by the Arabian Sea.
- It is landlocked by the three Indian states of Rajasthan, Madhya Pradesh and Maharashtra.

93(D). Soil pollution- the presence of toxic chemicals (pollutants or contaminants) in soil, in high enough concentration to pose a risk to human health and/or the ecosystem.

It can be also defined as the addition of substances to the soil, which adversely affects the physical, chemical, and biological properties of soil and reduces its productivity.

- Negative Pollution- Deterioration in the productivity of soil due to a reduction in quality or quantity of topsoil is called negative soil pollution. It is caused by over-use and erosion .
- Positive Pollution- It is a reduction in soil productivity and deterioration in the quality of plants.due to the addition of pollution from the air, faulty sanitation, industrial effluents, supra-optimum fertilizers, and pesticides.
- Third Pollution- It is landscape pollution in which the land is so severely misused that it becomes filthy and odorous because of the dumping of garbage, rubbish, sludge, ash, industrial wastes, etc. over it.

94(A). X, Y, and Z represent Virus, Direct contact, bacteria respectively.

The disease is defined as any condition which impairs health or interferes with the normal functioning of the body, It may be caused by some external agencies such as deficiency of nutrients, worms, viruses, bacteria, etc.

Polio:

- Polio is a dangerous disease for children.
- It is caused by the Enterovirus .
- The bacteria are spread through contaminated water , food, and milk .
- Symptoms are senseless, paralysis, deep sleep, etc.

Chickenpox:

- It is also a common disease in children.
- It is caused by the Varicella zoster virus.
- It spreads through direct contact.
- Symptoms are headache, high fever, blister or scab developed on the body, etc

Tuberculosis:

- It is an infectious disease.
- It is caused by the bacteria tuberculosis or mycobacterium.
- It is spread by direct and indirect contact.

Mechanical properties:

- ductility
- malleability
- hardness
- brittleness
- toughness
- tenacity
- elasticity

96(C). Rayleigh's law of scattering: According to Rayleigh's law of scattering, the intensity of light of wavelength λ present in the scattered light is inversely proportional to the fourth power of λ, provided the size of the scattering particles is much smaller than λ.

- Thus the scattered intensity is maximum for shorter wavelength .
- The sun looks reddish at the time of sunrise and sunset :
- At the time of sunrise and sunset , the sun is near the horizon . The rays from the sun have to travel a larger part of the atmosphere .
- As the wavelength of red color is more than that of blue color ($\lambda b \lll \lambda r$) and the intensity of scattered light is $\propto \dfrac{1}{\lambda^4}$, therefore, most of the blue light is scattered away .

97(A). The amplitude of a wave refers to the maximum amount of displacement of a particle from its rest position in a medium. The amplitude of a wave refers to the maximum amount of displacement of a particle from its rest position in a medium. The amplitude of the wave refers to the maximum amount of displacement of a particle from its rest position on the medium. Amplitude determines loudness, the greater the amplitude of a wave, the more thrust it produces. Sound intensity is defined as the sound power per unit area. Hence option (A) is correct.

98(B). The audible range for adult humans is 20 to 20,000 Hz.

Humans can detect sounds in the frequency range of about 20 Hz to 20 kHz. The number of sound vibrations emitted per second is known as frequency which is measured in hertz (Hz).

99(A). Earth's magnetism is due to dynamo effect.

It is a theory that explains the origin of the Earth's main magnetism in terms of a self-sustaining dynamo. In this dynamo mechanism, fluid motion in the Earth's outer core moves conducting material (liquid iron) across an already existing, weak magnetic field and generates an electric current. The electric current, in turn, produces a magnetic field that also interacts with the fluid motion to create a

100(B). Liquids have stronger interaction with neighboring atoms than gas. The wave travels due to the transfer of energy to a neighboring atom. Due to stronger interactions longitudinal wave travels faster in liquid than in gas.

$v_{solids} > v_{liquids} > v_{gases}$

Where V- speed of sound.

As we know water is a liquid state and air is a gaseous state so the sound will travel faster in water than air.

- Rigidity is the property of solids, not liquids (liquid's property is fluidity).
- Sound travels faster in rigid or stiff materials which do not deform easily.
- For this reason speed of sound in steel is more.
- From the above description, it is clear that the rigidity of the medium impact the speed of sound.
- The speed of sound is greater in water than in air.

Both statements are correct but (B) is not a correct explanation for (A).

101(B). The part of human alimentary canal where complete digestion of fats takes place is small intestine.

It is the site of complete digestion . Carbohydrates, protein, and fat are broken down here. It receives secretions from the liver and pancreas. Fats are present in the intestine in the form of large globules. Bile salts break them into smaller globules. The walls of the small intestine contain glands that secrete intestinal juice.

Intestinal enzymes convert :

- Proteins to amino acids
- Complex carbohydrates to glucose
- Fats to fatty acids and glycerol

Villi present on the surface increase area for absorption.

102(A). A rainbow is a natural spectrum appearing in the sky after a rain shower.

It is caused by the dispersion of sunlight by tiny water droplets, present in the atmosphere. A rainbow is always formed in a direction opposite the Sun. The water droplets act like small prisms. They refract and disperse the incident sunlight, then reflect it internally, and finally refract it again when it comes out of the raindrop. Due to the dispersion of light and internal reflection, different colours reach the observer's eye. Thus light energy escaping from the Sun can be spread by a shower of raindrops.

103(D). The basic formula for pressure is given by:

$$\Rightarrow \text{Pressure (P)} = \frac{\text{Force(F)}}{\text{Area(A)}}$$

- As we know, the SI unit of Force is Newton, and the unit of area is meter ^{2},

Students from UP $= 9\ \%$
Students from MP $= 1\,4\ \%$
Required Ratio = Students from UP : Students from MP $= 9 : 1\,4$

105(A). Given:
Number of students from Bihar
$= 4\% \times 8800$
$= \frac{4 \times 8800}{100}$
$= \frac{35200}{100}$
$= 352$
Number of students from UP $= 9\% \times 8800$
$= \frac{9 \times 8800}{100}$
$= \frac{79200}{100}$
$= 792$
Number of students passed from Bihar
$= 352 \times 50\%$
$= \frac{352 \times 50}{100}$
$= \frac{17600}{100}$
$= 176$
Number of students failed from UP
$= 792 - 176$
$= 616$
$\therefore$ % of Number of students failed from UP$=$
$\frac{\text{Number of students failed from UP}}{\text{Total number of students from UP}} \times 100$
$= \frac{616}{792} \times 100$
$= \frac{61600}{792}$
$= 77.7\%$

106(D). Since % of students passed from Faridabad is not given, we cannot calculate number of students who passed from Faridabad.

107(D). When scientists investigate the hypothesis, they follow a line of reasoning and eventually formulate a theory. Once a theory has been tested thoroughly and is accepted, it becomes a scientific law, Scientific laws (also known as natural laws)

imply a cause and effect between the observed elements and must always apply under the same conditions.

In order to be scientific law, a statement must describe some aspect of the universe and be based on repeated experimental evidence. A scientific theory may also be canceled or remain unaccepted if it fails to provide sufficient evidence.

108(D). Systematic application of scientific knowledge to practical tasks is termed as 'technology'. It is an activity in which human uses scientific knowledge, tools and procedures to turn resources into desired goods and services to meet the needs and purposes of society.

109(B). Edward C. Tolman (1886-1959) developed a theory of learning, combining the advantages of Stimulus-Response to S-R associationism. He developed a system which recognizes the cognitive aspect of behaviour without sacrificing the objectivity of behaviourism.

110(D). The radio is not an example of visual aids.

Visual aids are items of a visual manner, such as graphs, photographs, video clips, etc used in addition to spoken information. Visual aids are chosen depending on their purpose, for example, you may want to:

- Summarise information.
- Reduce the number of spoken words, for example, you may show a graph of your results rather than reading them out.
- Clarify and show examples.
- Emphasize what you're saying.
- Make a point memorable.
- Enhance your credibility.
- Engage the audience and maintain their interest.
- Make something easier for the audience to understand.

111(A). The technique of 'classroom questioning' in the teaching of Science can be more effectively used for Ensuring levels of learning It helps the teachers to plan and present the lesson coherently. There are different kinds of teaching-learning methods and techniques that make learning a fruitful process and the technique of classroom questioning is one of them.

112(C). Term-end achievement test assessment strategies is not suitable for formative assessment of learners in science. A term-end achievement test is a test designed to measure knowledge, understanding, and skills in a specified subject or a group of subjects. The term-end achievement test is a summative assessment tool for teachers for the evaluation of students at the end of the course.

113(C). A teacher before beginning to teach 'digestion' to class VI students provides them with the outline diagram of a human body and asks them to draw all parts, through which they think the food would travel from the mouth when they eat. Here, the teacher wants to investigate students' prior ideas related to the human body and digestion so that future teaching-learning sessions can be accordingly planned.

114(B). Turmeric is obtained from the stem part of the plant. Turmeric is the rhizome or underground stem of a ginger-like plant. The plant is a perennial, rhizomatous, herbaceous plant native to the Indian subcontinent and Southeast Asia. Turmeric powder has a warm, bitter

115(A). They are closed curves. Outside the magnet, they are from the north to south pole whereas, inside the magnet, it is the other way round. If the lines of force are crowded at a place, the field is strong. If the lines of force are parallel and equidistant, the concerned magnetic field will be uniform in nature. Two magnetic lines of force will near intersect each other. The tangent at any point on the field lines gives the direction of the magnetic field vector at that point. Magnetic monopoles do not exist.

116(C). Cockroaches have multi-chambered hearts that are shaped like tubes which are much more resistant to

failure than human hearts. But instead of shaping the heart as a tube, they've created the chambers in a series of concentric spheres like an onion. A cockroach belongs to the class Insecta of the phylum Arthropoda. Hence Statement 1 is correct. They are brown or black-bodied animals. The size ranges from 0.6-7.6 cm and consists of a long antenna, legs, and flat extension of the upper body wall that conceals the head.

117(A). EVS curriculum at the primary level has a lot of small experiments which are to be done to understand the concepts. The primary level is a base for the future, introducing experimentation here may develop critical thinking and problem-solving abilities in children. Rote learning can be prohibited in science and every

senses, or by documenting data with scientific techniques and devices. An observation is any data collected during an experiment. Hypothesis- It is a tentative, tested explanation for a natural occurrence. Many people refer to it as an "educated guess" based on prior knowledge and observation. Experimentation- It is a step in the scientific investigation that helps individuals choose between two or more competing hypotheses. Analysis- It is the process of interpreting the meaning of the data that has been collected, arranged and shown in a form of a table or graph. Conclusion- It is a statement based on experimental data and observations that includes a summary of the findings, a

determination of whether the hypothesis was supported, and the study's relevance recommendations for future research.

119(B). A test is a kind of assessment to measure the knowledge in a specified field. A test is being taken to test the knowledge, skills, and aptitude acquired by the students in a teaching-learning process. The tests can be of objective and subjective type:

Subjective tests :
- These tests are influenced by the views, thoughts, and ideas of an individual and can be done informally by doing general debates and discussions.
- These tests generally includes the essay type questions, short-answer type questions, and problem-solving test items. These tests include the open-

right/wrong questions that are used to measure educational achievement.
- These tests contains Qs which are highly reliable and valid as they require one-word answer thus minimize the subjective inference and judgment.

120(A). Given:

HCF $= 24$

LCM $= 168$

Ratio of numbers $= 1 : 7$.

Product of numbers $=$ LCM $\times$ HCF

Let numbers be x and $7x$.

$x \times 7x = 24 \times 168$

$\Rightarrow x^2 = 24 \times 24$

$\Rightarrow x = 24$

$\therefore$ Larger number $= 7x = 24 \times 7 = 168$.

Child Development and Pedagogy

1. While playing, a group of children enact scenes from a recent popular movie. This situation highlights that _______ is an important agency of socialization.
   (a) Family
   (b) Media
   (c) Peers
   (d) Religion

2. According to Kohlberg, which level of moral development of a child shows no internalization of moral values and the moral reasoning of the child is controlled by external

   (d) Universal ethical principle

3. Children in _______ stage have symbolic thinking but do not realize that actions can be reversed and their judgments are based on the immediate appearance of things.
   (a) Sensori-motor
   (b) Pre-operational
   (c) Concrete operational
   (d) Formal operational

4. Which of the following statement is not correct about development?
   (a) Each phase of the development has hazards
   (b) Development is not aided by stimulation
   (c) Development is affected by cultural changes
   (d) Each phase of the development has characteristics behaviour

5. When a child watches a nature documentary the child may discover new animals and add them to the existing group of animals in his memory. This is called:
   (a) Schema
   (b) Accommodation
   (c) Assimilation
   (d) Equilibration

6. During classroom discussions, the teacher pay attention to boys only rather than girls. This is an example of:
   (a) Gender bias
   (b) Gender identity
   (c) Gender equity
   (d) Gender constancy

7. Which kind of assessment 'Sums-up' how much a student has learned over a period of time?
   (a) Assessment as learning
   (b) Assessment for Learning
   (c) Assessment of learning
   (d) Assessment in Learning

8. Which of the following activities defines cephalocaudal principle?
   (a) Development of spinal cord after other parts of the body
   (b) Development of spinal cord before other parts of the body

9. According to Vygotsky, the upper limit of tasks that a learner can successfully perform with the assistance of a more competent individual is termed as:
   (a) Level of Potential Development
   (b) Actual Developmental Level
   (c) Zone of Proximal Development
   (d) All options are correct

10. Which of the following statement are best suited to cater to individual differences of students?
    (i) The curriculum should be organized and made flexible.
    (ii) A separate arrangement should be made for the education of exceptional children.
    (iii) The methods of teaching should be in keeping with the needs of the individuals.
    (iv) The division in classes should be in heterogenous groupings.
    (a) (i), (ii) and (iii)
    (b) (i), (ii) and (iv)
    (c) (ii), (iii) and (iv)
    (d) (i), (iii) and (iv)

11. What is egocentrism according to Piaget?
    (a) Environment is the center of knowledge.
    (b) School is the center of knowledge.
    (c) The child is the center of the world and everything revolves around him.
    (d) None of the above

12. Which of the following is likely to motivate students towards mastery learning?

    (a) Urge for competence
    (b) Urge for fame
    (c) Urge for money
    (d) Urge for power

13. Inclusive Education implies:
    (a) Ensuring learning outcome of every child to be the same
    (b) Including the disabled in the mainstream
    (c) Provides compulsory education for children below 14 years
    (d) Ensuring that no child is left behind in education

14. Which of the following best describes the extent of the effect of

    determinant of how far we can go
    (c) Heredity is the primary determinant of how far we will go
    (d) Heredity determines how far we can go

15. When the elder brother hides the toy, Karan looks for the toy and finds it. Karan's age according to Piaget is _______.
    (a) 2 year
    (b) 2 month
    (c) 8 to 12 month
    (d) 7 year

16. The young child learns to speak single, discrete words in the beginning. Later, he can join together these sentences in the form of language. Which principle of development is this?
    (a) Development follows a pattern
    (b) Development proceeds from general to specific
    (c) Development is continuous
    (d) Development leads to integration

17. In which stage, does the tendency of children to explore new and move around greatly increase?
    (a) Post Childhood
    (b) Infancy
    (c) Pre-childhood
    (d) None of these

18. Bani doesn't speak much at home, but speaks a lot in school. It shows:
    (a) She does not like her home

much.

(b) Her thoughts and ideas get importance in her school.

(c) Students get a lot of chance to speak in school.

(d) The teachers pay almost no attention to the discipline of classroom.

19. Which of the following does not determine problem solving:

(a) Insight

(b) Mental sets

(c) Entrenchment

(d) Fixation

20. Which of the following statements should not be considered a characteristic of the learning

(b) Learning is a comprehensive process.

(c) Learning is goal oriented.

(d) Un-learning is also a process of learning.

21. According to the principles of motivation, a teacher promotes learning through?

(a) As a teacher, care should be taken that children behave ethically

(b) Do not expect any kind from the students

(c) Having real expectations from students

(d) Forcing students for their knowledge

22. Which of the following is an instance of formal learning?

(a) Children learning through correspondence lessons

(b) Children learning to draw from their art teacher

(c) Children learning to cook from their parents

(d) Children learning a new game from friends

23. Which characteristic is a student with Attention Deficit Hyperactive Disorder (ADHD) likely to have?

(a) Tendency to sit and do work quietly

(b) Tendency to get distracted easily

(c) Tendency to listen to others carefully for long

(d) Ability to read long passages without breaks

24. Reena always thinks of varied

solutions for any problem given in the class. This is a characteristic of-

(a) Mental impairment

(b) Low comprehension

(c) Convergent thinking

(d) Divergent thinking

25. The 'fear of failure' needs to be discouraged in children within a classroom because:

(a) Children's fears cannot be handled within a classroom by a teacher

(b) School cannot take responsibility for emotional lives of children

(c) Failure and errors are a natural part of children's learning

(d) Children who experiences fear

pride and self respect

(b) To rechannel the motives he/she already has

(c) To threaten him/her with failure and punishment

(d) To tempt him/her with praise

27. A child belonging to a high-class family generally has a pool of information about new technologies but a mediocre child probably has a gist of the information. Which factor affecting learning showed by the statement?

(a) Heredity factor

(b) Personal factor

(c) Environmental factor

(d) Educational Factors

28. Teachers need to create a good classroom environment to facilitate children's learning. To create such a learning environment, which one of the given statements is not true?

(a) Compliance with teachers

(b) Acceptance of the child

(c) Positive tone of the teacher

(d) Approval of the child's efforts

29. Teachers blame learning problems in students based on:

(a) Lack of Motivation

(b) Very low intelligence

(c) Casual parental attitude

(d) None of the above

30. Special needs education is the type of education:

(a) Given to very special people

(b) Given to persons with disabilities

(c) Provided to intelligent people

(d) Established by colonial masters

Ques (31-39): Direction: Read the passage given below and answer the questions that follow by choosing the correct/most appropriate options:

Wimbledon is a tournament apart. It is delightfully anachronistic in that it is played on pristine grass courts, a throwback to the era when the sport was still called 'lawn tennis'. Star players, who otherwise resemble walking billboards, are required to be reticent and don spotless white attire, resonating with the tournament's strict policy of keeping the site relatively free of commercial

the event's magnetic pull that even the biggest crisis to hit tennis in recent times — of Wimbledon barring Russian and Belarusian players against the backdrop of the Russia-Ukraine war and the ATP and WTA retaliating by removing ranking points — did not turn into a smoky inferno. Rafael Nadal, who three weeks ago won his 14th French Open and a record-extending 22nd Grand Slam title literally on one leg, is set to feature after undergoing radiofrequency treatment. Seven-time singles champion Serena Williams has come out of a year-long semi-retirement. Roger Federer's grass-court majesty will be missed — for the first time since 1998 — but such is sport's uncanny knack to replenish itself that there will be enough verdant pomp and splendor as the iconic Centre Court celebrates its centenary year.

Nadal and three-time defending champion Novak Djokovic will be the biggest men's drawcards, along with eighth seed Matteo Berrettini who is seemingly back to his best after recovering from a hand injury. The absence of the top-two ranked men in Daniil Medvedev (barred) and Alexander Zverev (injured) are unfortunate, but the farthest they had progressed at SW19 was the fourth round. Nadal, who is halfway towards an improbable Grand Slam (winning all four Majors in a single year), can be a handful if he survives the first week when the grass is still lush and the bounce low and skiddy. Djokovic will be desperate to add to his 20 Slam titles and avoid the rare scenario where he would not be the reigning champion at any of the four Majors. Berrettini comes in with a grass-court win-loss record of 20-1 since Wimbledon 2019, including two titles at Queen's Club, one at Stuttgart, and a final at Wimbledon 2021. Among women, after the retirement of defending champion Ash Barty, Iga Swiatek has established herself as the numerouno. Grass is admittedly the Pole's weaker surface and there is a closely bunched group with established credentials comprising Serena, Petra Kvitova, Garbine Muguruza, Simona Halep, and Angelique Kerber. But Swiatek's splendid recent form — six titles including Roland-Garros and 35 consecutive match-wins on hard and clay — means she will not be short on confidence even without the specific skillsets demanded by grass courts.

31. Who among the following has a win loss record of 20-1?

(a) Matteo Berrettini

(b) Novak Djokovic

(c) Daniil Medvedev

Belarusian players?

(a) Due to doping issues

(b) Due to financial crisis

(c) As a part of COVID-19 protocols

(d) Due to the Russia-Ukraine war

33. In this question, a sentence (in bold) from the passage has been divided into five parts (A), (B), (C), (D), and (E). Read the sentence to find out whether there is any grammatical error in it. The error if any, will be in one part of the sentence. If there is no error, the answer is 'No error'. Ignore the error of punctuation if any.
The absence of the top-two ranked men (A)/ in Daniil Medvedev (barred) and Alexander Zverev (injured) are (B)/ unfortunate, but the farthest they (C)/ had progressed at SW19 was the fourth round. (D)/ No error (E)

(a) A   (b) B

(c) C   (d) D

34. Choose the synonym of the word 'Reticent'.

(a) Reserved   (b) Loquacious

(c) Gabby   (d) Expansive

35. Which of the following is/are correct according to the given passage?
A. Rafael Nadal will not participate at Wimbledon as he is undergoing radiofrequency treatment.
B. Serena Williams has made a return to the court after a semi-retirement.
C. Roger Federer is the defending Wimbledon men's champion.

(a) Only A   (b) Both A and B

(c) Only B   (d) Both B and C

36. Why is Rafael Nadal not able to participate at Wimbledon?

(a) Due to doping issues

(b) Due to retirement

(c) As he needs to undergo radiofrequency treatment

(d) All are false

37. Identify the part of speech of the underlined word:
Nadal and three-time defending champion Novak Djokovic will be the biggest men's drawcards.

(a) Adjective   (b) Adverb

(c) Noun   (d) Pronoun

38. Which of the following women

(c) Garbine Muguruza

(d) Simona Halep

39. Choose the antonym of the word 'Pristine'.

(a) Blemished   (b) Virgin

(c) Immaculate   (d) Flawless

Ques (40-45): Direction: Read the following poem and answer the questions by choosing the correct/most appropriate options:

When the humid shadows hover
Over all the starry spheres
And the melancholy darkness
Gently weeps in rainy tears,
What a bliss to press the pillow
Of a cottage-chamber bed
And lie listening to the patter
Of the soft rain overhead!
Every tinkle on the shingles
Has an echo in the heart;
And a thousand dreamy fancies
Into busy being start,
And a thousand recollections
Weave their air-threads into woof,
As I listen to the patter
Of the rain upon the roof.
Now in memory comes my mother,
As she used in years agone,
To regard the darling dreamers
Ere she left them till the dawn:
O! I feel her fond look on me
As I list to this refrain
Which is played upon the shingles
By the patter of the rain.

40. What is the meaning of the word 'melancholy'?

(a) Happiness   (b) Thoughtful

(c) Mysterious   (d) Sadness

41. What are the raindrops compared to in the poem?

(a) Drops   (b) Tears

(c) Pain   (d) Roof

42. Which figure of speech has been used in the line?
And the melancholy darkness

(a) Personification

(b) Anaphora

(c) Alliteration

(d) Repetition

43. The overall tone of the poem is:

(a) Gloomy   (b) Optimistic

(c) Challenging   (d) Bitter

44. Which figure of speech has been used in the line?
Now in memory comes my mother

(a) Onomatopoeia

45. What is the central idea of the poem?

(a) Aggravate rain

(b) Rain on the roof

(c) Power of weather

(d) Healing power of rain

46. While learning vocabulary, learners connect one word with its related words and the words which can occur before and after it. What is this technique called?

(a) Dictation

(b) Note making

(c) Collocation

(d) Conversation

47. The 'natural order' in the process of learning English suggests that children:

(a) Are able to speak first then listen

(b) Learn to read and write simultaneously

(c) Are slow at learning to speak when not in school

(d) Acquire some language structures earlier than others

48. The conduction of debate in a language classroom is useful for:
(i) Acquisition of new words
(ii) Fluency practice
(iii) Acquisition of grammatical rules
(iv) Developing the ability to express one's ideas

(a) (i) and (ii)   (b) (ii) and (iii)

(c) (ii) and (iv)   (d) (i) and (iii)

49. Which of the following is not the advantage of teaching by story telling students?

(a) Enhances a child's vocabulary

(b) Enhances speaking skills of children

(c) Encourage development of emotions and feeling in a child

(d) Makes learning easier

50. **A child is not able to pay attention in a language classroom and shows irrelevant and inappropriate behavior. Which of the following can be considered as the possible reason for this type of behavior of child?**

(a) Dyspraxia   (b) Autism

(c) Aphasia   (d) ADHD

51. **Authentic material can be used in the classroom:**

(c) to make language learning enjoyable

(d) All of the above

52. **The teacher prepares questions to see the language ability of the students. In this question, she omits every fifth word in a paragraph and asks students to search for that word. This method of test contrivance is called ______.**

(a) Cognitive test

(b) Vocabulary test

(c) Fill in the blanks test

(d) Bound question test

53. **In language teaching, creative expressions develop the ability to assimilate the concept efficiently by building creative thinking skills. Which is the best method to develop creative expression among students?**

(a) Write summary of the story that has read

(b) Write your experiences about the earthquake

(c) Write a letter for leave for two days

(d) Write an essay on - My Ideal School (in 100 words)

54. **Direction : Answer the following question by selecting the most appropriate option.**
Teachers can remediate for the student with language learning difficulty by:

(a) focusing on individual progress with individualized instruction

(b) providing notes that are summarized and simplified

(c) initially, giving information as reading only, no writing

(d) conduct extra classes for the student to 'catch up' with others

55. **Collection and organisation of ideas, sequencing, cohesion and use of vocabulary are subskills of _____.**

(a) listening   (b) speaking

(c) reading   (d) writing

56. **A teacher of class VII asks her learners to bring at least two or three objects from home and she asks them exchange the objects among themselves. She now asks them to describe the objects in their hands In at least ten sentences. What are the objects**

(b) Inputs for language learning

(c) Realia

(d) Home objects

57. **A child studying in Class V says, 'I drinked water.'**
It indicates that the child ___

(a) has not learnt grammar rules properly.

(b) should memorize the correct sentence.

(c) has over generated the rules for making past tense verbs showing that his learning is taking place.

(d) is careless and should be taught to be conscious of its errors.

58. **Which of the following defines "Innateness Hypothesis" of language acquisition?**

(a) Humans already possess the knowledge of language by birth.

(b) Humans have a natural tendency to acquire language.

(c) Humans are born to learn language.

(d) All of the above

59. **The textbooks included in the curriculum should have which of the following characteristics?**

(a) The introduction at the beginning and conclusion at the end of the chapter should be given in the textbook

(b) It should be content-oriented

(c) A standardized language should be used

(d) A speech on a particular topic should be organized among the students

60. **Which of the following is an**

example of active listening?

(a) Comprehensive Listening

(b) Critical Listening

(c) Therapeutic Listening

(d) All of the above

61. **Which of the following options is/ are correct in the context of nature of Mathematics?**

(a) 'Mathematics' is a broad term that encompasses many branches and components.

(b) Mathematics is a way of thinking and it is related to our life on daily basis.

(c) Mathematics should be

62. **Out of the following which is not the characteristic of reasoning in Mathematics?**

(a) Accuracy

(b) Certainty of result

(c) Originality

(d) Subjectivity

63. **Which of the following statement(s) is correct for keeping Mathematics in School curriculum?**
1) Mathematics provides a indefinite way of thinking.
2) Mathematics helps in character formation as well as morality.
3) Mathematics deals with significant, abstracts and consistent structures.
4) Mathematics generates logical attitude.

(a) 1 and 2   (b) 2 and 3

(c) 1 2, and 3   (d) 2, 3 and 4

64. **The NCF (2005) considers that Mathematics involves 'a certain way of thinking and reasoning'. From the statements given below, pick out one which does not reflect the above principle:**

(a) The way the material presented in the textbooks is written

(b) The activities and exercises chosen for the class

(c) The method by which it is taught

(d) Giving students set formulae to solve the numerical questions

65. **Which of the following statements is not true about 'mapping' in Mathematics?**

(a) Mapping strengthens spatial

thinking

(b) Mapping promotes proportional reasoning

(c) Mapping is not a part of the Mathematics curriculum

(d) Mapping can be integrated in many topics of Mathematics

66. **Which of the following is/are the cause of mathematics phobia?**
    (a) Inability to solve mathematics problems
    (b) Mathematics learning difficulty
    (c) Negative perception of community
    (d) All of the above

67. **Which of the following is true in context of evaluation in**

instructional programme

(c) It does not supports improvement of instruction

(d) It means giving test

68. **The main purpose of remedial teaching of mathematics is:**
    (a) To develop the talents of the students.
    (b) To change the behavior of students.
    (c) Teaching outside the curriculum.
    (d) Helping diverse learners individually.

69. **Which of the following is/are the problems in teaching and learning of mathematics?**
    (a) Inadequate of training for upgradation of learning strategies
    (b) Attitude towards mathematics relating fear of mathematics
    (c) Mathematical Anxiety
    (d) All of the above

70. **Which of the following is not true regarding the problems in teaching and learning mathematics?**
    (a) Positive attitude towards mathematics
    (b) Focus on problem solving approach
    (c) Cramming of all mathematical formulas
    (d) Connecting real life problems to mathematics

71. **Factors of $\left(25x^2 - 4y^2 + 28yz - 49z^2\right)$ are:**
    (a) $(5x + 2y - 7z)(5x - 2y - 7z)$
    (b) $(5x + 2y - 7z)(5x - 2y + 7z)$
    (c) $(5x - 2y - 7z)(5x + 2y + 7z)$
    (d) $(5x - 2y + 7z)(5x - 2y - 7z)$

72. **A car covers a distance of $48\,km$ at a speed of $40\,km/h$ and another $52\,km$ with a speed of $65\,km/h$. What is the average speed of the car (in km/h) for the total distance covered?**
    (a) 52
    (b) 50
    (c) 52.5
    (d) 53

73. **Given below is a data set of temperatures (in $°C$) : $-6, -8, -2, 3, 2, 0, 5, 4, 8$ What is the range of the data?**
    (a) $0°C$
    (b) $16°C$

profit percentage (approximate).
    (a) 35
    (b) 43
    (c) 52
    (d) 39

75. **The average score of 5 batches of $20, 25, 30, 15$ and 35 students respectively is $40, 35, 30, 40$ and 35. Find the average score of all the students put together.**
    (a) 36
    (b) 35.6
    (c) 34.3
    (d) 35.2

76. **At present, the ratio between the ages of Amit and Dhiraj is $5 : 4$. After 6 years, Amit's age will be 26 years. What is the age of Dhiraj at present?**
    (a) 6 years
    (b) 16 years
    (c) 12 years
    (d) 22 years

77. **4 bells ring at an interval of $4, 12, 20$ and 25 minutes. If they ring together at 8 a.m. then at what time they will ring together?**
    (a) 12 noon
    (b) 1 p.m.
    (c) 11 a.m.
    (d) 2 p.m.

78. **Simplify: $\sqrt{72\%}$ of $\sqrt{8} = ?$**
    (a) 5.6
    (b) 3.6
    (c) 2.4
    (d) 2.6

79. **The angles of a triangle are in the ratio $2 : 3 : 7$. The measure of the smallest angle is:**
    (a) $90°$
    (b) $60°$
    (c) $45°$
    (d) $30°$

80. **The angle of a triangle are $3x°, (2x - 7)°$ and $(4x - 11)°$. The value of x is:**
    (a) $18°$
    (b) $20°$
    (c) $22°$
    (d) $30°$

81. **The area of the rhombus, one side of which measure $25\,cm$ and diagonal $30\,cm$ is:**
    (a) $600\,sq.\,cm$
    (b) $250\,sq.\,cm$
    (c) $200\,sq.\,cm$
    (d) $150\,sq.\,cm$

82. **Two cubes each of volume $729\,cm^3$ are joined end to end. The total surface area of the resulting cuboid is:**
    (a) $841\,cm^2$
    (b) $729\,cm^2$
    (c) $810\,cm^2$
    (d) $720\,cm^2$

83. **Find the total no. of digits required to write the counting from 1 to 969.**
    (a) 2365
    (b) 2493
    (c) 2799
    (d) 1345

84. **In a division sum, the divisor is 5**

    (c) 75
    (d) 104

85. **A number consists of two digits whose sum is 7. If 9 is subtracted from the number, the digits are reversed. The number is:**
    (a) 43
    (b) 52
    (c) 70
    (d) 61

86. **Find the value '$p + q$', if mean of set of numbers $3, 6, 7, 14, p, 34, 26, q, 12$ is given as 22.**
    (a) 96
    (b) 88
    (c) 76
    (d) 75

87. **In a triangle $ABC, AB = 16\,cm, AC = 12\,cm$ and AD is the bisector of $\angle A$. If $BD = 4\,cm$, then what is CD equal to?**
    (a) $2\,cm$
    (b) $2.5\,cm$
    (c) $3\,cm$
    (d) $3.5\,cm$

88. **What is the condition that the roots of the equation $ax^2 + bx + c = 0$ are in the ratio $c : 1$?**
    (a) $b^2 = a(c + 1)^2$
    (b) $a^2 = b(c + 1)^2$
    (c) $b^2 = a(c - 1)^2$
    (d) $ab^2 = (c + 1)^2$

89. **A factor of $p(x) = 7x^2 - 4\sqrt{2}x - 6$ is:**
    (a) $x + \sqrt{2}$
    (b) $x + \sqrt{3}$
    (c) $4x + 3\sqrt{2}$
    (d) $7x + 3\sqrt{2}$

90. **The mean of the five observations $x + 1, x + 2, x + 3, x + 6, x + 8$ is 11, Then, the mean of the three middle observations is:**
    (a) 11
    (b) 10
    (c) $\frac{32}{3}$
    (d) 12

91. Boiled tapioca with any curry made using coconut is a preferred food of the people of:
(a) West Bengal   (b) Bihar
(c) Tamil Nadu   (d) Kerala

92. While discussing liking and disliking a student says, "I and my mother both love to eat snakes. Whenever we feel like eating snakes, we go to a nearby hotel and eat Ling-hu-fen." This student must belong to:
(a) Assam
(b) Hong Kong
(c) Odisha
(d) Arunachal Pradesh

93. Which one of the following is not a

94. Due to their semiconductor properties, which non-metals used in computers, T.V., etc.?
(a) Carbon   (b) Bromine
(c) Silicon   (d) Fluorine

95. Given below are two statements:
Assertion (A): Human body is incapable of digesting cellulose.
Reason (R): Starch degrading enzyme, diastase, is found in the human body.
Choose the correct answer from the code given below:
(a) Both (A) and (R) are true and (R) is the correct explanation of (A)
(b) Both (A) and (R) are true but (R) is not the correct explanation of (A)
(c) (A) is true but (R) is false
(d) (A) is false but (R) is true

96. An artificial source of light is:
(a) Sun   (b) Moon
(c) Candle   (d) Star

97. In the majority of higher animals and plants, ___ and ___ are mutually exclusive events.
(a) growth; nutrition
(b) nutrition; consciousness
(c) growth; reproduction
(d) reproduction; consciousness

98. Which of the following statement(s) is/are correct?
(a) Only living organisms grow.
(b) Plants grow only up to a certain age.
(c) The growth in living organisms is from inside.

(d) All of the above

99. Choose correct statements from the following:
a. Sound waves travel faster in solids than in gases.
b. Sound waves travel fastest through a vacuum.
c. Sound waves are longitudinal waves.
d. Sound waves travel slower in gases than in liquids.
(a) a, c and d only
(b) a and b only
(c) c and d only
(d) b and d only

100. Read the following sentences carefully, and choose the incorrect

(b) The movement of a bullet fired from a gun is an example of rectilinear motion.
(c) The motion of a sprinter (or short distance runner) running on a straight track is also rectilinear motion.
(d) The rectilinear motion may not take place in a fixed direction.

101. Paheli moves on a straight road from point A to point C. She takes 20 minutes to cover a certain distance AB and 30 minutes to cover the rest of the distance BC. She then returns back and takes 30 minutes to cover the distance CB and 20 minutes to cover the rest of the distance to her starting point. She makes 5 rounds on the road in the same way. Paheli concludes that her motion is:
(a) Only rectilinear motion
(b) Only periodic motion
(c) Rectilinear and periodic motion
(d) Neither rectilinear nor periodic motion

102. Animals are exploited for various reasons by humans. With regards to this match the animal with their economic application:

Name of animal	Economic Use
1-Elephant	a-Perfume
2-Musk deer	b- Medicine
3-Whales	c-Horn
4-Rhinoceros	d-Ivory

(a) 1-a, 2-b, 3-c, 4-d
(b) 1-b, 2-c, 3-d, 4-a
(c) 1-d, 2-a, 3-b, 4-c
(d) 1-d, 2-b, 3-a, 4-c

103. Vitamins protect our bodies from diseases and illnesses. Select the incorrect statement(s) with respect to vitamins from the codes given below:
A. Deficiency of vitamin A makes our bones weak.
B. Deficiency of iron causes paleness.

(a) A, B and C   (b) C and D only
(c) A and C only   (d) A, C and D

104. A bulb lights up only in:
(a) A closed circuit
(b) An open circuit
(c) Series connection
(d) None of these

105. Inside the magnet, the field lines move ________.
(a) from north to south
(b) from south to north
(c) away from south pole
(d) away from north pole

106. Match List I with List II and select the correct answer using the code given below the Lists:

	List I (Compound)		List II (Nature)
A.	Sodium hydroxide	1.	Strong acid
B.	Calcium oxide	2.	Alkali
C.	Acetic acid	3.	Weak acid
D.	Hydrochloric acid	4.	Base

(a) A - 2, B - 3, C - 4, D - 1
(b) A - 2, B - 4, C - 3, D - 1
(c) A - 1, B - 4, C - 3, D - 2
(d) A - 1, B - 3, C - 4, D - 2

107. The process of transfer of charges from a charged object to the earth is called ________.
(a) earthing
(b) lightning
(c) oscillation motion
(d) electron movement

108. A car towing another car using a chain, in this case, the force exerted on a chain is an example of which of the following force?

(a) Applied force

(b) Normal force

(c) Frictional force

(d) Tension force

109. Air is an example of __________.

(a) Paramagnetic material

(b) Diamagnetic material

(c) Ferromagnetic material

(d) Antiferromagnetic material

110. The most heat-resistant material in the world is ______.

(a) Titanium

111. In science teaching, which type of teaching should be planned after diagnosing the learning difficulties of the students?

(a) Team teaching

(b) Remedial teaching

(c) Micro-teaching

(d) Diagnostic teaching

112. Teaching of Science should be ______.

(a) Theoretical

(b) Textbook - centred

(c) Lead to innovation

(d) Examination oriented

113. To enrich teaching-learning experiences, a science teacher takes her students for a field trip. Which one of the following could be a suitable advantage of field trips?

(a) Provides first-hand experience which is not possible within the four walls of the classroom.

(b) Enriches the general knowledge of students which supplements classroom learning.

(c) Helps in broadening the outlook, deepens insight, and widens the vision of students.

(d) All of the above

114. Why constructivist approach is emphasized in teaching and learning of science?

(a) It enables students to engage in inquiry and hands-on activities to provide experiential learning.

(b) It reduces the burden on science teachers in the classroom and makes the classroom more fun.

(c) Teachers do not need to cater about the learning gaps of the learners in this approach.

(d) It is helpful for learners having parents with low educational backgrounds.

115. Which of the following statement does go along with the nature of science?

(a) At the time of an epidemic, scientists pray and seek divine intervention to save humanity.

(b) At the time of an eclipse, scientists pray against any ill effects flowing from the phenomenon.

(d) A scientist considers eclipse a natural phenomenon & tries to understand what caused the event.

116. What are the steps involved in Problem Solving method of the teaching-learning process?
I. Analysis of the problem.
II. Stating clearly the relationships between different concepts.
III. Testing hypothesis

(a) I and III   (b) I, II and III

(c) II and III   (d) I and II

117. Which of the following statements regarding the expository approach of teaching science is/ are correct?
I. Teaching-learning process is totally controlled by the teacher.
II. It is deductive thinking wherein abstract content is differentiated by the teacher giving appropriate examples to the students.

(a) Neither I nor II

(b) Only I

(c) Only II

(d) Both I and II

118. Which of the following contributes towards development of scientific attitude?

(a) Objective outlook, removal of superstition and aesthetic appreciation

(b) Removal of superstition, aesthetic appreciation and spirit of enquiry

(c) Aesthetic appreciation, spirit of enquiry and objecitve outlook

(d) Spirit of enquiry, objective outlook and removal of superstition

119. Match the diseases in Column I with their categories in Column II.

Column I	Column II
a) Polio	i) Sporadic
b) Rabies	ii) Pandemic
c) Malaria	iii) Epidemic
d) Covid-19	iv) Endemic

(a) a) iii, b) i, c) iv, d) ii

(b) a) iii, b) iv, c) i, d) ii

(c) a) iv b) i, c) ii. d) iii

(d) a) ii, b) iii , c)iv ,d) iii

will you teach such child?

(a) Show the chart having pictures of different types of rocks

(b) Take child to actual field to have a feel of the rock

(c) Give description of different types of rocks in the classroom

(d) All of the above

// Hints and Solutions //

1(B). While playing, a group of children enact scenes from a recent popular movie. This situation highlights that media is an important agency of socialization.

The process of learning to internalize the values and norms into itself or the mode of learning to live in society is called the process of socialization. There are many sources of socialization such as School, College, Friends, Society, Neighbourhood, Religion, Caste, Media, newspapers, Meetings, Events, etc.

Media is the source in which observational skills are considered, media such as Television, magazines, Mobile phone, reality shows, newspapers, etc.

2(A). According to Kohlberg the pre-conventional level of moral development of a child shows no internalization of moral values. In this level, the moral reasoning of the child is controlled by external rewards and punishment.

Pre-conventional Level:

- Obedience and Punishment: Based on avoiding punishment, a focus on the consequences of actions, rather than intentions; intrinsic deference to authority

- Individualism and Exchange: The "right" behaviours are those that are in the best interest of oneself, tit for tat mentality.

3(B). Children in Pre-operational stage have symbolic thinking but do not realize that actions can be reversed and their judgments are based on the immediate appearance of things.

Cognitive development involves cognitive processes such as knowing, thinking, remembering, recognizing, categorizing, imagining, reasoning, decision-making, and so forth. Cognitive development proceeds as children mature. Piaget divided cognitive development into four stages.

- Sensorimotor (Birth – 2 years) & Preoperational (2-7 years)
- Concrete Operational (7-11 years) & Formal Operational (11 years and above)

The Pre-operational Stage: This is the second stage of cognitive development which is basically a pre-logical stage as logic objects and store them in their minds for later use. For example, such a child can draw a picture of or pretend to play with a puppy that is no longer present there.

4(B). 'Development is not aided by stimulation' statement is not correct about development.

Development is aided by stimulation: While most development occurs as a result of maturation and environmental experiences, much can be done to aid development so that it will reach its full potential. Stimulation is especially effective at the time when the ability is normally developing, though it is important at all times.

5(C). Two basic processes are involved in adaptation: assimilation and accommodation.

- Assimilation takes place when people try to understand something new by fitting it into what they already know.
- For example, When a child watches a nature documentary the child may discover new animals and add them to the existing group of animals in his memory. The fitting of new experience into the already existing scheme is called Assimilation.
- The modification of existing schemes (and the development of new ones) in order to make sense of new experiences is called accommodation.
- For example, the child will keep calling a cat a "dog" until someone corrects him and made him understand the difference between a cat and a dog. He will now have a different scheme for understanding cats.

6(A). During classroom discussions, the teacher pay attention to boys only rather than girls. This is an example of Gender bias.

Gender Bias is behavior that shows favoritism toward one gender over another. Gender bias occurs when we make assumptions regarding the behaviors, abilities, or preferences of students based upon their gender. Therefore, During classroom discussions, when the teacher pays attention to boys only rather than girls. This shows the scenario of gender biaseness.

7(C). Assessment of learning evaluates student learning by comparing it against some standard or level. It 'Sums-up' how much a student has learned over a period of time. The main objective is to rank, grade, classify and compare students periodically that indicate their level of performance. It is considered a Formal method of Assessment proceeds to the rest of the body (head to foot).

The cephalocaudal principle refers to the general pattern of physical and motoric development followed from infancy into toddlerhood and even early childhood whereby development follows a head-to-toe progression.

9(A). According to Vygotsky, the upper limit of tasks that a learner can successfully perform with the assistance of a more competent individual is termed as level of Potential Development.

The zone of potential development is the upper limit of tasks that a learner can successfully perform with the assistance of a more competent individual. It can be understood as the difference/gap between the actual developmental level and potential developmental level (the upper limit of tasks that a learner can successfully perform with the assistance of a more competent individual) that can be identified while a child is working on a problem.

10(D). (i), (iii) and (iv) statement are best suited to cater to individual differences of students.

By individual differences, we mean physical and behavioural variations, seen in all species including human beings. Some of us are tall, some short, some bright and some are dull. Some of the instructional strategies are discussed below-

- The methods of teaching should be in keeping with the needs of the individuals.
- The curriculum should be organized and made flexible as per the needs and requirements of the individual.
- Instruction should aim at the development of the student's cognitive process beyond the attainment of information alone.
- In a heterogeneous classroom situation, you can organize instruction based on ability grouping where students are grouped according to the level of their ability, and instruction is modified as stated above to suit the level of their ability.
- The methods of teaching should be in keeping with the needs of the individuals.

11(C). Egocentrism can be defined as the child being the center of the world and everything revolves around him.

Egocentrism in early childhood refers to the tendency of young children to think that everyone sees things in the same way as the child.

12(A). Urge for competence is likely to they can demonstrate skills mastery.

13(D). Inclusive Education implies ensuring that no child is left behind in education.

Inclusive Education: It is concerned with the learning and participation of all students vulnerable to exclusionary pressures not only those with impairments or those who are categorised 'having special educational needs'. Inclusion is all about embracing all.

14(B). Heredity is the primary determinant of how far we can go this describes the extent of the effect of heredity upon development best.

Heredity provides a basis or potential for the development of any personality trait. Heredity influences physique, motor-sensory equipment and level of intelligence, certain diseases, and temperamental characteristics.

- Heredity is the primary determinant of how far we can go to develop the basis or potential of a child
- The bad environment can suppress good inheritance but the good environment is not a substitute for bad heredity
- Heredity sets the limit of the maximum development of a characteristic, which cannot be crossed by providing the best environment.
- Heredity is represented by 'genes' and the environment is represented by any stimulation minus genes. Thus we find that our body size, the color of skin and the ceiling of our intellectual capacities are all genetically determined but the final shape of our personalities emerges through our interactions with varied physical, geographical, social, and cultural environments that envelope us. Thus the development of personality is a dynamic process.

15(C). When the elder brother hides the toy, Karan looks for the toy and finds it. Karan's age according to Piaget is 8 to 12 months.

Knowing that objects and people exist even when you can't see or hear them is an important part of object permanence. Jean Piaget, a child psychologist, was the first to uncover this notion, and it is a critical milestone in a baby's brain development.

The capacity of a youngster to perceive that items remain even after they are no longer visible or audible is referred to as object permanence. When an object is concealed from view, infants under a particular age are frequently distressed that it has disappeared.

16(D). The young child learns to speak single, discrete words in the beginning.

Development leads to integration: Once the child learns specific or differentiated responses, then, as development continues, she can synthesise or integrate these specific responses to form a whole. For example, the young child learns to speak single, discrete words in the beginning. Later, he can join together these sentences in the form of language. Similarly, a young child may have a specific concept of a car. Later, as she grows, her concept expands as she is able to synthesise new aspects into it.

17(C). In pre-childhood, the tendency of children to explore new and move around greatly increases.

Pre-childhood covers the period from 2 to 6 years. It is also known as the preschool stage. The characteristics of pre-childhood are:
- Some parents feel that behavioral problems of the childhood period are more troublesome than physical care of infants.
- Some behavioral problems occur during this period such as obstinacy, stubbornness, disobedience, and antagonistic.
- It is a toy age because most of the time children are engaged with their toys. These toys are also helpful to educate the children. Toys are an important element of their play activities.
- The tendency of children to explore new and move around greatly increases.
- This is a period when a child is considered physically and mentally independent. This is also a school-going age.
- Children become more self-sufficient, and independent, and develop self-esteem.
- This is the age of foundations of social behavior. They are a more organized social life they will be required to adjust to when they enter first grade.
- Develop physical, cognitive, emotional, and social development.

18(B). Bani doesn't speak much at home, but speaks a lot in school. It shows her thoughts and ideas get importance in her school.

Selective Mutism is a complex childhood anxiety disorder characterized by a child's inability to speak and communicate effectively in select social settings. These children are able to speak and communicate in settings where they are comfortable, secure, and relaxed. This applies to Bani in the given example, she talks a lot in school because she feels comfortable, secure, and relaxed as her thoughts get acknowledged at school.

19(D). Fixation does not determine an end state (the goal). These two anchors are connected using several steps or mental operations.

Fixation, or hyper-focusing on a specific interest, is a recognized feature of autism. Fixations, along with other features or symptoms of autism like repetitive behaviors and cognitive inflexibility, may appear from the outside to be symptoms of obsessive-compulsive disorder (OCD).

Insight: Developing Insight is synthesizing the available information and facts to derive a new solution. Insight is preceded by a gradual process whereby relevant parts of the problem are identified.

Mental sets: A mental set is a tendency of a person to solve problems by following already tried mental operations or steps. However, this tendency also creates a mental rigidity that obstructs the problem solver to think of any new rules or strategies. Thus, while in some situations mental set can enhance the quality and speed of problem-solving, in other situations it hinders problem-solving.

Entrenchment- In this a person's not moving beyond how he or she has seen problems in the past. Thus it also determines problem-solving.

20(A). Educational institution is the only place where learning takes place statement should not be considered a characteristic of the learning process.

Learning is the process of being modified, more or less permanently, by what happens in the world around us, by what we do, or by what we observe.

The characteristics of the learning process are:
- Learning is a continuous process
- Learning is comprehensive
- Learning is goal-directed
- Learning is intentional
- Learning is an active process
- Learning is the outcome of the interaction of the individual with the environment
- Learning is individualistic
- Un-learning is also a process of learning
- Learning is transferable

21(A). According to the principles of motivation, a teacher promotes learning through as a teacher, care should be taken that children behave ethically.

Principle of the motivation in learning:
- Motivation is controlled both intrinsically and extrinsically.
- Motivation should encourage curiosity in the students.
- The motivation should be blended with both praise and encouragement to develop self-reliance among the students. The role of the teacher is to guide in the learning process so they take part in the process actively instead of feeling that learning is a burden, the students should feel learning is fun and interesting.
- When students start behaving ethically it will help to develop their character, they will be able to judge which is good or bad, which help them to understand the world.
- The teacher should motivate the students by guiding them, not by forcing and punishment because the child may learn in fear of punishment, but he will never understand the knowledge because he studies in fear of punishment.

22(B). Children learning to draw from their art teacher is an instance of formal learning.

Formal learning is also called structured learning or synchronous learning. Examples of formal learning include classroom instruction, web-based training, remote labs, e-learning courses, workshops, seminars, webinars, etc.

23(B). A student with Attention Deficit Hyperactive Disorder (ADHD) is likely to have the tendency to get distracted easily.

Developmental disorder refers to the severe, chronic disability of an individual which is likely to continue indefinitely. There are different kinds of developmental disorders and ADHD is one of them.

24(D). Reena always thinks of varied solutions for any problem given in the class. This is a characteristic of Divergent thinking.

Divergent Thinking: It is the ability of a student which create something new and present novel ideas. Divergent thinking students have the ability to use imagination and critical reasoning to create new and meaningful ideas.

25(C). Fear is an emotion that creates high levels of anxiety in a person and causes the loss of courage in a person.
- Fear of failure makes a person scared of failing. It commonly happens to the students. The reason for such fear is due to peer pressure, focusing on the outcome rather than concentrating on the learning.
- It even damages the mental and emotional state. Sometimes the fear overpowers the students in such a manner that they even commit drastic measures.
- Children should be counseled and should be made to understand that failure and errors are natural in the process of learning and they should not

the learning process to give insight into children's thinking. It helps the teacher to be aware of learners' learning styles, to cater to them according to their needs.

Thus, it is concluded that the 'fear of failure' needs to be discouraged in children within a classroom because failure and errors are a natural part of children's learning.

26(A). The best way to motivate a child to learn is to appeal to his/her sense of pride and self respect.

Learning is the acquisition of new behavior or the strengthening or weakening of old behavior as a result of experience. It represents progressive changes in behavior. It also involves the acquisition of knowledge, habits, and attitude.

Motivation refers to the process that guides an individual to achieve a goal. Motivation plays important role in the learning process. The teacher is an important person inside the classroom to motivate the child and provide rewards to induce interest in the learner.

27(B). A child belonging to a high-class family generally has a pool of information about new technologies but a mediocre child probably has a gist of the information. Personal factor affecting learning showed by the statement.

Any one of several internal, external, or unknown factors can influence learning. In this section, a classification of the factors influencing learning has been made under the broad headings physiological, personal, socio-emotional, and educational factors.

28(A). Teachers need to create a good classroom environment to facilitate children's learning. To create such a learning environment, compliance with teachers of the given statements is not true. The environment in which learning takes

place may be described as a composite of natural conditions, circumstances and influences, and sociocultural contexts in which an individual is situated. Therefore, you can say that the learning environment is the sum total of the surroundings in which individuals interact to enrich experiences and thus leading to learning.

29(A). Teachers blame learning problems in students based on lack of Motivation.

Learning may be defined as "any relatively permanent change in behavior or behavioral potential produced by experience".
- One must remember that some behavioral changes occur due to the use of drugs, or fatigue.
- Such changes are temporary. They are not considered learning.

of education given to persons with disabilities.

Special education is individualized education for children with special needs. Special education means, Specially designed instruction, to meet the unique needs of a child with special needs including instructions conducted in the classrooms, in the home, in hospital, and institutions and in other settings and instruction in physical education.

31(A). As we can see in the second paragraph of the passage, it is clearly mentioned that " Berrettini comes in with a grass-court win-loss record of 20-1 since Wimbledon 2019, including two titles at Queen's Club, one at Stuttgart, and a final at Wimbledon 2021".

Thus, it can be concluded that Matteo Berrettini has a win loss record of 20-1.

32(D). The fifth sentence of the first paragraph says "And such is the event's magnetic pull that even the biggest crisis to hit tennis in recent times — of Wimbledon barring Russian and Belarusian players against the backdrop of the Russia-Ukraine war and the ATP and WTA retaliating by removing ranking points — did not turn into a smoky inferno."

From the above sentence, we can say that according to the passage, Wimbledon barred Russian and Belarusian players due to the Russia-Ukraine war.

33(B). In the second part of the given sentence, the plural form of the verb 'are' is incorrect.

In the given sentence, the subject 'absence' is a singular subject.

We know that a singular subject always takes a singular verb.

The singular form of the verb 'is' should be used with the singular subject 'absence'.

Therefore, the singular form of the verb 'is' should be used in place of the plural form of the verb 'are'.

Correct sentence: The absence of the top-two ranked men in Daniil Medvedev (barred) and Alexander Zverev (injured) is unfortunate, but the farthest they had progressed at SW19 was the fourth round.

34(A). The word 'Reticent' means Not revealing one's thoughts or feelings readily; not wanting to tell people about things.

Example: She is so reticent about her achievements.

Reserved: slow to reveal emotion or opinions.

35(C). The sixth sentence of the first paragraph says "Rafael Nadal, who three weeks ago won his 14th French Open and a record-extending 22nd Grand Slam title

champion Novak Djokovic will be the biggest men's drawcards, along with eighth seed Matteo Berrettini who is seemingly back to his best after recovering from a hand injury".

From the above sentence, we can say that statements A and C are incorrect according to the given passage.

The seventh sentence of the first paragraph says "Seven-time singles champion Serena Williams has come out of a year-long semi-retirement."

From the above sentence, we can say that statement B is correct according to the given passage.

36(C). The sixth sentence of the first paragraph says "Rafael Nadal, who three weeks ago won his 14th French Open and a record-extending 22nd Grand Slam title literally on one leg, is set to feature after undergoing radiofrequency treatment".

Thus, it can be concluded that Rafael Nadal will not be able to participate at Wimbledon as he needs to undergo radiofrequency treatment.

37(A). Here the underlined word 'biggest' is an adjective i.e a word naming an attribute of a noun, such as sweet, red, or technical.

Biggest means of considerable size or extent; of considerable importance or seriousness.

For example:- I think her biggest fear was that she'd lose him.

38(B). Among women, after the retirement of defending champion Ash Barty, Iga Swiatek has established herself as the numerouno.

Grass is admittedly the Pole's weaker surface and there is a closely bunched group with established credentials comprising Serena, Petra Kvitova, Garbine

Muguruza, Simona Halep, and Angelique Kerber.

Thus, it can be deduced that Iga Swiatek has established herself better.

Numerouno means better, more important, or more popular than anything else or anyone else of its kind.

39(A). The word 'Pristine' means Clean and fresh as if new; spotless.

Example: He wasn't about to blemish that pristine record.

40(D). The meaning of the word 'melancholy' is Sadness.

The poet calls darkness as melancholy as it makes him sad.

The rain on the roof take the poet back to the sad memories of his mother when he was a child.

He gets lost in the feeling of being a child

falling from the eyes on dark gloomy nights. It represents the poet's sorrowful mood.

It is a representation of the bittersweet feelings that the rainy weather brings.

It shows the duality of enjoying the sound of rain yet thinking of sadness for which the clouds weep.

42(A). Here, personifies darkness who is presented to be in a melancholy mood and sheds tears in the form of raindrops.

It is shown as something with human attributes which is capable of feeling sad.

Personification: a figure of speech in which an idea or thing is given human attributes and/or feelings or is spoken of as if it were human.

Ex: In the poem: recollection is personified when he says that they weave dreams.

43(A). From reading the poem we can clearly see that the tone of this poem is full of sadness.

The poet is sad and thoughtful, and the rain also seems to mirror his emotions as it looks like tears falling softly from human eyes.

After some time the sound of raindrops helps him recover from his melancholic mood.

The poet remembers his mother and the poet takes on a nostalgic tone.

44(C). Alliteration: a literary device that reflects repetition in two or more nearby words of initial consonant sounds.

Alliteration does not refer to the repetition of consonant letters that begin words, but rather the repetition of the consonant sound at the beginning of words.

Ex: 'Darling dreamers' – 'd' sound is repeating

Thus, Alteration figure of speech has been used in these word in the above line: memory my mother

'Now in memory comes my mother' – 'm'

sound is repeating

45(D). The central idea of the poem is the healing power of rain.

The musical sound of raindrops falling on the rooftop at night has the ability to revive sweet memories and rouse fancies in an otherwise busy mind.

It represents controlling idea.

The rain has power of healing the mind and the heart of humans as it heals the earth.

46(C). Vocabulary learning includes knowing a word in the language. This means knowing several aspects of words, namely word form, word meaning, and word use. The aspect of word form alludes to the language, either speaking or written as well as the word parts in the language.

Collocation Technique: A collocation is described as a pair or group of words that

difficult for language learners, even at an advanced level.

47(D). Natural Approach theory is based on the radical notion that we all learn the language in the same way. And that way can be seen in how we acquire our first languages as children. The Natural Approach is a language learning theory developed by Stephen Krashen and Tracy Terrell.

Stephen Krashen, a linguist, propounded the "Theory of Second Language Acquisition", in which he proposed the five main hypotheses, natural order hypothesis is one of them.

The Natural Order Hypothesis in the Process of Learning English Suggests that:

- children acquire their first language in a predictable order.
- children acquire some language structures earlier than others.
- children's age, deliberate teaching, etc don't influence the natural order of acquisition.

The first stage in the natural approach is essentially a silent phase, where nothing seems to be happening.

In this approach, students are given plenty of comprehensible input by the teacher, which facilitates the acquisition of language.

Hence, it becomes clear that the 'Natural Order' in the process of learning English suggests that, children acquire some language structures earlier than others.

48(C). Language learning is the process of learning to speak and understand a foreign language. It helps children to acquire practical commands of language. It is a result of deliberate and conscious effort for a better understanding of foundational skills of language learning.

When a teacher uses the debate as a

framework for language learning, s/he hopes to get students to look at any issues from different angles, gather supporting evidence, engage in collaborative learning, delegate tasks, improve communication skills, and develop leadership and team skills - all at one go.

49(B). Storytelling refers to the art of narrating a story. It is used as a strategy in language teaching which broadens children reading choices.

Storytelling is the best teaching method to develop morals, values, and cultural norms among children at the primary level.

To develop morals, values, and cultural norms among children at the primary level Storytelling is the best teaching method, Because:

- Stories are universal in that they can

and differences.

- Stories function as a tool to pass on knowledge in a social context.
- Stories are effective educational tools because listeners become engaged and therefore remember which also makes learning easier.
- Storytelling is used as a tool to teach children the importance of respect through the practice of listening.
- As well as connecting children with their environment, through the theme of the stories, and giving them more autonomy by using repetitive statements, which improve their learning to learn competence.
- It is also used to teach children to have respect for all life, value inter-connectedness, and always work to overcome adversity which also encourages the development of emotions and feelings in a child.
- Children in indigenous communities can also learn from the underlying message of a story.
- It increases the child's vocabulary as they learn so many new words from the stories in different contexts.

50(D). Learning disabilities refer to certain kinds of disorders in the basic psychological processes of an individual. These disorders are mainly caused by nervous system dysfunction (brain or neurological damage impending one's motor or learning abilities) and also by genetic factor.

Attention Deficit Hyperactivity Disorder (ADHD):

- It is a complex neurodevelopmental disorder that leads to hyperactivity in a child's behavior.
- The child who is suffering from ADHD will show irrelevant and inappropriate behavior i.e., he will be constantly in

motion, tapping fingers, poking others for no apparent reason, talking out of turn, and fidgeting is often called hyperactive.
- These children also have difficulty in concentrating i.e., they would not be able to pay attention in class for long. So, they may not be able to complete the task on time and shy away from taking independent charge of doing tasks.
- ADHD leaves a negative impact on language learning as children can be easily distracted. Due to this, they are unable to learn and comprehend the language.
- They will continuously face problems like restlessness and impulsiveness. Their activities and movements seem haphazard which can be observable through their behavior in the classroom.

part of the teaching-learning program, also known as compensatory or corrective teaching.
The objective of remedial teaching is to give additional help to learners who have fallen behind the rest of the class in any topic or subject.
It is the process of identifying slow learners and providing them with the necessary help and guidance to overcome their problems.
Objectives of Remedial Teaching in the English language:
- To provide individualized teaching with intensive remedial support.
- To eliminate ineffective habits.
- To make learners learn better by giving additional help.
- To provide learning activities and practical experiences to pupils according to their abilities and

- It indicates that the child knows the rule of the past tense but couldn't make clear sentences.
- It also shows that his learning is taking place.
- The child is aware of the rule that we use the '-ed' form of the verb in the past tense, but he/she isn't aware of how to frame sentences.

From the above, we can say that the child has over-generated the rules for making past tense verbs showing that his learning is taking place.

58(B). The "Innateness Hypothesis" of language acquisition is also known as "Language Acquisition Device". It was proposed by Noam Chomsky. Language Acquisition Device or LAD is a hypothetical module of the human mind through which

teaching-learning process respects the diversity among students and the teacher follows different paths to achieve the goals of learning.
The teachers use different materials such as charts, models, film-strips, video clips, etc. to arouse the interest of students in learning and to keep them indulging actively in the teaching-learning process. These materials are known as "TLM" or "teaching-learning materials".

52(B). A test is a kind of assessment to measure the knowledge, skills, and aptitude in a specified field. A test is used to analyze the performance of the students and also to know the reliability of the teaching-learning process.
There are generally oral and written types of tests. The written tests can be short answer type, objective type, long answer type, and essay type tests.
The teacher usually takes the written test in a classroom and may or may not inform the students about the content, date, and duration of the test.

53(A). Creativity is the recombination or reconstruction of ideas that leads to a new thought, a new output, or a new product. Everyone has a need to express him/herself in a way that is unique to him or her and any such expression is creative.
- Creative thinking can be developed while promoting the acquisition of content knowledge through approaches that encourage exploration and discovery rather than rote learning and automation.
- While designing learning experiences, teachers can plan and frame the curriculum and provide tools that give students options, voice, and choice in order to enable them to be creative.

54(A). Remedial Teaching is an integral

with stimulating approaches.
- Help the pupils to get rid of their common or specific weaknesses.
- To transmit practical experiences to learners according to their diverse needs.

Hence, teachers can remediate for the student with language learning difficulty by focusing on individual progress with individualized instruction.

55(D). Collection and organisation of ideas, sequencing, cohesion and use of vocabulary are subskills of writing.
Sub-skill- A skill that makes up a part of a larger skill. The language skills of speaking, listening, writing, and reading is often divided into sub-skills, which are specific behaviors that language users do to be effective in each of the skills.

56(C). Teaching Learning Material (TLM), also known as instructional aids, facilitate a teacher in achieving the learning objectives formulated by her/him before starting teaching-learning activities. These are used by teachers to help learners to learn concept with ease and efficiency.
Realia refers to the objects associated with everyday life to be used in the classroom. Using realia in the language class means bringing real objects as teaching aids. It includes coin, newspaper, map, tickets, fruits, vegetables, etc.

57(C). Grammar has been succinctly defined as a study of the morphology and syntax of a language. In simple words, grammar has to do with the form and function of words and the way they are combined to form sentences. In essence, grammar is the study of how language functions.
A child studying in Class V says, 'I drinked water.'

59(A). The textbook is the area in which the language material presented is prescribed for teaching and learning. A good textbook not only teaches but it also tests. The content of the book should be very clear, a proper beginning is required to prepare the learners for the upcoming content and a perfect conclusion is required to assemble the entire learning.

60(D). All the given types of listening in the options are active form of listening. They require analysis and deep understanding of what is being said by the speaker. Active listening involves responding to the speaker so that she understands that the listeners are getting the message she wants to deliver. It is focused listening, where our aim is to gain something from the speaker. The qualities like empathy, attention and practice are very important for active listening. These qualities help the listener to understand the speaker and her message.

61(D). The basic structure of mathematics includes arithmetic, algebra, geometry, and trigonometry that helps in learning the techniques to handle abstractions and structures. The teaching of mathematics must develop attitudes to think, reason, analyze, and articulate logically. The nature of mathematics highly influences the nature of the teaching-learning process in mathematics.
Nature of mathematics:
- Mathematics should be visualised as the vehicle to train a child to think, reason, analyse, and articulate logically. Apart from being a specific subject, it should be treated as a concomitant to any subject involving analysis and meaning.
- 'Mathematics' is a broad term that encompasses many branches and components. It is a science that involves

dealing with numbers, measurement of shapes and structures, organisation and interpretation of data and establishing relationship among variables, etc.

- Mathematics is a way of thinking and it is related to our life on daily basis. Mathematics, as an expression of the human mind, reflects the active will, the contemplative reason, and the desire for aesthetic perfection.
- Mathematics is the "queen of all sciences" and its presence is there in all the subjects. Mathematics acts as the basis and structure of other subjects. Its basic elements are logic and intuition, analysis and construction, generality and individuality".

62(D). Subjectivity is not the characteristic of reasoning in Mathematics.

reasoning in mathematics:
- Simplicity: It is simple in the way that it involves problem-solving by following specific steps and nothing is rocket science.
- Accuracy: This property can be understood by the example that two and two are four in every part of the world, hence it does not change merely owing to perception.
- Certainty of Results: The beauty of maths is that every result is certain and can be derived using some logic and concept.
- Originality: It makes one to think independently and have novel ideas.
- Verification: Each statement in maths can be verified and if not, they are self-evident (axioms).

Therefore, we conclude that subjectivity is not the characteristic of reasoning in mathematics.

63(D). Mathematics is an important subject in school curriculum. It helps the child to develop as social and intellectual citizen. There are so many reasons for keeping Mathematics in School curriculum given below:

Mathematics provides a definite way of thinking.

Mathematics provides opportunity to develop mental abilities of the child.

The language of mathematics is universal.

Statement 1 is incorrect and rest of it are correct regarding the reasons for keeping mathematics in School curriculum.

64(D). As per NCF 2005 mathematics involves 'a certain way of thinking and reasoning'. The learning process should take place without any burden, learning should be an enjoyable activity with logical reasoning. Thus, giving students set formulae to solve the numerical questions

does not reflect the given principle.

65(C). Mapping is not a part of the Mathematics curriculum is not true about 'mapping' in Mathematics.

A map cannot be meaningful unless the reader is able to make out what the map contains. 'Map literacy' is essential for understanding maps.

- Children need to be able to read maps because maps are very much a part of their curriculum.
- They are expected to deal with maps of their district, state and country.
- The abilities required for dealing with them are a bit different from those needed for reading and drawing pictures.
- It may be surprising because maps are also 2D representations.

topics of Mathematics.

66(D). Causes of mathematics phobia: The following points may be the causes of mathematics phobia:
- Weak teaching method and weak mathematics background
- Teachers' aggressive, stressful and irritating characteristics
- Inability to solve mathematics problems iv) Bad relationships between a teacher and a student
- Inability to solve too many home assignment
- Not to understand mathematics in class
- Unable to solve mathematical tasks
- Use of abusive words by the teacher
- Negative attitude towards mathematics
- Not able to solve mathematics problem in time
- Not to be a child-friendly teaching environment
- Mathematics learning difficulty (dyscalculia)
- Community Influence (negative perception)
- Low self-esteem
- Lack of analogies

Therefore, we can conclude that all of the above are the cause of mathematics phobia.

67(B). A teacher of mathematics aims at making sure that his pupils learn mathematics and learn it well. The final test of a curriculum is its effectiveness in fostering learning. Every teacher has to find out the progress pupils have made towards accepted objectives. Note that evaluation:
- is concerned with the improvement of instruction.
- involves decisions regarding the effectiveness of the total instructional programme.

Therefore, we conclude that the evaluation involves decisions regarding the

effectiveness of the total instructional programme.

68(D). The main purpose of remedial teaching of mathematics is to help diverse learners individually.

Aims of the Remedial Teaching:
- Remedial Teaching identifies the backward learner's weaknesses and gives them the necessary guidance to overcome their problem after identifying their areas of difficulty.
- The objective of remedial teaching is to give additional help to pupils who are facing difficulties in understanding the concepts in the mathematics
- It is essential for the remedial teacher to understand the strength and weaknesses of their pupils so the appropriate teaching can be adapted to

mathematics.

69(D). Problems in teaching and learning of mathematics:
- Teacher Related: It is found less than half of mathematics teachers having a mathematics background is available at higher level but the majority were given training. Some teachers who are actually from other backgrounds have to teach mathematics and maximum math teacher have to teach other subjects like physics, chemistry, social science, religion, and physical education class as there is a shortage of teachers. More than half of teachers agreed with the fact that all teachers are not having sufficient training and therefore the quality of education failing to upgrade for all these problems.
- Attitude towards Mathematics: Mathematics is an important subject, but many of them do not at all like this subject at all. The reasons for disliking the subjects mentioned by the students were dissatisfactory results; lack of interest in the subject and in some cases complicacy with the subject contents. According to teachers, there are negative attitudes towards mathematics relating to fear of mathematics, examination system, and memorization. Students' attitudes towards mathematics have a great influence on their decision-making of choosing streams.
- Mathematical Anxiety: Most students mentioned that their poor result of mathematics creates lots of anxiety. Teachers' views also indicate this fact a problems for students. anxiety about getting zero if they solved their problems in a different way or through another method than those followed by teachers.

Therefore, we can conclude that all of the

above factors creating problems in teaching and learning mathematics.

70(C). "Cramming of all mathematical formulas" is not true regarding the problems in teaching and learning mathematics.
Problems of Teacher's attitude in teaching and learning of mathematics:
- It is the responsibility of a teacher to develop a liking and positive attitude for mathematics among the students.
- The attitude of students towards mathematics plays a significant role in their achievement. If the students learn mathematics with a positive attitude, interest, and liking then their level of achievement will go up.
- The teacher should encourage the students to use a problem-solving and stating the problems.
- The teacher tries to raise a problem in the minds of students so that it can stimulate purposeful reflective thinking to arrive at a solution.
- Also, it is necessary to connect real-life problems with mathematics to make the students familiar with the use of mathematics in their daily life.
- The teaching of mathematics is mainly focused on the practical usability of mathematics i.e., to enable the children to apply mathematics in their daily life situations.

71(B). We know that,
$(a-b)^2 = a^2 + b^2 - 2ab$
$(a-b)(a+b) = a^2 - b^2$
Now,
$25x^2 - 4y^2 + 28yz - 49z^2$
$\Rightarrow 25x^2 - (4y^2 - 28yz + 49z^2)$
$\Rightarrow 25x^2 - \{(2y)^2 - 2 \times 2 \times 7yz + (7z)^2\}$
$\Rightarrow 25x^2 - (2y - 7z)^2$
$\Rightarrow (5x)^2 - (2y - 7z)^2$
$\Rightarrow (5x - 2y + 7z)(5x + 2y - 7z)$

72(B). Given:
Speed $_1 = 40\ km/h$, Distance $_1 = 48\ km$
Speed $_2 = 65\ km/h$, Distance $_2 = 52\ km$
We know that,
Time $= \dfrac{\text{Distance}}{\text{Speed}}$
Average Speed $= \dfrac{\text{Total Distance}}{\text{Total Time}}$
Now,
Total Distance traveled $= 48\ km + 52\ km$
$= 100\ km$
Total Time $= \dfrac{48\ km}{40\ km/h} + \dfrac{52\ km}{65\ km/h}$
$= \dfrac{6}{5} + \dfrac{4}{5} = 2\ h$
Average Speed $= \dfrac{100}{2}\ km/h$
$\therefore$ The required Speed $= 50\ km/h$

73(B). Given:

$-6, -8, -2, 3, 2, 0, 5, 4, 8$
We know that,
The range of a set of data is the difference between the highest and the lowest value.
Now,
The highest value in the data $= 8$
The lowest value in the data $= -8$
Difference between the highest and the lowest data $= 8 - (-8) = 16$
$\therefore$ The required temperature is $16°C$.

74(B). Given:
Aakash sold an article and earned a profit equal to 30% of the selling price of that article.
We know that,
Profit % $= \left[\dfrac{(\text{S.P. -C.P.})}{\text{C.P.}}\right] \times 100$
Suppose $S.P. = $ Rs. x
So, Profit $= 0.3x$

$\therefore$ Profit percentage is 43%.

75(D). Given:
Number of students in each batch $= 20, 25, 30, 15$, and 35
Average score of each batch $= 40, 35, 30, 40$ and 35
We know that:
Total marks $=$ average marks $\times$ number of students
Average marks of 5 batches of $20, 25, 30, 15$ and 35 students are $40, 35, 30, 40$ and 35.
Therefore, the average score for all the students is:
$$= \dfrac{[(20 \times 40) + (25 \times 35) + (30 \times 30) + (15 \times 40) + (35 \times 35)]}{(20 + 25 + 30 + 15 + 35)}$$
$= \dfrac{4400}{125}$
$= 35.2$
Therefore, the average score of all the students put together is 35.2.

76(B). Let the present ages of Amit and Dhiraj be $5x$ years and $4x$ years respectively. Then,
After 6 years,
$5x + 6 = 26$
$\Rightarrow 5x = 20$
$\Rightarrow x = 4$
Dhiraj's age $= 4x = 16$ years

77(B). Given:
4 bells beep at an interval of 4, 12, 20 and 25 minutes.
Beep together at 8 a.m.
By using LCM method:
$4 = 2 \times 2$
$12 = 2 \times 2 \times 3$
$20 = 2 \times 2 \times 5$
$25 = 5 \times 5$
LCM of 4, 12, 20 and 25 $= 2 \times 2 \times 3 \times 5 \times 5$
$= 300$ minutes
$= 5$ hour
So, 8 a.m. $+ 5$ hour $= 13$ p.m. $= 1$ p.m.

$\therefore$ They will beep together again at 1 p.m.

78(C). Given:
$\sqrt{72\%}$ of $\sqrt{8}$
$= \sqrt{\dfrac{72}{100} \times 8}$
$= \sqrt{\dfrac{576}{100}}$
$= \dfrac{24}{10} = 2.4$

79(D). Let the angles be $(2x)°, (3x)°$ and $(7x)°$.
Then, $2x + 3x + 7x = 180$
$\Rightarrow 12x = 180$
$\Rightarrow x = 15$
Smallest angle $= (2x)° = 30°$

80(C). The sum of the angle of a triangle is $180°$.
$\therefore 3x° + 2x° - 7° + 4x° - 11° = 180°$

be $2x\ cm$.
We know that,
$a^2 = \left(\dfrac{d_1}{2}\right)^2 + \left(\dfrac{d_2}{2}\right)^2$ [where $a =$ side, d_1 and $d_2 =$ diagonals]
According to the question,
$25^2 = \left(\dfrac{30}{2}\right)^2 + \left(\dfrac{2x}{2}\right)^2$
$\Rightarrow 625 = 225 + x^2$
$\Rightarrow x^2 = 400$
$\Rightarrow x = 20$
Length of the second diagonal $= 2 \times 20 = 40\ cm$
Area of rhombus $= \dfrac{1}{2} \times$ product of diagonals
$\therefore$ Area of the rhombus $= \dfrac{1}{2} \times 30 \times 40 = 600\ sq.\ cm$

82(C).

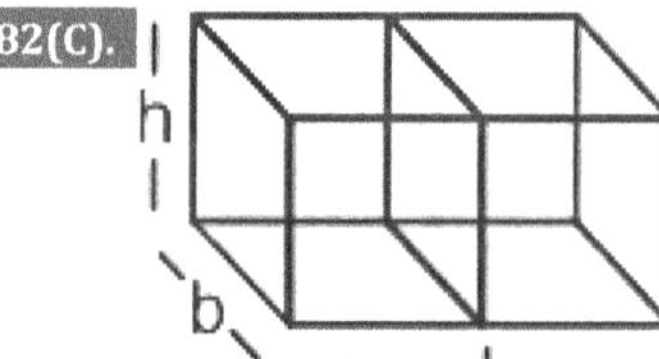

Volume of cube $= a^3$
$a^3 = 729$
$\Rightarrow a = 9\ cm$
Length of cuboid $= 9 + 9 = 18\ cm$
Breadth $= 9\ cm$
Height $= 9\ cm$
Total surface area of cuboid $= 2lb + 2bh + 2hl$ or $2(lb + bh + hl)$
Here l, b and h are length, breadth and height.
Total surface area of cuboid $= 2(18 \times 9 + 9 \times 9 + 9 \times 18) = 810\ cm^2$
$\therefore$ Total surface area of the cuboid is $810\ cm^2$.

83(C). 1 to 9 ... 9 numbers $= 9$ digits
10 to 99 ... 90 numbers $= 90 \times 2 = 180$ digits

100 to 969...870 numbers
$= 870 \times 3 = 2610$
So,
Total digits $= 9 + 180 + 2610 = 2799$

84(B). Given:
The divisor is 5 times the quotient.
The divisor is 4 times the remainder.
Remainder $= 5$
We know that,
Dividend $=$ Divisor $\times$ Quotient $+$ Remainder
Now,
Divisor $= 4\times$ Remainder $= 4 \times 5 = 20$
Divisor $= 5\times$ Quotient
Quotient $= \frac{20}{5} = 4$
Dividend $=$ Divisor $\times$ Quotient $+$ Remainder
$\Rightarrow 20 \times 4 + 5 = 85$

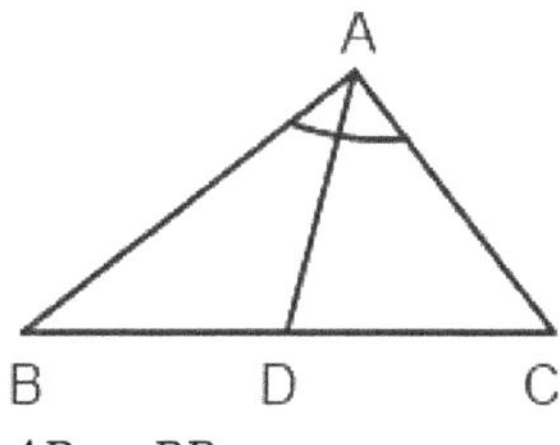

$\frac{AB}{AC} = \frac{BD}{CD}$
Now,

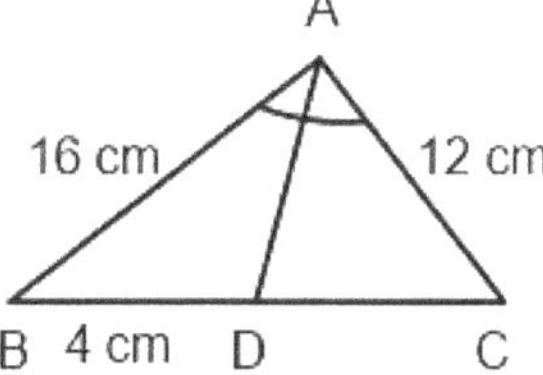

digits are reversed.
Now,
Let the digit at ones place be x.
Then digit at tens place be $7 - x$.
The number $= 10(7 - x) + x$
$= 70 - 9x$
The number obtained by reversing the digits,
$\Rightarrow 10x + 7 - x = 9x + 7$
According to the question,
It is given if 9 is subtracted from the number, it's digits are interchanged,
$70 - 9x - 9 = 9x + 7$
$\Rightarrow 54 = 18x$
$\Rightarrow x = 3$
Digit at ones place $= 3$
Digit at tens place $7 - 3 = 4$
$\therefore$ The number is $4 \times 10 + 3 = 43$

86(A). Given data: $3, 6, 7, 14, p, 34, 26, q$ and 12
Mean $= 22$
Mean
$(\bar{x}) = \dfrac{\text{Sum of all the observations}}{\text{Total number of observations}}$
$22 = \dfrac{3+6+7+14+p+34+26+q+12}{9}$
$\Rightarrow 22 = \dfrac{102+p+q}{9}$
$\Rightarrow 198 = 102 + p + q$
$\Rightarrow p + q = 198 - 102 = 96$

87(C). Given:
$AB = 16\ cm, AC = 12\ cm$ and $BD = 4\ cm$
And AD is the angle bisector of $\angle A$.
We know that,
Angle bisector theorem:
If AD is the angle bisector of $\angle A$, then

$\frac{12}{16} = \frac{x}{4}$
$\Rightarrow 16x = 48$
$\Rightarrow x = 3\ cm$
$\therefore$ The length of CD is $3\ cm$.

88(A). Given:
$ax^2 + bx + c = 0$ is a quadratice equation.
Roots are in the ratio $c : 1$
i.e $\alpha : \beta = c : 1$ or $\beta : \alpha = c : 1$
We know that,
Sum of roots $(\alpha + \beta) = -\frac{b}{a}$
Product of roots $(\alpha . \beta) = \frac{c}{a}$
Now,
Given:
$\alpha : \beta = c : 1 \quad ...(1)$
According to the question,
$(\alpha + \beta) = -\frac{b}{a} \quad ...(2)$
$(\alpha . \beta) = \frac{c}{a} \quad ...(3)$
On squaring the (1) equation, we get,
$\alpha^2 + \beta^2 + 2\alpha \cdot \beta = \frac{b^2}{a^2}$
Dividing the above equation by $\alpha . \beta$, we get,
$\dfrac{\alpha^2}{\alpha \cdot \beta} + \dfrac{\beta^2}{\alpha \cdot \beta} + 2 = \dfrac{\frac{b^2}{a^2}}{\frac{c}{a}}$
$\Rightarrow \dfrac{\alpha}{\beta} + \dfrac{\beta}{\alpha} + 2 = \dfrac{b^2}{ac}$
Now, from (1),
$c + \frac{1}{c} + 2 = \frac{b^2}{ac}$
Multiplying the above equation by ac both side, we get,
$ac^2 + a + 2ac = b^2$
$\Rightarrow a\left(c^2 + 1 + 2c\right) = b^2$
$\Rightarrow a(c + 1)^2 = b^2$
$\therefore$ The correct relation is $b^2 = a(c + 1)^2$.

89(D). Given:
$p(x) = 7x^2 - 4\sqrt{2}x - 6$
The above equation can be written as:
$p(x) = 7x^2 - 7\sqrt{2x} + 3\sqrt{2x} - 6$
$\Rightarrow p(x) =$
$\left\{ 7x^2 - 7\sqrt{2x} + 3\sqrt{2x} - (3\sqrt{2})\sqrt{2} \right\}$

$\Rightarrow p(x) = \{7x(x - \sqrt{2}) + 3\sqrt{2}(x - \sqrt{2})\}$
$\Rightarrow p(x) = (7x + 3\sqrt{2})(x - \sqrt{2})$
$(7x + 3\sqrt{2})$ and $(x - \sqrt{2})$ are the factor of the function $p(x)$.
$\therefore (7x + 3\sqrt{2})$ is the required factor.

90(C). Given:
Mean $= 11$
We know that,
Average $= \dfrac{\text{Sum of all observations}}{\text{Number of observations}}$
Now,
$11 = \dfrac{x+1+x+2+x+3+x+6+x+8}{5}$
By cross multiplication,
$55 = 5x + 20$
$\Rightarrow 35 = 5x$
$\Rightarrow x = 7$
Second observation $= 7 + 2 = 9$
Third obsevation $= 7 + 3 = 10$

$= \frac{32}{3}$
$\therefore$ Mean of three middle value is $\frac{32}{3}$.

91(D). Boiled tapioca with any curry made using coconut is a preferred food of the people of Kerala.
Tapioca is a starch extracted from the roots of the cassava plant. It can be made into flour and pearls of varying sizes and also used as a thickening agent in many foods. In southern parts of India, especially Kerala, tapioca is one of the most consumed staple foods after rice.

92(B). While discussing liking and disliking a student says, "I and my mother both love to eat snakes. Whenever we feel like eating snakes, we go to a nearby hotel and eat Ling-hu-fen." This student must belong to Hong Kong.
Ling-hu-fen is a Chinese dish consisting of starch jelly that is usually served cold, with a savory sauce, often in the summer. Therefore if someone is saying that he/she likes it, he/she must belong to the Chinese region (Hong Kong as per the options).

93(D). Silk is not a synthetic fibre.
Synthetic fibres are normally created from high heat polymerization of organic chemicals, accompanied by cooling to room temperature, leading to the creation of textile fibres. But from the silkworm, silk is produced. A cocoon of thread spins around the silkworm. It is used to safeguard silkworms. The silk thread is gathered from the cocoon and turned into a thread.

94(C). Due to their semiconductor properties, the non-metals used in computers, T.V., etc. is Silicon.
Semiconductors are materials that have neither the conductivity of a conductor nor the insulating properties of an insulator. They are formed of pure silicon crystal,

which is effectively pure silicon. Silicon is ideal for this lattice structure because its four valence electrons enable it to form perfect bonds with four of its silicon neighbours.

95(B). Both (A) and (R) are true but (R) is not the correct explanation of (A).
Humans are unable to digest cellulose because the appropriate enzymes to break down the beta acetal linkages are lacking. Undigestible cellulose is the fiber that aids in the smooth working of the intestinal tract.
In the digestive systems of humans and many other mammals, an alpha-amylase called ptyalin is produced by the salivary glands, whereas pancreatic amylase is secreted by the pancreas into the small intestine. The optimum pH of alpha-

can propagate faster. Solid having molecules compact together. So usually, the speed of sound is more in Solids compared to liquids and more in liquids than gases.

100(D). "The rectilinear motion may not take place in a fixed direction' this is an incorrect statement.
Motion in a straight line is called rectilinear motion. Some examples of rectilinear motion are the motion of a vehicle on a straight road, the motion of a train on a straight track, the motion of a falling stone, the motion of a ball rolling on the ground, etc. Rectilinear motion takes place in a fixed direction.

101(C). Paheli moves in a straight path from A to C and from C to A. So, the motion is rectilinear, further Paheli moves in a periodic motion because she makes 5

D		

Thus,
A. Deficiency of vitamin A makes our bones weak: Incorrect
B. Deficiency of iron causes paleness: Correct
C. Deficiency of vitamin D causes swollen and bleeding gums: Incorrect
D. The deficiency of vitamin B helps to increase our appetite: Incorrect

104(A). A bulb lights up only in a closed circuit.
In a complete circuit, the bulb glows because the current is flowing. A bulb requires proper current flow in order to glow. Once the current moves, the bulb's filament starts heating up and glowing which then emits heat and light. However, if the bulb is away, it will not let the current

parts, Natural and artificial:
Natural sources of Light: The sources of light which are part of our nature and universe like the Sun, and stars are natural sources of light.
Artificial sources of light: The sources of light which are developed by mankind for their convenience are called artificial sources of light. It includes candles, lamps, electric bulbs, LED bulbs, etc. The candle is made by humans so it is an artificial source of light.

97(C). In the majority of higher animals and plants, growth and reproduction are mutually exclusive events. Growth may be defined as a positive change in size, often over a period of time. Growth can occur as a stage of maturation or a process toward fullness or fulfillment. Reproduction may be defined as the production of progeny possessing features more or less similar to those of parents.

98(C). "The growth in living organisms is from inside" this statement is correct.
Growth is the act or process, or a manner of growing, development, or gradual increase. It is an exclusive event in the majority of the higher animals and plants. In plants, growth occurs continuously throughout their life span, and in animals, growth is seen only up to a certain age. In living organisms, growth is from the inside. Therefore, it cannot be taken as a defining property of living organisms.

99(A). Speed of Sound in a Medium: The speed of sound in a medium is decided by the density of that material, temperature and elasticity. The Sound wave is a type of longitudinal mechanical wave which propagates only through a medium by vibrating the molecules of its particle. If molecules are compact, the sound waves

102(C). The correct match is as follows:

Name of animal	Economic Use
1-Elephant	d-Ivory
2-Musk deer	a-Perfume
3-Whales	b-Medicines
4-Rhinoceros	c-Horn

Hunting and exploitation of animals and plants to fulfil human greeds are one of the major factors of losses of biodiversity. Hunting was considered a recreational sport in ancient times. Animals yield valuable substances that can yield good fortune.
For example, ivory obtained from an elephant's tusk is an expensive white material and is used to make jewelry. Whales pose a major threat as it is hunted for making lipsticks. Musk deer yields a very high-quality small amount of musk perfume and is hence hunted in large numbers. Rhinoceros are hunted for their horn.

103(D).

Vitamin/Mineral	Deficiency	Symptoms
Vitamin A	Night blindness	Poor vision, loss of vision in the darkness (night), sometimes complete loss of vision
Vitamin B1	Beri beri	Weak muscles and very little energy to work
Vitamin C	Scurvy	Bleeding and swollen gums, wounds take a longer time to heal
Vitamin	Rickets	Bones become soft and bent

move from north to south.
Magnetic field lines are continuous, forming closed loops without a beginning or end. They go from the north pole to the south pole.

106(B).

Compound	Nature
Sodium hydroxide	Alkali
Calcium oxide	Base
Acetic acid	Weak Acid
Hydrochloric acid	Strong Acid

Sodium hydroxide is also called caustic soda. Sodium hydroxide is highly soluble in water. Used in the manufacture of pulp and paper, drinking water, soaps, and detergents. Sodium hydroxide can be used for the detection of carbon monoxide poisoning.
Calcium oxide is commonly known as quicklime. Calcium oxide is usually made by the thermal decomposition of materials. When quicklime is heated to $2400°C$, it emits an intense glow known as the limelight.
Acetic acid is also called Ethanoic acid. It is a weak acid. Vinegar is made up of acetic acid and water. Acetic acid is a chemical reagent for the production of chemical compounds.
Hydrochloric acid is also called Muriatic acid. Hydrochloric acid was discovered by Jabir ibn Hayyan. It is a strong acidic. Used in the production of polyvinyl chloride for plastic.

107(A). The process of transfer of charges from a charged object to the earth is called earthing.
When a charged object comes in contact with the Earth, the charges flow into the Earth and the body gets discharged. This process is called earthing.